Mysteries of the Bible
Armageddon

The Christ & His Bride

vs.

The Antichrist & His
(Satan~Iran & Radical Islam~Mara Salvatrucha)

"I saw three unclean spirits like frogs come out of the mouth of the dragon, and out of the mouth of the beast, and out of the mouth of the false prophet. For they are the spirits of devils, working miracles, which go forth unto the kings of the earth and of the whole world, to gather them to the battle of that great day of God Almighty" (Rev 16:13-14).

JAMES V. POTTER, PH.D., PSY.D. & PAULA M. POTTER, MA
© 2009 JUBILEE ENTERPRISES
ADVOCARE PUBLISHING COMPANY - REDDING, CA 96099

MYSTERIES OF THE BIBLE: ARMAGEDDON
THE CHRIST & HIS BRIDE VS. THE ANTICHRIST & HIS

ISBN 978-1-9303-2754-2

Copyright © 2010 Jubilee Enterprises.
Authors, James V. Potter, Ph.D. & Paula M. Potter, MA

All rights reserved. No portion of this book and/or cover may be copied or reproduced in any form or media, except for brief quotations, without the prior written permission from the author and publisher.

Unless otherwise noted, all Biblical Scripture quotations in this volume are from the New International Version, Student Edition (NIV Study Bible), copyright © 1985 by the Zondervan Corporation, Grand Rapids, Michigan, USA

ISBN: 978-1-9303-2754-2 - 52195

Published by Advocare Publishing Co.
Redding, California 96001-9114, USA

Printed in the United States of America

Introduction

I, Jim, remember, during my college experience in 1955, when I first grasped the import of Scriptures that tell us God is the revealer of mysteries. Having shared some of the insights the Lord has given me over the years, our pastor asked us in June, 2007 to facilitate the midweek prayer service. My wife, Paula, and I, accepted his invitation. As prayer requests were made, I (Jim) would seek the Lord, asking for answers from Scripture and Paula served as our scribe, maintaining a journal of prayer requests and answers. **Over the next year, we experienced God moving in ours and other's lives, providing specific answers to innumerable prayers, increasing our trust in, and reliance on, God's guidance.**

In August, 2008, as our church prepared to move into a facility with much more room, our pastor asked that Paula and I prepare to teach a Sunday School class. After much prayer, we felt led to take others deeper into God's Word, encouraging them to seek out the hidden mysteries in Scripture that are so often overlooked. Feeling inadequate, but relying on the promise of James 1:5, that *"if any man lack wisdom, let him ask of God, who gives to all men liberally and withholds not,"* we began asking God to reveal the mysteries hidden within His Word.

Since that time, Paula's and my prayer has taken a new direction. We began meeting with the Lord, in prayer and meditation, each morning before undertaking any other activity. **In January, 2009, we felt led by God to add communion to our worship**, as we take a few minutes just to praise our Heavenly Father. Then, according to His promise, that: *"where two or three are gathered together in my name, there am I in the midst of them"* (Mt 18:20) -- we invite Father God, Holy Spirit, Jesus Christ and the heavenly host to be with us.

As facilitators of the midweek prayer service, members of our church's prayer-chain, and online instructors, mentoring college students for Vision International University, around the world, we usually have plenty to lift up to God in prayer. Based on our experience, we have confidence that He will fulfill His promise that: *"if two of you on earth agree about anything you ask for, it will be done for you by my Father in heaven"* (Mt 18:19). However, before lifting up our own, or other's requests, we first ask God what is on His heart that we may pray into. We then wait patiently and expectantly for His answer.

While we wait on the Lord, it is not uncommon to have our phone ring, and answering it to find someone seeking God's answer to a need in their life. As we lift up these requests to the Lord, God usually directs us to a text, or texts, that provide immediate answers to many of these prayer requests, even before we mention them. Frequently, we are given insight into current events, or events within the Body of Christ (the church). Often, we are blessed with new understanding of a portion of Scripture, as God reveals His secrets and principles.

Through this daily practice, our relationships with our Heavenly Father, Holy Spirit and our Elder Brother, Jesus Christ, have deepened tremendously, and our depth of understanding of His Word has expanded exponentially. However, that being said, we were not prepared for what was revealed to us recently that shook our understanding of the doctrine of salvation. The result has been a great deal of study and prayer for guidance as we embark on an assignment we felt being laid upon us -- to write what has shown us, and make it available to the church.

Before you begin to read, we recommend that you follow the practice of asking God to still your own thoughts and the imagination of your mind, and open your mind and heart to receive new revelation of His mysteries.

Contents

No.	Chapter Title	Page
Intro.	Introduction	i
Ch. 1	This Present Darkness	1
Ch. 2	The Apocrypha: The Hidden Secrets	11
Ch. 3	The Book of Enoch	25
Ch. 4	The Watchers	33
Ch. 5	Adam's & Eve's Conflict With Satan	47
Ch. 6	Life Outside The Garden of God	55
Ch. 7	Transmutation ~ Spiritual to Carnal Beings	65
Ch. 8	Paradise Lost	73
Ch. 9	Days of Creation	81
Ch. 10	The Seventh Day	97
Ch. 11	The Seal of God vs. The Mark of the Beast	105
Ch. 12	The Fall, Transmutation & The Mark of the Beast	117
Ch. 13	Christ's Victory Over Satan	127
Ch. 14	The History of Europe Foretold	133
Ch. 15	The Great Tribulation	143
Ch. 16	The Coming Beast & His Mark	155
Ch. 17	Biblical Numerology	163
Ch. 18	The Beast & The Number of His Name	179
Ch. 19	The Image of the Beast	195
Ch. 20	The Beast, His Kingdom & His Religion	209
Ch. 21	The Shadow of Armageddon ~ The Dragon	221
Ch. 22	The Armageddon Battle Plan	237
Ch. 23	The Intercontinental Leap	253
Ch. 24	Out of the Abyss	271
Ch. 25	The Gathering Storm	283
Ch. 26	The Conspirators Evil Scheme	295
Ch. 27	The Diaspora	311

Ch. 28 The Gathering — 327
Ch. 29 Armageddon: — 355
    (The Battle of the Great Day of the Lord)
Ch. 30 Divine War-Crime Tribunal — 373
Ch. 31 Hell Fire & Brimstone — 385
Ch. 32 New Beginnings — 405

Chapter One
This Present Darkness

"Man is born to trouble as surely as sparks fly upward. "But if it were I, I would appeal to God; I would lay my cause before him. He performs wonders that cannot be fathomed, miracles that cannot be counted. He bestows rain on the earth; he sends water upon the countryside. The lowly he sets on high, and those who mourn are lifted to safety. He thwarts the plans of the crafty, so that their hands achieve no success. He catches the wise in their craftiness, and the schemes of the wily are swept away. Darkness comes upon them in the daytime; at noon they grope as in the night" (Job 5:7-14).

The book, "This Present Darkness," by Frank Peretti, First published in 1986 was based on Ephesians 6:12 *"For our struggle is not against flesh and blood, but against the rulers, against the authorities, against the powers of this dark world and against the spiritual forces of evil in the heavenly realms."*

Peretti's book set the standard for suspense-filled spiritual warfare storytelling -- a benchmark that has rarely been equaled by his contemporaries. The story's setting is in the small, apparently innocent, town of Ashton, the scene of a terrific battle between the evil demons led by one Rafar, and the righteous forces led by the angelic being Tal. Into this battle -- this Present Darkness -- come an intrepid born-again Christian preacher and newspaper reporter. Collaboratively, they unearth a New Age plot to take over their local community and eventually conquer the entire world.

Nearly every page of Peretti's book describes sulfur-breathing, black-winged, slobbering demons engaged in a life and death battle with tall, handsome, angelic warriors in a dimension of reality that is just beyond the human senses. However, in Peretti's story, committed Christian believers and New Age demon-worshippers alike are able to influence these unseen forces, thus vicariously engaging in the clashes between good and evil, through the power of prayer and meditation.

The righteous human participants led by Marshall Hogan, editor of local newspaper, The Clarion, Pastor Hank Busche, their immediate friends, and groups of praying Christians, enter into a spiritual battle against the local witches and wicans, led by the fiendish Jack Sondericker. The battle wages fiercely, working up to a thrilling and satisfying climax. Peretti's violent descriptions of exorcisms are especially vivid. In one episode, he describes the battle, saying: *"There were fifteen [demons], packed into*

Carmen's body like crawling, superimposed maggots, boiling, writhing, a tangle of hideous arms, legs, talons, and heads."

Perretti's book, while not for the squeamish, is a page-turning spiritual suspense, and one that's hard to beat. Even more important, while completely allegorical, it graphically depicts the intensity of the unseen, but universally experienced, battle between good and evil. Its reading provides one new insight into the plans of the powers of darkness for universal dominance and the impact those plans upon the earth and the family of man. Anyone reading Peritti's book will have a better understanding of how God sees what planet earth has become -- a place of spiritual darkness -- its inhabitants filled more with despair than with hope.

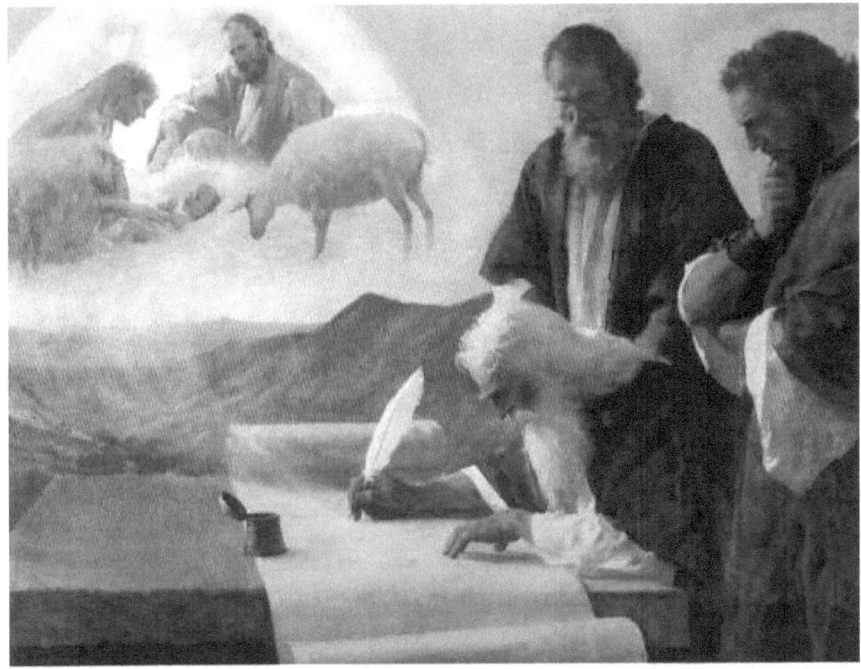

The prophet Isaiah paints a vivid portrait of this present darkness: *"But your iniquities have made a separation between you and your God, and your sins have hidden His face from you, so that He will not hear. For your hands are defiled with blood and your fingers with iniquity; your lips have spoken lies, your tongue mutters wickedness. None sues or calls for righteousness [except for the sake of doing injury to others — to take some undue advantage]; no one goes to law honestly and pleads [his case] in truth; they trust in emptiness, worthlessness and futility, and speaking lies! ...*

"Their feet run to evil, and they make haste to shed innocent blood. Their thoughts are thoughts of iniquity; desolation and destruction are in their paths and highways. The way of peace they know not, and there is no justice or right in their goings. They have made them into crooked paths; whoever goes in them does not know peace.

"Therefore justice and right are far from us, and righteousness and salvation do not overtake us. We expectantly wait for light, but [only] see darkness; for brightness, but we walk in obscurity and gloom. We grope along the wall like the blind, yes, we grope like those who have no eyes. We stumble at noonday as in the twilight; in dark places and among those who are full of life and vigor, we are as dead men. We all groan and growl like bears and moan plaintively like doves.

"We look for justice, but there is none; for salvation, but it is far from us. For our transgressions are multiplied before You [O Lord], and our sins testify against us; for our transgressions are with us, and as for our iniquities, we know and recognize them [as]: Rebelling against and denying the Lord, turning away from following our God, speaking oppression and revolt, conceiving in and muttering and moaning from the heart words of falsehood.

"[So] justice is turned away backward, and righteousness (uprightness and right standing with God) stands far off; for truth has fallen in the street (the city's forum), and uprightness cannot enter [the courts of justice]. Yes, truth is lacking, and he who departs from evil makes himself a prey."

Isaiah then concludes his prophetic portrait by revealing God's perspective of this chaos: **"And the Lord [looked down and] saw it, and it displeased Him that there was no justice. He saw that there was no man [righteous] and marveled [was appalled] that there were no intercessors [no one to intervene on behalf of truth and right]"** (Is 59:2-16).

This is not the only biblical reference that mentions the connection between evil and darkness. Quite the contrary. The Scriptures are replete with comments concerning the two, and the relationship between them. For example, King Solomon -- ascribed as being the wisest man to ever live -- wrote: *"The path of the righteous is like the first gleam of dawn, shining ever brighter till the full light of day. But the way of the wicked is like deep darkness ; they do not know what makes them stumble"* (Pro 4:18-19).

Isaiah, in addition to his detailed description of the darkness of the fallen world mentioned above, provides this summary: **"See, darkness covers the earth and thick darkness is over the peoples"** (Is 60:2).

Luke counsels us to remember that: *"Your eye is the lamp of your body. When your eyes are good, your whole body also is full of light. But when they are bad, your body also is full of darkness. See to it, then, that the light within you is not darkness. Therefore, if your whole body is full of light, and no part of it dark, it will be completely lighted, as when the light of a lamp shines on you"* (Lk 11:34-36).

The apostle, Paul, speaking of those controlled by the powers of darkness, wrote: *"All have turned away, they have together become worthless; there is no one who does good, not even one. Their throats are open graves; their tongues practice deceit. The poison of vipers is on their lips. Their mouths are full of cursing and bitterness. Their feet are swift to shed blood; ruin and misery mark their ways, and the way of peace they do not know. There is no fear of God before their eyes"* (Ro 3:12-18).

Paul also warns Christians against becoming engaged with those in darkness: *"Let no one deceive you with empty words, for because of such things God's wrath comes on those who are disobedient. Therefore do not be partners with them. For you were once darkness , but now you are light in the Lord. Live as children of light (for the fruit of the light consists in all goodness, righteousness and truth) and find out what pleases the Lord. Have nothing to do with the fruitless deeds of darkness, but rather expose them"* Eph 5:6-11).

Peter, referring to this same group, says: *"These men are springs without water and mists driven by a storm. Blackest darkness is reserved for them"* (2 Peter 2:17). And, the apostle John tells us how to identify those who are in darkness: *"Anyone who claims to be in the light but hates his brother is still in the darkness. Whoever loves his brother lives in the light, and there is nothing in him to make him stumble. But whoever hates his brother is in the darkness and walks around in the darkness; he does not know where he is going, because the darkness has blinded him"* (1 Jn 2:9-11).

The Origin of Spiritual Darkness:
The Book of Jude, the next to last, and one of the shorter books of the Bible, provides us with some interesting insight into the origin of this present darkness, saying: **"And the angels who**

did not keep their positions of authority but abandoned their own home — these he has kept in darkness, bound with everlasting chains for judgment on the great Day" (Jude 6).

The book of Revelation also chronicles this event, correlating the identity of Satan with the devil: *"And there was war in heaven. Michael and his angels fought against the dragon, and the dragon and his angels fought back. But he was not strong enough, and they lost their place in heaven. The great dragon was hurled down — that ancient serpent called the devil, or Satan, who leads the whole world astray. He was hurled to the earth, and his angels with him"* (Rev 12:7-9).

The prophet **Isaiah also references this universal tragedy and its cause**, saying: *"How art thou fallen from heaven, O Lucifer, son of the morning! how art thou cut down to the ground, which didst weaken the nations! For thou hast said in thine heart, I will ascend into heaven, I will exalt my throne above the stars of God: I will sit also upon the mount of the congregation, in the sides of the north: I will ascend above the heights of the clouds; I will be like the most High. Yet thou shalt be brought down to hell, to the sides of the pit.*

They that see thee shall narrowly look upon thee, and consider thee, saying, Is this the man that made the earth to tremble, that did shake kingdoms; That made the world as a wilderness, and destroyed the cities thereof; that opened not the house of his prisoners?" (Is 14:12-17).

Job, the oldest book in the Bible, confirms that Lucifer and Satan are one, the same entity as the son of the morning (or of light) that was cast down: *"Now there was a day when the sons of God came to present themselves before the Lord, and Satan came also among them. And the Lord said unto Satan, "Whence comest thou?" Then Satan answered the Lord, and said, "From going to and fro in the earth, and from walking up and down in* it"" (Job 1:6-7). ... "*Again there was a day when the sons of God came to present themselves before the Lord, and Satan came also among them to present himself before the LORD. And the Lord said unto Satan, "From whence comest thou?" And Satan answered the Lord, and said, "From going to and fro in the earth, and from walking up and down in it"*" (Job 2:1-2).

Jude, in addition to identifying the origin of this present darkness, describes how it infested the ancient world, and predicted it would ultimately corrupt whole earth: *"In a similar way, Sodom and Gomorrah and the surrounding towns gave themselves up to sexual immorality and perversion. They serve as an example of those who suffer the punishment of eternal fire.*

"In the very same way, these [present-day] dreamers pollute their own bodies, reject authority and slander celestial beings. But even the archangel Michael, when he was disputing with the devil about the body of Moses, did not dare to bring a slanderous accusation against him, but said, "The Lord rebuke you!" Yet these men speak abusively against whatever they do not understand; and what things they do understand by instinct, like unreasoning animals — these are the very things that destroy them. Woe to them! They have taken the way of Cain; they have rushed for profit into Balaam's error; they have been destroyed in Korah's rebellion.

"These men are blemishes at your love feasts, eating with you without the slightest qualm — shepherds who feed only themselves. They are clouds without rain, blown along by the wind; autumn trees, without fruit and uprooted — twice dead. They are wild waves of the sea, foaming up their shame; wandering stars, for whom blackest darkness has been reserved forever. Enoch, the seventh from Adam, prophesied about these men: "See, the Lord is coming with thousands upon thousands of his holy ones to judge everyone, and to convict all the ungodly of all the ungodly acts they have done in the ungodly way, and of all the harsh words ungodly sinners have spoken against him."

"These men are grumblers and faultfinders; they follow their own evil desires; they boast about themselves and flatter others for their own advantage. But, dear friends, remember what the apostles of our Lord Jesus Christ foretold. They said to you, "In the last times there will be scoffers who will follow their own ungodly desires." These are the men who divide you, who follow mere natural instincts and do not have the Spirit" (Jude 6-19).

Perretti, in his book, "This Present Darkness", provides an excellent allegory depicting the dual-dimensional reality we live in: spiritual vs. Mortal, heavenly vs. Earthly. Nowhere, however, is the origin, and scope of this present darkness more succinctly described than in the book Jude was quoting from -- the ancient Book of Enoch.

While the Bible that most Christians use today contains only brief references to the patriarch, Enoch, more copies of the book ascribed to him -- the Book of Enoch -- or portions thereof, have been discovered, and found in more locations around the world, than any book of the canonized Bible. At least 40 manuscripts, or fragments thereof, of the ancient scroll, The First Book of Enoch, have been discovered in places as diverse as the Netherlands, Ethiopia, Syria and the Qumran Caves.

The Book of Enoch, together with a number of other ancient writings, have been included in the Apocrypha, a collection of works that many Christians hold to be spurious at best and at worst, a deception of the enemy of our souls. However, this collection of ancient writings was once held in great honor by Jewish and Christian theologians, historians and scholars alike.

If valid, the Book of Enoch and some of the other so called apocryphal books, provide the clearest insight into this dual-dimenstional reality, in which we live and breath and have our being. But, if spurious, the apocrypha could -- as some have claimed -- spawn heresy within the church. Before drawing a conclusion regarding the authenticity of these ancient writings, it's important to take the time to carefully examine the origin of the Apocrypha. Beginning in the next chapter, we provide a brief introduction to some of these ancient writings.

Chapter Two
The Apocrypha: The Hidden Secrets

The Apocrypha:
The Book of Enoch are a part of the Apocrypha, a collection of ancient writings that were originally considered too deep, too lofty in subject matter, for all but those initiated into the deeper mysteries of God. Then, over time, they came to be thought of as heretical and banned. To better understand the reasons for this ban, and the modern-day church's omission of the apocryphal books from the biblical cannon, the term "apocryphal" must be considered and properly understood.

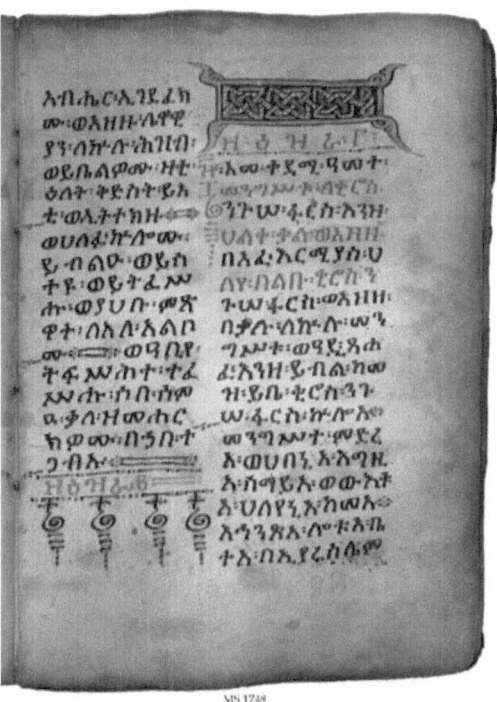

MS 1748
Ezra. In Ge'ez. Ethiopia, ca. 1350-1430

The word, 'apocryphal' is derived from a Greek word that means "hidden" or "secret." Originally, this was a complimentary term, and when applied to sacred writings, it meant that their contents were considered too exalted, too profound, or too deep, to be made available to the general public. Some members of the church orthodoxy were even kept in the dark, not being taught the teachings of these books, since they were considered to be unschooled in such matters. As a result, the concept gradually evolved, from the clergy itself, that these ancient scrolls -- once read only by the very wise -- were not to be read at all.

From that time on, the apocryphal books were read primarily by mystics and examined by esoteric circles of devout believers. The clergy members of the early church that were not admitted into such circles -- because they were thought not to be sufficiently enlightened -- retaliated. They effectively banned all apocryphal material, labeling it heretical, which meant it was forbidden to be read in the church, and prohibited reading for any Christian.

While the apocryphal books are included in modern Douay-Rheims Versions of the Bible -- the version relied on by Catholics -- Protestant traditions cite Revelation 22:18-19 as laying a potential curse on those who attach any canonical authority to extra-biblical writings, including the Apocrypha. However, a strict exegesis of this text clearly indicates it referred only to the Book of Revelation.

Revelation 22:18-19 (KJV) states: *"For I testify unto every man that heareth the words of the prophecy of this book, If any man shall add unto these things, God shall add unto him the plagues that are written in this book: And if any man shall take away from the words of the book of this prophecy, God shall take away his part out of the book of life, and out of the holy city, and from the things which are written in this book."* Holding to strict hermeneutics, the "book of prophecy" mentioned here does not refer to the Bible as a whole, but only to the Book of Revelation.

The Origin of the Cannon:
The biblical cannon that has been handed down to us, contains only those books that the First Council of Nicaea decided we should have. The First Council of Nicaea was convened in Nicaea in Bithynia (now a town in Turkey) by the Roman Emperor Constantine I in 325 AD. The Council of Nicaea is believed to have been the First Ecumenical council of the Christian Church, and was attended by the Assyrian Church of the East, the Oriental Orthodox, the Eastern Orthodox, the Roman Catholics, the Old Catholics, and a number of other Western Christian groups. The council's deliberations resulted in the first uniform Christian doctrine, called the Nicene Creed.

With the creation of this creed, a precedent was established for subsequent general (ecumenical) councils of Bishops' (Synods) for the development of statements of belief and canons of doctrinal orthodoxy — their intent being to define unity of beliefs for the whole of Christendom. From Koine Greek, the word, *'oikoumenikos'*, that has been translated into English as "ecumenical," literally means worldwide, however, the council of Nicaea was hardly worldwide. It was generally limited to the church officials within the Roman Empire.

One of the most important, and perhaps most infamous, acts of the Council of Nicaea involved decisions made concerning which of the many ancient scrolls and books would be retained in the official cannon of Scriptures -- the Bible. Most people today receive the writings that this council considered inspired, arranged and bound together in a book (Bible) identified as 'The

Holy Bible'. They unquestionably accept it as true, simply because that is what they found bound together under that title in their bookstore.

Many Protestants believe that when choosing a Bible at their favorite book store, they 'must avoid' the shelf labeled "Roman Catholic Bibles," since these are -- they believe -- designed to promote Catholic beliefs. They also contain some books that most Protestants do not even accept as Scripture — specifically those referred to as belonging to the "Apocrypha." Many simply reject these books without ever considering why they were omitted in the Protestant cannon and included in the Roman Catholic cannon.

In truth, very few -- even among the clergy -- have ever even read the apocryphal books, or evaluated them personally. In actuality, many Christians have never even read all of the books which they, and their pastor, consider to be Holy Scripture. It is evident then, that most people accept certain books and essentially reject others -- not because they have personally evaluated them -- but because they trust someone else who they believe has evaluated them, and made a decision for them in concerning this vital matter. A credible question then becomes: Who made this decision for us, and were they really competent to make this decision for all?

The Development of the Cannon:
In 367 AD, an influential bishop named Athanasius published a list of books authorized to be read in the churches under his supervision. This list included precisely those books we have in our Protestant Bibles today (except — he included the book of Baruch but deleted the book of Esther from the Old Testament). Other lists had previously been published, by other church historians and theologians, as early 170 AD. None of these lists received the full agreement of all the bishops.

Then there is another pertinent question. Who authorized the men who published these lists to decide which books should be accepted as Scripture?

Historians and scholars studying this issue closely have concluded that these lists of books merely ratified decisions made by the majority of churches from the earliest days of Christendom.

Irenaeus, born somewhere between 120 to 140 AD, in Asia Minor, and dying somewhere between 200 and 203 AD. Irenaeus lived in the days before anyone felt it necessary to identify and list 'the approved books'. He quotes as Scripture 'all of those books available'. As a boy, he had listened to the great bishop and martyr, Polycarp of Smyrna, who was a highly regarded disciple of Christ's apostles.

Irenasus later published a list containing only those books that appeared in another person's list, originally published on another continent, by Origen, who was born in 185 AD. Still other early Christian theologians developed other divergent lists. It is evident then, that the elders of each local congregation approved certain writings and rejected others as they became available to them, and were evaluated by them.

Prominent first through the forth century teachers were also influential in this process. About this time in history, bishops began to prevail over the Church, acting as governors over groups of churches. They in turn simply ratified earlier lists, prepared by others. These 'approved' books were then referred to as the "canon" of Scripture, "canon" being a Greek word meaning "rod" or "ruler." The approved books constituted the standard, or rule of faith, for all the churches under their governance. The canon was not imposed by ecclesiastical authority, it merely evolved through independent decisions of elders who were responsible for their congregations alone.

On what basis then did these church elders decide which writings should be read in their church as authoritative? Most simply received, without question, the writings of the apostles and their closest companions, as well as other writings endorsed by them. The entire Old Testament we use today was received pretty much intact by the implicit endorsement of the apostles. The single exception to this was the Book of Ecclesiastes. This book was omitted from many of the cannons until the authorized King James version was printed in 1611.

Their reasoning was that the Gospel of Matthew was written by an apostle; The Gospel of Mark was written by the apostle Peter's closest disciple; The Gospel of Luke was written by the apostle Paul's close companion; The Gospel of John was written by an apostle; And, the Acts of the Apostles was written by Luke, Paul's close companion.

Thirteen letters, now referred to as epistles were written to various churches by Paul, and were accepted by the church elders as authoritative. The epistle to the Hebrews was received by most, believing it too was from Paul. However, current thought suggests another author, or co-author was responsible for the book. The epistle of James was attributed to the brother of the Lord, who exercised authority in Jerusalem with the apostles. However, the authenticity of this book is to this day, still questioned by some. The epistle of Jude was from another brother of the Lord. The two epistles of Peter were from an apostle. And the three epistles of John are from an apostle, who many also credited with writing the Revelation. However, there is growing dispute about its authorship.

How did the early church elders know that these writings were not forgeries? They were not received them from strangers; but were hand-delivered by friends of the apostles to the church elders, many of whom also knew the apostles personally. Forgeries, they reasoned, would be obvious, especially if the writing promoted strange doctrines. However, some of the elders of various churches became wary, even beginning to doubt some of the writings they had formerly received, principally because they were copies from other churches' copies.

Writings that at one time or another have come under question include: Hebrews, James, Jude, 2 Peter, 2 and 3 John, and the Revelation of John. The reasons for doubt have been various. The author of Hebrews never identifies himself. James was not an apostle, and his message seems on some points to contradict Paul's message. Jude was not an apostle, and he quotes from the Book of Enoch, which the church had come to suspect. 2 Peter, was not widely distributed at first.

The author of 2 and 3 John doesn't identify himself plainly. The author of the Revelation identifies himself as John, but does not say that he is the apostle John. Moreover, the style of the Revelation is quite different from that of the Gospel of John, leading some to believe it may have been written by John the Baptist. Nevertheless, the majority of churches received and used the books contained in our present cannon of Scripture, without questioning them, while vigorously rejecting all others.

Jesus quoted from the Septuagint version of the Old Testament, so it would seem natural that if we could locate a copy of this document, it might be the most reliable. However, it is inaccurate to talk about the Septuagint as though it were a single book. During apostolic times, the various writings existed as separate scrolls. They were not bound together in a single volume until the middle of the second century AD, when the codex or physical "book" as we know it was invented.

Before this time, people didn't have books or bookshelves, but cabinets or large clay pots filled with scrolls. The codex was adopted by the early Christians who desired a more convenient way of referencing Scripture, and the Greek Old Testament was one of the first collection of writings to be put in this form. When compiled, there were certain writings referred to as Apocryphal. These were highly regarded by the Greek-speaking Jews, and were bound in the same volume with the other books.

Eventually, **the Septuagint came to be regarded as a kind of inspired scriptural paraphrase by teachers in the churches,** principally because the apostles had used it. However, some suspected that the Jews had deliberately corrupted the Hebrew text in certain anti-Christian ways since it was translated. This suspicion eventually led to the deletion of a number of writings, including even Ecclesiastees, which was not restored until 1611 AD. Other writings, many of them mentioned by name in the early 'approved writings', became particularly suspect, and were subsequently removed by church councils.

There are still surviving manuscripts of the early Christian Bible that include at least some of the Apocrypha as well as other disputed books. After the Protestant and Catholic canons were defined by Luther and Trent respectively, early Protestant and Catholic editions of the Bible did not at first omit these books, but placed them in a separate Apocrypha section apart from the

Old and New Testaments, to indicate their status. Even then there were variations in which books were considered authentic.

Jerome's Vulgate Prologues:
Jerome completed his version of the Bible, the Latin Vulgate, in 405. In the Middle Ages the Vulgate became the de facto standard version of the Bible in the West. These Bibles were divided into Old and New Testaments only; there was no separate Apocrypha section. Nevertheless, the Vulgate manuscripts included prologues which clearly identified certain books of the Vulgate Old Testament as apocryphal or non-canonical.

In the prologue to the books of Samuel and Kings, which is often called the Prologus Galeatus, Jerome described those books not translated from the Hebrew as apocrypha; he specifically mentions that Wisdom, the book of Jesus son of Sirach, Judith, Tobias, and the Shepherd 'are not in the canon'. In the prologue to Esdras he mentions 3rd. and 4th. Esdras as being apocrypha. In his prologue to the books of Solomon, he mentioned "the book of Jesus son of Sirach and another pseudepigraphos, which is titled the Wisdom of Solomon". He says of them and Judith, Tobias, and the Books of the Maccabees, that the Church "has not received them among the canonical scriptures".

He mentions the book of Baruch in his prologue to the Jeremiahs and does not explicitly refer to it as apocryphal, but he does mention that "it is neither read nor held among the Hebrews". In his prologue to the Judith he mentions that "among the Hebrews, the authority [of Judith] came into contention", but that it was "counted in the number of Sacred Scriptures" by the First Council of Nicaea.

Although in his Apology against Rufinus, Book II he denied the authority of the canon of the Hebrews, this caveat does not appear in the prologues themselves, nor in his prologues does he specify the authorship of the canon he describes. Whatever its origin or authority, it was this canon without qualification which was described in the prologues of the Bibles of Western Europe.

The Gutenberg Bible:
The famous Gutenberg Bible edition of the Vulgate was published in 1455. Like the manuscripts on which it was based, the

Gutenberg Bible lacked a specific Apocrypha section; its Old Testament included those books that Jerome considered apocryphal, and those which Clement VIII would later move to the appendix. The Prayer of Manasses was located after the Books of Chronicles, and 3rd. and 4th. Esdras followed 2nd. Esdras (Nehemiah), and the Prayer of Solomon followed Ecclesiasticus.

The Martin Luther Bible:
Martin Luther translated the Bible into German during the early part of the 16th century, first releasing a complete Bible in 1534. His Bible was the first major edition to have a separate section called the Apocrypha. Books and portions of books not found in the Hebrew Tanakh were moved out of the principal body of the Old Testament to this section. Luther placed these books between the Old and New Testaments. For this reason, these works are sometimes known as the inter-testamental books. The books 1st. and 2nd. Esdras were omitted by Martin Luther entirely. Many twentieth century editions of the Luther Bible omit the Apocrypha section all together. Luther also expressed some doubts about the canonicity of four New Testament books, although he never called them apocrypha. These included the Epistle to the Hebrews, the Epistles of James and Jude, and the Revelation to John. He did not put them in a separate section, but he did move them to the end of the New Testament.

The Clementine Vulgate:
In 1592 Pope Clement VIII published his revised edition of the Vulgate. He moved three books not found in the canon of the Council of Trent into an appendix, "ne prorsus interirent," "lest they utterly perish". These included: the Prayer of Manasses; 3rd. Esdras (1st Esdras in the early King James Bible); 4th. Esdras (2nd. Esdras in the early King James Bible). All the other books of the Old Testament, including the deuterocanonical books, were placed in their traditional positions.

The Geneva Bible:
The Geneva Bible is one of the most historically significant translations of the Bible in the English language, preceding the King James translation by 51 years. It was the primary Bible of the 16th Century Protestant movement and was the Bible used by William Shakespeare, Oliver Cromwell, John Milton, John Knox, John Donne, and John Bunyan, author of Pilgrim's Progress. It was one of the Bibles taken to America on the Mayflower, it was used by many English Dissenters, and it was still respected by Oliver Cromwell's soldiers at the time of the English Civil War.

Because the language of the Geneva Bible was more forceful and vigorous, most readers strongly preferred this version over the Bishops' Bible -- the translation authorized by the Church of England under Elizabeth I. In the words of Cleland Boyd McAfee, *"it drove the Great Bible off the field by sheer power of excellence"*.

The first full edition of this Bible, with a further revised New Testament, appeared in 1560, but it was not printed in England until 1575 for the New Testament and 1576 for the complete Bible. Over 150 editions of the Geneva Bible were issued; the last probably in 1644. The annotations are an important part of the Geneva Bible, and were Calvinist and Puritan in character. As such, they were disliked by the ruling pro – government Protestants of the Church of England, as well as King James I, who commissioned the "Authorized Version," or King James Bible, in order to replace it. The 1560 edition -- published specifically for the Protestant Reformers, played an important role in the development of the US Declaration of Independence and the Constitution.

The 1599 edition, that is highly publicized as the Bible of our founding fathers was not the edition used, It omitted the apocrypha and was thus rejected by the Protestant Reformers, The 1560 edition -- published at their request -- contained the entire apocrypha and extensive annotations.

The differences between the 1599 Geneva Bible and the 1611 King James Version of the Bible are apparent in many ways. The King James Version of the Bible eliminated the marginal notes that had been a popular feature for those who used them as a study guide in the 1599 Geneva Bible. The translation difference in each of the books of the Old Testament is also apparent in that the 1560 and 1599 Geneva Bible's Old Testament was translated directly from the Greek Old Testament and the Hebrew Septuagint scriptures, while the 1611 King James Version of the Bible was complied from previous English translations of the Old Testament.

After King James I commissioned the creation of the King James Version of the Bible, the realm's tolerance of Protestants and Puritans using the 1560 and 1599 Geneva Bible version became nonexistent. King James I and the Church of England wanted only their English translation version of the Bible to be in use. The Protestants and Puritans' only choices were to stay and live with the oppression or create another life for themselves in another country. Some followers of the Protestant Reformation moved north to The Netherlands and others went across the Atlantic Ocean to the American colonies.

The Original King James Version (including the Apocrypha):
The English-language King James Version of 1611 followed the lead of the Luther Bible in using an inter-testamental section labeled "Books called Apocrypha", or just "Apocrypha" at the running page header. The section contains the following books:

- 1 Esdras (Vulgate 3rd. Esdras)
- 2 Esdras (Vulgate 4th. Esdras)
- Tobit
- Judith
- The rest of Esther (Vulgate Esther 10:4-16:24)
- The Wisdom of Solomon (also referred to as Wisdom)
- Ecclesiasticus (also known as Sirach)
- Baruch and the Epistle of Jeremy (all part of Vulgate Baruch)
- Song of the Three Children (Vulgate Daniel 3:24-90)\
- Story of Susanna (Vulgate Daniel 13)
- The Idol Bel and the Dragon (Vulgate Daniel 14)
- The Prayer of Manasses
- 1st. Maccabees
- 2nd. Maccabees

Included in this list are those books of the Vulgate which were not in Luther's canon. These are the books which are most frequently referred to by the casual appellation "the Apocrypha".

These same books are also listed in Article VI of the Thirty-Nine Articles of the Church of England. Despite them being placed in the section titled the Apocrypha, in the table of lessons, located at the front of the King James Bible, these 'apocryphal' books are included in the Old Testament.

Additional Early Bible Editions:

All English translations of the Bible printed in the sixteenth century included a section or appendix for Apocryphal books. Matthew's Bible, published in 1537, contains all the Apocrypha of the later King James Version in an inter-testamental section. The 1538 Myles Coverdale Bible contained an Apocrypha which excluded Baruch and the Prayer of Manasseh. The 1560 Geneva Bible placed the Prayer of Manasseh after 2nd. Chronicles and the rest of the Apocryphal books were placed in an inter-testamental section. The Douay-Rheims Bible (1582-1609) placed the Prayer of Manasseh and 3rd. and 4th. Esdras into an Appendix of the second volume of the Old Testament.

In the Zürich Bible (1529-30) the apocryphal books are placed in an Appendix. They include 3rd. Maccabees, along with 1st. Esdras & 2nd. Esdras. The 1st edition omitted the Prayer of Manasseh and the Rest of Esther, although these were included in the 2nd edition. The French Bible (1535) of Pierre Robert Olivétan placed them between the Testaments, with the subtitle, "The volume of the apocryphal books contained in the Vulgate translation, which we have not found in the Hebrew or Chaldee".

In 1569 the Spanish Reina Bible following the example of the pre-Clementine Latin Vulgate contained the deuterocanonical books in its Old Testament. Valera's 1602 revision of the Reina Bible moved these books into an inter-Testamental section following the other Protestant translations of its day.

The Disappearing Apocrypha:
All King James Bibles published before 1640 included the complete Apocrypha. In 1826, the British and Foreign Bible Society (BFBS) decided that no more BFBS funds were to be used to pay for the printing of any Apocryphal books, anywhere. Since that time, most modern editions of the Bible and re-printings of the King James Bible omit the Apocrypha section.

In the 18th century, the Apocrypha section was omitted from the Challoner revision of the Douay-Rheims version. In the 1979 revision of the Vulgate, the section was dropped. Modern reprinting of the Clementine Vulgate commonly omits the Apocrypha section. Many reprintings of older versions of the Bible now omit the apocrypha and many newer translations and revisions have never included them at all.

There are some exceptions to this trend, however. Some editions of the Revised Standard Version of the Bible include not only the Apocrypha listed above, but also include the third and fourth books of the Maccabees, and Psalm 151; the RSV Apocrypha also lists the Letter of Jeremiah (Epistle of Jeremy in the KJV) as separate from the book of Baruch, following the Orthodox tradition.

Reemergence of the Apocrypha:
The American Bible Society lifted its restrictions on the publication of Bibles with the Apocrypha in 1964. The British and Foreign Bible Society followed in 1966. The Stuttgart edition of the Vulgate (the printed edition only -- not most of the on-line editions), published by the United Bible Society (UBS), contains the Clementine Apocrypha as well as the Epistle to the Laodiceans and Psalm 151.

Brenton's edition of the Septuagint includes all of the Apocrypha found in the King James Bible with the exception of 2nd. Esdras, which was not in the Septuagint and is no longer extant in Greek. He places them in a separate section at the end of his Old Testament, following English tradition. In Greek circles, however, these books are not traditionally called Apocrypha, but **Anagignoskomena**, and are integrated into the Old Testament.

The Anagignoskomena:
The Septuagint, the preeminent Greek version of the Old Testament, contains a number of books that are not present in the Hebrew Bible. These texts are not traditionally segregated into a separate section, nor are they usually called apocrypha. Rather, they are referred to as the Anagignoskomena ("things that are read"). The anagignoskomena included the books of Tobit, Judith, Wisdom of Solomon, Wisdom of Jesus Sirach, Baruch, Epistle of Jeremy (in the Vulgate this is chapter 6 of Baruch), additions to Daniel (The Prayer of Azarias, Sosanna and Bel and the Dragon), additions to Esther, 1st. Maccabees, 2nd. Maccabees, 3rd. Maccabees, 1st. Esdras, and Psalm 151. 4th. Maccabees is relegated to an appendix in modern editions of the Greek Bible. Some editions add the Odes, including the Prayer of Manasses. And some Slavonic Bibles add 2nd Esdras.

The Apocrypha vs. the Pseudegrapha:
Technically a pseudepigraphon is a book written in a particular biblical style which is ascribed to an author who did not actually write it. In common usage, however, the term pseudepigrapha is often misused to refer to the apocryphal writings which do not appear in printed editions of the Bible, as opposed to the apocryphal texts listed above.

Examples of these unprinted ancient writings, that are often misrepresented as pseuidegraphical, include the following books:

- The Letter of Aristeas
- The Martyrdom and Ascension of Isaiah
- Joseph and Aseneth
- Life of Adam and Eve
- Lives of the Prophets
- The Ladder of Jacob
- Jannes and Jambres
- The History of the Rechabites
- Eldad and Modad
- The History of Joseph
- The Odes of Solomon
- The Prayer of Joseph
- The Prayer of Jacob.

Often included among the pseudepigrapha are 3rd. and 4th. Maccabees because they are not traditionally found in most western Bibles, although, they were included in the Septuagint. Similarly, the Book of Enoch, the Book of Jubilees and 4th. Baruch are often listed with the pseudepigrapha although they are included in most Ethiopian and Syriac Bibles. The Psalms of Solomon are also included in some editions of the Septuagint.

In his spiritual autobiography, titled: "Grace Abounding to the Chief of Sinners," John Bunyan, author of "Pilgrim's Progress," recounts how God strengthened him against the temptation to despair of his salvation by inspiring him with the words, *"Look at the generations of old and see: did any ever trust in God, and were confounded?"*

John Bunyan -- Author of Pilgrim's Progress

Regarding the Apocrypha, Bunyan says: *"At which I was greatly encouraged in my soul... So coming home, I presently went to my Bible, to see if I could find that saying, not doubting but to find it presently... Thus I continued above a year, and could not find the place; but at last, casting my eye upon the Apocrypha books, I found it in Ecclesiasticus, chap. ii. 10. This, at the first, did somewhat daunt me; because it was not in those texts that we call holy*

and canonical; yet, as this sentence was the sum and substance of many of the promises, it was my duty to take the comfort of it; and I bless God for that word, for it was of good to me. That word doth still ofttimes shine before my face."

The Apocrypha of the King James Bible constitutes the books of the Vulgate that are present neither in the Hebrew Old Testament nor the Greek New Testament. Since these are derived from the Septuagint, from which the old Latin version was translated, it follows that the difference between the KJV and the Roman Catholic Old Testaments is traceable to the difference between the Palestinian and the Alexandrian canons of the Old Testament. This is only true with certain reservations, as the Latin Vulgate was revised by Jerome according to the Hebrew, and, where Hebrew originals were not found, according to the Septuagint.

Furthermore, the Vulgate omits 3rd. and 4th. Maccabees, which generally appear in the Septuagint, while the Septuagint and Luther's Bible omit 2nd. Esdras, which is found in the Apocrypha of the Vulgate and the King James Bible. Luther's Bible, moreover, also omits 1st. Esdras. It should further be observed that the Clementine Vulgate places the Prayer of Manasses and 3rd. Esdras and 4th. Esdras in an appendix after the New Testament as apocryphal.

It is hardly possible to form any classification -- or cannon -- of Scripture which is not open to some objection. Scholars are still divided as to the original language, date, and place of composition of some of the books which must come under this provisional attempt at order. (Thus some of the additions to Daniel and the Prayer of Manasseh are most probably derived from a Semitic original written in Palestine, yet in compliance with the prevailing opinion they are classed under Hellenistic Jewish literature. Again, the Slavonic Enoch goes back undoubtedly in part to a Semitic original, though some of it may have been written by a Greek Jew in Egypt.)

In order to vicariously sit on the Council of Nicaea and participate in their deliberations concerning these ancient writings, come with me while we examine exerts from these ancient patriarchs, prophets and scribes.

CHAPTER THREE
THE BOOK OF ENOCH

The Book of Enoch, also known as Ethiopic Enoch, Ist. Enoch, and **The Book of Henoch" was once highly revered by the Jews and Christians alike,** but it fell into disfavor among powerful theologians of the second century AD because of its controversial descriptions of the nature and deeds of the fallen angels. The Enochian writings and others, such as The Books of Tobias and Esdras, were omitted (or lost) from the Bible. The Book of Enoch, was for a very long time considered by the early church fathers to be among the biblical apocryphal writings.

The writings referred to as the Book of Enoch were banned as heretical by Church fathers much later than many of the other banned ancient writings. Its ban resulted mainly because of its theme concerning the nature and actions of the fallen angels. In fact, Enoch's record of this event, briefly recorded in Genesis 6, actually infuriated some of the Church fathers. In time, some Jewish Rabbis followed their lead, even refusing to give credence to these writings they once held as among the most sacred. The Books of Enoch -- relied on for doctrine by Jesus and his brother, Jude -- were ultimately considered such a sacrilege that they were denounced, cursed, banned, and no doubt burned and shredded. As a result, the book of Enoch was conveniently lost for about a thousand years. But, with ironical persistence -- and unquestionably in God's perfect timing -- the Book of Enoch eventually reappeared.

Once banned, the reasons for the church having suppressed and forbidden the book so became much more illusive after the Book of Enoch was rediscovered. Rumors of a surviving copy of the book surfaced in 1773, sending **Scottish explorer, James Bruce**, off to distant Ethiopia in search of it. Arriving there, Bruce discovered that the Ethiopic church had not only saved the Book of Enoch; indeed they kept it alongside all the other sacred books of the Bible.

James Bruce was in time, able to secure not just one, but three copies of the Ethiopic Book of Enoch, which he brought back to Europe and England. Nearly a half-century after its rediscovery, in 1821, Dr. Richard Laurence, an Oxford Hebrew professor, produced the first English translation of the Books of Enoch. This translation gave the world its first glimpse of the once cherished, and then later forbidden, Enochian mysteries pertaining to the watchers and their offspring, the Nephilim.

Recent discoveries have produced additional copies of the book, found among the Dead Sea Scrolls at Qumran. This find proved beyond a shadow of doubt that the **Book of Enoch was well accepted, and in existence before the time of Jesus Christ**. The date of the original writing, upon which the second century BC, Qumran copies were based, is shrouded in obscurity. However, it is, in a word, old -- very, very old. Early Christians accepted the words of this Book of Enoch as authentic scripture, especially those portions that were later most questioned -- those describing the fallen angels, their intermarriage with the daughters of men, and their prophesied judgment.

Many of the key concepts taught by Jesus Christ, and recorded by his apostles, seem to have been drawn from, or at least directly connected to, terms and ideas contained in the Book of Enoch. Thus, it is hard to avoid the conclusion that Jesus not only accepted the book, and studied it, but also respected it highly enough to adopt, and elaborate on, its specific descriptions of the coming kingdom and its theme of an inevitable judgment descending upon "the wicked ones." This term -- 'the wicked ones' was most often used throughout the Old Testament to describe a group of angels known as the 'Watchers'. There is, in fact, **abundant proof that Christ not only approved of, but actually taught from, the Book of Enoch**. More than one hundred phrases in the New Testament find their precedents nowhere else, but in the Book of Enoch.

The time span between the writings of Enoch and those of Jude (pictured left) is approximately 3400 years. Therefore, Jude's reference to the Enochian prophesies strongly supports the conclusion that these written prophecies were both available to him and others at that time, they were apparently accepted without question. Long after Jude, many respected early church fathers, including: Tatian (110-172); Irenaeus, Bishop of Lyons (115-185); Clement of Alexandria (150-220); Tertullian (160-230); Origen (186-255); Lactantius (260-330); Methodius of Philippi, Minucius Felix, Commodianus, and Ambrose of Milan accepted the Enochian writings as inspired.

Even St. Augustine (354-430) said he supposed the work to be the genuine work of the patriarch, Enoch. Given this sound endorsement of authenticity, let's personally examine a few exerts from the Book of Enoch. The first glimpse will be that which may have been the very information Moses relied on when he compiled the first eleven books of Genesis -- often referred to as 'Primeval History'.

Most commonly, the phrase, "Book of Enoch" refers to solely to the First Book of Enoch, which is wholly extant only in the Ethiopic language, with Aramaic fragments from Qumran and medieval Greek fragments found in a number of other locations. In addition to this book, there are two other books named "Enoch": The Second Book of Enoch (surviving only in Old Slavonic, with an English translation by R. H. Charles (1896); and the Third Book of Enoch (surviving in Hebrew, and attributed to about the fifth-sixth century). The numbering of these texts has been applied by scholars to distinguish the texts from one another. The remainder of our discussion her deals exclusively with the First Book of Enoch.

While the Book of Enoch does not form part of the Canon of Scripture used by most Protestant Christian Churches today, it was quoted as a prophetic text in the New Testament (see the Letter of Jude, also the reference to it in I Peter 3:19,20). It is also considered by many to be the original source for many of the Old Testament references to giants, including those in Genesis 6, which is believed to describe a time when fallen angels (or Watchers) took wives of the children of men, giving birth to giants mentioned by historians throughout the first 3,000 years of biblical history.

The **Book of Enoch was also quoted by many of the early Church Fathers, and the Ethiopian Orthodox Christian Church still regards it to be inspired Scripture**. The currently known copies of this work are usually dated sometime during the Second Temple period, that is between the fourth or third century BC, and the first century AD.

The First Book of Enoch consists of five distinct major sections:

1. The Book of the Watchers (1 Enoch 1 – 36).

2. The Book of Parables of Enoch (1 Enoch 37 – 71) (Also called the Similitudes of Enoch).

3. The Astronomical Book (1 Enoch 72 – 82) (Also called the Book of the Heavenly Luminaries or Book of Luminaries).

4. The Book of Dream Visions (1 Enoch 83 – 90) (Also called the Book of Dreams).

5. The Epistle of Enoch (1 Enoch 91 – 108).

The results of contemporary scholarly research covering the First Book of Enoch are well represented by the monumental Commentary published in 2001 by **George W. E. Nickelsburg** in the Hermeneia Series. The shared view of contributing scholars is that these five sections were originally independent works, themselves a product of much editorial arrangement, that were later redacted into what we now call the First Book of Enoch.

This view is, however, opposed by a few authors who maintain the literary integrity of the Book of Enoch. One of the most recent proponents of this latter concept being Wossenie Yifru (1990).

Before the discovery of the Dead Sea Scrolls, a great deal of the undercurrent regarding the narrative of these sections was aimed at the apparent similarity of literature from the era of the Maccabees. For that reason, the First Book of Enoch had mistakenly been dated during (or after) the 2nd century BC. However, the discovery at Qumran of ancient pre-Maccabean fragments of the Book of the Watchers and the Astronomical Book have proven this not to be the case.

1 Enoch 6–11, a part of the Book of Watchers, is now believed to have been written much earlier, and is understood to contain the original core of that Book, around which the remainder may have been added at some later time. Only the "Book of Dream Visions", that contains a prophetic vision of the history of Israel, all the way down to what the majority of scholars have interpreted as the revolt of the Maccabees, could possibly be dated during Maccabean times.

The Book of Parables appears to be based on the Book of Watchers, including a portion that may have been a later development of the idea of final judgment and eschatology, concerned not only with the destiny of the fallen angels but also with the destiny of the evil kings of the Earth. The Book of Parables contains several references to a Messiah, Son of Man, as well as including a number of messianic themes. As no fragments of this work were found at Qumran, historian Józef Milik took the view that this section dates from later, Christian times. However, since the term "Son of Man" is a Semitic phrase, and since the Book of Daniel also refers to a Son of Man, in a context of judgment, most ancient philology specialists now maintain that the work is a Second Temple Jewish document, copied from much earlier writings, and compiled as early as the late 1st century BC or the very beginning of the 1st century AD.

As for the Second Book of Enoch, almost all scholars that deal with this book believe it was translated into Old Church Slavonic from an earlier Greek edition, perhaps by Saints Cyril and Methodius. In addition to the five sections identified above, historian, Józef Milik, has suggested that the "Book of Giants", discovered among the Dead Sea Scrolls should be accepted as part of the collection of the works of Enoch and included after the Book of Watchers. The traditional view of the Ethiopic Orthodox Church, which reckons the First Book of Enoch to be an inspired document, is that the Ethiopic text is the original one, written by Enoch himself. In their view, the opening sentence of Enoch is the first and oldest sentence ever written in any human language, since Enoch, by his own declaration, was the first human to write letters. Translated, these words read as follows: *"Word of blessing of Henok (Enoch), wherewith he blessed the chosen and righteous who would be alive in the day of tribulation for the removal of all wrongdoers and backsliders."*

The **Book of Enoch describes the fall of a number of the Watchers, a special class of angels** who were assigned to watch over and protect mankind. These fallen Watchers were those angels who took human wives and fathered the Nephilim (cf. the bene Elohim, Genesis 6:1-2), both before the flood and at other times in history (Genesis 6:4). The fallen angels went to

Enoch asking him intercede on their behalf before God, after he declared to them their doom.

The remainder of the book describes Enoch's visit to Heaven in the form of a vision, and his revelations. The book also contains descriptions of the movements of heavenly bodies (in connection with Enoch's trip to Heaven). It has been speculated that certain portions of this provide instructions for the construction of a solar declinometer (an instrument for measuring magnetic declination).

The Book of the Watchers is further divided into several sections that have been placed into chapters by modern translators:

- I-V. Parable of Enoch on the Future Lot of the Wicked and the Righteous.

- VI-XI. The Fall of the Angels: the Demoralization of Mankind: the Intercession of the Angels on behalf of Mankind. The Dooms pronounced by God on the Angels of the Messianic Kingdom.

- XII-XVI. Dream-Vision of Enoch: his Intercession for Azazel and the fallen angels: and his Announcement of their first and final Doom.

- XVII-XXXVI. Enoch's Journeys through the Earth and Sheol.

    - XVII-XIX. The First Journey.
    - XX. Names and Functions of the Seven Archangels.
    - XXI. Preliminary and final Place of Punishment of the fallen Angels (stars).
    - XXII. Sheol or the Underworld.
    - XXIII. The fire that deals with the Luminaries of Heaven.
    - XXIV-XXV. The Seven Mountains in the North-West and the Tree of Life.
    - XXVI. Jerusalem and the Mountains, Ravines, and Streams.
    - XXVII. The Purpose of the Accursed Valley.
    - XXVIII-XXXIII. Further Journey to the East.
    - IV-XXXV. Enoch's Journey to the North.
    - VI. The Journey to the South.

In the introduction to the Book of Enoch, the author tells us that he is *"a just man, whose eyes were opened by God so that he saw vision of the Holy One in the heavens, which the sons of God showed to me, and from them I heard everything, and I knew what I saw, but [these things that I saw will] not [come to pass] for this generation, but for a generation that has yet to come."* The book then goes on to prophetically describe God coming to Earth, on Mount Sinai, with his hosts to pass judgment on mankind. It also tells us about the luminaries of the skies rising and setting in their order and in their own time, that never changes.

Our purpose for incorporating part of this information is not to reopen the debate concerning whether or not the Book of Enoch rightfully belongs in the cannon of Scriptures, but merely to provide additional information on the origin of this present darkness over the earth, drawn from the same source that has been cited by a number of biblical authors, whose works we accept without question as being inspired.

While no claim of authenticity is being made for these books by the authors, it is important to note that an increasing number of Christian Theological Seminaries now rely on, and teach from, the Books of Enoch, as well as several other of the apocryphal books. The result is that more and more clergy and Bible students are becoming acquainted with these important historical works. Biblical study and translation software vendors have begun meeting their expressed need by including the Books of Enoch, and some of the other apocryphal writings, in their program's resources, making these important writings available once more to the church.

Chapter Four
The Watchers

The story of The Watchers, mentioned in brevity in Genesis 6, is consistent with, and appears to have been taken directly from, the Book of Enoch. The primary difference between the sources is that the record provided in the Book of Enoch provides far more detail.

First Book of Enoch:

Chapter 7: *"It happened after the sons of men had multiplied in those days, that daughters were born to them, elegant and beautiful. And when the watchers (angels, the sons of heaven), beheld them, they became enamored of them, saying to each other, Come, let us select for ourselves wives from the progeny of men, and let us beget children.*

"Then their leader Samyaza said to them; I fear that you may perhaps be indisposed to the performance of this enterprise; And that I alone shall suffer for so grievous a crime. But they answered him and said; We all swear; And bind ourselves by mutual execrations, that we will not change our intention, but execute our projected undertaking" (Vs 1-6).

"Then they swore all together, and all bound themselves by mutual execrations. Their whole number was two hundred, who descended upon Ardis, which is the top of mount Armon. That mountain therefore was called Armon, because they had sworn upon it, and bound themselves by mutual execrations. These are the names of their chiefs: Samyaza, who was their leader, Urakabarameel, Akibeel, Tamiel, Ramuel, Danel, Azkeel,

Saraknyal, Asael, Armers, Batraal, Anane, Zavebe, Samsaveel, Ertael, Turel, Yomyael, Arazyal. These were the prefects of the two hundred angels, and the remainder were all with them" (Vs 7-9).

[The Aramaic texts preserve an earlier list of names of these Watchers: Semihazah; Artqoph; Ramtel; Kokabel; Ramel; Danieal; Zeqiel; Baraqel; Asael; Hermoni; Matarel; Ananel; Stawel; Samsiel; Sahriel; Tummiel; Turiel; Yomiel; Yhaddiel] (Milik, p. 151).

"Then they took wives, each choosing for himself; whom they began to approach, and with whom they cohabited; teaching them sorcery, incantations, and the dividing of roots and trees. And the women conceiving brought forth giants, whose stature was each three hundred cubits. These devoured all which the labor of men produced; until it became impossible to feed them; when they turned themselves against men, in order to devour them; and began to injure birds, beasts, reptiles, and fishes, to eat their flesh one after another (one another's flesh), and to drink their blood" (Vs 10-14).

Chapter 8: "Moreover Azazyel taught men to make swords, knives, shields, breastplates, the fabrication of mirrors, and the workmanship of bracelets and ornaments, the use of paint, the beautifying of the eyebrows, the use of stones of every valuable and select kind, and all sorts of dyes, so that the world became altered. Impiety increased; fornication multiplied; and they *transgressed and corrupted all their ways. Amazarak taught all the sorcerers, and dividers of roots: Armers taught the solution of sorcery; Barkayal taught the observers of the stars (Astrologers), Akibeel taught signs; Tamiel taught astronomy; And Asaradel taught the motion of the moon, And men, being destroyed, cried out; and their voice reached to heaven."*

Chapter 9: *"Then Michael and Gabriel, Raphael, Suryal, and Uriel, looked down from heaven, and saw the quantity of blood which was shed on earth, and all the iniquity which was done upon it, and said one to another, It is the voice of their cries; The earth, deprived of her children has cried even to the gate of heaven. And now to you, O you holy one of heaven, the souls of men complain, saying, "Obtain Justice for us with the Most High." Then they said to their Lord, the King, "You are Lord of lords, God of gods, King of kings.*

"The throne of your glory is for ever and ever, and for ever and ever is your name sanctified and glorified. You are blessed and glorified. Obtain justice for us with (Literally, "Bring judgment to us from." You have made all things; you possess power over all things; and all things are open and manifest before you. You behold all things, and nothing can be concealed from you. You have seen what Azazyel has done, how he has taught every species of iniquity upon earth, and has disclosed to the world all the secret things which are done in the heavens. Samyaza also has taught sorcery, to whom you have given authority over those who are associated with him. They have gone together to

the daughters of men; have lain with them; have become polluted; And have discovered (revealed) crimes to them.

"**The women likewise have brought forth giants**. Thus has the whole earth been filled with blood and with iniquity. And now behold the souls of those who are dead, cry out. And complain even to the gate of heaven. Their groaning ascends; nor can they escape from the unrighteousness which is committed on earth. You know all things, before they exist. You know these things, and what has been done by them; yet you do not speak to us. What on account of these things ought we to do to them?" (Vs 3-14).

Chapter 10: "Then the Most High, the Great and Holy One spoke, And sent Arsayalalyur to the son of Lamech, Saying, Say to him in my name, Conceal yourself. Then explain to him the consummation which is about to take place; for all the earth shall perish; the waters of a deluge shall come over the whole earth, and all things which are in it shall be destroyed. And now teach him how he may escape, and how his seed may remain in all the earth." (Vs 1-5).

"Again the Lord said to Raphael, Bind Azazyel hand and foot; cast him into darkness; and opening the desert which is in Dudael, cast him in there. Throw upon him hurled and pointed stones, covering him with darkness; There shall he remain for ever; cover his face, that he may not see the light. And in the great day of judgment let him be cast into the fire. Restore the earth, which the angels have corrupted; and announce life to it, that I may revive it. All the sons of men shall not perish in consequence of every secret, by which the Watchers have destroyed, and which they have taught, their offspring. All the earth has been corrupted by the effects of the teaching of Azazyel. To him therefore ascribe the whole crime" (Vs 6-12).

"**To Gabriel also the Lord said**, Go to the biters (more accurately bastards), to the reprobates, to the children of fornication; and destroy the children of fornication, the offspring of the Watchers, from among men; bring them forth, and excite them one against another. Let them perish by mutual slaughter; for length of days shall not be theirs. They shall all entreat you, but their fathers shall not obtain their wishes respecting them; for they shall hope for eternal life, and that they may live, each of them, five hundred years" (Vs 13-14).

"**To Michael likewise the Lord said**, Go and announce his crime to Samyaza, and to the others who are with him, who have been associated with women, that they might be polluted with all their impurity. And when all their sons shall be slain, when they shall see the perdition of their beloved, bind them for seventy generations underneath the earth, even to the day of judgment, and of consummation, until the judgment, the effect of which will last for ever, be completed. Then shall they be taken away into the lowest depths of the fire in torments; and in confinement shall they be shut up for ever. Immediately after this shall he, (Samyaza) together with them, burn and perish; they shall be bound until the consummation of many generations. Destroy all the souls addicted to dalliance, (lust) and the offspring of the Watchers, for they have tyrannized over mankind. Let every oppressor perish from the face of the earth; Let every evil work be destroyed" (Vs 15-20).

"The plant of righteousness and of rectitude appear, and its produce become a blessing. Righteousness and rectitude shall be for ever planted with delight. And then shall all the saints give thanks, and live until they have begotten a thousand children, while the whole period of their youth, and their sabbaths shall be completed in peace. In those days all the earth shall be cultivated in righteousness; it shall be wholly planted with trees, and filled with benediction; every tree of delight shall be planted in it. In it shall vines be planted; and the vine which shall be planted in it shall yield fruit to satiety; every seed, which shall be sown in it, shall produce for one measure a thousand; and one measure of olives shall produce ten presses of oil" (Vs 21-24).

"Purify the earth from all oppression, from all injustice, from all crime, from all impiety, and from all the pollution which is committed upon it. Exterminate them from the earth. Then shall all the children of men be righteous, and all nations shall pay me divine honors, and bless me; and all shall adore me. The earth shall be cleansed from all corruption, from every crime, from all punishment, and from all suffering; neither will I again send a deluge upon it from generation to generation for ever. In those days I will open the treasures of blessing which are in heaven, that I may cause them to descend upon earth, and upon all the works and labor of man. Peace and equity shall associate with the sons of men all the days of the world, in every generation of it" (Vs 25-29).

Chapter 12: *"Before all these things Enoch was concealed; nor did any one of the sons of men know where he was concealed, where he had been, and what had happened. He was wholly engaged with the holy ones, and with the Watchers in his days. "I, Enoch, was blessing the great Lord and King of peace. And behold the Watchers called me Enoch the scribe." Then the Lord said to me: "Enoch, scribe of righteousness, go tell the Watchers of heaven, who have deserted the lofty sky, and their holy everlasting station, who have been polluted with women. And have done as the sons of men do, by taking to themselves wives, and who have been greatly corrupted on the earth; That on the earth they shall never obtain peace and remission of sin. For they shall not rejoice in their offspring; they shall behold the slaughter of their beloved; shall lament for the destruction of their sons; and shall petition for ever; but shall not obtain mercy and peace."*

Chapter 13: *"Then Enoch, passing on, said to Azazyel: You shalt not obtain peace. A great sentence is gone forth against you. He shall bind you; Neither shall relief, mercy, and supplication be yours, on account of the oppression which you have taught; And on account of every act of blasphemy, tyranny, and sin, which you have discovered to the children of men. Then* departing from him I spoke to them all together; And they all became terrified, and trembled; Beseeching me to write for them a memorial of supplication, that they might obtain forgiveness; and that I might make the memorial of their prayer ascend up before the God of heaven; because they could not themselves thenceforwards address him, nor raise up their eyes to heaven on account of the disgraceful offense for which they were judged" (Vs 1-6).

"Then I wrote a memorial of their prayer and supplications, for their spirits, for everything which they had done, and for the subject of their entreaty, that they might obtain remission and rest. Proceeding on, I continued over the waters of Danbadan, which is on the right to the west of Armon, reading the memorial of their prayer, until I fell asleep. And behold a dream came to me, and visions appeared above me. I fell down and saw a vision of punishment, that I might relate it to the sons of heaven, and reprove them. When I awoke I went to them. All being collected together stood weeping in Oubelseyael, which is situated between Libanos and Seneser, (near Damascus) with their faces veiled. I related in their presence all the visions which I had seen, and my dream; And began to utter these words of righteousness, reproving the Watchers of heaven" (Vs. 7-14).

Chapter 14: "This is the book of the words of righteousness, and of the reproof of the Watchers, who belong to the world,

(who are from eternity) according to that which He, who is holy and great, commanded in the vision. I perceived in my dream, that I was now speaking with a tongue of flesh, and with my breath, which the Mighty One has put into the mouth of men, that they might converse with it. And understand with the heart. As he has created and given to men the power of comprehending the word of understanding, so has he created and given to me the power of reproving the Watchers, the offspring of heaven. I have written your petition; and in my vision it has been shown me, that what you request will not be granted you as long as the world endures" (Vs 1-2).

The End of the Giants:

"Judgment has been passed upon you: your request will not be granted you. From this time forward, never shall you ascend into heaven; He has said, that on the earth He will bind you, as long as the world endures. But before these things **you shall behold the destruction of your beloved sons;** you shall not possess them, but they shall fall before you by the sword. Neither shall you entreat for them, not for yourselves; But you shall weep and supplicate in silence. The words of the book which I wrote" (Vs 3-7).

"A vision thus appeared to me. Behold, in that vision clouds and a mist invited me; agitated stars and flashes of lightning impelled and pressed me forwards, while winds in the vision assisted my flight, accelerating my progress. They elevated me aloft to heaven. I proceeded, until I arrived at a wall built with stones of crystal. A vibrating flame (a tongue of fire) surrounded it, which began to strike me with terror. Into this vibrating flame I entered; And drew nigh to a spacious habitation built also with stones of crystal. Its walls too, as well as pavement, were *formed with stones of crystal, and crystal likewise was the ground. Its roof had the appearance of agitated stars and flashes of lightning; and among them were cherubim of fire in a stormy sky. (a heaven of water) A flame burned around its walls; and its portal blazed with fire. When I entered into this dwelling, it was hot as fire and cold as ice. No trace of delight or of life was there. Terror overwhelmed me, and a fearful shaking seized me. Violently agitated and trembling, I fell upon my face"* (Vs 8-13).

*"In the vision **I looked. And behold there was another habitation more spacious than the former,** every entrance to which was open before me, erected in the midst of a vibrating flame. So greatly did it excel in all points, in glory, in magnificence, and in magnitude, that it is impossible to describe to you either the splendour or the extent of it. Its floor was on fire; above were lightnings and agitated stars, while its roof exhibited a blazing fire. Attentively I surveyed it, and saw that it contained an exalted throne; The appearance of which was like that of frost; while its circumference resembled the orb of the brilliant sun; and there was the voice of the cherubim. From underneath this mighty throne rivers of flaming fire issued"* (Vs 14-19).

"To look upon it was impossible. One great in glory sat upon it: whose robe was brighter than the sun, and whiter than snow. No angel was capable of penetrating to view the face of Him, the Glorious and the Effulgent; nor could any mortal behold Him. A fire was flaming around Him. A fire also of great extent

continued to rise up before Him; so that not one of those who surrounded Him was capable of approaching Him, among the myriads of myriads who were before Him. To Him holy consultation was needless. Yet did not the sanctified, who were near Him, depart far from Him either by night or by day; nor were they removed from Him. I also was so far advanced, with a veil on my face, and trembling. Then the Lord with his own mouth called me, saying, Approach hither, Enoch, at my holy word. And He raised me up, making me draw near even to the entrance. My eye was directed to the ground" (Vs 20-25).

Chapter 15: "Then addressing me, He spoke and said, Hear, neither be afraid, O righteous Enoch, you scribe of righteousness: approach hither, and hear my voice. Go, say to the Watchers of heaven, who have sent you to pray for them, You ought to pray for men, and not men for you. Wherefore have you forsaken the lofty and holy heaven, which endures for ever, and have lain with women; have defiled yourselves with the daughters of men; have taken to yourselves wives; have acted like the sons of the earth, and have begotten an impious offspring? (literally giants). You being spiritual, holy, and possessing a life which is eternal, have polluted yourselves with women; have begotten in carnal blood; have lusted in the blood of men; and have done as those who are flesh and blood do. These however die and perish" (Vs 1-4).

"Therefore have I given to them (humans) wives, that they might cohabit with them; that sons might be born of them; and that this might be transacted upon earth. But you from the beginning were made spiritual, possessing a life which is eternal, and not subject to death for ever. Therefore I made not wives for you, because, being spiritual, your dwelling is in heaven. Now the giants, who have been born of spirit and of flesh, shall be called upon earth evil spirits, and on earth shall be their habitation. Evil spirits shall proceed from their flesh, because they were created from above; from the holy Watchers was their beginning and primary foundation. Evil spirits shall they be upon earth, and the spirits of the wicked shall they be called. The habitation of the spirits of heaven shall be in heaven; but upon earth shall be the habitation of terrestrial spirits, who are born on earth" (Vs 5-8).

"**The spirits of the giants shall be like clouds, which shall oppress, corrupt, fall, content, and bruise upon earth.** They shall cause lamentation. No food shall they eat; and they shall be thirsty; they shall be concealed, and shall rise up against the *sons of men, and against women; for they come forth during the days of slaughter and destruction"* (Vs 9-10).

This reference, briefly cited by Moses in Genesis 6, is the first mention of evil spirits, or demons. **Prior to the death of the giants (Nephilim) there were no 'evil' spirits** [Compare the last text quoted from the Book of Enoch with Jude 12 & 13: *"These men are blemishes at your love feasts, eating with you without the slightest qualm — shepherds who feed only themselves. They are clouds without rain, blown along by the wind; autumn trees, without fruit and uprooted — twice dead. They are wild waves of the sea, foaming up their shame; wandering stars, for whom blackest darkness has been reserved forever"*].

The Origin of Evil Spirits:
Chapter 16: *"And as to the death of the giants, wheresoever their spirits depart from their bodies, let their flesh, that which is perishable, be without judgment. (or be destroyed before the judgment) Thus shall they perish, until the day of the great consummation of the great world. A destruction shall take place of the Watchers and the impious. And now to the Watchers, who have sent you to pray for them, who in the beginning were in heaven, say, In heaven have you been; secret things, however, have not been manifested to you; yet have you known a reprobated mystery. And this you have related to women in the hardness of your heart, and by that mystery have women and mankind multiplied evils upon the earth. Say to them, Never therefore shall you obtain peace."*

Chapter 19: *"Then Uriel said, Here the angels, who cohabited with women, appointed their leaders; and being numerous in appearance (assuming many forms) made men profane, and caused them to err; so that they sacrificed to devils as to gods.*

"For in the great day there shall be a judgment, with which they shall be judged, until they are consumed; and their wives also shall be judged, who led astray the angels of heaven that they might salute them. And I, Enoch, I alone saw the likeness of the end of all things. Nor did any human being see it, as I saw it."

Chapter 20: "[And] These are the names of the angels who watch. Uriel, one of the holy angels, who presides over clamor and terror. Raphael, one of the holy angels, who presides over the spirits of men. Raguel, one of the holy angels, who inflicts punishment on the world and the luminaries. Michael, one of the holy angels, who, presiding over human virtue, commands the nations. Sarakiel, one of the holy angels, who presides over the spirits of the children of men that transgress. Gabriel, one of the holy angels, who presides over Ikisat, (over paradise, and over the cherubim)."

Summary:
The Book of Enoch graphically portrays the onset of this present darkness that covers the earth, the gross darkness that shrouds the people, referred to by the prophet Isaiah (Is 60:2). Lured by Satan, known as Lucifer, the Covering Cherub, before his rebellion, the Watchers -- the very angelic beings who were appointed to watch over mankind -- yielded to Satan's temptations and became engaged in a diabolic plot to destroy the children of God, claim the earth for themselves, and take over the universe. But God, in His divine omniscience, had -- prior to creation -- devised a sovereign plan to defeat their diabolical scheme.

The prophet Isaiah foresaw this event and wrote: "How you have fallen from heaven, O morning star, son of the dawn! You have been cast down to the earth, you who once laid low the nations! You said in your heart, "I will ascend to heaven; I will raise my throne above the stars of God; I will sit enthroned on the mount of assembly, on the utmost heights of the sacred mountain. I will ascend above the tops of the clouds; I will make myself like the Most High." But you are brought down to the grave, to the depths of the pit" (Isaiah 14:12-15).

The prophet Ezekiel also describes Satan's origin and fall: "Son of man, take up a lament ... and say ...: *"This is what the Sovereign LORD says: "'You were the model of perfection, full of wisdom and perfect in beauty. You were in Eden, the garden of God; every precious stone adorned you: ruby, topaz and emerald, chrysolite, onyx and jasper, sapphire, turquoise and beryl. Your settings and mountings were made of gold; on the day you were created they were prepared. You were anointed as a guardian cherub , for so I ordained you. You were on the holy mount of God; you walked among the fiery stones. You were blameless in your ways from the day you were created till wickedness was found in you.*

"Through your widespread trade you were filled with violence, and you sinned. So I drove you in disgrace from the mount of God, and I expelled you, O guardian cherub, from among the fiery stones" (Ezekiel 28:12-16).

God's sovereign plan of triumphant victory for His children was conceived before the foundations of the world were laid (Matthew 13:34-35; 25:31-34; 1 Peter 1:18-20, etc.), but for a time, Satan's diabolical scheme prevailed, resulting in this present darkness -- a stark comparison to the world that existed prior to man's rebellion and fall.

The austere dissimilarity of life on earth, before and after the fall, is graphically related in another ancient narrative omitted from our current cannon of Scripture -- the "First Book of Adam and Eve": also referred to as "The Conflict of Adam and Eve with Satan". In our next chapter, we will examine this fascinating book.

CHAPTER FIVE
ADAM'S AND EVE'S CONFLICT WITH SATAN

Present day controversy rages over the authenticity of the Scriptures, particularly over the apocryphal books, and over how human life began on this planet. To answer these questions, the serious, open minded individual must pause in their quest to carefully consider the Genesis Adam and Eve story. Where does the story come from? What does it mean?

The familiar Genesis story is clearly not the source of this foundational epoch. Nor it is not a spontaneous, Heaven-born account that first sprang into place in the Old Testament. The first eleven books of Genesis -- often referred to as the record of the primeval era -- was compiled from a number of older writings, many of which have been found and translated. This compilation was apparently undertaken by Moses, who as a prince of Egypt, had access to the extensive Egyptian libraries that served as the repository for literally thousands of ancient documents, many of which were considered sacred. Thus, **the first eleven books of Genesis represented one of the first attempts to canonize the available sacred writings.**

Genesis provides us with one version of the creation story, unexcelled no doubt, but still a version of an epoch event, a story handed down by word of mouth from generation to generation. Through the primeval, unrecorded ages of man, the story springs forth -- like an inextinguishable ray of light that reveals the moment when human life began. It is a story, born of an epoch that occurred before the human mind need express itself in writing to leave an account for others. This, is the most ancient story in the world, and has survived generation after generation because it embodies a concern common to all -- the origin of the universe and of human life.

The facts that have not changed a single iota; amid all time and the myriad of superficial changes of civilization's vivid array, are these: The origin of the universe; the Origin of Man; the Conflict of Good and Evil; the Fight between Mankind and the Devil; and the Eternal Struggle of Human Nature Against Sin.

That the Adam and Eve story, we will turn to shortly, pervaded the thoughts of ancient writers is evident from the large number of versions of the Book of Adam and Eve (The Conflict of Adam and Eve with Satan) that still exist. Their origin may be traced, through the ancient writings of the Greeks, Syrians, Egyptians,

Abyssinians, Hebrews, and other ancient peoples. As any Forensic Scientist, who examines so much apparently unrelated evidence, would testify: the record is so voluminous, so compelling, there simply must be something to it.

The version of the origin of man related in this ancient writing is the work of unknown ancient authors -- most likely from Egypt. The lack of an accurate historical allusion makes it impossible to date the writing. Portions of this version of the creation story are found in the Old Testament, the Talmud, the Koran, and in other early writings, showing what a vital role it played in the original literature of human wisdom. The Egyptian author of the version we will cite from first wrote it in Arabic, contributing to its authenticity, validating that was the original manuscript.

Over time, copies of it have found its way further south, and eventually it was translated into Ethiopic. For the present English translation we are indebted to Dr. S. C. Malan, Vicar of Broadwindsor, who worked from the Ethiopic edition edited by Dr. E. Trumpp, Professor at the University of Munich. Dr. Trumpp had a distinct advantage in his undertaking this work, having also had access to the Arabic original. Thus, through the work of Drs. Trumpp and Malam, the gap of many centuries can be bridged with relative certainty.

The reading of these books is truly an adventure. You will find the mind of man fed by the passions, hopes, and fears of the new and strange earthly existence described, through this ancient author's riotous, unrestrained, zestful and illumined expressions. Through his creative account of this epoch, you will find yourself suddenly staring at commonplace unvarnished events experienced by Adam and Eve: all the troubles, all the petty disagreements, and the taking sides with, and against, one another, that is commonplace today. They experienced the bothers of moving, of going without, and "staying with the baby," that still mark family life today.

One critic commenting on this writing, said: **"This is we believe, the greatest literary discovery that the world has known. Its effect upon contemporary thought in molding the judgment of the future generations is of incalculable value.** *The treasures of Tut-ank-Amen's Tomb were no more precious to the Egyptologist than are these literary treasures to the world of scholarship."* But, we prefer to let the reader complete his or her own exploration and form his or her own opinion. The writing is arresting enough to inspire very original thoughts concerning it.

In general, this account begins where the Old Testament, Genesis story, of Adam and Eve leaves off. Thus the two accounts can not be compared like they were parallel accounts. Rather, what is here presented is a new chapter -- a sort of sequel to the Genesis story. Here we discover the story of the twin sisters of Cain and Abel, and it is notable that in this account, the blame for the first murder is placed squarely at the door of jealousy over a Woman.

The plan of these books is as follows:

Book I:

- The careers of Adam and Eve, from the day they left the Garden of Eden;

- Their fist dwelling outside the garden. in the Cave of Treasures;

- Their trials and temptations;

- Satan's manifold apparitions to them.

- The birth of Cain, of Abel, and of their twin sisters;

- Cain's love for his own twin sister, Luluwa, whom Adam and Eve wished to have marry Abel;

- The details of Cain's murder of his brother; and Adam's sorrow and death.

Book II:

- The history of the patriarchs who lived before the Flood;

- The dwelling of the children of Seth on the Holy Mountain -- Mount Hermon -- until they were lured by Henun and by the daughters of Cain, to come' down from the mountain.

- Cain's death, when slain by Lamech the blind; and

- The lives of other patriarchs up to and including the birth of Noah.

Book I - Expelled from the Garden of Eden:
Chapter 1: *"On the third day, God planted the garden in the east of the earth, on the border of the world eastward, beyond which, towards the sun-rising, one finds nothing but water, that encompasses the whole world, and reaches unto the borders of heaven. And to the north of the garden there is a sea of wafer, clear and pure to the taste, like unto nothing else; so that, through the clearness thereof, one may look into the depths of the earth. And when a man washes himself in it, becomes clean of the cleanness thereof, and white of its whiteness -- even if he were dark"* (Vs 1-3).

"And God created that sea of His own good pleasure, for He knew what would come of the man He should make; so that after he had left the garden, on account of his transgression, men should be born in the earth, from among whom righteous

ones should die, whose souls God would raise at the last day; when they should return to their flesh; should bathe in the water of that sea, and all of them repent of their sins. But when God made Adam go out of the garden, He did not place him on the border of it northward, lest he should draw near to the sea of water, and he and Eve wash themselves in it, be cleansed from their sins, forget the transgression they had committed, and he no longer reminded of it in the thought of their punishment" (Vs 4-5)

"Then, again, as to the southern side of the garden, God was not pleased to let Adam dwell there; because, when the wind blew from the north, it would bring him, on that southern side, the delicious smell of the trees of the garden. Wherefore God did not put Adam there, lest he should smell the sweet smell of those trees forget his transgression, and find consolation for what he had done, take delight in the smell of the trees, and not be cleansed from his transgression. Again, also, because God is merciful and of great pity, and governs all things in a way He alone knows -- He made our father Adam dwell in the western border of the garden, because on that side the earth is very broad. And God commanded him to dwell there in a cave in a rock -- the **Cave of Treasures below the garden**" (Vs 6-9).

Chapter 2: "But, when our father Adam, and Eve, went out of the garden, they trod the ground on their feet, not knowing they were treading. And when they came to the opening of the gate of the garden, and saw the broad earth spread before them, covered with stones large and small, and with sand, they feared and trembled, and fell on their faces, from the fear that came upon them; and they were as dead. Because -- whereas they had hitherto been in the garden-land, beautifully planted with all manner of trees -- **they now saw themselves, in a strange land, which they knew not, and had never seen. And because at that time they were filled with the grace of a bright nature, and they had not hearts turned towards earthly things.**

"Therefore had God pity on them; and when He saw them fallen before the gate of the garden, He sent His Word unto father Adam and Eve, and raised them from their fallen state."

Chapter 3: "God said to Adam, "I have ordained on this earth days and years, and thou and thy seed shall dwell and walk in it, until the days and years are fulfilled; when **I shall send the Word that created thee,** and against which thou hast transgressed, the Word that made thee come out of the garden and that raised thee when thou wast fallen. **Yea, the Word that will again save thee when the five days and a half are fulfilled"** (Vs 1-2) ...

"But God had before that made this covenant with our father, Adam, in the same terms, ere he came out of the garden, when he was by the tree whereof Eve took the fruit and gave it him to eat. Inasmuch as when our father Adam came out of the garden, he passed by that tree, and saw how God had then changed the appearance of it into another form, and how it withered. And as Adam went to it he feared, trembled and fell down; but God in His mercy lifted him up, and then made this covenant with him.

And, again, when Adam was by the gate of the garden, and saw the cherub with a sword of flashing fire in his hand, and the cherub grew angry and frowned at him, both Adam and Eve became afraid of him, and thought he meant to put them to death. So they fell on their faces, and trembled with fear" (Vs 7-10). ...

Chapter Six
Life Outside the Garden of God

Chapter 4: *"But, Adam and Eve wept for having come out of the garden, their first abode. **And, indeed, when Adam looked at his flesh, that was altered, he wept bitterly, he and Eve, over what they had done**.*

*"**And they walked and went gently down into the Cave of Treasures.** And as they came to it Adam wept over himself and said to Eve, "Look at this cave that is to be our prison in this world, and a place of punishment! "What is it compared with the garden? What is its narrowness compared with the space of the other? "What is this rock, by the side of those groves? What is the gloom of this cavern, compared with the light of the garden?*

"What is this overhanging ledge of rock to shelter us, compared with the mercy of the Lord that overshadowed us? "What is the soil of this cave compared with the garden-land? This earth, strewed with stones; and that, planted with delicious fruit-trees?" (Vs 1-7).

*"And Adam said to Eve, "Look at thine eyes, and at mine, which afore beheld angels in heaven, praising; and they, too, without ceasing. **"But now we do not see as we did: our eyes have become of flesh; they cannot see in like manner as they saw before." Adam said again to Eve, "What is our body today, compared to what it was in former days, when we dwelt in the garden?"** After this Adam did not like to enter the cave, under the overhanging rock; nor would he ever have entered it. But he bowed to God's orders; and said to himself,*

"Unless I enter the cave, I shall again be a transgressor" (Vs 8-11).

Chapter 5: "Then, Adam and Eve entered the cave, and stood praying, in their own tongue, unknown to us, but which they knew well. And as they prayed, Adam raised his eyes, and saw the rock and the roof of the cave that covered him overhead, so that he could see neither heaven, nor God's creatures. So he wept and smote heavily upon his breast, until he dropped, and was as dead. And Eve sat weeping; for she believed he was dead. Then she arose, spread her hands towards God, suing Him for mercy and pity, and said, "O God, forgive me my sin, the sin which I committed, and remember it not against me. "For I alone caused Thy servant to fall from the garden into this lost estate; from light into this darkness; and from the abode of joy into this prison" (Vs 1-5).

"O God, look upon this Thy servant thus fallen, and raise him from his death, that he may weep and repent of his transgression which he committed through me. "Take not away his soul this once; but let him live that he may stand after the measure of his repentance, and do Thy will, as before his death. "But if Thou do not raise him up, then, O God, take away my own soul, that I be like him; and leave me not in this dungeon, one and alone; for I could not stand alone in this world, but with him only.

"For Thou, O God, didst cause a slumber to come upon him, and didst take a bone from his side, and didst restore the flesh in the place of it, by Thy divine power. "And Thou didst take me, the bone, and make me a woman, bright like him, with heart, reason, and speech; and in flesh, like unto his own; and Thou didst make me after the likeness of his countenance, by Thy mercy and power. "O Lord, I and he are one and Thou, O God, art our Creator, Thou are He who made us both in one day" (Vs 6-11). ...

Chapter 8: "Then Adam wept and said, "O God, when we dwelt in the garden, and our hearts were lifted up, we saw the angels that sang praises in heaven, but now we do not see as we were used to do; nay, when we entered the cave, all creation became hidden from us." Then God the Lord said unto Adam, **"When thou wast under subjection to Me, thou hadst a bright nature within thee, and for that reason couldst thou see things afar off. But after thy transgression thy bright nature was withdrawn from thee; and it was not left to thee to see things afar off, but only near at hand; after the ability of the flesh; for it is brutish."** When Adam and Eve had heard these words from God, they went their way; praising and worshipping Him with a sorrowful heart. And God ceased to commune with them."

Chapter 10: "*And Adam said, after he was raised, "O God, while we were in the garden we did not require, or care for this water; but since we came to this land we cannot do without it." Then God said to Adam, "While thou wast under My command and wast a bright angel, thou knewest not this water. "But after that thou hast transgressed My commandment, thou canst not do without water, wherein to wash thy body and make it grow; for it is now like that of beasts, and is in want of water."* When Adam and Eve heard these words from God, they wept a bitter cry; and Adam entreated God to let him return into the garden, and look at it a second time" (Vs 4-7).

Chapter 11: "Both Adam and Eve then withdrew from the water, and drank none of it at all; but came and entered the Cave of Treasures. But when in it Adam could not see Eve; he only heard the noise she made. Neither could she see Adam, but heard the noise he made. Then Adam wept, in deep affliction, and smote upon his breast; and he arose and said to Eve, "Where art thou?" And she said unto him, "Lo, I am standing in this darkness." **He then said to her, "Remember the bright nature in which we lived, while we abode in the garden!**

"O Eve! remember the glory that rested on us in the garden. *O Eve! remember the trees that overshadowed us in the garden while we moved among them.*

"O Eve! remember that while we were in the garden, we knew neither night nor day. Think of the Tree of Life, from below which flowed the water, and that shed luster over us! Remember, O Eve, the garden-land, and the brightness thereof! ***"Think, oh think of that garden in which was no darkness, while we dwelt therein***. *"Whereas no sooner did we come into this Cave of Treasures than darkness compassed us round about; until we can no longer see each other; and all the pleasure of this life has come to an end." (Vs 3-11).*

Chapter 12:
"Then Adam arose in the cave and said, ***"O God, wherefore has light departed from us, and darkness come over us?*** *Wherefore dost Thou leave us in this long darkness? Why wilt Thou plague us thus?* ***"And this darkness, O Lord, where was it ere it came upon us? It is such, that we cannot see each other.*** *"For, so long as we were in the garden, we neither saw nor even knew what darkness is. I was not hidden from Eve, neither was she hidden from me, until now that she cannot see me; and no darkness came upon us, to separate us from each other.*  ***"But she and I were both in one bright light.*** *I saw her and she saw me.*

Yet now since we came into this cave, darkness has come upon us, and parted us asunder, so that I do not see her, and she does not see me. "O Lord, wilt Thou then plague us with this darkness?" (Vs 7-11).

Chapter 13: "Then, when God, who is merciful and full of pity, heard Adam's voice, He said unto him: **"O Adam, so long as the good angel was obedient to Me, a bright light rested on him and on his hosts.**

"But when he transgressed My commandment, I deprived him of that bright nature, and he became dark. "And when he was in the heavens, in the realms of light, he knew naught of darkness. "But he transgressed, and I made him fall from heaven upon the earth; and it was this darkness that came upon him. "And on thee, O Adam, while in My garden and obedient to Me, did that bright light rest also. But when I heard of thy transgression, I deprived thee of that bright light. Yet, of My mercy, I did not turn thee into darkness, but I made thee thy body of flesh, over which I spread this skin, in order that it may bear cold and heat. (Vs 1-7).

"If I had let My wrath fall heavily upon thee, I should have destroyed thee; and had I turned thee into darkness, it would have been as if I killed thee. "But in My mercy, I have made thee as thou art; when thou didst transgress My commandment, O Adam, I drove thee from the garden, and made thee come forth into this land; and commanded thee to dwell in this cave; and darkness came upon thee, as it did upon him who transgressed My commandment. "Thus, O Adam, has this night deceived thee. It is not to last for ever; but is only of twelve hours; when it is over, daylight will return" (Vs 8-10). ...

"For I made thee of the light; and I willed to bring out children of light from thee and like unto thee. "But thou didst not keep one day My commandment; until I had finished the creation and blessed everything in it. "Then I commanded thee concerning the tree, that thou eat not thereof. Yet I knew that Satan, who deceived himself, would also deceive thee. "So I made known to thee by means of the tree, not to come near him. And I told thee not to eat of the fruit thereof, nor to taste of it, nor yet to sit under it, nor to yield to it. (Vs 14-17).

Chapter 14: *"Then Adam said unto God: "O Lord, take Thou my soul, and let me not see this gloom any more; or remove me to some place where there is no darkness."* But God the Lord said to Adam, "Verily I say unto thee, this darkness will pass from thee, every day I have determined for thee, until the fulfillment of My covenant; when **I will save thee and bring thee back again into the garden, into the abode of light thou longest for, wherein is no darkness. I will bring thee, to it -- in the kingdom of heaven"** (Vs 1-2).

Chapter 22: *"And Adam said to God, "While I was in the garden I knew neither heat, nor languor, neither moving about, nor trembling, nor fear; but now since I came to this land, all this affliction has come upon me."* **Then God said to Adam, "So long as thou wast keeping My commandment, My light and My grace rested on thee**. But when thou didst transgress My commandment, sorrow and misery befell thee in this land" (Vs 3-4).

Chapter 25: *"But Adam said unto God, "It was in my mind to put an end to myself at once, for having transgressed Thy commandments, and for my having come out of the beautiful garden; and for the bright light of which Thou hast deprived me; and for the praises which poured forth from my mouth without ceasing, and for the light that covered me"* (Vs 3).

Chapter 34: *"And after their prayers Adam began to entreat 'God, saying, "O my Lord my God, and my Creator, thou didst command the four elements to be gathered together, and they were gathered together by Thine order.* **"Then Thou spreadest Thy hand and didst create me out of one element, that of dust of the earth; and Thou didst bring me into the garden at the third hour, on a Friday, and didst inform me of it in the cave.** "Then, at first, I knew neither night nor day, for

I had a bright nature; neither did the light in which I lived ever leave me to know night or day" (Vs. 4-6).

Chapter 37: *"Then Adam said to Eve, "**Seest thou not these figs and their leaves, with which we covered ourselves when we were stripped of our bright nature?** But now, we know not what misery and suffering may come upon us from eating them. "Now, therefore, O Eve, let us restrain ourselves and not eat of them, thou and I; and let us ask God to give us of the fruit of the Tree of Life." Thus did Adam and Eve restrain themselves, and did not eat of these figs. But Adam began to pray to God and to beseech Him to give him of the fruit of the Tree of Life, saying thus: **"O God, when we transgressed Thy commandment at the sixth hour of Friday, we were stripped of the bright nature we had, and did not continue in the garden after our transgression**, more than three hours"* (Vs 1-4).

Chapter 44: *"Then Adam said to Eve, "See this fire of which we have a portion in us: which formerly yielded to us, but no longer does so, now that **we have transgressed the limit of creation, and changed our condition, and our nature is altered**. But the fire is not changed in its nature, nor altered from its creation. Therefore has it now power over us; and when we come near it, it scorches our flesh."*

Chapter 45: *"O Adam, how Satan has exalted thee! **He has deprived thee of the Godhead, and of an exalted state like unto Me**, and has not kept his word to thee; but, after all, is become thy foe. It is he who made this fire in which he meant to burn thee and Eve. "Why, O Adam, has he not kept his agreement with thee, not even one day; **but has deprived thee of the glory that was on thee -- when thou didst yield to his command**? "Thinkest thou, Adam, that he loved thee when he made this agreement with thee? Or, that he loved thee and wished to raise thee on high?*

*"But no, Adam, he did not do all that out of love to thee; **but he wished to make thee come out of light into darkness, and from an exalted state to degradation; from glory to***

abasement; from joy to sorrow; and from rest to fasting and fainting." (Vs. 5-8).

Chapter 51: "Then came the Word of God to Adam and Eve, and said to them, **"This is he who was hidden in the serpent, and who deceived you, and stripped you of the garment of light and glory in which you were.** "This is he who promised you majesty and divinity. Where, then, is the beauty that was on him? Where is his divinity? Where is his light? Where is the glory that rested on him? "Now his figure is hideous; he is become abominable among angels; and he has come to be called Satan" (Vs 5-7).

Chapter 55: "Then Adam, when he heard the Word of God, and the fluttering of the angels whom he did not see, but only heard the sound of them with his ears, he and Eve wept, and said to the angels:-- **"O Spirits, who wait upon God, look upon me, and upon my being unable to see you! For when I was in my former bright nature) then I could see you. I sang praises as you do; and my heart was far above you. "But now, that I have transgressed, that bright nature is gone from me, and I am come to this miserable state. And now am I come to this, that I cannot see you, and you do not serve me As you were wont. For I am become animal flesh"** (Vs 2-4).

"Then the angels said unto Adam, "Thou didst hearken to Satan, and didst forsake the Word of God who created thee; and thou didst believe that Satan would fulfill all he had promised thee.

"But now, O Adam, we will make known to thee, what came upon us through him, before his fall from heaven. "He gathered together his hosts, and deceived them, promising them to give them a great kingdom, a divine nature; and other promises he made them. "His hosts believed that. his word was true, so they yielded to him, and renounced the glory of God. "He then sent for us according to the orders in which we were-to come under his command, and to hearken to his vain promise. But we would not, and we took not his advice.

"Then after he had fought with God, and had dealt forwardly with Him, he gathered together his hosts, and made war with us. And if it had not been for God's strength that was with us, we could not have prevailed against him to hurl him from heaven. "But when he fell from among us, there was great joy in heaven, because of his going down from us. For had he continued in heaven, nothing, not even one angel would have remained in it. **"But God in His mercy, drove him from among us to this dark earth; for he had become darkness itself and a worker of unrighteousness**" (Vs 7-14).

Adam and Eve by Béla Klimkovics

Chapter 65: "**Then Adam and Eve came back into the cave sorrowful and weeping because of the alteration in their nature. And they both knew from that hour that they were altered beings**, that their hope of returning to the garden was now cut off; and that they could not enter it. **For that now their bodies had strange functions; and all flesh that requires food and drink for its existence, cannot be in the garden. Then Adam said to Eve, "Behold, our hope is now cut off; and so is our trust to enter the garden.**

"We no longer belong to the inhabitants of the garden; but henceforth we are earthy and of the dust, and of the inhabitants of the earth, We shall not return to the garden, *until the day in which God has promised to save us, and to bring us again into the garden, as He promised us"* (Vs 7-9).

What does all this mean to Christians -- to you and I, and the end-times in which we live? Come with us, into chapter six as we begin to compare the words of this book with the words of those we have come to rely on -- Jesus Christ and the New Testament apostles.

CHAPTER SEVEN
TRANSMUTATION: SPIRITUAL TO CARNAL BEINGS

The principle concept reiterated in the Book of Adam and Eve: the idea that mankind's very nature was altered at the fall -- somehow mutating beings of light into beings of flesh and blood, covered with skin -- was the fundamental tenet that those opposing this book's inclusion in the Sacred Cannon centered on. However, this permutation of man's nature, **is precisely what the apostle Paul seems to describe** in 2 Corinthians 4:6 through chapter 5.

"For it is the God who once said, ***"Let light shine out of darkness," who has made his light shine in our hearts, the light of the knowledge of God's glory shining in the face of the Messiah Yeshua.*** *But we have this treasure in clay jars, so that it will be evident that such overwhelming power comes from God and not from us.* We have all kinds of troubles, but we are not crushed; we are perplexed, yet not in despair; persecuted, yet not abandoned; knocked down, yet not destroyed. **We always carry in our bodies the dying of Yeshua, so that the life of Yeshua may be manifested in our bodies too**.

"For we who are alive are always being handed over to death for Yeshua's sake, so that Yeshua's life also might be manifested in our mortal bodies. Thus death is at work in us but life in you" (2 Co 4:6-12). **[Note: the bracketed information in the following texts are based on a more literal transliteration of the Greek text.]**

"*The Tanakh (Torah) says,* **"I trusted, therefore I spoke." Since we have that same Spirit who enables us to trust, we also trust** [are persuaded] **and therefore speak**; because we know that he who raised the Lord Yeshua will also raise us with Yeshua and bring us along with you into his presence. All this is for your sakes, so that as grace flows out to more and more people, it may cause thanksgiving to overflow and bring glory to God" (4:13-15).

"This is why we do not lose courage [despair]. **Though our outer self is heading for decay, our inner self is being renewed daily**. For our light and transient troubles are achieving for us an everlasting glory whose weight is beyond description. We concentrate not on what is seen but on what is not seen, since things seen are temporary [temporal (pertaining to this world, worldly)], but things not seen are eternal [everlasting]" (4:16-18).

"**We know that when the tent** [hut or temporary residence] **which houses us here on earth is torn down** [disintegrates]**, we have a permanent building** [structure] **from God, a building** [a home] **not made by human hands** [unmanufactured and inartificial]**, to house us in heaven** [everlasting in the heavens]. **For in this tent** [habitation]**, our earthly body, we groan** [murmur] **with desire** [yearning] **to have around us** [to be wrapped in] **the home** [habitation] **from heaven that will be ours.** [Indeed] **With this around us** [divesting ourselves of this wrapper (of flesh)] **we will not be found** [perceived] **naked** [disembodied]" (5:1-3).

"**Yes, while we are in this body** [hut or temporary residence]**, we groan** [murmur and grumble, sighing] **with the sense of being oppressed** [burdened down]: it is not so much that we want [are disposed] to take something off [to strip, or divest ourselves], but rather to put something on over it [to wrap ourselves in a wrapper]; so that what must die [our mortality] may be swallowed up [devoured] by the [that] Life. **Moreover, it is God who has prepared us** [fashioned us] **for this very thing, and as a pledge** [earnest money, guarantee]**, He has given** [bestowed upon] **us his** [The] **Spirit**.

"So [therefore] we are always confident — we know [understanding] that so long as we are at home in the body [while in our present body], we are away from our home with the Lord [absent from the Lord]; for we live by trust, not by what we see [for by reason of our faith we walk not according to what is seen]. **We are confident, then,** [and moreover willing] **and would much prefer to leave our home in the body and come to** [be present] **our home with** [in the house of] **the Lord**" (5:4-8).

"Therefore, whether at home or away from home, we try our utmost to please him; for we must all appear before the Messiah's court of judgment, where everyone will receive the good or bad consequences of what he did while he was in the body. So it is with the fear of the Lord before us that we try to persuade people. Moreover, **God knows us as we really are**; and I hope that in your consciences you too know us as we really are. We are not recommending ourselves to you again but giving you a reason to be proud of us, so that you will be able to answer those who boast about a person's appearance rather than his inner qualities" (5:9-12).

[The CJB, KJV and NIV versions seemed so convoluted, compared to the original Greek text, that bracketed inserts seemed insufficient to bring clarity. Therefore, the following alternative translation of these verses has been provided for your consideration.]

["Therefore, whether at home or absent from home, we endeavor to be well pleasing to Him; for we must all declare ourselves before the judgment seat of Christ, that everyone may bring the deeds committed in the body, whether beneficial or flawed. Accordingly, being fully aware of the impending, exceeding terror of the Lord, we endeavor to persuade men Godward. "Moreover, I have confidence we are to appear (there), moreover also, in that (day) your own moral conscience will be made manifest (show forth). Furthermore, we never commend ourselves to you, but provide occasion for you to rejoice on our behalf so that you may be able to rejoice in that appearance and not be broken hearted.]

"If we are insane, it is for God's sake; and if we are sane, it is for your sake. For the Messiah's love has hold of us, **because we are convinced that one man died on behalf of all mankind (which implies that all mankind was already dead), and that he died on behalf of all in order that those** *who live should not live any longer for themselves but for the one who on their behalf died and was raised. So from now on, we do not look at anyone from a worldly viewpoint. Even if we once regarded the Messiah from a worldly viewpoint, we do so no longer"* (5:13-16).

Once again, we found it difficult to interject bracketed information, and provide the following translation for your consideration. *[Therefore, whether (if) we are beside ourselves with amazement to God; (or) whether (if) we are sober-minded with you, seeing that the love of Christ compels us conclude the same, that because one on behalf of everyone was slain, truly everyone was slain; therefore on behalf of everyone he was slain, so that they who live no longer live for themselves, but on behalf of Him who was slain and rose from the dead. Wherefore, from this time, henceforth, we consider nobody according to carnality, though we (once) perceived Christ according to his carnality, nevertheless, we henceforth perceive (Him) no longer.]*

"Therefore, if anyone is united with the Messiah, he is a new creation — the old has passed; look, what has come is fresh and new! *And it is all from God, who through the Messiah has reconciled us to himself and has given us the work of that reconciliation, which is that God in the Messiah was reconciling mankind to himself, not counting their sins against them, and entrusting to us the message of reconciliation. Therefore we are ambassadors of the Messiah; in effect, God is making his appeal through us. What we do is appeal on behalf of the Messiah, "Be reconciled to God! God made this sinless man be a sin offering on our behalf, so that in union with him he might fully share in God's righteousness"* (2 Cor 5:17-21 CJB).

[Therefore if anyone is positionally in Christ, he is a new creation -- the old has passed away. Behold! They arise new! Moreover, everything originates from God, the One who reconciles us (to) himself through Christ, and granted us this ministry, that of restoration to divine favor; to wit: because God was in Christ reconciling the cosmos to himself, not taking an inventory of their unintentional lapses and deviations; and appointing unto us the preaching, that of restoration to divine favor. Now then, on behalf of Christ, we serve as ambassadors, even as if God himself called (beseeched) through us; we call (beseech) in Christ's stead -- be reconciled Godward!] One who knew not sin, on our behalf he appointed (laid on him) our offenses, so that we might arise justified Godward in Him.]

The Impotence of Metamorphism

In these texts we are presented with an analogy -- a metaphor -- of changing clothes: of taking off our decaying, mortal body and putting on our eternal, spiritual body. We are also presented with the fact that in so doing, one is faced with a dilemma: the longing to be clothed with our promised spiritual body, fused with the desire to hang onto our carnal being. Caught in this dilemma we seem impotent.

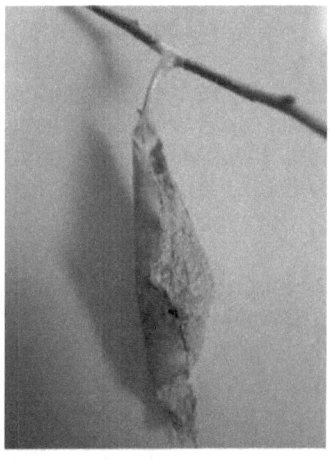

This deeply felt impotence is the cardinal characteristic of metamorphism, without which transformation -- the process of change -- and transfiguration -- the manifestation of a new being -- cannot occur. To comprehend this, lets consider the plight of the lowly caterpillar whose destiny it is to transcend its life of creeping in the dirt and eating bitter plants, to flitting in the breeze to search out the nectar of choice blossoms. Something deep within a caterpillar compels it to entomb itself inside a cocoon (chrysalis) from whence ***it*** will never emerge. Yet, something within this creature gives it hope in a future destiny -- a state of being -- never before experienced.

The apostle, Paul, expounds on man's desire to experience a similar transformation in Romans, chapter 8. *"For I reckon that the sufferings of this present time are not worthy to be compared with the glory which shall be revealed in us. For the earnest expectation of the creature waiteth for the manifestation of the sons of God. For the creature was made subject to vanity, not willingly, but by reason of him who hath subjected the same* in hope, Because the creature itself also shall be delivered from the bondage of corruption into the glorious liberty of the children of God" (vs.., 18-21).

Referring back to the Greek text, we read: *["Therefore, I conclude concerning the affliction of this present season, not even comparable when compared to that honor and glory (dignity) hereafter revealed among us. Indeed, that earnest expectation of this creature waiting expectantly for the coming manifestation as the offspring, the kinship of God. Because, from moral depravity this creature was subjected to obedience, not voluntarily but by reason of the one who subjected him to obedience in confidence, because this creature shall also be liberated out of that slavery to spontaneous ruin into that glorious freedom of the children of God."]*

"For we know that the whole creation groaneth and travaileth in pain together until now. And not only they, but ourselves also, which have the firstfruits of the Spirit, even we ourselves groan within ourselves, waiting for the adoption, to wit, the redemption of our body" (Ro 8:22-23).

Referring to the Greek text again, we read: *["Therefore, we understand that the entire creation experiencing this calamity (animate and inanimate) collectively moans and simultaneously travails in pain until this present time; and not alone. Even we ourselves, who possess the Holy Spirit's firstfruits; even we ourselves agonize within ourselves, awaiting adoption as children, the ransom in full of our body"]*

"For in this hope we were saved. But hope that is seen is no hope at all. Who hopes for what he already has? But if we hope for what we do not yet have, we wait for it patiently" (Ro 8:24-25).

Referring again to the Greek, we read: *["Because of this confident expectation (faith/hope) we are saved (made whole); but confident expectation (faith/hope) of things seen is not confident expectation (faith/hope) at all. For why would any man have confident expectation for what he beholds? But, if fully expecting, we trust in things not seen, we cheerfully endure.]*

To fully understand what Paul is speaking about, it is imperative that we comprehend that this present darkness, including our existent state of death, dying and decay, is not normal. It is crucial that we comprehend the entirety of what happened at the fall. We must grasp the scope of the change that occurred when mankind became subject to the transmutation from spirit to carnality, before we can begin to fathom what it means to put off this old body, be born-again, and be clothed in the spirit, thereby becoming a fully-realized Child of God.

The event that initiated this state of being, we refer to as 'the fall' or the rebellion of Adam and Eve. The consequence of that event is the state of being we presently endure, which we have titled: "Paradise Lost", the title of the next chapter.

CHAPTER EIGHT
PARADISE LOST

As descriptive as the text of The First Book of Adam and Eve may be, it scarcely begins to portray the enormity of our first parents' losses on that day when they were expelled from the Garden of Eden. Exiled from their Edenic home, it was not simply the comforts and pleasures of living in the Garden of God that Adam and Eve missed. Their loss was far greater than the loss of their shining glory -- the light they had been clothed with since creation. **Their loss was indeed, the loss of paradise and all it represented, including eternal life.**

Exiled from their Garden of Eden, Adam and Eve were banished to a hostile land: a land that was cursed, a land that had lost its strength, a land that began producing thistles and thorns; a land that would require painful toil to produce a crop (Gen 3:17-19; Lev 26:20). God's commission to Adam and Eve to *"Be fruitful and increase in number; fill the earth and subdue it"* (Gen 1:28); a commission that established man co-creators, also took on a new dimension. Childbirth would now be attended by pain and suffering (Gen 3:16).

Adam and Eve were also deprived of their primary diet -- the fruit from the tree of life -- without which their bodies would be subject to aging, decay and death (Gen 3:22). In death, they would once again become part and parcel of the elements of the earth, from which their bodies of flesh and blood, [clarified in the Hebrew text as being an outer wrapper], had been created (Gen 1:27; 2:7; 3:19 & 23). Far worse than any of these losses, the loss of their shining glory represented more than the mere loss of physical brilliance. Referring to the Hebrew, it was the loss of their [haw-dawr` - kaw-bode`], God's magnificence, His Shekinah Glory, that had enveloped their spirits (Ps 8:6).

Reflecting back to 2 Cor 5:1-9, Paul describes the agony experienced in being 'unclothed' -- that is, of having neither a physical (mortal) substance, nor a spiritual (immortal) body. The Greek word Paul used to describe this state is: (*'gumnos'*), most often translated naked or unclothed, but more succinctly referring to a soul or spirit without a body -- (a disembodied soul or spirit). It was this abysmal sense of nakedness that produced in Adam and Eve, their profound shame and fear (Gen 3:9).

They were so fearful, so ashamed, they hid from God, their Creator, seeking to cover themselves [to gird themselves, or armor themselves] with some foreign substance, inaccurately referred to in some translations as fig leaves! (Gen 3:7).

The Scriptures give us some idea of the degree of sheer panic, shame and fear experienced, from their subsequent dialogue with God: *"Then the eyes of both of them were opened, and they realized they were naked; so they sewed fig leaves together and made coverings for themselves.* **Then the man and his wife heard the sound of the Lord God as he was walking in the garden in the cool of the day, and they hid from the Lord God among the trees of the garden. But the Lord God called to the man, "Where are you?" He answered, "I heard you in the garden, and I was afraid because I was naked; so I hid"** (Gen 3:7-10 KJV).

Referring to the Hebrew text, we read: [Wati - paw-kakh' - ah' - yin' - shen-ah'-yim - yaw-dah' - kee - ay-rome' - haym], meaning: *"And the senses of the couple were awakened and they recognized their nakedness."* [Wayi-taw-far' - aw-leh' - teh-ane' - waya'-suw - laahem - chagorot], meaning: *"And they sewed together a foreign substance to bring forth armor (an apron) for their purpose"]*

Remembering that their spiritual bodies of honor and glory (the Shekiniah Glory of God) had departed, there was nothing to see. Having their carnal senses awakened they recognized the gravity of their condition and sought to cover themselves (to make themselves visible bodies) of some foreign substance.

It was while in this state of being that they heard the sound of the Lord [Hebrew: Yahweh - Elohiym, meaning (Yeshua of the Godhead)] as he approached, walking [Hebrew: haw-lak', meaning "he came forward" in the garden in the cool of the evening. [This last phrase stems from a single Hebrew word (roo'-akh) referring to spirit.] This would seem to infer that a better translation might read: *"They were alarmed at the sound of Yeshua of the Godhead as he came forward in his spirit."*

The Hebrew says Yeshua of the Godhead called them by name, saying where/how are you? Then the next sentence, which in the KJV reads: **He answered, "I heard you in the garden, and I was afraid because I was naked; so I hid"**, in Hebrew, reads: [Wayo'-mer - qolkaa - shaama'tiy - bagaan - waa'ryaa' - kiy - 'eeyrom - 'aanokiy - waa'eechaabee'], meaning: *"He* answered, I heard you calling in the garden and was dreadfully frightened because of my nakedness and I secreted myself."

The level of fear expressed far exceeded what one might expect if they were merely naked or unclothed. After all, God had made them and knew everything about them. But, being disembodied -- having lost their covering of the Shekinah Glory of God -- they were distressed. Then, hearing God advancing in the spirit -- their distress turned to sheer panic, which is quite understandable.

Following their initial encounter, Yeshua lovingly endeavors to draw a confession out of man, which man counters with a 'blame-game' -- Adam and Eve blaming each other, Adam blaming God for giving him Eve as his wife, and their blaming the serpent. Following this mealy-mouthed confession, there ensues a tragic dialogue between God and man that continues through verse 20, where God explains the consequences of their act of rebellion. Finally, in verse 22, we are told briefly, that: *"The LORD God made garments of skin for Adam and his wife and clothed them"* (Gen 3:21).

Coats of Skin:
Through the years, we have heard a number of sermons preached on this text -- all interpreting it to mean that God conducted the first holocaust (animal sacrifice), afterward clothing Adam and Eve in the animal skins.

However, the Hebrew for this phrase (wayal^abisheem 'owr kaat^anowt), when literally translated, says: "Yeshua of the Godhead brought forth (produced, or created) robes (garments, coats) of hide (skin) for Adam and his woman." The Hebrew does not even suggest that God performed an animal sacrifice and wrapped Adam and Eve in their skins. It merely says God covered them with skin, or hide. Adam and Eve were no longer enveloped within the Shekinah Glory of God.

They were no longer bright and shining, illumined beings. In stark contrast, they were now covered with skin, or hide (with flesh and blood), created from the elements (dust) of the earth. Originally created in the image and likeness of God, and enveloped with His Shekinah Glory, they now looked more like the beasts of the field. **Their bodies of glory and honor had been stripped away, to be replaced with mortal, carnal, decaying bodies of flesh and blood.**

To fully grasp the import of this, it is imperative for us to go back to the Genesis story -- back in time to the beginning of creation. In six days (eras or dimensions) *"... the Lord made the heavens and the earth, the sea, and all that is in them"* ... then *"he rested on the seventh day ... blessed the Sabbath day and made it holy"* (Exodus 20:11). The creation of the heavens, the earth and sea, and all that is in them, was a progressive event. In the first day, or era, God called light into existence, saying *"Light Be"* and light was* (Genesis 1:3 ARBT).

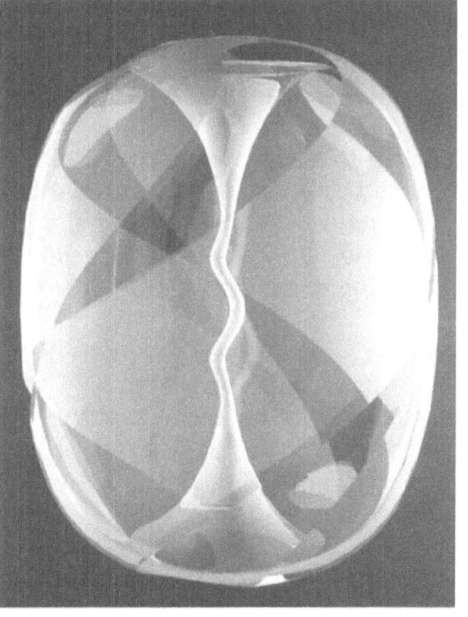

The Hebrew word *['owr]*, translated into the Aramaic Septuagint as *'phos'*, refers to phosphorescence, or phosphorescent light -- a light emitted by photons. Phosphorescence is a form of light that results in objects glowing in the dark. In physics, **the photon is the elementary particle responsible for all electromagnetic phenomena**. The photon is the carrier of electromagnetic radiation of all wavelengths, including gamma rays, X-rays, ultraviolet light, visible light, infrared light, microwaves, radio waves, etc.

The photon differs from many other elementary particles, such as the electron and the quark, in that it has zero rest mass; therefore, it travels (in a vacuum) at the speed of light. **Like all quanta, the photon has both wave and particle properties ("wave-particle duality").** It is this, the elementary particle of the cosmos, the photon, that God called into existence in the first day (era) of creation. It is that which modern astronomists believe was constituted during the first era (dimension) of creation -- which they refer to as the "**Big Bang**."

Not until the last century did science discover that all matter is made up of energy, or power. The atomic bombs that exploded over Japan during the World War II helped prove that all the material elements are actually made out of, or expressions of, energy, or power. Interestingly, the Bible was far ahead of 'modern' science. It taught man this 2900 years ago, telling us that the heavens were made by the power of God, by His Word: *"By the word of the Lord the heavens were made, and by the breath of His mouth all their host. For He spoke, and it was done; He commanded, and it stood fast"* (Ps 33:6,9).

Biblical Foreknowledge of Scientific Facts:
Long ago, in the book of Hebrews, it was recorded that visible matter -- all that is seen -- is made out of what is not seen. *"By faith we understand that the worlds were prepared by the word of God, so that what is seen was not made out of things which are visible"* (Heb 11:3). All elemental things can be seen, however, antimatter (power, or energy), can not be seen. In this we have evidence of scientific foreknowledge in the Bible. Where did this information come from? Certainly not from science during the era when the Bible was being recorded. God, who created the heavens and earth, unquestionably provided this information. *"For prophecy came not in old time by the will of man: but holy men of God spake as they were moved by the Holy Ghost"* (2 Pe 1:21),

Gen 1:3 begins with the conjunction, 'and', letting us know it is part of a continuing action. God was still on the surface of the earth. *"And God said, 'Let there be light,' and there was light."* [A literal translation if this text is: "Light Be: Light Was".] Where was this light? It' was on the surface of the earth for the first time. Where did this light come from. The text does not say directly, but it gives us some clues. It says that God said: *"light be."* Let's read the remainder of what occurred on the first day to discover the clues. *"And God saw that the light was good; and God separated the light from the darkness. And God called the light day, and the darkness He called night. And there was evening and there was morning, one day."* (Gen 1:4-5).

How long was this Day One? Many Christians assume that all the Genesis creation days were exactly 24-hours long. Neither the Gen 1 account nor any other Bible verses directly address how long the first day was. However, we do know that there were a lot of things that happened on the first day -- God created the entire universe.

There are other Bible verses that reveal, at least in part, how God created the universe, giving a hint about the time involved. No fewer than eleven verses from five different inspired biblical authors (patriarchs and prophets) claim that God 'stretched out the heavens' (i.e., Ps 136:6; Is 45:12; Jer 10:12; 32:17; 51:15).

Many of these verses use the present tense, indicating that God is still stretching out the heavens. How long did it take to stretch out the trillions and trillions of stars? The Bible doesn't say, but if we measure the current rate that the universe is still being stretched out, and the distance from some of the distant stars to the earth, measured in light-years, it would suggest that this occurred over a very long time.

Chapter Nine
Days of Creation

In our last chapter, we reviewed the events that occurred in the first day, or era, of creation. Light was called into existence by the Word of the Living God. When He said "Light Be!" He called into existence the photon -- the basic unit of the universe: both of matter and of antimatter. This event is referred to in the scientific world as the **'Big Bang.'** In other words, when God said, "Light be", He called into existence, the building blocks of our universe. With this in place, the orderly creation of all things could proceed.

Day Two:
The second day (era or dimension) of the creation week, God created an expanse and called the expanse sky (Gen 1:6-8) The phrase used here comes from the Hebrew word *"mabdiyl"* translated as 'to divide' (or to create an expanse). The word literally means to separate. In this era, or dimension, of creation, the **photons** were, according to astronomers and scientists, separated, creating the vast expanses of the universe.

About 2200 years ago, philosophers in Alexandria, Egypt taught that the planets were held up by solid crystalline spheres. Long before this, however, the Bible conveyed the truth. The Hebrew word **(rakia)** was translated in Greek literature to mean a firm or **solid structure (stereoma).** However, the Hebrew word actually refers to an expanse. All Hebrew lexicons show that the word **"rakia"** means **expanse**. Thus, it was apparently the translators who were believers in a false scientific theory, leading them to change the meaning of the word to fit their own preconceived theory.

This mistranslation, first made in early Greek literature, was later replicated by the translators of the Bible into modern languages. Sadly, this mistranslation still persists, even though modern philologists and most theologians know better. In many translations today one still finds the word translated **"firmament" (meaning solid ground)**, (e.g., Gen 1:1-17). However, based on the original Hebrew word, **"rakia,"** it should be translated using the English word "expanse." In the Torah of the Jewish Publication Society of America, 1962, **"rakia"** is

81

consistently -- and correctly -- translated "expanse." This is true also for the New American Standard Bible. Once again we see that the original Scriptures were scientifically accurate, thousands of years before 'men of science' discovered that the planets are not held up by a solid structure.

During the second day (era or dimension) of the creation week, God also consolidated materials within this expanse and separated the solid elements from the water, causing the seas to form and dry land to appear. Subsequent to this, on both land, and in the seas, He called forth living things (Gen 1:9-13). If such consolidation had occurred without Divine intervention, one would expect that the liquids (including water) would contain all of the elements found in the earth. In this case, the undifferentiated mass would become thicker, or more dense, over time. However, only through God's ability to separate the water from the other elements, did dry earth and the seas appear, making life on earth, and in the seas possible. **After all, murky water and mud sustains very, very little, if any, life.**

The "Creation Psalm" (Ps 104) describes how God accomplished the materialization of land. According to the Psalmist, writing under Divine inspiration, *"The mountains rose; the valleys sank down to the place which Thou didst establish for them."* (vs.. 11). This description suggests that God's declaration employed a form of tectonic activity to form the dry land. If tectonic activity were indeed used by God to form the dry land, this would suggest that the third day (era or dimension) occurred over a very long period of time.

God also established the boundaries, or limits of the seas: *"Or who shut up the sea with doors, when it brake forth, as if it had issued out of the womb? When I made the cloud the garment thereof, and thick darkness a swaddling-band for it, and brake up for it my decreed place, and set bars and doors, and said, "Hitherto shalt thou come, but no further: and here shall thy proud waves be stayed"?"* (Job 38:8-11).

Before the time of Columbus, most philosophers and early scientists believed that the earth was flat. They feared that if one sailed too close to the edge, they might drop off into space and be lost forever. However, the Bible contained the truth about the shape of the earth more than 2,100 years before Columbus. Isaiah, the prophet, writing under inspiration from God, said: *"It is He that sitteth upon the circle of the earth, ..."* (Is 40:22; Pro 8:27.)

Notice the expression "**circle of the earth**." The original Hebrew word used here is **('chug')**, which means **circle and sphere**. This Hebrew word contains the scientific truth that the earth is round and is a sphere. Obviously, Isaiah did not get his information from the scientists of his day, since all believed and taught that the earth was flat. His information must have come from a better, a higher, source. Isaiah himself claims that what he wrote came from the Great Scientist, The Creator of the heavens and the earth, and all that is in them.

How long was Day Two? Once again, it is difficult to say just how long the second day, or era, was. Part of the verse indicates that God *"let the separation be"* (suggesting a natural process). Scripture goes on to explain that **God "made" the separation**. The Hebrew word *'asah'* translated **"made"** suggests that **God formed the separation from existing materials**, rather than creating it brand new. As such, the formation could involve both supernatural and natural processes. If the separation was allowed to form on its own, it would be expected that the second day (dimension, era) might represent a very long period of time.

Day Three:
Once the earth was formed and the limits of the waters established, "God said, *"Let the earth sprout vegetation, plants yielding seed, and fruit trees bearing fruit after their kind, with seed in them, on the earth"; and it was so. And the earth brought forth vegetation, plants yielding seed after their kind, and trees bearing fruit, with seed in them, after their kind; and God saw that it was good"* (Gen 1:11-12). On the third day God allowed the earth to produce plants through germination (sprouting) and He directed them to grow until fruit bearing seeds were produced.

The Hebrew word *'dasha'* used here **refers to a plant that sprouts from a seed until the seedling turns green**. This Hebrew verb tells us that God used natural processes identical to what we observe on the earth today. The plants spouted, grew to maturity, and produced fruit with seeds. Several species of plants are described here. The Hebrew word *'deshe'* **refers primarily to grasses; while the word *'eseb'* refers primarily to herbs; and the words *'peri'* and *'ets'* both refer to fruit trees.**

How long was Day (dimension) Three? It must have been fairly long since there is no plant in the world that can germinate, mature, and produce fruit and seeds within a 24-hour time period. From here on the interpretation of a creation day representing a literal 24 hour day is more problematic for each succeeding creation day. In the Genesis scenario, we not only find plants that sprout, we also have trees that grow to maturity and produce fruit with seeds in it. It takes fruit trees several years of growth to mature sufficiently before they produce any fruit. Of course, God could have caused everything to happen super-quick. However, this is not what the record says: God said, *"Let the earth sprout vegetation..."* and Scripture continues, saying, **"And the earth brought forth vegetation..."**

In order to claim that God miraculously created all the plants, seeds, etc., calling them into existence in 24-hours, one would have to claim that God is a liar, since He says the earth brought forth the vegetation. Not a good accusation to make! So, from this statement, we know that the second part of the third day alone had to be at least several years long.

Day Four:

In the forth day (era or dimension) of creation, *God established (or appointed) the two great lights; the greater (in Hebrew, older) light to govern the day, and the lesser (in Hebrew, younger) light to govern the night; He made the stars also. And God placed them in the expanse of the heavens to give light on the earth.* (Gen 1:16,17). Modern astronomy has demonstrated beyond a reasonable shadow of doubt that the sun is much older than the moon, and that stars are still being created -- providing additional evidence that each creation day refers to an era or dimension of time and space.

Many people believe that the text concerning day four of creation says that God created the Sun, moon and stars on the fourth day. However, this is not what the text actually says. Let's read it again for clarity:

- *"Then God said, "Let there be lights in the expanse of the heavens to separate the day from the night, and let them be for signs, and for seasons, and for days and years"* (Gen 1:14) ...

- *"and let them be for lights in the expanse of the heavens to give light on the earth"; and it was so"* (Gen 1:15) ...

- *"And God made the two great lights, the greater light to govern the day, and the lesser light to govern the night; He made the stars also"* (Gen 1:16) ...

- *"And God placed them in the expanse of the heavens to give light on the earth"* (Gen 1:17) ...

- *"and to govern the day and the night, and to separate the light from the darkness; and God saw that it was good"* (Gen 1:18).

In verse 14 we have that unusual word construction once again: *"let there be."* This is not a statement of creation, but rather, a statement of permitting its appearance or state of being. At this point in the creation process, the clouds that appeared during the initial creation of the earth were completely removed so that the celestial bodies themselves were visible for the first time from the surface of the earth. The passage tells us that the lights were allowed "to be" so that they could be for signs to demark the seasons, days, and years. It was absolutely necessary for the life and well-being of the creatures created during day 5, that the heavenly bodies be visible.

We know for example, that many of the migratory birds (created on day 5) require visible stars to navigate by, hence their need to actually see these celestial bodies. Verse 18 provides yet another hint concerning the length of the creation days. The lights, it says, were placed in the sky to *"separate the light from the darkness."* Does this sound familiar? This is the identical Hebrew phrase used for God's creative work during the first day when, *"God separated the light from the darkness"* (Gen 1:4)

By employing this phrase, the text appears to be recounting the formation of the Sun, moon and stars, which Scripture says were created on the first day. If we accept that God created the Sun, moon and stars on the fourth day, then He didn't really create the heavens in verse one, as stated in the Genesis record. Thus, it seems that these celestial bodies were created during day one, and first became visible, from the earth's surface, during day four. Once again, the 24-hour period, of the word translated day, suffers a serious contradiction between Gen 1:1 and Gen 1:16.

How can a day be longer than 24-hours? Even though the Genesis text clearly suggests that the creation days are much longer than 24-hours each, some individuals still insist that any interpretation of Gen 1 that deviates from a literal 24-hour day interpretation is not biblical, and is perhaps even heresy.

However, the real problem in comprehending the actual time involved in the creation week, is our misunderstanding of the Hebrew word **'yom'.** Translated as day in Genesis, the word yom -- **based on its usage -- has several definitions. It can mean a 12 hour daylight period, a 24 period of time, a long, but indefinite period of time, or a dimension of time and space.** A careful reading of the Genesis creation account reveals that the 24-hour interpretation is ruled out by the original Genesis text itself.

How many stars are there? Do you know? Do astronomers know? Does anyone know? The Bible recorded that God promised Abraham, He would multiply his descendants as the stars of the heavens (Gen 22:17; 26:4). One can hardly count the descendants of Abraham since, they continue to multiply with every succeeding generation. In like manner, the Bible states that the stars cannot be numbered. In Jer 33:22, we read that the host of heaven cannot be counted: *"I will make the descendants of David my servant and the Levites who minister before me as countless as the stars of the sky and as measureless as the sand on the seashore.'"*

Science-minded individuals have repeatedly attempted to count the stars. Hipparchus (c190 BC) listed 1,056 visible stars. Ptolemy (90-168 AD), stated that about 3,000 could be counted. Within a short time after God entered into His covenant promise with Abram, Abram had more than 3,000 descendants. His descendants later numbered in the millions. How then is it that the Bible says that the stars could not be numbered, yet scientists have counted them? Was the Bible wrong? Not at all. Science, through increased technology, has learned that there are far more stars than they once believed. Of course, this was not discovered until the invention of the telescope. Moreover, we know today that the number of stars is not finite; it continues to increase. The Bible was right about it all the time -- neither the number of stars, nor the descendants of Abraham can be counted.

Abraham lived about 3,700 years before the invention of the telescope. Jeremiah lived 2,200 years before the telescope was invented. How then could Jeremiah have known that the stars could not be counted? The scientists of his time didn't believe this. In fact, Jeremiah could not have known this, except that God told him. Jeremiah, recording what God said, wrote: *"Thus says the Lord ... As the host of heaven cannot be counted, and the sand of the sea cannot be measured, so I will multiply the descendants of David My servant and the Levites who minister to Me"* (Jer 33:22). In this instance, the Bible was at least 2,200 years ahead of astronomy -- another reason to believe that the Bible is the word of God.

Day Five:
During the fifth day (era) of the creation week, God created the animals, represented by the Hebrew word **'nephesh'**, referring to **beings that breathe and have mental processes (a soul).**

- Then God said, *"Let the waters teem with swarms of living creatures [nephesh], and let birds fly above the earth in the open expanse of the heavens."* (Gen 1:20) ...

- *"And God created the great sea monsters, and every living creature [nephesh] that moves, with which the waters swarmed after their kind, and every winged bird after its kind; and God saw that it was good"* (Gen 1:21) ...

- *"And God blessed them, saying, "Be fruitful and multiply, and fill the waters in the seas, and let birds multiply on the earth"* (Gen 1:22)

The word **nephesh**, is used of both animals and human beings. It incorporates the meanings **to 'have breath' and 'soul.'** This term **encompasses the aspects of intellect, emotion, instinct, etc.**. These characteristics apply to all 'higher animals' -- those that require air, such as the birds and mammals. These creatures include many different kinds of birds (Gen 1:21) as well as the "great sea monsters," no doubt referring to whales (also referred to as nephesh beings). These creatures were created in great abundance, as indicated by the verbs **'sharats' and 'ramas'**. Fossil record confirms that there was a massive introduction of bird and mammal species at the beginning of what has been called the Tertiary Age.

The Sixth Day:
The sixth day (dimension) of the creation week describes the creation of animals that interact with mankind as well as the creation of mankind himself.

- *"Then God said, "Let the earth bring forth living creatures [nephesh] after their kind: cattle and creeping things and beasts of the earth after their kind"; and it was so"* (Gen 1:24) ...

- *"God made the beasts of the earth after their kind, and the cattle after their kind, and everything that creeps on the ground after its kind; and God saw that it was good"* (Gen 1:25) ...

  - *"Then God said, "Let Us make man in Our image, according to Our likeness; and let them rule over the fish of the sea and over the birds of the sky and over the cattle and over all the earth, and over every creeping thing that creeps on the earth"* (Gen 1:26) ...

- *"God created man in His own image, in the image of God He created him; male and female He created them"* (Gen 1:27)

The sixth day (dimension) commences with the creation of more **nephesh** creatures. These include the **'behemah' (large vegetation eating quadrupeds), creeping 'remes' nephesh (probably reptiles and rodents), and "beasts 'chay' of the earth" (wild beasts, including those that eat raw flesh -- the wild carnivores).**

After having created these animals, the record says: **"And God saw that it was good"** (Gen 1:25). This is the phrase that is introduced at the end of the activity of day three (vs.., 12); day four (vs.., 18); and day five (vs.., 21). After completing the primary tasks of creation day six, beholding the finished product, and proclaiming the result good (vs.., 25), God [Elohiym (the Supreme Ones, the Godhead)] declare their intention to create children -- made in their own image and likeness, children who were to be given dominion over the earth and everything thereon.

"Then God said, "Let us make man in our image, in our likeness, and let them rule over the fish of the sea and the birds of the air, over the livestock, over all the earth, and over all the creatures that move along the ground" (Ge 1:26).

Thus, the ultimate nephesh (breathing creature with a soul) -- mankind -- was created during a separate expanse of time -- at, or near the end of the sixth day (era). After being created, man is given dominion over the earth and everything thereon, and commissioned to govern, or manage, it (Gen 1:26 & 27). This record tells us that God (Elohiym, a plural noun) created mankind (plural) during a separate span of time from the animals. Not only was man created during a separate span of time, he was created as a distinctly different species -- made in the image and likeness of God -- created as males and females.

"So God created man in his own image, in the image of God he created him; male and female he created them. God blessed them and said to them, "Be fruitful and increase in number; fill the earth and subdue it. Rule over the fish of the sea and the birds of the air and over every living creature that moves on the ground." Then God said, "I give you every seed-bearing plant on the face of the whole earth and every tree that has fruit with seed in it. They will be yours for food. And to all the beasts of the earth and all the birds of the air and all the creatures that move on the ground — everything that has the breath of life in it — I give every green plant for food." And it was so. God saw all that he had made, and it was very good. And there was evening, and there was morning — the sixth day. Thus the heavens and the earth were completed in all their vast array" (Ge 1:27-2:1).

The Hebrew word **'tselem'** translated image, **literally refers to a mirror image or idol.** The Hebrew word, **'demuwth'**, translated likeness, **denotes a concrete similitude in shape and manner.**

Genesis 2 provides us with additional clues about the activities that occurred during the sixth day (or era) of creation. From Gen 1:27, we know that the sixth day extended at least through the creation of Eve, since the text indicates that God created mankind, both male and female on the sixth day. In Gen 2:7, it says that *"the Lord God formed the man from the dust of the ground and breathed into his nostrils the breath of life, and the man became a living being"* (Ge 2:7).

According to the Genesis 2 account, the following events all took place after the creation of Adam.

- ★ God planted a **Garden in Eden** (Gen 2:8) ... in the Genesis 1 account, this activity occurred on day three.

* God caused the garden to sprout and grow (Gen 2:9) ... once again, the Genesis 1 account states this occurred on day three.

These events, if they all transpired on the sixth day rather than the third, would have required a time span much longer than 24 hours. The Hebrew text clearly indicates that God planted a garden or plantation. This garden was not planted full-grown, since once again the Hebrew text clearly states that **the trees were caused to sprout or grow (Hebrew 'tsamach')**. The amount of time allowed for the garden to grow is not stated, but presumably, it would take much longer than 24-hours.

According to the Genesis 2 account, it was after the garden had grown sufficiently to support life, that man was placed in the garden to cultivate it. By this time, the trees were producing fruit so that Adam could eat. It was, apparently, after this that:

* God brought all the birds, cattle and wild animals to Adam to name (Gen 2:19-20) ... animals which were, according to the Genesis 1 account, created on days five and six.

Adam was next given the assignment of naming the birds, the cattle and wild animals. The list here includes only birds and mammals and does not mention fish or other lower life forms. Even so, it would require that Adam name at least 14,600 species (8,600 species of birds and 4,000 species of mammals)

during a single day. This would require Adam to name more than 10 species per minute (assuming he had the entire 24 hours)! For those who believe in a 'young earth,' this would require that Adam name not only all of the existing birds and mammals on earth today, but also all the ones in the fossil record, since they would all have to be alive on day 6 since no animal death occurred prior to the fall. Such a task would probably double the number of species to be named.

The problem is, Adam did not have the entire 24 hours. According to the Genesis 2 account, part of the day was required for the planting and growing of the garden, and Adam tending the garden. Realistically, Adam would have to name at least 20 species per minute, including all the species found in the fossil record, to accomplish this within a literal 24 hour day; and since part of the day was consumed for other tasks, he would have had to work at the task much faster.

Next, according to the Genesis 2 account, God put Adam to sleep, took a part of him and formed Eve (Gen 2:21-22) ... an event, which seemingly contradicts the Genesis 1 account, where God apparently created mankind (male and female) simultaneously.

Following his naming of the animals, no suitable helper was found for Adam. So, God -- according to the Genesis 2 story -- put Adam into a deep sleep, took at piece of Adam's side, and created Eve. Being awakened, Adam's response to Eve's creation is also telling. Upon seeing Eve for the first time, Adam says (as stated in Hebrew). *"at last."* This is not exactly the response one would expect from a person who had waited for less than one day for his bride. So, based on the evidence presented, we must conclude that the sixth day was most certainly much longer than 24 hours, probably taking at least several years, given Adam's response.

We are really left with only one internally consistent interpretation of the word '*yom*' regarding the days of Genesis 1 and Genesis 2. The meaning of '**yom'** as used in Genesis must refer to an unspecified, lengthy period of time. Since the Genesis text clearly establishes that the third day alone must -- at a minimum -- have been several years long, none of the other days would be expected to be limited to 24-hours. All, or nearly all, of the other creation days also appear to require an extensive period of time to complete the activities related to that day. This supports the interpretation that each creation day was in reality an era, or dimension of change within the cosmos.

Accepting this concept resolves most, but not all, of the apparent conflicts between the first and second chapters of Genesis. The principle issue remaining to be resolved is when mankind appeared on the scene. Was it before or after the Garden of Eden was planted? Was it before or after plants had matured and produced fruit? And, why was the creation of mankind separated from the creation of the animals **IF** mankind is -- as scientists attest -- part of the animal kingdom?

Understanding the creation days as eras, or dimensions of time and space, helps us resolve this problem. According to this interpretation, God (Elohiym, the Supreme Ones, or the Godhead), completed all the other features of creation during six long eras (or dimensions of time and space). Then, sometime toward the end of this era, before resting from His creative process, God created mankind (male and female) in their own image and likeness.

Adam and Eve were not there during those six long eras of time -- that commenced when God said *"Light be."* They were not there when God pronounced the animals that He created, good (vs.., 25). Mankind was called into existence after this time, bearing God's image and likeness, and of male and female gender. They were -- as God's representatives -- to govern, or rule over, all things created during the previous six dimensions of time and space (Gen 1:28). Thus, in essence, mankind, while created at the end of the sixth ear -- before their fall -- apparently dwelt in the seventh dimension -- in the presence of God.

Chapter Ten
The Seventh Day

In further support of the concept that each day of the creation week represented an era or dimension, consider what we are told concerning the seventh day. *"God saw all that he had made, and it was very good. And there was evening, and there was morning — the sixth day. Thus the heavens and the earth were completed in all their vast array.* **By the seventh day God had finished the work he had been doing; so on the seventh day he rested from all his work. And God blessed the seventh day and made it holy, because on it he rested from all the work of creating that he had done.**

This is the account of the heavens and the earth when they were created. When the Lord God made the earth and the heavens" (Gen 1:31-2:4).

Opponents of the era/dimensional interpretation of the Hebrew word **'yom'** most frequently refer to the fourth commandment -- and the command to observe the seventh day, perpetually from week to week, as a Sabbath, holy unto the Lord. *"The seventh day is a Sabbath to the Lord your God. On it you shall not do any work, neither you, nor your son or daughter, nor your manservant or maidservant, nor your animals, nor the alien within your gates. For in six days the Lord made the heavens and the earth, the sea, and all that is in them, but he rested on the seventh day. Therefore the Lord blessed the Sabbath day and made it holy"* (Ex 20:10-11).

While on the surface, this position seems viable, further consideration gives one cause to challenge this belief. A careful evaluation of the facts appears to support the fact that the weekly **Sabbath was a symbol**, established as a memorial of remembrance of God's creative acts. In support of this, consider the following text:

The author of the Book of Hebrews cautioned: *"See to it, brothers, that none of you has a sinful, unbelieving heart that turns away from the living God. But encourage one another daily, as long as it is called Today, so that none of you may be hardened by sin's deceitfulness. We have come to share in Christ if we hold firmly till the end the confidence we had at first. As has just been said: "Today, if you hear his voice, do not harden your hearts as you did in the rebellion." Who were they who heard and rebelled? Were they not all those Moses led out of Egypt? And with whom was he angry for forty years? Was it not with those who sinned, whose bodies fell in the desert? And to whom did God swear that they would never enter his rest if not to those who disobeyed? So we see that they were not able to enter, because of their unbelief."*

"Therefore, since the promise of entering his rest still stands, let us be careful that none of you be found to have fallen short of it. For we also have had the gospel preached to us, just as they did; but the message they heard was of no value to them, because those who heard did not combine it with faith. Now we who have believed enter that rest, just as God has said, "So I declared on oath in my anger, 'They shall never enter my rest.'" And yet his work has been finished since the creation of the world."

"For somewhere he has spoken about the seventh day in these words: "And on the seventh day God rested from all his work." And again in the passage above he says, "They shall never enter my rest." It still remains that some will enter that rest, and those who formerly had the gospel preached to them did not go in, because of their disobedience. Therefore God again set a certain day, calling it Today, when a long time later he spoke through David, as was said before: "Today, if you hear his voice, do not harden your hearts." **For if Joshua had given them rest, God would not have spoken later about another day. There remains, then, a Sabbath — rest for the people of God; for anyone who enters God's rest also rests from his own work, just as God did from his**. Let us, therefore, make every effort to enter that rest, so that no one will fall by following their example of disobedience" (Heb 3:12-4:11).

Most theologians agree that this text clarifies the fact that the Sabbath day was a memorial of creation, commemorative of God's Sovereignty, and prophetically, it specifically symbolizes the Christian's rest from the law, in and through the Gospel of Jesus Christ. This concept is wholly supportive of the dispensational doctrine, that we presently live in the church dispensation, rather than under the law. As such, **this dispensation -- the church age is correlative to both an era and a dimension, rather than a 24 hour day.**

Concerning its correlation to an era, not one of us knows how long this dispensation (or era) will last -- not even Christ himself: *"Heaven and earth shall pass away: but my words shall not pass away. But of that day and that hour knoweth no man, no, not the angels which are in heaven, neither the Son, but the Father. Take ye heed, watch and pray: for ye know not when the time is"* (Mk 13:31-33).

Regarding the relationship between the Sabbath day representing a dimension, consider what Christ himself said concerning the Kingdom of God, as recorded by Mark: *"After John was put in prison, Jesus went into Galilee, proclaiming the good news of God.* **"The time has come,"** *he said.* **"The kingdom of God is near.** *Repent and believe the good news!"* (Mk 1:14-15); *"And he said to them, "I tell you the truth,* **some who are standing here will not taste death before they see the kingdom of God come with power**" (Mk 9:1); **"You are not far from the kingdom of God"** (Mk 12:34).

Luke records the following words of Christ: **"The knowledge of the secrets of the kingdom of God has been given to you**, *but to others I speak in parables, so that, "'though seeing, they may not see; though hearing, they may not understand'"* (Lk 8:10); *"The Law and the Prophets were proclaimed until John. Since that time,* **the good news of the kingdom of God is being preached, and everyone is forcing his way into it**" (Lk 16:16); **"The kingdom of God does not come with your careful observation,** *nor will people say, 'Here it is,' or 'There it is,' because* **the kingdom of God is within you**" (Lk 17:20-21).

Jesus, speaking to Nicodemus said: *"I tell you the truth,* **no one can see the kingdom of God unless he is born again"** (Jn 3:3). And the apostle Paul wrote: *"For* **the kingdom of God is not a matter of eating and drinking, but of righteousness, peace and joy in the Holy Spirit**" (Rom 14:17); **"For the kingdom of God is not a matter of talk but of power"** (1 Cor 4:20); *"I declare to you, brothers, that* **flesh and blood cannot inherit the kingdom of God**, *nor does the perishable inherit the imperishable"* (1 Cor 15:50).

In Collosians, Paul encouraged his disciples to: *"be strengthened with all power according to his glorious might so that you may* **have great endurance and patience, and joyfully giving thanks to the Father, who has qualified you to share in the inheritance of the saints in the kingdom of light.** *For* **he has rescued us from the dominion of darkness and brought us into the kingdom of the Son he loves**" (Col 1:11-13).

It goes without question that the rest, the author of Hebrews encourages us to make every effort to enter (Heb 3:10-4:11), is our **entering into the Kingdom of God and, in faith, resting in Christ's victory over the powers of darkness**. This dimensional change is further explained by the author of Hebrews who wrote: *"For the* **law having a shadow of good things to come**, *and not the very image of the things, can never with those sacrifices which they offered year by year continually make the comers thereunto perfect"* (Heb 10:1); and by the words of the apostle Paul, who wrote: *"***Let no man therefore judge you** *in meat, or in drink, or* **in respect of an holy day, or of the new moon, or of the Sabbath days: Which are a shadow of things to come; but the body is of Christ"** (Col 2:16-17).

The apostle Paul reminds us that: *"The Scripture, foreseeing that God would justify the heathen through faith, preached before the gospel unto Abraham, saying, In thee shall all nations be blessed.* **So then they which be of faith are blessed with faithful Abraham. For as many as are of the works of the law are under the curse:** *for it is written, Cursed is every one that continueth not in all things which are written in the book of the law to do them. But that* **no man is justified by the law in the sight of God,** *it is evident: for,* **The just shall live by faith. And the law is not of faith**: *but, The man that doeth them shall live in them. Christ hath redeemed us from the curse of the law, being made a curse for us: for it is written, Cursed is every one that hangeth on a tree"* (Gal 3:8-13).

The Old Testament covenant law (the Ten Commandments) was provided as a guide, tutor, or mentor until Christ came. Paul elaborates on this, saying: *"But the scripture hath concluded all under sin, that the promise by faith of Jesus Christ might be given to them that believe.* **But before faith came, we were kept under the law**, *shut up unto the faith which should afterwards be revealed.* **Wherefore the law was our schoolmaster to bring us unto Christ, that we might be justified by faith. But after that faith is come, we are no**

longer under a schoolmaster. *For ye are all the children of God by faith in Christ Jesus"* (Gal 3:22-26).

While the whole Old Testament covenant law served, both as a schoolmaster and a shadow of things to come, (i.e., the incarnation, sacrificial death and resurrection of our Lord and Savior, Jesus Christ); the Sabbath served a particular purpose. It was a constant reminder of God's Sovereignty, and it foreshadowed (foretold) the time when God's people would be able, in faith, to rest in the completed redemptive work of Christ, rather than striving to keep the law.

It is equally evident that the Kingdom of God is not a time-limited event nor a space-limited reality. Quite the contrary! The Kingdom of God is limitless -- having neither limits in time (Rev 10:5,6), nor boundaries within the expanse of the universe (Is 66:1).

Summary
Having completed the creation of His handiwork sufficiently to support life -- the life of His Children --man -- created in His image, God entered the seventh day (dimension) -- the dimension of rest. He planted a garden -- the "Garden of God" (the Garden of Eden, also called The Holy Land) (Eze 28:13; 31:8,9; Dan 11:31), and invited his children, Adam and Eve, to dwell there with Him. They had access to the Tree of Life that arched over, and was watered by the River of Life, flowing from the throne of God, providing them with life-giving fruit -- a different fruit for each month of the year (Rev 22:1,2).

Adam and Eve enjoyed a face to face, intimate relationship with God. God personally placed them in the Garden (Gen 12:15), and came to the garden -- His Garden -- on a daily basis, in the cool of the evening, to visit with them (Gen 3:8). It was there, in the Garden of God -- the **Seventh Dimension of Reality** -- that humanity began, and it is there that redeemed mankind will one day again enjoy God's presence:

"Then the angel showed me the river of the water of life, as clear as crystal, flowing from the throne of God and of the Lamb down the middle of the great street of the city. On each side of the river stood the tree of life, bearing twelve crops of fruit, yielding its fruit every month. And the leaves of the tree are for the healing of the nations. No longer will there be any curse.

"The throne of God and of the Lamb will be in the city, and his servants will serve him. They will see his face, and his name will be on their foreheads. There will be no more night. They will not need the light of a lamp or the light of the sun, for the Lord God will give them light. And they will reign for ever and ever. The angel said to me, "These words are trustworthy and true. The Lord, the God of the spirits of the prophets, sent his angel to show his servants the things that must soon take place" (Rev 22:1-6).

It was also in the Garden of Eden -- the Kingdom of God -- where Adam and Eve succumbed to temptation, rebelled, becoming subject to the curse and the profound transmutation that all mankind now experiences. And it is in (and through) this 'garden' -- the Kingdom of God -- where man will be restored to the family of God. In the Kingdom of God, there will be no more death and dying. While on earth, *"Jesus went through all the towns and villages, teaching in their synagogues, preaching the good news of the kingdom and healing every disease and sickness"* (Mt 9:35).

He commissioned his disciples, saying: *"All authority in heaven and on earth has been given to me. Therefore go and make disciples of all nations, baptizing them in the name of the Father and of the Son and of the Holy Spirit, and teaching them to obey everything I have commanded you. And surely I am with you always, to the very end of the age"* (Mt 28:18-20). ... *"As you go, preach this message: 'The kingdom of heaven is near.' Heal the sick, raise the dead, cleanse those who have leprosy, drive out demons. Freely you have received, freely give"* (Mt 10:7-8).

Jesus, as he walked the earth, said: *"Be sure of this: the Kingdom of God is near"* (Lk 10:11). And, his apostle, John, prophesying of last-day events, wrote: *"The seventh angel sounded his trumpet, and there were loud voices in heaven, which said: "The kingdom of the world has become the kingdom of our Lord and of his Christ, and he will reign for ever and ever"* (Rev 11:15). ... *"Now have come the salvation and the power and the kingdom of our God, and the authority of his Christ. For the accuser of our brothers, who accuses them before our God day and night, has been hurled down"* (Rev 12:10).

Prior to the ushering in of God's Kingdom, all mankind will be identified with a mark: His Children with the Seal of God; and those who deny Him with the Mark of the Beast. This drama, and how it is played out, comprises the remainder of this book.

Chapter Eleven
The Seal of God vs. The Mark of the Beast

Sealed with a mark.
In our earlier book, "Mysteries of the Bible - Adam to Abram: The Primeval Era", we provided substantial evidence that the two trees in the Garden of Eden (The Tree of Life and The Tree of The Knowledge of Good and Evil) represent two families, or kingdoms: the Family, or Kingdom of God; and the Family, or Kingdom of Satan. Every person who has ever lived, or who will live, upon the earth, will -- according to their personal choice -- be a member of one of these families, serving one of these kingdoms. As such, all will be sealed with a mark of Authority.

The Purpose of the Seal:
What is the purpose of a King's seal? The Bible tells us it is to mark the possessions of the king: including those individuals who are members of His kingdom. In the Old Testament, we read that God chose Israel and marked the people as his:

"Now the glory of the God of Israel went up from above the cherubim, where it had been, and moved to the threshold of the temple. Then the Lord called to the man clothed in linen who had the writing kit at his side and said to him, *"**Go throughout the city of Jerusalem and put a mark on the foreheads of those who grieve and lament over all the detestable things that are done in it.**" As I listened, he said to the others, "Follow him through the city and kill, without showing pity or compassion. Slaughter old men, young men and maidens, women and children, but **do not touch anyone who has the mark**. Begin at my sanctuary." So they began with the elders who were in front of the temple"* (Eze 9:3-6).

The King's seal is a statement concerning his authority: a declaration that his decrees are binding upon all his subjects and are NOT to be changed by anyone. Thus, in a sense, the king's seal, or mark, is a token, symbolizing his authority and laws.

God's Seal:
Confirming that the Torah, or Decalogue, is the Seal of God, the Old Testament says:

- *"Bind up the testimony, Seal the law among my disciples."* (Is 8:16)

- *"These Commandments [the Torah or Decalogue] that I give you today are to be upon your hearts. ... Tie them as symbols on your hands and bind them on your foreheads."* (Dt 6:6-8).

Further validation that God's law is His seal, is provided by the prophet Jeremiah, who declared: *"The time is coming," declares the Lord, "when I will make a new covenant with the house of Israel and with the house of Judah. It will not be like the covenant I made with their forefathers when I took them by the hand to lead them out of Egypt, because they broke my covenant, though I was a husband to them," declares the Lord.* **"This is the covenant I will make with the house of Israel after that time," declares the Lord. "I will put my law in their minds and write it on their hearts.**

"I will be their God, and they will be my people. No longer will a man teach his neighbor, or a man his brother, saying, 'Know the Lord,' because they will all know me, from the least of them to the greatest" (Jer 31:31-34).

The fulfillment of this prophecy was delayed, pending a climactic event -- the crucifixion of Christ. This delay and subsequent fulfillment is recorded in Hebrews: *"Since that time he waits for his enemies to be made his footstool, because by one sacrifice he has made perfect forever those who are being made holy. The Holy Spirit also testifies to us about this. First he says:* **"This is**

the covenant I will make with them after that time, says the Lord. I will put my laws in their hearts, and I will write them on their minds" (Heb 10:13-16).

The Effects of God's Seal:
The following verses make reference to the benefits that accrue to those marked with the seal of God.

- *"Do not labor for the food which perishes, but for the food which endures to everlasting life, which the Son of Man will give you, because God the Father has set His seal on Him"* (John 6:27).

- *"Now He who establishes us with you in Christ and has anointed us is God, 22 who also has sealed us and given us the Spirit in our hearts as a guarantee"* (2 Cor 1:21-22).

- *"In Him you also trusted, after you heard the word of truth, the gospel of your salvation; in whom also, having believed, you were sealed with the Holy Spirit of promise"* (Eph 1:13).

- *"And do not grieve the Holy Spirit of God, by whom you were sealed for the day of redemption"* (Eph 4:30).

- *"Nevertheless the solid foundation of God stands, having this seal: "The Lord knows those who are His," and, "Let everyone who names the name of Christ depart from iniquity"* (2 Ti 2:19).

The disciples of God are *sealed with His law.* The seal of God is imprinted on their foreheads (minds) and tied on their hands.

The Mystery of Transfiguration:
Sealed with His seal, God's disciples will experience the reality of one of His most precious mysteries -- a reality that Christ's disciples, Peter, James and John, witnessed when Jesus, Moses and Elijah were transfigured before them: *"Take notice! I tell you a mystery (a secret truth, an event decreed by the hidden purpose or counsel of God).*

We shall not all fall asleep [in death], but we shall all be changed (transfigured).

"In a moment, in the twinkling of an eye, at the [sound of the] last trumpet call. For a trumpet will sound, and the dead will be raised imperishable (free and immune from decay), and we shall be changed (transfigured). For this perishable [our flesh and blood] must put on the imperishable [spiritual nature], and this mortal [nature that is subject to death and dying] must put on immortality (eternal life)" (1 Cor 15:51-53 AMP)

The Mark of the Beast:
When asked their understanding of the Mark of the Beast, most Christians respond by stating that the Mark of the Beast is the number 666. Is this really true, or have we already been deceived at this point in our understanding? In actual fact, Rev 13:17 clearly indicates that the Mark of the Beast is different than his number, that number representing the number of man. Reading the verse carefully. It states: *"And that no man might buy or sell, save he that had the mark, or the name of the beast, or the number of his name."*

Satan counterfeits many things of God, such as physical and psychological healing, tongues, signs and wonders, and other miracles. Is it conceivable that Satan is also going to counterfeit God's mark, referred to as the Seal of God? To help gain understanding of this, consider whether the mark the Lord set upon Cain was a physical mark or a spiritual mark? Genesis 4:15 reads, *"... the LORD set a mark upon Cain, lest any finding him should kill him."* Did Cain actually spend the rest of his life with writing on His forehead? Assuming that this were true, would others living at that time have known about it meaning, or bothered to take notice of any such mark on Cain's head?

Some have interpreted the mark of the beast as a tattoo of some sort. Others suggest it may be a microchip injected into the hand or the forehead. Still others think it is connected to a credit card, a national health card, the bar code, or the currency of a one-world order. From a practical standpoint, think what a monumental task it would be to effect any of these on a worldwide basis.

An alternate interpretation, held by some, that you may not have heard about before, or seriously considered, lies in the fact that Satan is a liar -- the father of lies. He consistently endeavors to counterfeit God's works. Pursuing this thought, if God's law is the symbol (or seal) of His authority, isn't it reasonable to assume that Satan would attempt to counterfeit this?

Revelation 9, 13, 14 & 19 all indicate that those who receive the Mark of the Beast will die the second death. For example, in Rev 19, we read: *"[When] The fifth angel sounded his trumpet ... I saw a star that had fallen from the sky to the earth. ... given the key to the shaft of the Abyss. ... When he opened the Abyss, smoke rose from it .. And out of the smoke [similar ones] came down upon the earth like locusts and were given power like that of scorpions of the earth. They were told not to harm the grass of the earth or any plant or tree, but only those people who did not have* **the seal of God on their foreheads**" *(Rev 9:1-4);* **"[but] them that had received the mark of the beast, and them that worshipped his image. These both were cast alive into a lake of fire burning with brimstone"** (Rev 19:20).

Consider also the words of the apostle, Paul who wrote: **"But I see another law at work in the members of my body, waging war against the law of my mind and making me a prisoner of the law of sin at work within my members**. *What a wretched man I am! Who will rescue me from this body of death? Thanks be to God — through Jesus Christ our Lord! So then, I myself in my mind am a slave to God's law, but in the sinful nature (the flesh) a slave to the law of sin. Therefore, there is now no condemnation for those who are in Christ Jesus, because through Christ Jesus the law of the Spirit of life set me free from the law of sin and death"* (Ro 7:23-8:2).

The Mark of the Beast: The Law of Sin and Death: If **the Mark of the Beast, is the "law of sin and death"** it is imperative that we know what is included within this law of sin which produces death. Reflecting back to the Garden of Eden, God forewarned Adam and Eve about this law, declaring: *"You* may freely eat from every tree in the garden except the tree of the knowledge of good and evil. You are not to eat from it, because on the day that you eat from it, it will become certain that you will die" (Ge 2:16-17).

In the sentence, *"You are free to eat from any tree in the garden; but you must not eat from the tree of the knowledge of good and evil, for when you eat of it you will surely die",* the Hebrew reads: ['akal' (aw-kal'), 'akal' (aw-kal'), literally meaning 'eat, eat' (or eat liberally); [from] ['kol' (kole), meaning any or all [the] [`ets (ates) trees (wood stalk) [but] ['lo' (lo) not, or never], [from] the tree ['a`ath (dah'-ath), the knowledge of ['towb' (tobe), an adjective meaning of good things, pleasures or prosperity]; 'and evil' ['ra' (rah), referring to adversity, affliction, bad, calamity].

Thus, a better translation of this Scripture might read: *"The Lord God enjoined (instructed) mankind concerning the garden: 'eat liberally from any and all the trees, but never eat from the tree of pleasures and prosperity: adversity, affliction and calamity."*

This 'Tree of Knowledge of Good and Evil' (providing both pleasures and prosperity: adversity, affliction and calamity), can only be fully understood within the context of the symbolism of the trees in the Garden of Eden representing two family trees [see "Mysteries of the Bible - Adam to Abram: The Primeval Era," Potter, J. V., and Potter, P. M., 2009, The Mystery of the Two Trees, pg. 53-59.]

The Seed of Satan:
The 'family tree' which brought previously unknown 'pleasure and prosperity: adversity, affliction and calamity' upon mankind was the seed of Satan -- the offspring of the Watchers and the daughters of men, referred to in Genesis 6:1-4, and expounded on in the above referenced book, in the chapters on 'The Mystery of Enoch and The Watchers', and 'The Mystery of the Nephilim'. In that book, we quote at length from the ancient

writing referred to as The Book of Enoch, which in part reads as follows:

"And it came to pass when the children of men had multiplied that in those days were born unto them beautiful and comely daughters. And the angels, the children of the heaven, saw and lusted after them, and said to one another: 'Come, let us choose us wives from among the children of men and beget us children.' And Semjâzâ, who was their leader, said unto them: 'I fear ye will not indeed agree to do this deed, and I alone shall have to pay the penalty of a great sin.' And they all answered him and said: 'Let us all swear an oath, and all bind ourselves by mutual imprecations not to abandon this plan but to do this thing.'

"Then sware they all together and bound themselves by mutual imprecations upon it. **And they were in all two hundred; who descended in the days of Jared on the summit of Mount Hermon**, and they called it Mount Hermon, because they had sworn and bound themselves by mutual imprecations upon it. And these are the names of their leaders: Sêmîazâz, their leader, Arâkîba, Râmêêl, Kôkabîêl, Tâmîêl, Râmîêl, Dânêl, Êzêqêêl, Barâqîjâl, Asâêl, Armârôs, Batârêl, Anânêl, Zaqîêl, Samsâpêêl, Satarêl, Tûrêl, Jômjâêl,
Sariêl. These are their chiefs of tens" (En 6).

Giants in the Earth:
"**And all the others together with them took unto themselves wives, and each chose for himself one, and they began to go in unto them and to defile themselves with them**, and they taught them charms and enchantments, and the cutting of roots, and made them acquainted with plants. **And they became pregnant, and they bare great giants, whose height was three thousand ells**: Who consumed all the acquisitions of men. **And when men could no longer sustain them, the giants turned against them and devoured mankind.**

And they began to sin against birds, and beasts, and reptiles, and fish, and to devour one another's flesh, and drink the blood. Then the earth laid accusation against the *lawless ones*" (En 8).

"And **they have gone to the daughters of men upon the earth, and have slept with the women, and have defiled themselves, and revealed to them all kinds of sins. And the women have borne giants**, and the whole earth has thereby been filled with blood and unrighteousness. And now, behold, the souls of those who have died are crying and making their suit to the gates of heaven, and their lamentations have ascended: and cannot cease because of the lawless deeds which are wrought on the earth" (En 9:1-10).

While the initial intrusion of the Watchers offspring, the Nephilim, were destroyed in Noah's flood, the Bible clearly indicates that this was not their end. The record of Genesis reads: **"There were giants in the earth in those days; and also after that**, when the sons of God came in unto the daughters of men, and they bare children to them, the same became mighty men which were of old, men of renown" (Gen 6:4).

The Bible mentions more than one reoccurrence of "giants," seen by the Israelites, specifically the giant-races of

Canaanites. There were apparently a number of such tribes, including: the Anakites, the Rephaim, the Emim, the Horim, and Zamsummim. All were giants. The fact that giants lived on the earth after the flood, is confirmed by many of the Old Testament writers.

Concerning the second invasion of the Nephilim, another ancient scroll: "The Jubilees" states: And, *"In the twenty-ninth jubilee, in the first week [1373 A.M.], ... Arpachshad took to himself a wife ... and went to seek for himself a place where he might seize for himself a city. And he found a writing which former generations had carved on the rock, and he read what was thereon, and he transcribed it and sinned owing to it; for it contained the teachings of the Watchers in accordance with which they used to observe the omens of the sun and moon and stars in all the signs of heaven. And he wrote it down and said nothing regarding it; for he was afraid to speak to Noah about it lest he should be angry with him on account of it. ..."* (BJ 8:1-5).

Following this, the writer records the return of the Nephilim, documenting that: *"... in the third week of this jubilee the unclean demons began to lead astray the sons of Noah. And to make to err and destroy them. And the sons of Noah came to Noah their father, and they told him concerning the demons which were leading astray and blinding and slaying his sons' sons.*

Then, *"In the three and thirtieth jubilee, in the first year in the second week, Peleg [great grandson of Noah] took to himself a wife ... and she bear him a son ... and he called his name Reu; for he said: "Behold, the children of men have become evil through the wicked purpose of building for themselves a city and a tower in the land of Shinar." ... For in the days they built the city and tower, saying: "Come to, let us ascend thereby unto heaven." ...*

"And, the Lord our God said unto us: "Behold they are one people, and this they begin to do, and now nothing will be withholden from them. Come to, let us go down and confound their language, that they may not understand one another's speech ...

And the Lord descended, and we went with Him to see the city and the tower which the children of men had built. And He confounded their language, and they no longer understood one another's speech, and they ceased to build the city and the tower. For this reason the whole land of Shinar is called Babel, because the Lord did there confound all the language of the children of men, and from thence they were dispersed into their cities, each according to his language and nation" (BJ 10:18-26).

It is here, in the land of Shinar, in a City called Babel, that we pick up our story. Here Nimrod, an evil giant, founded the Tower of Babel and established the ancient Mystery Religions, which have perpetuated -- even to our times -- the 'knowledge of good and evil.' The tower may be long gone, the ancient city of Babylon deserted; but the demonic mystery religions founded by Nimrod and his queen, Semiramis, have contaminated the whole world, even to our time. It is these mystery religions about which John the Revelator wrote:

"Then the angel carried me away in the Spirit into a desert. There I saw a woman sitting on a scarlet beast that was covered with blasphemous names and had seven heads and ten horns. The woman was dressed in purple and scarlet, and was glittering with gold, precious stones and pearls. She held a golden cup in her hand, filled with abominable things and the filth of her adulteries. This title was written on her forehead: MYSTERY BABYLON THE GREAT THE MOTHER OF PROSTITUTES AND OF THE ABOMINATIONS OF THE EARTH" (Rev 17:3-5).

Thus, we if we can gain an insight into the origins of the many mystery religions, which we discuss briefly in the following chapter, we should be able to unravel many of the mysteries of Revelation.

Chapter Twelve
The Fall, Transmutation & the Mark of the Beast

The Fall:
Adam and Eve were originally -- like the angelic host -- illumined, or clothed in light. They were, after all, created in the image of God (Gen 1:26,27; 2:7), who is The Light of the world [cosmos] (Jn 8:12). As a result of their rebellion, their illumined bodies were removed, and they became disembodied souls. Feeling naked, ashamed and dreadfully fearful, they hid from their loving Heavenly Father when, in the cool of the evening, He came walking in the garden to visit.

God already knew what they had done, but in His love and mercy, He came seeking them. He Found them hiding in the shadows, immobilized with shame and fear as they tried to cover themselves with some foreign substance (Gen 3:7-10). Approaching them, God first cursed the serpent for allowing itself to be used by Satan to tempt His children (vs.. 14); then He sadly related to Adam and Eve the consequences of their rebellion (vs.. 16-20). Finally, before He departed and ordered them to be exiled from His garden lest they eat of the Tree of Life and become eternal rebels, without hope of restoration, He covered them with skin (hide or flesh and blood).

Transmutation
As a result of their rebellion, Adam and Eve were changed, transmutated, from glory to shame -- from beings of light, reflecting God's image; into creatures of flesh, manifesting a similitude of the animal kingdom. Created in the image and likeness of God, they had reflected His image -- even having their souls clothed in light like their Heavenly Father and the angels. After their sin, they

became, for brief moment unclothed -- disembodied souls -- which caused them to experience terror and shame. Then, through God's loving mercy and kindness, their very beings were altered, changing them from illumined beings of light into creatures with flesh and blood, covered with skin -- creatures no longer fit to live in the presence of God. This act of mercy, while saving their lives, simultaneously altered their very nature.

The Garden of God -- their Heavenly home -- is in the **Seventh Dimension**, where God, resting from His creative acts, dwells with all the hosts of holy angels. In that dimension, there is no illness, suffering, death nor dying. There is no night there and no need of sun, moon nor lamp to light one's way. **In that dimension, lies the Holy City, the home of God's throne, from whence the River of Life -- clear as crystal -- flows, watering the whole earth.** And, down the middle of the Great Street of the city, stands the Tree of Life, rooted on both sides of the river, providing life-giving fruit -- a different variety for each month of the year (Rev 22:1-6).

We have been given but brief glimpses into the 'Paradise Lost' that Adam and Eve once enjoyed. Christ's disciple, John, author of the Book of Revelation, and Enoch, author of the Book of Enoch, which Jesus frequently quoted from, provide us brief snapshots into the seventh dimension. Yet even John, Christ's beloved apostle, who was caught up into paradise, *"saw and heard things that were not lawful for him to utter or write about"* (2 Cor 12:2-4). Paul declared that: *"Eye hath not seen, nor ear heard, neither have entered into the heart of man, the things which God hath prepared for them that love him"* (1 Cor 2:9).

The Mark of The Beast

When Adam and Eve fell, it was not merely a fall from grace, such as Paul describes of those who, having been saved by faith, seek once again to be justified by keeping the law. Their fall was far more profound.

They fell from the seventh dimension -- from Paradise and the Garden of God -- into the sixth dimension -- the dimension of the animal kingdom. As a result of their fall from the seventh, into the sixth dimension, they became carnal creatures with flesh and blood; subject to pain and suffering, death and dying. **They no longer mirrored back God's**

image, or mark. Instead, they bore the image or mark of a beast!

Of all mankind, only Adam and Eve have seen God face to face in all His glory. They were, after all made in His image and likeness, being -- according to the Hebrew Scriptures -- mirror images of God. **Created as beings of light, they bore in their beings, the image, or mark of their Creator**. But, through their rebellion, they became subject to a transmutation -- changed from beings of light into carnal, animalistic beings. **As such, they took upon themselves, The Mark of the Beast!**

Anyone who has been a Christian for any length of time has heard of "The Mark of the Beast." Throughout the Christian era, there have been an almost innumerable number of books written on the subject and hundreds of thousands of sermons preached on the topic. To grasp the interest that this theme arouses, one need only do a web-search. One year ago (June, 2008) my web-search located more than one million, seven hundred and forty thousand hits on the mark of the beast. On June, 2009, my web-search located nine million, eight hundred twenty thousand hits; and today (January 15, 2010, that number has swelled to over twelve million, five hundred thousand (12,500,000)! Certainly this exponential growth speaks to the relevance of this study on **The Seal of God** vs., **The Mark of the Beast.**

Most of these web-sites, as well as the thousands of books and sermons dealing with this topic, base their interpretations on the limited biblical texts discussing this topic found within the book of Revelation. There, we are told that a time would come when only those bearing the mark of the beast will be able to buy or sell (Rev 13:16-18). Following this, John the Revelator provides a clue for us to be able to identify the beast. It is this clue that has raised concern, confusion and controversy within the body of Christ -- the church.

This controversy centers around Rev 13:18, where John says: *"This calls for wisdom. If anyone has insight, let him calculate the number of the beast, for it is man's number. His number is 666."* Over the years, there have been those who have assigned this number to Rome, to the Catholic church, to Emperor Nero, Emperor Caligula, Domitian, the Papacy, Apostacy in general, Hitler, Palaibaskanos (an ancient sorcerer),

Kakos Odegos (a wicked guide), the UPC Bar Code, the Microchip, the United States of America and even one's individual Social Security number! Most believing they have solved this clue, have applied similar techniques: applying the letters (letter-values) commonly used for numbers in Hebrew, Latin or Greek.

Surely John the revelator (the revealer of mysteries) didn't include this clue to cause his readers such confusion, nor to create division within the Body of Christ as has occurred, with this number being assigned to various nations, their leaders, a number of churches and various church leaders. In fact, even the number itself has been cause for confusion.

In May 2005, it was reported that biblical scholars at Oxford University, using advanced imaging techniques, had been able to read previously illegible portions of the earliest known copy of the Book of Revelation, from the Oxyrhynchus site: Papyrus 115 or (P115), which dates to the mid to late third century. **This fragment identifies the Number of the Beast as 616 (chi, iota, stigma), rather than the majority text 666 (chi, xi, stigma). Another early witness, Codex Ephraemi Rescriptus, has this same number written out in full: hexakosiai deka hex (lit. six hundred sixteen).**

Comparative Manuscripts:
Significantly, Papyrus 115 aligns with Codex Alexandrinus (A) and Codex Ephraemi Rescriptus (C) which are generally regarded by biblical philologists (specialists in comparative linguistics) as those providing the best testimony to Revelation. Thus, P115 is considered to provide superior testimony to that of P47 which aligns with Codex Sinaiticus, together forming the second-best witness to the Book of Revelation. This has led more and more biblical scholars to conclude that 616 is the original number of the beast rather than 666.

Dr. Paul Lewes in his book, "A Key to Christian Origins" (1932) wrote: *"The figure 616 is given in one of the two best manuscripts, C (Codex Ephraemi Rescriptus, Paris), by the Latin version of Tyconius (DCXVI, ed. Souter in the Journal of Theology, SE, April 1913), and by an ancient Armenian version (ed. Conybaere, 1907). Irenaeus knew about it [the 616 reading], but did not adopt it (Haer. v.30,3), Jerome adopted it*

(De Monogramm., ed. Dom G Morin in the Rev. Benedictine, 1903). It is probably original. The number 666 has been substituted for 616 either by analogy with 888, the [Greek] number of Jesus (Deissmann), or because it is a triangular number, the sum of the first 36 numbers (1+2+3+4+5+6...+36 = 666)."

Considering the question of the numerology involved, it would at first glance appear that the best information provided to identify this beast -- by the most reliable source available: John the Revelator -- may be even more confusing. However, it seems highly unlikely that John would have provided this clue and encouraged those who have wisdom to calculate the number (Rev 13:18), if it could not be done. Surely, the Holy Spirit who inspired John's writing (2 Tim 3:16), knew in advance that the diverse manuscripts would vary. Having this foreknowledge, it is unlikely that the Holy Spirit -- the revealer of all mysteries (Jer 33:3) -- provided a clue that could not lead to understanding.

Perhaps, we need to reread this text carefully, and prayerfully. *"**And I beheld another beast coming up out of the earth**; and he had two horns like a lamb, and he spake as a dragon. And he exerciseth all the power of the first beast before him, and causeth the earth and them which dwell therein to worship the first beast, whose deadly wound was healed. And he doeth great wonders, so that he maketh fire come down from heaven on the earth in the sight of men, And deceiveth them that dwell on the earth by the means of those miracles which he had power to do in the sight of the beast; saying to them that dwell on the earth, that they should make an image to the beast, which had the wound by a sword, and did live. And he had power to give life unto the image of the beast, that the image of the beast should both speak, and cause that as many as would not worship the image of the beast should be killed.*

"And he causeth all, both small and great, rich and poor, free and bond, to receive a mark in their right hand, or in their foreheads: And that no man might buy or sell, save he that had the mark, or the name of the beast, or the number of his name. Here is wisdom. Let him that hath understanding count the number of the beast: for it is the number of a man; and his number is Six hundred threescore and six" (Rev 13:11-18 KJV).

To provide additional clarity, lets look at a couple of other translations. The Amplified, for example, says: **"Then I saw another beast rising up out of the land [itself];** he had two horns like a lamb, and he spoke (roared) like a dragon. **He exerts all the power and right of control of the former beast in his presence, and causes the earth and those who dwell upon it to exalt and deify the first beast**, whose deadly wound was healed, and to worship him. **He performs great signs (startling miracles), even making fire fall from the sky to the earth in men's sight.** And because of the signs (miracles) which he is allowed to perform in the presence of the [first] beast, he deceives those who inhabit the earth, commanding them to erect a statue (an image) in the likeness of the beast who was wounded by the [small] sword and still lived. [Dt 13:1-5.]

"And he is permitted [also] to impart the breath of life into the beast's image, so that the statue of the beast could actually talk and cause to be put to death those who would not bow down and worship the image of the beast. [Dan 3:5.] Also **he compels all [alike], both small and great, both the rich and the poor, both free and slave, to be marked with an inscription [stamped] on their right hands or on their foreheads,** So that no one will have power to buy or sell unless he bears the stamp (mark, inscription), [that is] the name of the beast or the number of his name. **Here is [room for] discernment [a call for the wisdom of interpretation]. Let anyone who has intelligence (penetration and insight enough) calculate the number of the beast, for it is a human number [the number of a certain man]; his number is 666"** (Rev 13:11-18 AMP).

The Amplified translation of verse 18 reads, *"it is a human number,"* which is consistent with Darby's translation that says" *"Here is wisdom.* **He that has understanding let him count the number of the beast: for it is a man's number;** *and its number [is] six hundred [and] sixty-six"* (Rev 13:18 Darby). While the Amplified and Darby versions of this text provide some clarification, most translations miss one very important point. The Greek word αντηρωπου, **translated *"of a man"* would more correctly be translated *"of man".***

While it is true that the word is in the masculine, singular form, it is also the form used when speaking of mankind in general, as in Mt 4:4, where Jesus said: *"It is written: '***Man** *does not live on bread alone, but on every word that comes from the mouth of God.'"* Making this correction, Rev 13:18 would read: "Here is wisdom. He that has understanding let him count the number of *the beast: for **it is man's number**; and its number [is] six hundred [and] sixty-six."* [or six hundred sixteen.]

This may sound like a small thing to trifle about, however, there is a profound difference between our applying this number mankind in general, vs., attempting to apply it to some particular individual, at some time, in some locale, in history, either the past, present, or the future. More importantly, this seemingly 'small change' gives the entire passage internal consistency. This change also enables one to comprehend current events in a brand new light. To explain what we mean by this, lets look once more at the passage in full, within its overall context.

The initial beast -- that this new 'unknown beast' -- is made in the image of -- comes to the forefront in Rev 12: *"A great and wondrous sign appeared in heaven: a woman clothed with the sun, with the moon under her feet and a crown of twelve stars on her head. She was pregnant and cried out in pain as she was about to give birth. Then another sign appeared in heaven: an enormous red dragon with seven heads and ten horns and seven crowns on his heads. His tail swept a third of the stars out of the sky and flung them to the earth (vs.. 1-4).*

[Most theologians agree that **the woman clothed with the sun, with the moon under her feet and a crown of twelve stars on her head -- who was pregnant and cried out as she was about to give birth -- represents the church.** Likewise, most agree that the **enormous red dragon -- who swept a third of the stars out of the sky, flinging them to**

earth -- represents Satan, who deceived one-third of the angelic host, causing them to be cast out of heaven with him, to the earth].

"The dragon stood in front of the woman who was about to give birth, so that he might devour her child the moment it was born. She gave birth to a son, a male child, who will rule all the nations with an iron scepter. And her child was snatched up to God and to his throne" (vs.. 4-5).

[Once again, theologians are in agreement that these texts refer to the birth, ministry, death, resurrection and ascension of Jesus Christ.]

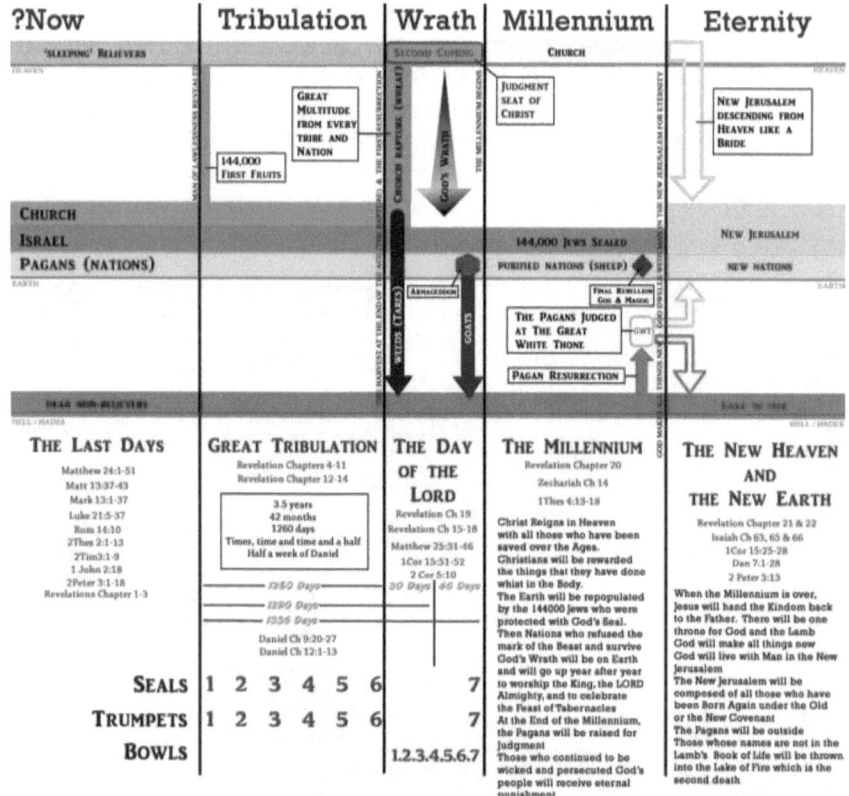

The End Times Prophesies of the Bible

"The woman fled into the desert to a place prepared for her by God, where she might be taken care of for 1,260 days. And there was war in heaven. Michael and his angels fought against the dragon, and the dragon and his angels fought back. But he was not strong enough, and they lost their place in heaven. The great

dragon was hurled down — that ancient serpent called the devil, or Satan, who leads the whole world astray. He was hurled to the earth, and his angels with him" (vs.. 6-9).

[Most biblical historicists agree that the "1,260 days" spanned the Middle Ages, a time when early Christians were persecuted for their beliefs, a period concluding within the early modern or modern era. Although various dates have been proposed for the start and finish of the "1,260 days", three time spans have proven overwhelmingly popular. The majority of historicists throughout history have identified the "1,260 days" as being fulfilled by one or the other of the following three time spans:
- 312 AD to 1572
- 606/610 AD to 1866/1870
- 533/538 AD to 1793/1798

Event ==>	(Seven Seals) Moth Code found on "Ten Days of Awe"	Flu Prophecy posted on forum And one-month margin	Non-event	Swine Flu (First known Flu death on April 12)	Swine Flu Vaccine and second wave of flu?	???
Regular date ==>	2002 Sept. 9-16 SARS began 2 months later	2005 Aug. 24-31 to Sept. 23-30	2006 Feb. 20-27 to March 22-29	2009 March 6-13 to April 5-12	2009 Sept. 2-9 to Oct. 2-9	2012 Aug. 17-24 to Sept. 16-23
Above date on Jewish Calendar ==>	Tishri 3-10 (Week up to "Day of Atonement") Note the 3+7-days that foretold next 3+7 years of chart, called "The Ten Days of Awe!"	Av. 19-26 to Elul 19-26	Shebat 22-29 to Adar 22-29 (Religious New Year begins end of Adar 29)	Adar 10-17 to Nisan 8-18 (Purim and half of Passover week)	Elul 13-20 to Tishri 14-21 (Tishri = week of Tabernacles)	Av. 29-Elul 6 to Elul 29 – Tishri 7 (First week of Civil New Year, i.e., anniversary of Creation week)
Above date on 360-calendar ==>	6th mth, 15-22 day	6th to 7th mth, 15-22 day (7th mth = Week of Tabernacles)	12th to 1st mth, 15-22 day (1st mth = Passover week)	12th to 1st mth, 15-22 day (1st mth = Passover week)	6th to 7th mth, 15-22 day (7th mth = Week of Tabernacles)	6th to 7th mth, 15-22 day (7th mth = Week of Tabernacles)
7+3=10 pattern	7 years (3.5 + 3.5 yrs, that is, 1260 + 1290 days)				3 yrs (1080 days)	
3+7=10 pattern	3 yrs (1080 days)	7 years (3.5 + 3.5 yrs, that is, 1290 + 1260 days) (1290 + 1260 years back to fall of Babylon in Sept., 539 BC)				
	10 years (3630 days plus the 1-month margin)					

[For example: many believe that this prophecy stretches from 538 AD to 1798 AD, allegedly relating to a period of papal supremacy.] The outcome of this prophecy concludes in Rev

12:10, where our next chapter commences. Others believe that the 1260 years is now coming to a close, as depicted in the included graphs.

The differences in these graphs merely testify to the truth of Jesus' words: *"Therefore keep watch, because you do not know the day or the hour"* (Mt 25:13). ... *"Of that day and hour knoweth no man, no not the angels of heaven, but my Father only"* (Mt 24:16).

All we can really know for certain is that since no man knows the day of hour, it behooves us to be ready when that day arrives. As the apostle, Peter advised: *"But the day of the Lord will come like a thief. The heavens will disappear with a roar; the elements will be destroyed by fire, and the earth and everything in it will be laid bare. Since everything will be destroyed in this way, what kind of people ought you to be? You ought to live holy and godly lives as you look forward to the day of God and speed its coming. That day will bring about the destruction of the heavens by fire, and the elements will melt in the heat. But in keeping with his promise we are looking forward to a new heaven and a new earth, the home of righteousness. So then, dear friends, since you are looking forward to this, make every effort to be found spotless, blameless and at peace with him"* (2 Pe 3:10-14).

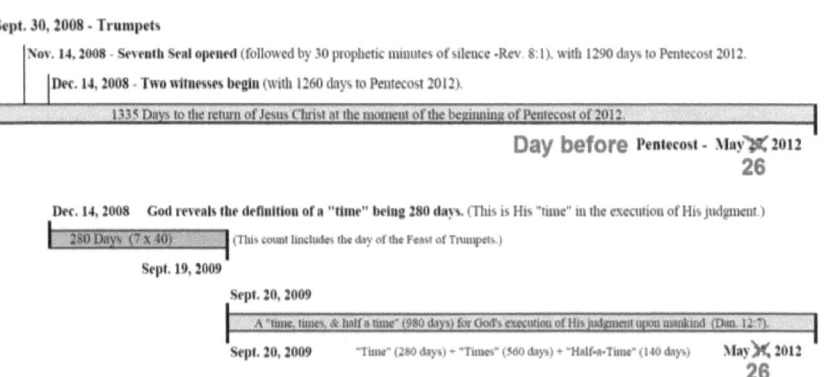

Chapter Thirteen
Christ's Victory Over Satan

Early Church fathers, and modern-day theologians, uniformly accept Revelation 12:10 to the chapter's end, as a prophecy that sets forth the declaration of Christ's conclusive victory and Satan's ultimate defeat.

"Then I heard a loud voice in heaven say: "Now have come the salvation and the power and the kingdom of our God, and the authority of His Christ. For the accuser of our brothers, who accuses them before our God day and night, has been hurled down" (vs.. 10).

"They overcame him by the blood of the Lamb and by the word of their testimony; they did not love their lives so much as to shrink from death. Therefore rejoice, you heavens and you who dwell in them! But woe to the earth and the sea, because the devil has gone down to you! He is filled with fury, because he knows that his time is short" (vs.. 11,12).

[The 'they' referred to in this text is believed by most theologians to refer to all Christians from the dawn of Christianity down through time to the present moment, particularly all Christian martyrs.]

"When the dragon saw that he had been hurled to the earth, he pursued the woman who had given birth to the male child. The woman was given the two wings of a great eagle, so that she might fly to the place prepared for her in the desert, where she would be taken care of for a time, times and half a time, out of the serpent's reach." (vs.. 13,14).

[**When the dragon (Satan) realized that he was cast down to the earth, he persecuted the woman (the church)** which brought forth the man child. (**Jesus Christ**)]. To the woman were given two wings of a great eagle] -- or in Greek: **'tou aetou tou megalou.'** The great eagle mentioned here seems unquestionably to represent the emblem of the Roman empire. The Roman power was referred to as an eagle, based on its legionary military standard, introduced among the Romans in the second year of the Consulate of C. Marius (102 AD). Previous to that time, their standards exhibited wolves, leopards, horses, boars, and eagles indiscriminately, according to the humor of the commander. Some even exhibited minotaurs (an idol depicting a creature that was part man, and part bull), honoring ancient Babylon, whose founder, Nimrod, was allegedly reincarnated as a bull.

The Roman eagles were figures in relief made of silver or gold, borne on the tops of the pikes, or standards. The wings were often displayed as in flight, and frequently, the eagle held a thunderbolt in its talons. Under the eagle, on the pike, were carved or cast bucklers (or mini-shields), and often small crowns. The two wings of the great eagle appear to refer to the two grand independent divisions of the Roman empire. On January 17, AD 395, Constantine declared Christianity as the official religion of the 'Roman empires' -- being, in his words: "both a civil and sacred empire."

The mention of the church flying into the wilderness, to a place prepared for her is an apparent repetition of what is mentioned in vs. 6. Many theologians have considered the former passage as a prophecy in anticipation of what was to occur; since the woman (the church) did not 'fly into the wilderness' (or hide from civil authorities) till several years after the pseudo-conversion of Constantine. However, there is evidence that the true Church, began to flee into the wilderness a considerable time before the division of the great Roman empire into two independent monarchies.

The word translated fled is not to be taken in that peculiar sense as if the woman, in the commencement of her flight, had been furnished with wings. The original word is **'efugen'**, meaning that the woman began to make rapid strides towards the desert almost immediately after her elevation to 'the heaven' (e.g., the throne of the Roman empire). To aid her in her flight she was furnished with the wings of the great eagle **'ina pethtai'** (indicating speed) that she might rapidly disappear from general recognition, hiding, as it were, in that place prepared by God, where she should be fed (nurtured or cared for) a thousand two hundred and threescore days (or years).

It is said here that the period for which the woman should be nourished in the wilderness would be a time, times, and a half (three and one-half years, computed at 360 days per year -- the calendar length of one year at that time -- or, a period of 1260 years). Thus, this period coincides with the twelve hundred and sixty days of vs. 6.

In no other sense can these prophetic periods be considered to be the same other than by understanding 'a time' to signify one year; 'times', two years; and half a time, half a year; i.e., totaling three years and a half. Each prophetic year in the Old Testament contains three hundred and sixty days (believed at that time to be the length of the year), so three and one half years would contain precisely twelve hundred and sixty days.

The Apocalypse being highly symbolical, it is reasonable to expect that its periods of time will also be represented symbolically, and that the prophecy may be homogeneous (manifest uniformity) in all its parts. The Holy Spirit, when speaking of years symbolically, invariably represents them by days, employing the principal of one prophetic day equaling one actual year. *["For forty years — one year for each of the forty days you explored the land — you will suffer for your sins and know what it is like to have me against you"* (Nu 14:34); *"I have assigned you 40 days, a day for each year"* (Eze 4:6). The one thousand two hundred and threescore days, that the woman is fed (cared for) in the wilderness, must therefore, be understood symbolically and must, consequently, denote that many natural years.

The 'wilderness' into which the woman fled was apparently the Greek and Latin empires (pictured in a first century map on the following page). She is conveyed into her place by means of the two wings of the great eagle representing her speedy declension from her state of prominence and great prosperity to a forlorn and desolate condition, where it was not safe for a Christian to publicly acknowledge their faith. The woman was nourished for one thousand two hundred and threescore years from the face of the serpent,

The empires in the east and west were destined, in the course of the Divine providence, to support the Christian religion, at least nominally while the rest of the world remained in pagan idolatry, under the influence of the dragon, the serpent (or Satan, since 'he deceiveth the whole world.'

The accuracy of the words of this prophecy are remarkable. **The Christian Church is symbolized as being supported by both eastern and western empires, two mighty denominations (Roman Catholicism and the Eastern Orthodox)**. The split of the church commenced under the reign of Constantine, during the Council of Nicea in 325 AD, and was formalized in the mid 1400's. At the same time the church is situated in the wilderness, strongly denoting that, though many persons professed Christianity, there were but very few who truly "kept the commandments of God, and had the testimony of Jesus Christ."]

Continuing on in the Revelation, John wrote: *"Then from his mouth the serpent (Satan) spewed water"* [water in prophecy representing multitudes of people, nations and languages (Rev 17:15)]. These pagan nations functioned as though they were *"like a river, to overtake the woman and sweep her away with the torrent"* (vs.. 15).

[**Represented symbolically here is the inundation of the church by the heathen barbarous nations that descended upon the Roman empire**; and the purpose that the dragon had in view by this inundation -- to cause the woman (the Christian Church) -- To be carried away (or destroyed) by the flood. [Satan no doubt hoping that she would be entirely swept away -- off the face of the earth.]

In the fifth century, the Goths, the Heruli, the Franks, the Huns, and Vandals, with other fierce and warlike nations, strangers to Christianity, invaded the Roman empire. During these invasions the Christians were grievously persecuted. This transmigration of nations continued invading the Roman empire, until they had decimated the eastern empire, from Constantinople to the gates of Byzantium, (see map of empire following) and finally took possession of the western empire.]

John writing prophetically during the first century, wrote: *"But the earth helped the woman by opening its mouth and swallowing the river that the dragon had spewed out of his mouth"* (vs.. 16).

[The outcome of the invasion of the Roman empire and the utter subversion of the Christian Church to the many barbarous nations proved contrary to human expectation. The earth symbolically swallowed up the flood -- that is, **the barbarians were ultimately swallowed up by the Romans, rather than the Romans by the barbarians**. The heathen conquerors, instead of imposing their own values on the conquered people, submitted to the religion of the conquered Roman Christians. They not only embraced the religion, but even adopted the laws, the manners, the customs, the language, and the very name -- Romans -- so that **the victors were in a manner, swallowed up (absorbed or lost) among those who they sought to vanquish.**]

"Then the dragon (Satan) was enraged at the woman (the church) and went off to make war against the rest of **her offspring — those who obey God's commandments and hold to the testimony of Jesus**" (vs.. 15-17).

[The heathen hordes, foiled in their subtle attempt to destroy Christianity, were enraged. They endeavored to incite the hatred of the multitude against the religion of Jesus. They even alleged that before the coming of Christ into the world, they were blessed with peace and prosperity; but that since the proliferation of the Christian religion, their gods, were filled with indignation to see their worship neglected and their altars abandoned. They had thus, visited upon the earth -- they claimed -- those plagues and desolations which were increasing every year.]

Satan Switches Tactics:
Thus, the dragon (Satan) now redirects his efforts to make war with the remnant of 'her seed' (the Christian remnant who survived the persecutions). The dragon [Greek **'aphlqe'**], pursuing the woman (the church), now departed into the wilderness, following the church where she had fled. In so doing, a new focus of persecution was instituted, one directed only against the 'remnant of her seed' -- *'those who keep the commandments of God, and have the testimony of Jesus Christ.'*

[The term 'her seed', referring to the Peshitta Aramaic-English Interlinear New Testament, reads: *"Her seed is the Messiah and no other; the remnant are those who believe in and follow Him."* The word translated 'seed' always refers to a son.]

Thus ends Rev 12, after setting the stage, as it were, for a new drama to be played out in Revelation 13, where the image to the beast is introduced and a numerical clue to its identity given.

CHAPTER FOURTEEN
THE HISTORY OF EUROPE FORETOLD

"And the dragon stood on the shore of the sea. And I saw a beast coming out of the sea. He had ten horns and seven heads, with ten crowns on his horns, and on each head a blasphemous name. The beast I saw resembled a leopard, but had feet like those of a bear and a mouth like that of a lion. The dragon gave the beast his power and his throne and great authority" (Rev 13:1-2). [The literal sea shore that John was standing on, or near, when he wrote the Apocalypse, was the shores of the Mediterranean Sea.

At the same time, represented here symbolically, we are introduced to the sea (or multitudes) of people of the Gentile nations. The beast [which in the Greek is the word, **'therion'**, refers to a dangerous, venomous beast, or monster.] Like the dragon, this monster has seven heads and ten horns. But from this point on, the order of symbolism is reversed from that of the red dragon (Satan) introduced in Rev 12.

The dragon (Satan) in Rev 12, was described as having seven heads, with ten horns and seven diadems on his heads. The monster is described as having ten horns and seven heads and ten diadems upon his heads, also [having] blasphemous names upon his heads. Then, in Rev 13, the horns are not described as being on the heads, but rather on the beast itself, seemingly on its body, rather than on its head. Glancing ahead, in Rev 17:12, we read that *"the ten horns which thou sawest are ten kings which have received no kingdom as yet; but receive power as kings one hour* [Greek **'hora'** literally meaning in an instant, or short time period], *with* [Greek **'meta'**, meaning among, or along with], *the beast (monster)."*

In Rev 12, the Dragon and his angels were cast out onto the earth. Here, in Rev 13, John beholds in his vision this beast, or monster, with seven heads, and ten horns rising out of this sea of Gentile Nations. It is also clear from Rev 17, that the ten horns, were to become manifest at a later date, since, *'they had received no kingdom as yet.'*

This monster shares some features with the great dragon, but also exhibits some characteristics that are reminiscent of beasts the prophet, Daniel, beheld and described. To comprehend the meaning of the monster in this chapter, we must first search the Scriptures to clarify the identity of the dragon, and this beast, both of which have with seven heads and ten horns, but exhibit other, dissimilar features. In Rev 13:2, we read: *"And the monster which I saw was like a leopard, and its feet like a bear, and its mouth like a lion's mouth. And the dragon gave to him, his power and his throne and great authority."* Clearly then, **if the dragon empowered and enthroned this monster, the monster and the dragon cannot be one in the same.** The answer to this dilemma is, I believe, found in Daniel 7 and 8.

"In the first year of Belshazzar king of Babylon Daniel had a dream and visions of his head upon his bed: then he wrote the dream, and told the sum of the matters. Daniel spake and said, I saw in my vision by night, and, behold, the four winds of the heaven strove upon the great sea. **And four great beasts came up from the sea**, *diverse one from another.* **The first was like a lion**, *and had eagle's wings: I beheld till the wings thereof were plucked, and it was lifted up from the earth, and made stand upon the feet as a man, and a man's heart was given to it"* (Dan 7:1-4).

"And behold another beast, **a second, like to a bear**, *and it raised up itself on one side, and it had three ribs in the mouth of it between the teeth of it: and they said thus unto it, Arise, devour much flesh. After this I beheld,* **and lo another, like a leopard**, *which had upon the back of it four wings of a fowl; the beast had also four heads; and dominion was given to it.* **After this I saw in the night visions, and behold a fourth beast, dreadful and terrible, and strong exceedingly; and it had great iron teeth**: *it devoured and brake in pieces, and stamped the residue with the feet of it: and* **it was diverse from all the beasts that were before it; and it had ten horns"** (vs.. 5-7).

"I considered the horns, and, behold, there came up among them another little horn, before whom there were three of the first horns plucked up by the roots: and, behold, in this horn were eyes like the eyes of man, and a mouth speaking great things. *I beheld till the thrones were cast down, and the Ancient of days did sit, whose garment was* white as snow, and the hair of his head like the pure wool: his throne was like the fiery flame, and his wheels as burning fire. A fiery stream issued and came forth from before him: thousand thousands ministered unto him, and ten thousand times ten thousand stood before him: the judgment was set, and the books were opened" (vs. 8-10).

"I beheld then because of the voice of the great words which the horn spake: I beheld even till the beast was slain, and his body destroyed, and given to the burning flame. As concerning the rest of the beasts, they had their dominion taken away: yet their lives were prolonged for a season and time. I saw in the night visions, and, behold, one like the Son of man came with the clouds of heaven, and came to the Ancient of days, and they brought him near before him. And there was given him dominion, and glory, and a kingdom, that all people, nations, and languages, should serve him: his dominion is an everlasting dominion, which shall not pass away, and his kingdom that which shall not be destroyed" (vs. 11-14). ...

"These great beasts, which are four, are four kings, which shall arise out of the earth. But the saints of the most High shall take the kingdom, and possess the kingdom for ever, even for ever and ever. Then I would know the truth of the fourth beast, which was diverse from all the others, exceeding dreadful, whose teeth were of iron, and his nails of brass; which devoured, brake in pieces, and stamped the residue with his feet; And of the ten horns that were in his head, and of the other which came up, and before whom three fell; even of that horn that had eyes, and a mouth that spake very great things, whose look was more stout than his fellows" (vs. 17-20).

"I beheld, and the same horn made war with the saints, and prevailed against them; Until the Ancient of days came, and judgment was given to the saints of the most High; and the time came that the saints possessed the kingdom. Thus he said, The fourth beast shall be the fourth kingdom upon earth, which shall be diverse from all kingdoms, and shall devour the whole earth, and shall tread it down, and break it in pieces" (vs. 21-23).

"And the ten horns out of this kingdom are ten kings that shall arise: and another shall rise after them; and he shall be diverse from the first, and he shall subdue three kings. And he shall speak great words against the most High, and shall wear out the saints of the most High, and think to change times and laws: and they shall be given into his

hand until a time and times and the dividing of time*. But the judgment shall sit, and they shall take away his dominion, to consume and to destroy it unto the end. And the kingdom and dominion, and the greatness of the kingdom under the whole heaven, shall be given to the people of the saints of the most High, whose kingdom is an everlasting kingdom, and all dominions shall serve and obey him"* (vs. 24-27).

In Dan 7, The angel tells the prophet, Daniel, that **the four beasts are four kings or kingdoms that will arise on the earth**. The angel also explains to Daniel that the **ten horns are ten kings that will arise out of the last beast, or world wide kingdom, in existence before Jesus comes and sets up His kingdom.** From these passages in Daniel, we can begin to make sense of the beast in Rev 13.

"And the beast which I saw was like unto a leopard, and his feet were as the feet of a bear, and his mouth as the mouth of a lion: and the dragon gave him his power, and his seat, and great authority" (Rev 13:2).

John, the Revelator, picks up on this theme of the seven kingdoms, saying: *"And there are seven kings: five are fallen, and one is, and the other is not yet come; and when he cometh, he must continue a short space"* (Rev 17:10).

The fact that Satan is the power behind, or supporting, the beasts described in Rev 13:2, has already been established since Satan is the dragon, and it is the dragon who empowers and enthrones the monster. The seven heads on the beast appear to represent the seven ancient Gentile world empires. John says, 'five are fallen, one now is, and the other is not yet come. The world empires that had fallen include Egypt, Assyria, Babylon, Media-Persia and Greece. The world empire holding dominion during John's lifetime Was the Roman Empire. Rev 13:2 describes certain attributes of these last four beasts or world empires.

The descriptions given here are in reverse order to those provided by Daniel, since Daniel was looking forward in time, while in Revelation, John's vision begins by looking back in time. Putting these two together it seems clear that the Leopard was the Greek empire, the Bear was the Medo-Persian Empire and the Lion was the Babylonian Empire. The forth beast, or world empire, as described by Daniel, would have the combined attributes of the three before it. The Roman Empire fits the description of the fourth Beast that rises out of the sea, making it the seventh head of the dragon.

The Roman empire died of entropy (collapsing from within). However, the wreckage (the fractured portions thereof), survived and have continued to exist to the present time. Several kings, presidents and other leaders have tried unsuccessfully to put the Roman empire back together again. The last historical attempt was Germany under Hitler. Presently, we see renewed efforts to revive the old Roman Empire taking shape in Europe. It is called the European Union (EU). The EU as of this writing has 27 members.

The territory of the EU consists of the combined territories of its 27 member states with some exceptions outlined below. The territory of the EU is not the same as that of Europe, as parts of the continent are outside the EU, such as Iceland, Switzerland, Norway, and European Russia. Some parts of member countries are not part of the EU, despite their forming part of the European continent (for example the Channel Islands and Faroe Islands). Several territories associated with member states that are outside geographic Europe are also not part of the EU (such as Greenland, Aruba, the Netherlands Antilles, and all the non-European territories associated with the United Kingdom). Some overseas territories are part of the EU even though they are not geographically part of Europe, such as the Azores, the Canary Islands, French Guiana, Guadeloupe, Madeira, Martinique, Réunion, Saint Barthélemy, and Saint Martin.

The EU's member states cover a combined area of 4,422,773 square kilometers (1,707,642 sq. mi.). The total territory of the EU -- pictured right -- is larger than all but six countries. Its highest peak is Mont Blanc in the Graian Alps, 4807 meters above sea level. The landscape, climate, and economy of the EU are influenced by its coastline, which is

69,342 kilometers (43,087 mi.) In length. The EU has the world's second longest coastline, after Canada.

The combined member states of the EU share borders with 21 other, nonmember states for a total border of 12,441 kilometers (7,730 mi.), the fifth longest border in the world. The EU's intent is for all members to join together in one central government, having a single constitution and currency. According to the EU constitution, **there are, and will be, only ten (10) full charter members comprised of the old European countries -- portions of the old Roman empire.**

This **number (10) has significance, since it represents the number of independent states that the Roman empire collapsed into, depicted by the ten horns on the beast of Daniel 7 and Revelation 12-17.** It is the express goal of the EU, at some point -- in the not too distant future -- to evolve back into a unified Europe, fulfilling the prophecy of Revelation 17:12-13. This revived Roman Empire is further defined in Daniel's prophetic explanation of the vision of the statue in Nebuchadnezzar's dream. The meaning of the statute and its differing parts, was revealed to Daniel, for him to be able to relate it the king (Dan 2). This vision describes all the Gentile world powers from Babylon to the return of Christ, when God will set up His kingdom on the earth. The feet and ten toes on Nebuchadnezzar's image, or statue, represent the ten kings that existed during the last phase of the Roman Empire.

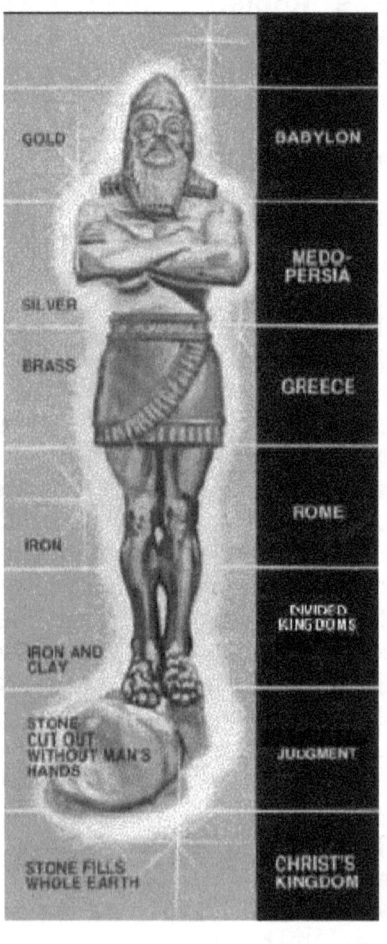

According to the vision of Daniel 2, at the end of the time -- while the nations represented still exist -- a rock, cut out without hands, descends and hits the toes of the image, pulverizing it. The ten toes in this vision of Daniel represent the same leaders of the same nations as do the ten horns in Revelation. The ten toes are equivalent to the ten horns that will share power with the Beast for one hour (or in one era). It is these same nations that will be crushed by the stone cut out of the mountain, made without hands, which represents Christ -- Petra [the rock (Mt 16:18)] -- returning in His glory).

Daniel spoke to the king of Babylon explaining the king's dream, saying: *"And after thee shall arise another kingdom inferior to thee, and another third kingdom of brass, which shall bear rule over all the earth. And the fourth kingdom shall be strong as iron: forasmuch as iron breaketh in pieces and subdueth all things: and as iron that breaketh all these, shall it break in pieces and bruise. And whereas thou sawest the feet and toes, part of potters' clay, and part of iron, the kingdom shall be divided; but there shall be in it of the strength of the iron, forasmuch as thou sawest the iron mixed with miry clay. And as the toes of the feet were part of iron, and part of clay, so the kingdom shall be partly strong, and partly broken. And whereas thou sawest iron mixed with miry clay, they shall mingle themselves with the seed of men: but they shall not cleave one to another, even as iron is not mixed with clay"* (Daniel 2:39-43).

"And in the days of these kings shall the God of heaven set up a kingdom, which shall never be destroyed: and the kingdom shall not be left to other people, but it shall break in pieces and consume all these kingdoms, and it shall stand for ever. Forasmuch as thou sawest that the stone was cut out of the mountain without hands, and that it brake in pieces the iron, the brass, the clay, the silver, and the gold; the great God hath made known to the king what shall come to pass hereafter: and the dream is certain, and the interpretation thereof sure" (vs.. 44-45).

John, the Revelator (the revealer of mysteries) picks up where Daniel left off, saying: *"One of the heads of the beast seemed to have had a fatal wound, but the fatal wound had been healed. The whole world was astonished and followed the beast. Men worshiped the dragon because he had given authority to the beast, and they also worshiped the beast and asked, "Who is like the beast? Who can make war against him?" The beast was given a mouth to utter proud words and blasphemies and to exercise his authority for forty-two months"* (Revelation 13:3-5).

[Here John reiterates a portion of his prophetic commentary concerning the 1260 years of persecution of the early church. This time period, understood on the basis of one prophetic day equaling one literal year, is the same as the "time, times and half a time" mentioned in Dan 7:25; 12:7; Rev 12:14, and the "forty-two months" mentioned in Rev 13:5]

"He (the beast, or Satan) opened his mouth to blaspheme God, and to slander his name and his dwelling place and those who live in heaven. He was given power to make war against the saints and to conquer them. And he was given authority over every tribe, people, language and nation. All inhabitants of the earth will worship the beast — all whose names have not been written in the book of life belonging to the Lamb that was slain from the creation of the world" (Rev 13:6 & 8). Here John elaborates on the activity of the beast (Satan) as he pursues the converts of the early church into every nation, kingdom, people and tribe.

Satan's involvement is further attested to by John, when he speaks of "*the beast that was, and is not,*" explaining that "*even he is the eighth, and is of the seven, and goeth into perdition*" (Rev 17:11).

The Great Tribulation:
After this, John turns his attention to the coming 'great tribulation' -- a time of trouble (for God's children) such as has never been, nor will ever be again. John says: "*He who has an ear, let him hear. If anyone is to go into captivity, into captivity he will go. If anyone is to be killed with the sword, with the sword he will be killed. This calls for patient endurance and faithfulness on the part of the saints*" (Rev 13:9-10).

This great tribulation appears to be the same tribulation period addressed in Rev 7, following the description of the 144,000 -- 12,000 from each of the 12 tribes of Israel -- who were sealed.

"*After this I looked and there before me was a great multitude that no one could count, from every nation, tribe, people and language, standing before the throne and in front of the Lamb. They were wearing white robes and were holding palm branches in their hands. And they cried out in a loud voice: "Salvation belongs to our God, who sits on the throne, and to the Lamb." All the angels were standing around the throne and around the elders and the four living creatures. They fell down on their faces before the throne and worshiped God. ...*

"Then one of the elders asked me, "These in white robes — who are they, and where did they come from?" I answered, "Sir, you know."

And he said, **"These are they who have come out of the great tribulation; they have washed their robes and made them white in the blood of the Lamb.** Therefore, "they are before the throne of God and serve him day and night in his temple; and he who sits on the throne will spread his tent over them. Never again will they hunger; never again will they thirst. The sun will not beat upon them, nor any scorching heat. For the Lamb at the center of the throne will be their shepherd; he will *lead them to springs of living water. And God will wipe away every tear from their eyes"* (Rev 7:9-17).

The great tribulation -- commenced when Christ was crucified, and will culminate when he is glorified. This our focus in the next chapter, where we pinpoint the part it plays in the identification of the beast and it's image.

Chapter Fifteen
The Great Tribulation

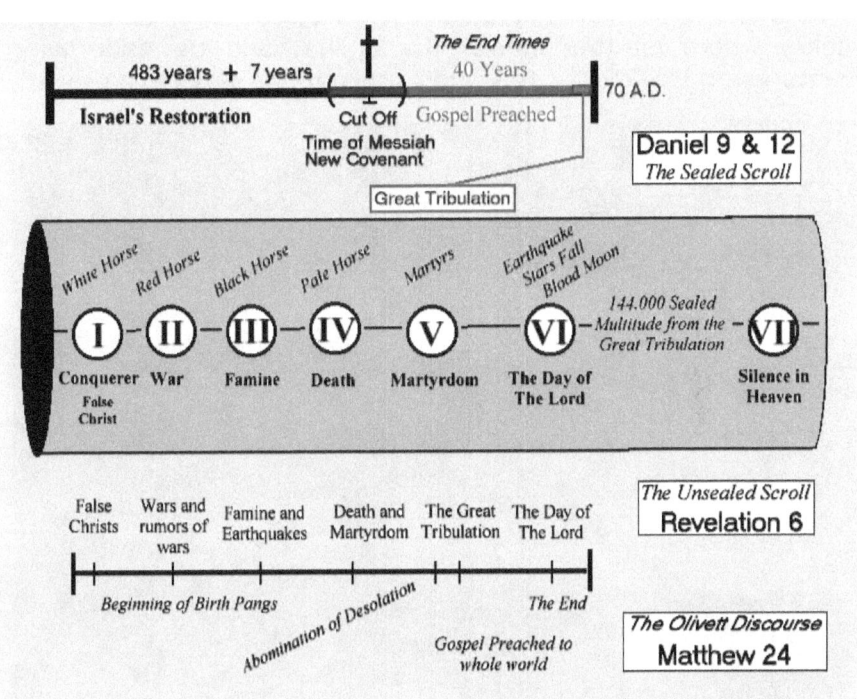

After elaborating on the history of nations and Satan's pursuit of the church into the wilderness, John turns his attention to the coming great tribulation -- a time of trouble (for God's children) such as has never been, nor will ever be again. He says: *"He who has an ear, let him hear. If anyone is to go into captivity, into captivity he will go. If anyone is to be killed with the sword, with the sword he will be killed. This calls for patient endurance and faithfulness on the part of the saints"* (Rev 13:9-10).

This appears to be the same tribulation period that is addressed in Rev 7, following the description of the 144,000 -- 12,000 from each of the 12 tribes of Israel -- who were sealed. John says: *"I saw another angel coming up from the East, having the seal of the living God. He called out in a loud voice to the four angels ... Do not harm the land or the sea or the trees until we put a seal on the foreheads of the servants of our God. Then I heard the number of those who were sealed: 144,000 from all the tribes of Israel"* (Rev 7:2-4).

John continues: *"After this, I looked and there before me was a great multitude that no one could count, from every nation,* tribe, people and language, standing before the throne and in front of the Lamb. They were wearing white robes and were holding palm branches in their hands. And, they cried out in a loud voice: "Salvation belongs to our God, Who sits on the throne, and to the Lamb" (vs.. 9-10). After this, John describes a scene, where all the angels, the elders, and the four living creatures praise God. At this end of this praise service, he says:

"Then one of the elders asked me, "These in white robes — who are they, and where did they come from?" I answered, "Sir, you know." And he said, "These are they who have come out of the great tribulation; they have washed their robes and made them white in the blood of the Lamb. Therefore, "they are before the throne of God and serve him day and night in his temple; and he who sits on the throne will spread his tent over them. Never again will they hunger; never again will they thirst. The sun will not beat upon them, nor any scorching heat. For the Lamb at the center of the throne will be their shepherd; he will lead them to springs of living water. And God will wipe away every tear from their eyes."

The 144,000:
While the subject of the 144,000 is not our principle focus, the symbolism involved here is important. To the Israelites, the number twelve (12) represented completeness, or governmental perfection. The number one thousand (1,000) was their highest

numerical value, beyond which things were numbered in multiples of thousands, rather than the millions, billions, trillions, etc., that we use today. Thus, the 144,000 who were sealed, represented the highest number conceivable from each of the twelve tribes, who were sealed.

The seal here appears to have dual applicability. First, they were all sealed with the seal of the living God, which according to Paul, is the Holy Spirit of God (Eph 4:30). Secondly, considering the use of a king's seal, it was used both as a mark of his authority, and to seal, or close, scrolls, or writing (documents), which were to be opened at a later date, but only by the one so designated. So the sealing of the 144,000 appears to represent the fact that God's work in and through Israel, was sealed, or closed, until a later date, when it would be reopened by the one authorized (Yeshua the Messiah).

This interpretation is further supported by the fact that John now has his focus redirected to the vast multitude, who originated from every nation, tribe, people and language; a multitude who have come out of great tribulation and have washed their robes and made them white in the blood of the Lamb. **This clearly represents the fact that at Christ's death, the Old Testament (Covenant) was closed, and the New Testament (Covenant) implemented.** This fact is further attested to by the author of the book of Hebrews, who wrote:

"For this reason Christ is the mediator of a new covenant, that those who are called may receive the promised eternal inheritance — now that he has died as a ransom to set them free from the sins committed under the first covenant. ***In the case of a will, it is necessary to prove the death of the one who made it, because a will is in force only when somebody has died; it never takes effect while the one who made it is living"*** (Heb 9:15-17).

The fact that this unnumbered multitude emanated from every nation, describes the major change that took place when the New Testament, or Covenant, was implemented -- the good news of the Kingdom of God, was now delivered, not only to the Jewish nation, but to all the Gentile nations, throughout the earth. This fact became part and parcel of Christ's commission of his disciples.

"He said to them, "Go into all the world and preach the good news to all creation. Whoever believes and is baptized will be saved, but whoever does not believe will be condemned" (Mk

16:15-16); *"Then Jesus came to them and said, "All authority in heaven and on earth has been given to me. Therefore go and make disciples of all nations, baptizing them in the name of the Father and of the Son and of the Holy Spirit, and teaching them to obey everything I have commanded you. And surely I am with you always, to the very end of the age"* (Mt 28:18-20).

Another critical factor to consider is that: *"These are they who have come out of the great tribulation; they have washed their robes and made them white in the blood of the Lamb."* **In other words, this unnumbered multitude -- those under the New Covenant, who have washed their robes and made them white in blood of the Lamb -- have also endured the great tribulation.**

This suggests that the great tribulation is not a thing of the future to fearfully dread, but an era that commenced at Christ's death, when the New Covenant went into effect; and something that continues until the Great Day of God Almighty (Rev 16:14). Jesus Christ was, himself, the first martyr of the New Covenant, followed by the apostle, Stephen (Acts 7), whom the apostle, Paul identified as one of Jesus' martyrs (Acts 20:20).

The history of Christian martyrs does not end with Stephen's death. During the first century after Jesus' death nearly all of his disciples suffered martyrdom for His sake. James the son of Zebedee was beheaded in approximately 44 AD Philip was crucified in 54 AD Matthew was killed with a halberd, an ax-like weapon, in 60 AD James, who is thought to be the brother of Jesus, was beaten to death, Matthias was beheaded, Andrew was crucified, Mark was torn to pieces, and Peter was crucified upside down. Jude, Bartholomew, and Thomas were also martyred. Paul suffered martyrdom in Rome where he was beheaded. Other early apostles, including: Luke, Barnabas, Timothy, and Simon were also martyred for the sake of Christ.

This history of Christian martyrdom did not end with the death of the disciples. Thousands willingly gave their lives for Christ under Roman persecution by the emperors Nero, Domitian, Trajan, Marcus Aurelius, Maximus, Decius, Valerian, Aurelian, and Diocletian. The Roman persecution lasted well into the fourth century AD and did not end until Emperor Constantine declared Christianity the official religion of his empire. During the same time period, the Gospel had quickly spread throughout the kingdom of Persia, where, many more thousands were martyred for their faith.

Unfortunately, the history of Christian martyrs did not end with Constantine, and the demise of the Persian kingdom. Throughout the intervening centuries, up to the present time, Christians continue to suffer martyrdom. This persecution has been effected by means of other Christians, those of other faiths, and political powers. This ongoing martyrdom gives testimony to Jesus' prophetic utterance: *"Remember the words I spoke to you: 'No servant is greater than his master.' If they persecuted me, they will persecute you also. If they obeyed my teaching, they will obey yours also. They will treat you this way because of my name, for they do not know the One who sent me"* (Jn 15: 20-21).

Dying for Christ seems almost surreal to most Westerners. We live in that part of the world where Christianity rarely makes the news unless it is to be mocked or defamed. Otherwise, the media is strangely silent about modern Christian martyrdom. *"Three things distinguish anti-Christian persecution and discrimination around the world,"* said Denver's Archbishop Charles Chaput to the US Commission on International Religious Freedom. *"First, it's ugly. Second, it's growing. And third, the mass media generally ignores or downplays its gravity."*

The secular West has been looking the other way when religious persecution occurs, for such a long time, the average western churchgoing Christian has no idea that 45.5 million of the estimated 70 million (or 65%), of the Christians who have been martyred for Christ, were killed within the last century. It is for this reason that scholars such as Robert Royal, president of the Faith and Reason Institute in Washington, DC, and author of The Catholic Martyrs of the Twentieth Century, refer to the twentieth century as one of the darkest periods of martyrdom since the birth of Christianity.

These appalling numbers even prompted Pope John Paul II to urge the faithful to do everything possible to recover the names and stories of individual martyrs. *"At the end of the second millennium, the Church has once again become a Church of martyrs,"* the Pope wrote in his 1994 apostolic letter Tertio Millennio Adveniente. He said, *"This witness must not be forgotten,"* and to assure that it is not, he established a special "Jubilee Year Commission on New Martyrs," whose task was to amass the martyrs' stories. This endeavor resulted in the publication of the names and stories of more than thirteen thousand Catholic, Orthodox, and Protestant martyrs for the faith.

Millions of Christians were martyred during the last century because of their resistance to Communism. In China alone, estimates of those martyred under Communism run as high as 50 million. Communism in the Soviet Union claimed another 25 million. While not all of those killed were Christians, researchers believe that these numbers are so high because this is where the majority of Christian victims lost their lives during the twentieth century. As the Soviet dissident, Vladimir Bukovsky, so aptly put it, Communism typically killed as many people in one day as the Roman Inquisition killed during all prior centuries since the death of Christ.

Rebellions, civil wars, and dictatorships have taken their toll on Christianity as well. At the end of Spain's civil war in 1939, the names and stories of more than 7,000 martyrs were submitted to the Pope. In North Korea, during the past fifty years alone, more than 300,000 Christians have vanished without a trace.

Other genocidal conflicts that occurred in the later part of the twentieth century were also costly for Christians. The press was largely silent about the deaths of 200 priests, sisters, bishops, seminarians, and thousands of laymen who gave their lives during the Rwanda struggle, for refusing to renounce the gospel and accede to the genocide.

Events hardly mentioned by the press, include, the many reports about martyrdom in Darfur, Sudan, where the government of Khartoum waged a campaign of terror against Christians. Various relief agencies reported widespread persecution of Christians who were raped, tortured, enslaved and even burned alive. Christian Solidarity International reports that an estimated 25,000 Christian Sudanese children were sold into slavery.

While Christians in the secular West languish in spiritual mediocrity, Christianity remains a deadly serious matter nearly everywhere else on planet earth. The world's 2.1 billion Christians are a religious minority in eighty-seven countries. The Geneva Report of 2002, estimates that upwards of 200,000,000 Christians are being denied their full human rights, as defined by the United Nations Declaration of Human Rights, simply because they are Christians. Since 2000, there have been verifiable deaths attributable to anti-Christian violence, in at least forty countries.

According to one report, **Asia and the Middle East are the most dangerous places in the world for Christians.** These areas represent six of the eleven countries listed as "Countries of Particular Concern" by the US Commission on International Religious Freedom, due to their "ongoing egregious violations of religious freedom."

The situation for Christians in Iran continues to deteriorate. During President Mahmoud Ahmadinejad's first six months in power, he called for an end to the development of Christianity in the country. A report by the US Commission on International Religious Freedom found that Christians were increasingly subject to harassment, arrests, close surveillance, imprisonment and torture. The head of Iran's Guardian Council, Ayatollah Ahmad Jannati, publicly referred to non-Muslims as "sinful animals."

An Assyrian-Chaldean Christian organization in Iraq reported scores of Christian victims of violence since 2003. Dozens of churches have been bombed or attacked by Muslim extremists, and the tiny Christian minority has become a target of Sunni Arabs, Shiites, and Kurds. Hundreds of thousands of Christians have been forced to flee the country.

In Egypt, citizens are frequently arrested, tortured, and imprisoned just for converting to Christianity. In early 2005, one man, Gaseer Mohamed Mahmoud, a Christian convert, was tortured for refusing to renounce Christ. His toenails were pulled out and he was kept in a water-filled room, beaten, whipped, and confined to a mental hospital. Only pressure from the international community saved his life. But, even though he was eventually released, he must still live his life in hiding.

In Saudi Arabia, it is considered a religious obligation for Muslims to hate Christians and Jews. Apostasy from Islam warrants a death sentence. The Saudi Ministry of Education textbooks for elementary and secondary school children demonize Christians, Jews, and non-Wahhabi Muslims. Reports of the harassment, surveillance, arrest, and torture of Christians in Saudi Arabia are too numerous to keep track of.

In Bangladesh, Christians are denied access to public water wells, and are frequently targets of physical violence and the intentional destruction of their private property. In Turkey, Christians are denied civil and military jobs. It is nearly impossible to build a Christian church. Since Islamic Law was proclaimed in twelve northern states in Nigeria in 2004, clashes between Christians and Muslims have claimed more than 12,000 lives.

The situation in India has become particularly problematic. According to one report, there have been hundreds of episodes of anti-Christian violence during this year (2009) alone. These acts include the gang rape of Christian women and children, the murder of missionaries, pastors and priests, sexual assaults on female church workers, ransacking and burning of churches and convents, desecration of cemeteries, and Bible burnings by the government.

One of the most gruesome killings in India involved the 1999 slaying of Graham Staines, a fifty-eight-year-old Australian-born Christian missionary. He was sleeping in his car with his two sons when a large group of extremists doused the car with gasoline and set it on fire. Staines, his ten-year-old son Philip, and seven-year-old son Timothy were found curled up on a back seat, their bodies burned beyond recognition.

In Indonesia, the world's largest Muslim nation, this year has seen three Christian school girls captured on their way to school and beheaded, and a Christian market bombed. The president of the country recently refused to overturn a controversial death sentence looming over the heads of three Catholic men.

International groups have recorded at least 134 reports of violence perpetuated against Christians by extremist groups since 2000. These incidents included church bombings, altar desecrations, killings, and false imprisonments.

Voice of the Martyrs, a worldwide organization offering support to persecuted Christians, reports that extremist groups in Indonesia are responsible for the deaths of more than 8,000 people and the destruction of more than 600 churches since 1996. This is in addition to the bloody twenty-five-year occupation of the small, heavily Christianized, country of East Timor that ended in 1999. This military occupation left one-third of the Timorese population (200,000) dead, and an estimated 100,000 more are still being held as political prisoners.

North Korea is among the most repressive regimes in the world. In 2004, a North Korean refugee told the US Commission on International Religions Freedom that not only are Christians being persecuted in that country, but that through forced sterilization, *"their next generation and the next generation and the second and third generation will be liquidated as well."* Soon Ok Lee, a woman who survived seven years in a North Korean women's prison, reported watching prison guards murder Christians by pouring molten iron on those who refused to renounce their faith.

The Chinese government continues to detain and repress thousands of Christians and other religious minorities each year. Anyone caught worshiping outside the state-controlled churches is subject to arrest. Since late 1999, the Chinese government has destroyed more than 1,200 Christian churches in one eastern province alone.

There are no public churches in China because they are illegal there. Prayer services, even praying over the dead is considered illegal and subversive by the Chinese government. Religious services can be only secretly conducted in private homes or deserted fields. The Chinese government deems these private gatherings as illegal, unauthorized, subversive, and punishable by exorbitant fines, detention, house arrests, jails, labor camps, or even death. Because fact-finding in China is so difficult, the exact number of people who have been incarcerated or killed in the past century because of their loyalty to Christ will probably never be known.

Missionaries and lay people alike are being "taken out of the way" because they are inconvenient. Most of their deaths are ascribed to robberies or other crimes. Christians are the most persecuted religious group in the world today, suffering the greatest number of victims, reports Nina Shea, director of Freedom House's Puebla Program on Religious Freedom, who said: *"The most atrocious human rights abuses are committed against Christians solely because of their religious beliefs and activities — atrocities such as torture, enslavement, rape, imprisonment, killings, and even crucifixion. Roman Catholics, together with Protestant evangelicals, are the prime targets."*

The four primary reasons for the increase in the persecution of Christians worldwide are: resurgent communism, religiously intolerant forms of Islam, and reemerging nationalism, and the continued ignorance or indifference of Christians in the developed West.

Brother Andrew, founder of Open Doors, an international organization supporting persecuted Christians, wrote in "The Calling" -- *"We in the Western Church don't come close to matching the level of commitment, determination, and strength of many Muslim groups. Until we do, Islam will continue to be the world's fastest growing religion, not because of its strength but because of our weakness. We can and should do much more to support persecuted Christians in the developing world. Financial and prayerful support for the missions is essential, but so is developing an increased awareness of and involvement in the fight for human rights."*

After John's parallel prophecy of the rise and fall of nations with those events described in Daniel's visions, he introduces the beast whose identity we are most concerned with in these last days -- the beast which is the focus of our next chapter.

Chapter Sixteen
The Coming Beast And His Mark

Concerning the beast and his mark, John wrote: *"Then I saw another beast, coming out of the earth. He had two horns like a lamb, but he spoke like a dragon. He exercised all the authority of the first beast on his behalf, and made the earth and its inhabitants worship the first beast, whose fatal wound had been healed. And he performed great and miraculous signs, even causing fire to come down from heaven to earth in full view of men. Because of the signs he was given power to do on behalf of the first beast, he deceived the inhabitants of the earth.*

"He ordered them to set up an image in honor of the beast who was wounded by the sword and yet lived. He was given power to give breath to the image of the first beast, so that it could speak and cause all who refused to worship the image to be killed" (Rev 13:11-15).

There are several important factors we need to address regarding the differences between the identity of this beast and the others mentioned thus far:

First, unlike all of the other beasts of Daniel and Revelation, each of which came up out of the seas [representing peoples, multitudes, nations and languages (Rev 17:15), **this beast came up out of the earth** (Rev 13:11), which might indicate that it arose in an area that marked the absence of many peoples, multitudes, nations and languages. This could refer to a relatively uninhabited area, or "the earth", indicating it would be a worldwide kingdom.

155

Second, this beast is not identified as a nation per. se., as each of the others are, but rather, as a man, or as man. At the same time, since all of the beasts mentioned in these prophecies deal with national identities, it is doubtful that the prophetic symbols would be altered in the middle of a prophecy. It is more probable that this beast correlates with the seventh king mentioned: *"And there are seven kings: five are fallen, and one now is, and* **the other is not yet come; and when he cometh, he must continue a short space** *[in time]"* (Rev 17:10).

Nations have boundaries, kingdoms do not: remember that Christ's and Satan's kingdoms cover the whole earth, and God's kingdom embraces the entire universe. Based on this comparison, it suggests that this kingdom (of the seventh beast) will be a worldwide kingdom, without geographic borders or boundaries. It Similar to (a counterfeit of) the kingdom of our God under the authority of Christ; this kingdom will be that of the dragon (Satan), under the authority of the beast.

Third, this beast originates from the earth itself. The root meaning of the Hebrew word *'ghay',* translated 'earth' in this text, is contracted from a primary word referring to soil or dust; or as some translations render it -- out of the earth, or the dust (elements), itself. Another Hebrew word translated earth -- *'aphar'* -- refers to ashes, dust or powder This terminology, is reminiscent of the Genesis story where man was formed of the soil, dust (or elements) of the earth:

Consider the following references to our being created from the dust -- or elements -- of the earth: **"The LORD God formed the man from the dust of the ground** *and breathed into his nostrils the breath of life, and the man became a living being"* (Genesis 2:7); *"By the sweat of your brow you will eat your food* **until you return to the ground, since from it you were taken; for dust you are and to dust you will return**" (Genesis 3:19); *"Then* **Abraham spoke** *...: "Now that I have been so bold as to speak* **to the Lord, though I am nothing but dust and ashes**" (Genesis 18:27).

Job and other biblical authors reiterate this truth stating: *"If it were his intention and he [God] withdrew his spirit and breath, all mankind would perish together and* **man would return to the dust**" (Job 34:14-15). David likewise validates this truth, declaring: *"Before the mountains were born or you brought forth the earth and the world, from everlasting to everlasting you are God.* **You turn men back to dust, saying, "Return to dust, O**

sons of men" (Psalm 90:2-3); "*As a father has compassion on his children, so the LORD has compassion on those who fear him; for **he knows how we are formed, he remembers that we are dust***" (Psalm 103:13-14).

Solomon, in Ecclestiastes, laments this fact, saying: "*Man's fate is like that of the animals; the same fate awaits them both: As one dies, so dies the other. All have the same breath; man has no advantage over the animal. Everything is meaningless.* **All go to the same place; all come from dust , and to dust all return**. *Who knows if the spirit of man rises upward and if the spirit of the animal goes down into the earth?*" (Eccl 3:19-21); "*Remember him — before the silver cord is severed, or the golden bowl is broken; before the pitcher is shattered at the spring, or the wheel broken at the well, and **the dust returns to the ground it came from, and the spirit returns to God who gave it***" (12:6-7).

The apostle, Paul, documents this fact as well, comparing the composition of man's fallen, carnal body with the nature of the spiritual body of Christ and those who are redeemed:

"*There are also heavenly bodies and there are earthly bodies; but the splendor of the heavenly bodies is one kind, and the splendor of the earthly bodies is another. The sun has one kind of splendor, the moon another and the stars another; and star differs from star in splendor. So will it be with the resurrection of the dead. The body that is sown is perishable, it is raised imperishable; it is sown in dishonor, it is raised in glory; it is sown in weakness, it is raised in power; it is sown a natural body, it is raised a spiritual body. If there is a natural body, there is also a spiritual body. So it is written: "The first man Adam became a living being"; the last Adam, a life-giving spirit. The spiritual did not come first, but the natural, and after that the spiritual.* **The first man was of the dust of the earth, the second man from heaven**" (1 Corinthians 15:40-48).

John wrote: "*He [the beast, the dragon or Satan, represented by his image (believed to represent man)] also forced everyone, small and great, rich and poor, free and slave, to receive a mark on his right hand or on his forehead, so that no one could buy or sell unless he had the*

mark, which is the name of the beast or the number of his name" (Rev 13:16,17).

[The concept of 'The Mark' as employed here -- based on history of biblical times -- is believed to refer to the official mark or seal of authority -- such as a king's signet, seal or mark. **An official seal, or mark of authority always contains three key elements:**

1. The Name of the one in authority

2. The Title of the one in authority, and

3. The territory over which the one in authority rules.

There are numerous references to an official mark, or seal, being placed on an individual -- commonly on one's forehead, as depicted on this bust of an ancient king's guard.

One of the first instances of this practice, recorded in the Bible, is found in Ezekiel: *"And I saw six men coming from the direction of the upper gate, which faces north, each with a deadly weapon in his hand. With them was a man clothed in linen who had a writing kit at his side. They came in and stood beside the bronze altar. Now the glory of the God of Israel went up from above the cherubim, where it had been, and moved to the threshold of the temple. Then the LORD called to the man clothed in linen who had the writing kit at his side and said to him, "Go throughout the city of Jerusalem and put a mark on the foreheads of those who grieve and lament over all the detestable things that are done in it"* (Ezekiel 9:2-4).

Reviewing the context of this Scripture, we see, in addition to the identity of those who were to be marked:

1. The Name of the one in authority: God

2. The title of the one in authority: God of Israel, and

3. The territory over which the one in authority rules: the City of Jerusalem

In this case, those with the mark of God were to be spared the punishment declared for those guilty of idolatry: *"Slaughter old men, young men and maidens, women and children, but do not touch anyone who has the mark . Begin at my sanctuary." So they began with the elders who were in front of the temple"* (Ezekiel 9:6).

The observance of the Feast of Unleavened Bread, was said to be like a sign, symbol, or mark, in the forehead and the hand; demonstrating that manifest obedience -- or disobedience -- leaves a mark of identity on the individual:

"Eat unleavened bread during those seven days; nothing with yeast in it is to be seen among you, nor shall any yeast be seen anywhere within your borders. On that day tell your son, 'I do this because of what the LORD did for me when I came out of Egypt.' ***This observance will be for you like a sign on your hand and a reminder on your forehead that the law of the LORD is to be on your lips****. For the LORD brought you out of Egypt with his mighty hand"* (Exodus 13:7-9).

This concept -- of being marked, or sealed, as a manifestation of whose authority one is under -- is used throughout the New Testament. For example: Paul wrote: *"Now it is God who makes both us and you stand firm in Christ. He anointed us,* **set his seal of ownership on us***, and put his Spirit in our hearts as a deposit, guaranteeing what is to come"* (2 Corinthians 1:21-22); *"Having believed,* **you were marked in him with a seal , the promised Holy Spirit***, who is a deposit guaranteeing our inheritance until the redemption of those who are God's possession"* (Ephesians 1:13-14).

John, in Revelation, just prior to the outpouring of the final plagues, states that God's faithful are sealed: *"After this I saw four angels standing at the four corners of the earth, holding back the four winds of the earth to prevent any wind from blowing on the land or on the sea or on any tree. Then* **I saw another angel coming up from the east, having the seal of the living God. He called out in a loud voice to the four** angels who had been given power to harm the land and the sea: *"Do not harm the land or the sea or the trees until we put a seal on the foreheads of the servants of our God"* (Revelation 7:1-3).

Those with this seal, will be protected from the plagues: *"The fifth angel sounded his trumpet, and I saw a star that had fallen from the sky to the earth. The star was given the key to the shaft of the Abyss. When he opened the Abyss, smoke rose from it like the smoke from a gigantic furnace. The sun and sky were darkened by the smoke from the Abyss. And out of the smoke locusts came down upon the earth and were given power like that of scorpions of the earth.* **They were told not to harm the grass of the earth or any plant or tree, but only those people who did not have the seal of God on their foreheads"** (Revelation 9:1-4).

[Man (*'adam'* - the human species) was originally created [male and female (genesis 1:27)] in the image and likeness of God. **Man bore both His Creator's image and likeness -- His seal, symbol or 'mark'.** Man was, like his Creator, clothed in light. Like his Creator, Man held dominion over a delineated territory: *the earth*. Within his own dominion, or dimension, man had the position of authority and, as co-creator with God through the gift of procreation, the first of mankind -- (Adam and Eve) -- would leave a mark on all mankind. Man's sign, seal, or mark of authority:

1. His name was Adam -- mankind -- (Genesis 1:26,27)

2. His title was Ruler (Genesis 1:28; Psalm 8:6)

3. His territory was the Earth (Genesis 1:28-30; Psalm 8:6-8)

Man lived with God in the Seventh Dimension; dwelling in Garden of God (the Garden of Eden); enjoying the presence of God, Who came to visit them in the cool of the evening. Then, man rebelled and fell from grace (Hebrew *'chen"* - being 'subjective kindness and favor with objective beauty). The fall resulted in man being exiled from the Garden of God (the seventh dimension); being transformed in nature, taking on flesh and blood, covered with skin -- like an animal: the Mark of the Beast.

The Seventh Kingdom and its Ruler:
Concerning the seventh kingdom mentioned in Revelation 17, and its ruler, the beast of Revelation 13, his mark, or seal of authority, is identified as follows:

1. His name is **Man** [*"This calls for wisdom. If anyone has insight, let him calculate the number of **the beast**, for it **is man's number**"* (Rev 13:18)].

2. His title is **The Lawless One** [*"And then the lawless one will be revealed, whom the Lord Jesus will overthrow with the breath of his mouth and destroy by the splendor of his coming. The coming of the lawless one will be in accordance with the work of Satan displayed in all kinds of counterfeit miracles, signs and wonders"* (2 Th 2:8-9)].

3. His territory **The Earth** [*"All the world wondered after the beast. And they worshipped the dragon which gave power unto the beast"* (Rev 13:3-4)].

The Ruler's Identification:
Referring back to the verse that inspired this dialogue -- the verse so many have mistaken as identifying the "Mark of the Beast." However, **this number is -- as demonstrated -- not his mark at all, but rather a clue to the identity of the one who will leave this mark on all mankind:**

"This calls for wisdom. If anyone has insight, let him calculate the number of the beast, for it is man's number. His number is 666" (Revelation 13:18): [The number of the beast (man) is 666 or 616 -- depending on which manuscript one references!]

Which of these numbers is correct? More notably, if this is such an important clue regarding such an important matter, why was it allowed to become garbled? To answer this question, we need to consider some of the biblical and historical evidences pertaining to numerology.

First and foremost, it is quite obvious that the Bible employs numerical symbolically, often using a numerical pattern to represent a truth. For example: who can deny that the number 40 is significant in Scripture? The rain storm contributing to Noah's flood lasted 40 days. Moses was on Mount Sinai for 40 days before he descended with God's law, written on the tablets of stone. Jesus was in the desert fasting for 40 days. The Israelites wandered in the desert for 40 years. The twelve spies scouted out the promised land for 40 days. God directed Jonah to warn Nineveh for 40 days.

Whether or not the analysis of these numerical symbols and patterns mentioned in Scripture are accurate is open for debate. But to help you decide for yourself, we offer the following information pertaining to biblical numerology condensed from the book, "Numbers in Scripture", by Bullinger.

One of the fascinating aspects of numerology in Scripture is that neither Hebrew or Greek have numeric characters in their written language. Where we have numbers and letters, the Hebrew or Greek text has only letters. **In each language, certain letters, or combinations of letters are understood as numbers.** In a small way we use this same concept in English. For example: "O" is both a number and a letter of in the alphabet. "I" may be a one, the letter I, or a small L? When these are used, only the context tells us which is which, yet we have no problem understanding it. The same principle holds true for those writing and reading Hebrew and Greek. Even though they used the same symbol, the writers knew when they were writing numbers and when they were writing letters.

Another very interesting thing is that when a word is written, it also has a numeric equivalent. For example, the word "Jesus" in Greek is *"iasous."* Since each letter has a numeric equivalent, we can add up each number and get a value. The value is the 'gammatria.' Therefore, the gammatria of "Jesus" in Greek is 888 because i = 10, a = 8, s = 200, o = 70, u = 400, and s = 200. We have a similar pattern in English, with our use of Roman numerals: i.e., I = 1, V = 5, X =10, L = 50, Etc. There are many interesting 'games' that can be played using this feature of Greek, Hebrew or English, and much of it is mindless absurdity. However, some of the numeric relationships in Scripture are more than 'just interesting'.

To lean more about the identity of this beast and the nature of his kingdom, we must first solve his identity, using the clue provided in Rev 13:18, regarding the number of his name. To this end, we turn now to a brief lesson in biblical numerology.

Chapter Seventeen
Biblical Numerology

According to biblical numerologists, here are the meanings of the Greek and Hebrew numbers:

1. **THE NUMBER OF UNITY**

    - Deuteronomy 6:4 "Hear, O Israel: The LORD our God, the LORD is one;

    - Ephesians 4:5 "one Lord, one faith, one baptism."

    - The number one is also used to denote the beginning.

2. **THE NUMBER OF DIVISION; UNION & WITNESSING**

    - Christ Jesus has two natures: human and divine;

    - There are 2 Testaments: the Old and New;

    - Man is two -- Male and Female;

    - Romans 9 speaks of two vessels: one for honorable use and the other for dishonorable use;

    - Two types of people: Sheep and Goats;

    - There are two ages, this age and the age to come (Matthew 12:32; 13:39,40,49; Mark 10:30).

    - The number two is used throughout Scripture to denote the number of witnesses necessary to verify a fact (Num 35:30; Dt 17:6; 19:15; 2 Cor 13:1; 1 Ti 5:19; Heb 10:28; Rev 11:3).

3. **THE NUMBER OF COMPLETENESS & DIVINE PERFECTION**

- The Divine Trinity consists of Father, Son, and Holy Spirit;
- There are three qualities of the universe: Time, Space, and Matter.
- To exist (except for God), all three are required;
- Each quality consists of three elements.
- Therefore, we live in a trinity of trinities.
- The three qualities of universe are each three:
    - Time is one yet three -   Past, Present & Future
    - Space is one yet three - Height, Width & Depth
    - Matter is one yet three - Solid, Liquid. & Gas

We truly live in a Trinity of Trinities - Romans 1:20 says, "For since the creation of the world ...

- His invisible attributes,
- His eternal power and
- Divine nature ... have been clearly seen, being understood through what has been made..."

The divine attributes are three fold: God is:

- Omniscient, Omnipresent & Omnipotent
- Love, Light & Spirit
- Holy, Righteous & Just

4. THE NUMBER OF CREATION/CREATIVE WORKS

- Four directions: North, South, East, West;
- Four Seasons: Spring, Summer, Fall, Winter;
- The 4th commandment -- the first that refers to the earth;

- The 4th clause of the Lord's Prayer is the first that mentions the earth;

- The materials used in the construction of the tabernacle were four and so were the coverings and the ornamentation.

5. THE NUMBER OF GRACE/GOD'S GOODNESS

- The Pentateuch (the first five books of the Old Testament) contain the full plan of man's salvation;

- Redemption - Israel came out of Egypt 5 in rank (Ex 13:18);

- David picked up 5 smooth stones to fight Goliath (1 Sam. 17:40);

- The Holy Anointing Oil was pure yet composed of 5 different oils (Ex. 30:23-25).

6. THE NUMBER OF MAN

- Man was created on the 6th day;

- Man was to labor 6 days only;

- The Serpent that deceived man was created on the 6th day;

- The beasts, whose likeness man took on after the fall, was created on the 6th day;

- The 6th commandment is "Thou shalt not murder";

- The manifestations of sin are six;

- The evil nature of Satan is manifest six ways;

- **Six words are used in the Bible to identify man: Adam, ish, Enosh, gehver, anthropos, anar.**

- The total numerical value of these six words is said to equal 666. This means that the name of fallen man in Greek adds up to 666. This is considered a mockery of the Trinity.

7. THE NUMBER OF SPIRITUAL PERFECTION

- Seven days in a week;

- Seven colors in the spectrum;

- Seven of the 10 commandments begin with the word "not";

- There are in Revelation, 7 seals, 7 trumpets, 7 churches, 7 thunders, 7 lamp stands, 7 stars, 7 spirits; a beast with 7 horns, 7 angels and y last plagues.

- There 7 parables in Matthew, and 7 promises to the churches,

- There are 7 "eternals" in Hebrews: A priest for ever (1:6); Eternal salvation (1:9); Eternal judgment (6:2); eternal redemption (9:12); eternal spirit (9:14); eternal inheritance (9:15); and everlasting covenant (13:20).

- Jesus is attributed with 7 last sayings on the cross:
  - 1) Luke 23:34 "Jesus said, "Father, forgive them, for they do not know what they are doing." And they divided up his clothes by casting lots;

  - 2) Luke 23:43 - Jesus answered him, "I tell you the truth, today you will be with me in paradise";

  - 3) Matthew 27:46 About the ninth hour Jesus cried out in a loud voice, "Eloi, Eloi, lama sabachthani?" -- which means, "My God, my God, why have you forsaken me?";

  - 4) John 19:26 "When Jesus saw his mother there, and the disciple whom he loved standing nearby, he said to his mother, "Dear woman, here is your son";

- 5) John 19:28 "Later, knowing that all was now completed, and so that the Scripture would be fulfilled, Jesus said, "I am thirsty."

- 6) John 19:30 "When he had received the drink, Jesus said, "It is finished." With that, he bowed his head and gave up his spirit"; and

- 7) Luke 23:46 "Jesus called out with a loud voice, "Father, into your hands I commit my spirit." When he had said this, he breathed his last."

8 THE NUMBER OF NEW BEGINNINGS

- 8 people were saved on Noah's Ark (2 Pet. 2:5);

- Circumcision occurred on 8th day (Gen. 17:12);

- God made 8 covenants with Abraham

9 THE NUMBER OF DIVINE COMPLETENESS

- God's Judgment. There are 9 Greek words derived from the root word meaning judgment = dikay.

- The following words relating to God's judgment, each occur 9 times in the Bible: abussos (bottomless pit); asebee (ungodly); aselgeia (lasciviousness); and astrapee (lightning).

- The gifts of the spirit are 9 in number (1 Corinthians 12:8-10): the word of wisdom, the word of knowledge, faith, healing, miracles, prophecy, discerning of spirits, tongues, and interpretation of tongues.

10 THE NUMBER OF DIVINE LAW & TESTIMONY

- There are 10 commandments (Ex. 20);

- 1/10 of one's increase is a tithe (tribute) belonging to God;
- There were 10 plagues on Egypt (Ex. 9:14f);
- There were 10 x 10 silver sockets that formed the foundation of the Tabernacle (Ex 38:27);
  - There are 10 "I AM's spoken by Jesus as his testimony, in the Book of John:

    1) I am the Bread of Life (6:35);

    2) I am the Bread of Life which came down from heaven (6:41);

    3) I am the Living Bread (6:51);

    4) I am the Light of the world (8:12);

    5) I am One that bears witness of Myself (8:18);

    6) I am the Door of the sheep (10:7,9);

    7) I am the Good Shepherd (10:14);

    8) I am the Resurrection and the Life (14:6);

    9) I am the Way, the Truth, and the Life (11:25); and

    10) I am the True Vine (15:1,5).

11. THE NUMBER OF INCOMPLETENESS, DISORDER & JUDGMENT

- The number of Jacob's sons after Joseph was sold into slavery, prophetically foretold (Gen 37:9).
- The number of apostles after Judas' betrayal of Christ

12. THE NUMBER OF GOVERNMENTAL PERFECTION

- Jacob, the son of promise, had 12 sons (Gen 35:22).
- Ishmael, the son of Hagar, had 12 sons (Gen 17:20; 25:16),
- There were 12 tribes of Israel (Gen 49:28).

- The High Priest's Ephod had 12 stones, engraved with the names of the 12 tribes of Israel (Ex 39:14),

- The number of the plates and sprinkling bowls of silver, and the gold bowls filled with incense, that were used in the dedication of the altar in the tabernacle (Num 7)

- The 12 staffs, or standards, representing the 12 tribes of Israel (Num 17:2-6).

- The 12,000 armed men (1,000 from each tribe) that fought against and defeated, the Midianites (Num 31:5).

- The 12 stones, one for each of the 12 tribes, used in the construction of the monument of remembrance (Jos 4:3-9).

- The 12 Governors who ruled over the 12 districts of Israel (1 Ki 4:7).

- The 12 bronze bulls that held up the bronze bath (1 Ki 7:44), and the 12 lions that stood on the steps to Solomon's palace (1 Ki 10:20).

- The 12 stones Elijah used when he built the altar on Mt. Carmel, where the prophets of Baal were defeated (1 Ki 18:31).

- Elisha's team of 12 Oxen, yoked together, that he was plowing with when God called him (1 Ki 19:19).

- The 12 Apostles (Mt 10:1).

- The 12 baskets full of bread left over from Jesus' miracle of feeding 5,000 men plus women and children (Mt 14:20).

- The 12 thrones the followers of Christ will sit on to judge the 12 tribes of Israel (Mt 19:28).

- The 12 legions of angels at Christ's disposal (Mt 26:53).

- The 12 foundations of the walls in the heavenly Jerusalem inscribed with the names of the 12 apostles, the 12 gates, made of 12 pearls, with 12 angels watching over the gates, above which are inscribed the names of the 12 tribes of Israel (Rev 21:12-14);

- The 12 angels. The measurements of New Jerusalem are 12,000 furlongs or stadia, while the wall will be 144 (12 x 12) cubits (Rev. 21:16-17).

- The 12 fruits the tree of life produces, one for each of the 12 months (Rev 22:2).

13. THE NUMBER OF APOSTASY, DEPRAVITY & REBELLION

- Ishmael, the rebel, was circumcised when 13 (Gen 17:25).

- The 13 rebellious cities assigned to Simeon (Jos 19:6).

- Solomon's palace, which he out of the tributes of Israel, took 13 years to complete (1 Ki 7:1).

14. THE NUMBER OF DELIVERANCE OR SALVATION

- Jacob worked for his uncle Laban 14 years to deliver himself, his family and his possessions (Gen 31:41).

- Solomon and the people of Israel observed a 14 day festival to celebrate the completion of the temple courtyard, which symbolized God's deliverance (1 Ki 8:64-65).

- The 14 sons the Lord gave Job after delivering him from the hand of Satan (Job 42:12).

- There were 14 generations from Abraham to David, 14 generations from David to the exile from Babylon, and 14 generations from the exile to Christ (Mt 1:17).

- The 14 days the soldiers and sailors transporting prisoners, including the apostle Paul, were in constant suspense, going without food (Acts 27:33).

15. THE NUMBER OF RESTORATION

- Aged men of Israel, over 60, were assigned a value of fifteen shekels (Lev 27:7).

- The Levites pasturelands by statute, extended fifteen hundred feet beyond their towns' walls (Num 35:4).

- God added 15 years to Hezekiah's life after restoring his health (2 Ki 20:6).

- Hosea bought his wife back from prostitution for fifteen shekels of silver, and restored her as his wife (Hos 3:2).

- Zechariah's flying scroll was 15 feet wide and 30 (15 x 2) feet long (Zec 5:2).

16. THE NUMBER OF PRODUCTIVITY

- The total number of children born to Jacob and Zilpah, Leah's handmaid, were 16 (Gen 46:18).

- Shimei had 16 sons and daughters (1 Ch 4:27).

- Eleazar descendants included 16 heads of families (1 Ch 24:4).

17. THE NUMBER OF VICTORY

- Jacob lived in the land of Egypt 17 years, his descendants were given the land of Goshen, and nearing his death, Jacob -- foreseeing victory -- asked that his bones be buried with his forefathers in the Cave of Machpelah (Gen 47:28).

- Rehoboam, the son of Solomon, was victorious over others' challenges to Solomon's throne and reigned 17 years (1 Ki 14:21).

- Israel's "Mighty Men of Valor" numbered 17,000 and 200 -- all fit for battle (1 Ch 7:11).

18. THE NUMBER OF BONDAGE

- The Israelites were in bondage to Eglon, king of Moab, for 18 years (Jdg 3:14).

- As a consequence of serving Baal and Ashtoreth, God gave the Israelites into the hands of the Philistines, who kept them in bondage for 18 years (Jdg 10:6-8).

- 18 were killed when the tower in Siloam collapsed, an event related by Christ to depict the consequences of the bondage to sin (Lk 3:1-5).

- Jesus noted that a woman whom he set free, had been bound with an infirmity, by Satan for 18 long years (Lk 13:16).

20. THE NUMBER OF REDEMPTION

- Joseph was redeemed from the pit and sold to the Midianites for 20 shekels of silver (Gen 37:28).

- The Israelites over 20 years of age, whom God redeemed and allowed to enter the promised land, were to give an offering to the Lord (Ex 30:14).

- All Israeli men, 20 and older, were to serve in the army (Num 1:3).

- Solomon's Temple, which foreshadowed God's redemption of mankind, was 20 cubits wide, the portico was 20 cubits wide and 20 cubits long, the Holy Place was 20 cubits wide and 20 cubits long, and the Most Holy Place was 20 x 20 x 20 cubits, and the building was 20 cubits high (2 Ch 3:3-8).

- The wingspan of the cherubim over the Mercy Seat of the Arc of the Covenant, was 20 cubits, touching the wall on both sides (2 Ch 3:11-13).

- The altar of sacrifice was 20 cubits wide (2 Ch 4:1).

- Ezekiel's Temple, which was shown him by vision, was to be 20 cubits wide, the outer sanctuary 20 cubits wide and 20 cubits long, the inner sanctuary, or Most Holy Place, was of the same dimensions -- 20 x 20 cubits. Around the temple were rooms for the priests, each measuring 20 x 20 cubits (Eze 41:4-10).

21. THE NUMBER OF EXCEEDING WICKEDNESS

- Laban deceived Jacob, resulting in Jacob serving him for 21 years before he was able to return to his homeland (Gen 24-31).

- Zedekiah, one of Israel's most wicked kings who deceived God, Israel and the king of Babylon, was 21 when he became king (2 Ki 24:18; 36:11; Jer 52:1).

- The prince (spiritual principality) of the Persian empire resisted Michael, the chief prince of God, for 21 days, delaying God's answer to Daniel's prayer (Dan 10:13).

22. THE NUMBER OF FEAR & DESTRUCTION

- 22,000 men turned back when Gideon, preparing to attack the Midianites, said "Anyone who trembles with fear may turn back and leave Mount Gilead" (Jdg 7:3).

- The Benjamites at Gibeah cut down 22,000 Israelites in battle (Jdg 20:21).

- David struck down 22,000 Arameans of Damascus (2 Sa 8:5; 1 Ch 17:5).

- Solomon sacrificed 22,000 cattle when he dedicated the temple of the Lord (1 Ki 8:63).

- Abijah, who had 22 sons, inflicted more than 500,000 causalities among Israel's able men (2 Ch 13:21).

- Ahaziah, one of the more evil kings of Judah, of whom it is said that he walked in the ways of Ahab, began his reign when he was 22 (2 Ch 22:2).

- Amon, another evil king, who sacrificed to idols, began his reign when 22 (2 Ch 33:21).

23. THE NUMBER OF DEATH

- Aaron was one hundred and twenty-three (23) when he died on Mount Hor (Num 33:39).

- Tola, son of Puah, son of Dodo, rose up to save Israel. He led Israel 23 years then died and was buried in Shamir (Jdg 10:2).

- Jehoahaz was 23 when he became king, and reigned only three months before he was put to death (2 Ki 23:31).

- As a consequence of their ongoing sexual immorality, 23,000 Israelites died (1 Co 10:8).

24. THE NUMBER OF THE PRIESTHOOD

- David appointed 24,000 priests to supervise the work of the temple of the Lord (1 Ch 23:4).

- In the heavenly tabernacle, there are 24 thrones surrounding God's throne, and seated on them are 24 elders dressed in white (Rev 4:4).

- The 24 elders worship God day and night, saying: *"You are worthy, our Lord and God, to receive glory and honor and power, for you created all things, and by your will they were created and have their being"* (Rev 4:10; 5:8; see also 11:6; 19:4).

25. THE NUMBER OF FORGIVENESS & REDEMPTION

- Only those Levites 25 and older were to serve in the tabernacle (Num 8:24).

- Jehoshaphat, of whom it is recorded that in everything, he did what was right in the eyes of the Lord, reigned in Jerusalem for 25 years, bringing peace to the land (1 Ki 22:42; 2 Ch 20:31).

- Amaziah, son of Joash, who did what is right in the eyes of the Lord, began his twenty-nine year reign when 25 (2 Ki 14:2; 2 Ch 25:1).

- Jotham, son of Uzziah, began his reign when he was 25 and did what was right in the eyes of the Lord (2 Ki 15:33,34; 2 Ch 27:1).

- Hezekiah, son of Ahaz, began his reign when he was 25 and did what was right in the eyes of the Lord (2 Ki 18:2; 2 Ch 29:1).

29. THE NUMBER OF LONGEVITY OF AUTHORITY

- Amaziah, son of Joash, did what was right in the eyes of the Lord and reigned over Judah for 29 years (2 Ki 14:2; 2 Ch 25:1).

- Hezekiah, son of Ahaz, did what was right in the eyes of the Lord, and reigned over Judah for 29 years (2 Ki 18:2; 2 Ch 29:1).

30. THE NUMBER OF DEDICATION & WISDOM

- Joseph was 30 when he entered the service of Pharaoh, king of Egypt (Gen 41:46).

- Saul was 30 when he became king (1 Sa 13:1).

- David was 30 when he became king (2 Sa 5:4).

- 30 local tribes dedicated their men to the service of David, under the unction of the Spirit (1 Ch 12:18).

- Solomon wrote 30 sayings of counsel and wisdom (Pr 22:20).

- Jesus was 30 when he began his ministry (Lk 3:23).

40. THE NUMBER OF PROBATION OR TRIAL.

- In the days of Noah, God sent rain and opened the fountains of the deep to cleanse the earth (Gen 7).

- After being in the ark for 40 days, Noah opened the window and sent out a dove to test whether or not the flood waters had receded (Gen 8:6).

- When Moses went up on Mt. Sinai, to receive God's law, he was there for 40 days and 40 nights, without eating or drinking, while God was testing Israel (Ex 24:18).

- The representatives of the twelve tribes of Israel spied out the land of Canaan for 40 days (Num 13:25).

- Because of their lack of faith in God's ability to drive the Canaanites out of the land promised them, the Israelites spent 40 years wandering in the wilderness -- one day for each day the spies had explored the land (Num 14:33,34).

- God led Israel in the desert for 40 years to test them and humble them (Dt 8:2).

- God protected the Israelites and preserved their clothing and shoes for 40 years while they wandered in the wilderness (Dt 8:4).

- The Lord delivered Israel into the hands of the Philistines for 40 years a probation for their having disobeyed Him (Jdg 13:1)

- Goliath, the Philistine Giant, taunted Israel for 40 days, until David slew him (1 Sa 17).

- Elijah traveled 40 days and 40 nights until he reached Mt. Horeb (1 Ki 19:8).

- Jonah warned Nineveh that unless the people repented, the city would be destroyed by fire in 40 days (Jnh 3).

- Jesus was tempted by Satan for 40 days (Mt 4:2).

- Jesus, after his suffering and resurrection, appeared to his disciples for 40 days before ascending into heaven (Acts 1).

- The apostle, Paul received 40 lashes, minus 1, on five occasions (2 Co 11:24).

50. THE NUMBER OF THE HOLY SPIRIT: PENTECOST

- Moses, under divine direction, established the foreshadowing of the Day of Pentecost, declaring that Israel was to count off 50 days after the seventh Sabbath, and then present the offering of new grain to the Lord (Lev 23:16).

- This foreshadowing, whose reality was in Christ, was fulfilled on the day of Pentecost, when Holy Spirit anointed those waiting in the upper room (Acts 2:1).

60. THE NUMBER OF SELF-SUFFICIENCY OR PRIDE

- When one reached 60 in Israel, they were thought to be filled with wisdom (Lev 27:7).

- Israel was filled with pride over having taken 60 cities from king Og, without losing one (Dt 3:4; Jos 13:30).

- Israel was filled with pride over the size of Solomon's temple, that was 60 cubits long (1 Ki 6:2).

- Rehoboam was proud that he had 60 concubines and 60 daughters, and in his pride, he abandoned the law of the Lord (2 Ch 11:21-12:1).

- Because of Rehoboam's pride and unfaithfulness, God sent Shishak, king of Egypt with 60,000 horsemen to capture the cities of Judah as far as Jerusalem (2 Ch 12:3,4).

- Solomon, in his pride, had 60 warriors escort his carriage, wherever he went (SS 3:7).

70. THE NUMBER OF PUNISHMENT & RESTORATION

- As a result of their idolatry, Israel was taken captive by Assyria but were restored to their homeland 70 years later (2 Ch 36:21).

- The city of Tyre was forgotten as a center of trade for 70 years, after which her fortunes were restored (Is 23:15-18).

- Judah was taken into captivity into Babylon for her idolatry, but was restored 70 years later (Jer 25:11,12).

- At the end of her 70 years in Babylonian Captivity, God delivered Judah and promised her: "I know the plans I have for you," declares the Lord, "plans to prosper you and not to harm you, plans to give you hope and a future" (Jer 29:10,11).

- I, Daniel, understood from Scripture, according to the word of the Lord given to Jeremiah the prophet, that the desolation of Jerusalem would last 70 years (Dan 9:2).

Biblical numerology is interesting, and you may find it useful in the future, when studying the biblical prophecies and interpreting biblical symbolism. Our purpose for including it here is merely to validate what we have demonstrated through biblical exegesis -- that the number 6 refers to, and identifies, mankind in general, rather than referencing a particular individual.

Chapter Eighteen
The Beast & The Number of His Name

Clarifying The Number: 616 or 666?
To properly interpret Revelation 13:18, we still need to address an apparent discrepancy between the numbers 666 and 616. There is, we believe a clear explanation for this discrepancy -- an explanation that further validates our assertion that John was referring to mankind, or a category of men, represented by the beast of Revelation 13:8. To determine who it is that will set up an image to the beast that was before, let's consider each of these numbers in the light of biblical numerology.

666

One of the methods employed in biblical times to emphasize a point was repetition. For example: **Christ, after his resurrection, asked Peter three times if he loved him** (John 21:15-17). Then, after Peter confirmed his love for the master, **Jesus thrice told him to feed, or care for his sheep (disciples).** Likewise, the apostle, Paul, seeking to emphasize the profound effect of spiritual transformation of the mind, wrote: *"Do not conform any longer to the pattern of this world, but be transformed by the renewing of your mind. Then you will be able to test and approve what God's will is — **his good, pleasing and perfect will"*** (Romans 12:2).

Employing this concept, take another look at the words of John, in Revelation 13:18, while temporarily assuming that the number intended was 666. John wrote: *"This calls for wisdom. If anyone has insight, let him calculate the number of the beast, for it is man's number. His number is 666."* Relying on the principle of emphasis by repetition, this text would be best understood as follows: 'If anyone has wisdom let him calculate the number of the beast -- for it is 666 -- **the number of Man, Man, Man**!

616

On the other hand, assuming that the earlier manuscripts we have previously identified, which state the number in Revelation 13:8 as 616, are correct, we need to consider once more the biblical numerology involved. **The number one in Scripture consistently stands for unity; the number six, as indicated above, consistently represents mankind.** Therefore, if the number of the beast is 616, it would more likely represent two humans who are as one in unity and purpose -- representing solidarity, or one person with a duality of nature.

This is exactly what Scripture says about the nature of mankind in Genesis 1! God created man (the human species) both male and female (Genesis 1:26). To denote their unity, **God called Them by one Name -- ADAM (meaning MAN).** After presenting the man's counterpart (woman) to him, God spoke of the unity they would share, saying: *"For this reason a man will leave his father and mother and be united to his wife, and they will become one flesh"* (Genesis 2:24). It is important to note that it was not God who named the first woman Eve, but Adam, after their rebellion and fall (Genesis 3:20).

Jesus confirmed mankind's unique oneness of 'unity through duality,' saying: *"Haven't you read,"* ... *"that **at the beginning the Creator 'made them male and female**,' and said, 'For this reason a man will leave his father and mother and be united to his wife, and **the two will become one flesh'? So they are no longer two, but one**. Therefore what God has joined together, let man not separate"* (Matthew 19:4-6; Mark 10:6-9).

The apostle, Paul also commented on this unity, comparing it to the unity between Christ and the church, saying: *"For this reason **a man will leave his father and mother and be united to his wife, and the two will become one flesh." This is a profound mystery** — but I am talking about Christ and the church"* (Ephesians 5:31-32).

In further consideration of the number 616, and the interpretation given above, reflect once more on what John the Revelator (the revealer of mysteries) penned when this beast was first introduced. He says: *"Then I saw another beast, coming out of the earth. He had two horns like a lamb, but he spoke like a dragon"* (Revelation 13:11).

Jesus Christ was prophetically symbolized as a lamb throughout the Old Testament and is, throughout the New Testament, referred to as "The Lamb of God." Similarly, as we have noted, Scripture consistently represents Satan by employing the symbol of a dragon. Jesus is referred to both as the 'only-begotten' of the Father (i.e., Jn 1:14), and as the 'first-begotten' of the dead (Rev 1:5).

Jesus ~ First-begotten or Only-begotten?
The term 'only-begotten' stems from the Greek word, *'monogenes'*, meaning one-of-a-kind, while the term 'first-begotten' is a translation of the Greek word, *'prototokos'*, which literally translated means *'prototype.'* The preincarnate

Christ was one-of-a-kind: the only member of the Godhead (Elohiym) Who had stepped into the physical world of matter. In contrast to this typology, the incarnate Christ, *"who was tempted in every way, just as we are, yet without sin"* (Heb 4:15), who suffered and died, then rose again, became the prototype, or pattern, for redeemed man.

Man was originally created in the image and likeness of the only-begotten of the Father (in the image and likeness of God). In Christ, redeemed man, is 'born-again' (a term from the Greek *genneethee' a'noothen*, meaning to be gened anew, or 're-gened'). To be re-gened' infers one undergoing a total change. This is the degree of change described by the apostle, Paul, who admonished newborn Christians to be transformed by the renewing (renovation, retrofitting, or regeneration) of their mind.

Clearly, the man represented by the beast of Revelation 13:11 has not experienced this transformation. In contrast, the man represented here, was originally created in the image of God, since he has two horns like a lamb (the Lamb of God -- the prototype). But, in John's metaphor, man has reached the point where he speaks like the dragon (Satan). Horns are consistently used in prophetic symbolism to represent authority and power (i.e., Dan 7:7,8; Rev 13:1; 17:12). In the case before us, we have a beast who is one, yet has duality of authority represented by the two horns.

As God's children, man (male and female) have attributes similar to our Elder Brother, Christ -- the 'first begotten' of The Father. Created in the image and likeness of God, man has both a physical nature and a spiritual nature. Although they were created in God's image and likeness, Adam and Eve, subsequent to their rebellion and fall, began taking on certain traits of the dragon (Satan). For example, they Immediately began lying, trying to deceive, hiding from God, and blaming one another.

God addressed this profound change that took place, declaring: *"The man has now become like one of us, knowing good and evil"* (Gen 3:22). Clearly, God was speaking to Satan since he was the archetype rebel who had earlier, because of his rebellion, been stripped of his glorious body of light and exiled from God's presence. Satan is also called a liar and the father of lies (Jn 8:44).

The King James Version translation of God's warning to Adam and Eve says: *"But of the tree of the knowledge of good and evil, thou shalt not eat of it: for in the day that thou eatest thereof thou shalt surely die"* (Gen 2:17).

The death that occurred when Adam and Eve violated God's command was not their physical death since Adam lived nine hundred and thirty years. Their death was not mental and/or emotional (soulish) since God continued to reason with mankind (Is 1:18). Moreover, regarding the nature of the soul, we are told that we should not fear man who can destroy our body, but fear God who can destroy both our body and our soul (Mt 10:28). Nor was the death Adam and Eve experienced 'in the day they ate of the Tree of Knowledge of Good and Evil, spiritual death. The Old Testament is replete with references to man's spirit and notes that God communed with man, spirit to spirit.

The death that Adam and Eve suffered the day they ate of the forbidden fruit was none of these, yet it was profound. Immediately, God's Shekinah Glory (Hebrew 'kaw-bode') departed from them, and Holy Spirit, Who indwelled man, departed. Having lost their body of glory and honor, and sensing a profound emptiness within, they became disembodied, empty spirits. This resulted in such profound shame, fear and panic, they hid from God when He came to visit them in the cool of the day.

After confronting Adam and Eve for their rebellion and pronouncing the consequences of their action, God, In His love, fashioned bodies for them from the elements of the earth. This resulted in their now reflecting the image of the animal kingdom [the mark of the beast], rather than that of their heavenly Father. [For more information on this subject, see "Mysteries of The Bible - Creation to The Fall of Babylon: The Primeval Era", Potter, James V., and Paula M., Advocare Publishing, 2009.]

Adam and Eve's fall resulted in another death related experience. They experienced immediate death of relationship intimacy -- their intimate relationship with God their Father, indwelling Holy Spirit, and Yeshua (the preincarnate Christ), was severed. Moreover, their intimate, oneness in relationship with one another, ended, manifest in their accusation and blaming of one another. [See "Soul Care: An Introduction to Pastoral Care", Potter, James V., and Paula M., Advocare Publishing, 2009.]

Shortly after the fall of man, another event occurred that contributed even more to mankind's degradation than Adam's and Eve's initial rebellion. We read about this event in Genesis 6.

*"Now it came about, when men began to multiply on the face of the land, and daughters were born to them, that **the sons of God saw that the daughters of men were beautiful; and they took wives for themselves, whomever they chose.** Then the Lord said, "My Spirit shall not strive with man forever, because he also is flesh; nevertheless his days shall be one hundred and twenty years." **The Nephilim (Giants) were on the earth in those days, and also afterward, when the sons of God came in to the daughters of men, and they bore children to them**. Those were the mighty men (giants) who were of old, men of renown"* (Ge 6:1-4 NAS).

The Nephilim were by nature, beings with a dual nature. They were descendants of both flesh and spirit -- born of human mothers who were impregnated by the fallen Watchers, a category of angels God had commissioned to watch over man. [For more details on the origin, work and destiny of the Watchers, see: The Mysteries of the Bible: The Primeval Era, James V. And Paula M. Potter, Advocare Publishing, 2009.] The original invasion of Nephilim occurred shortly after Adam and Eve left the Garden of Eden.

The Book of Enoch (one of the ancient apocryphal books that have been omitted from our modern Bibles) discusses their invasion in detail. He states that they taught mankind all manner of wickedness and finally turned against mankind and began consuming them. They were indeed 'beasts' who performed miraculous signs and made, or enticed, man to worship the dragon (Satan).

As a result of their invasion and wicked activities: *"God [looked down and] saw that the wickedness of man was great in the earth, and that every imagination of the thoughts of his heart was only evil continually"* (Genesis 6:5). To cleanse the earth of the Nephilim and their evil influence, God destroyed both evil man and the Nephilim in Noah's flood. Unfortunately, this was not the end of the Nephilim. The Genesis account says: *The Nephilim (Giants) were on the earth in those days,* **and also afterward***, when the sons of God [the watchers] came in to the daughters of men, and they bore children to them."*

We know that the Nephilim repeated their invasion of the earth after the flood, since Scripture records that there were, during the time of Israel's settling in Canaan, once again giants in the land. Their presence seems to have commenced with the ancestors of Nimrod the mighty hunter of men. Nimrod and his queen, Semiramis, founded several ancient cities, including Nineveh and Babel. It was Nimrod who conceived of, and directed the construction of, the Tower of Babel. Nimrod, Semiramis and their followers were also responsible for founding the ancient Mystery Religions. These 'Mystery Religions' are those referred to in Rev. 17:5, that have polluted the whole earth.

Nimrod and his ilk constructed a number of city states surrounding the land God had promised to Abram and his descendants, blocking every traveled ingress. The purpose was to prevent the descendants of Shem -- the Israelites -- from entering the land of Canaan and settling there. The Nephilim's presence, and the fact that they were giants, is well documented. The twelve operatives that Moses commissioned to spy out the land of Canaan, returned to report their presence. Ten of the twelve said:

"We be not able to go up against the people; for they are stronger than we. And they brought up an evil report of the land which they had searched unto the children of Israel, saying, The land, through which we have gone to search it, is a land that eateth up the inhabitants thereof; and **all the people that we saw in it are men of a great stature. And there we saw the giants***, the sons of Anak, which come of the giants: and we were in our own sight as grasshoppers, and so we were in their sight"* (Nu 13:31-33).

Satan's Scheme:
Satan, prior to man's creation, was the highest, most noble created being. But, with the entrance of man onto the stage of the cosmos, Satan would not only have to take a back seat, he would be required to worship these 'humans' since they would be Children of God: part of the Family of God, After all, it was the

family of God who Satan and the other angels had been created to worship, minister to and serve. The author of the Book of Hebrews acknowledges this, saying: *"Are not all angels ministering spirits sent to serve those who will inherit salvation"* (Heb 1:14).

GOD IS ALIVE....
....SO IS SATAN

Incensed with the very thought of worshipping and serving another created being, Satan purposed in his heart: *"I will scale the heavens, I will raise my throne above God's stars. I will sit on the Mount of Assembly far away in the north. I will rise past the tops of the clouds, I will make myself like the Most High"* (Is 14:13-14 CJB).

As a result of his pride and rebellion, Satan was cast down. The prophet, Isaiah, declared: *"Instead, you are brought down to Sheol, to the uttermost depths of the pit. Those who see you will stare at you, reflecting on what has become of you: 'Is this the man who shook the earth, who made kingdoms tremble, who made the world a desert, who destroyed its cities, who would not set his prisoners free?' "All other kings of the nations, all of them, lie in glory, each in his tomb. But you are discarded, unburied, like a loathed branch, clothed like the slain who were pierced by the sword, then fall to the stones inside a pit, like a corpse to be trampled underfoot"* (Is 14:15-19 CJB).

Having rebelled, Satan and the host of heaven who defected with him were doomed. Undaunted, Satan devised a plan so diabolical, that if successful, it would destroy the image and likeness of God in man, and reinstate him as the highest, most noble created being. To comprehend Satan's scheme, we need to refer to The Wisdom of Solomon, another of the ancient books no longer included in our modern Bibles. In its opening lines we find a major clue to Satan's diabolical scheme to destroy mankind.

"Devious thoughts cut men off from God, and the divine power, when made trial of, exposes the foolish. For **Wisdom** *will not enter a fraudulent mind, nor make* **Her** *home in a body*

mortgaged to sin. The **Holy Spirit, that divine tutor**, will fly from cunning stratagem; **She** will withdraw from unintelligent thoughts and will take umbrage at the approach of injustice.

"**Wisdom** is a **benevolent Spirit** and **She** will not hold a blasphemer immune from his own utterances; because God is a witness of his thoughts, the real guardian of his mind, who hears every word. For the **Spirit of the Lord fills the world**, and that which holds all things together has knowledge of all articulate sound. No one, therefore, who celebrates injustice will escape notice, nor will justice the accuser pass him by" (WS 1:2-8).

Following man's rebellion, Holy Spirit, Who indwelled man, enveloping them with the glory and honor (the Shekinah Glory) of God, departed. **Man's own spirit was now empty -- devoid of God's guiding presence.** It was this tragedy that gave rise to Satan's fiendish plot. If he could entice some of the Watchers to defect and join his ranks, his prize, he reasoned, would soon be his. After all, the Watchers, who were commissioned to watch over man, could appear in the form of a man, masquerading as one of them, and entice them to do what he, himself, could never accomplish.

Having been God's covering cherub, Satan -- formerly Lucifer, the light-bearer (or standard bearer of colors) -- understood many of God's mysteries. The prophet, Ezekiel, alludes to this saying: "This is what the Sovereign Lord says: *"You were the model of perfection, full of wisdom and perfect in beauty. You were in Eden, the garden of God; every precious stone adorned you: ruby, topaz and emerald, chrysolite, onyx and jasper, sapphire, turquoise and beryl. Your settings and mountings were made of gold; on the day you were created they were prepared. You were anointed as a guardian cherub, for so I ordained you. You were on the holy mount of God; you walked among the fiery stones"* (Eze 28:12-14).

The Potential for Possession:
Surely, Satan must have reasoned, if the Watchers can assume human form, they must also be able to manifest human capabilities, yet remain spirits. This being the case, they could inhabit the spirits of man, usurping the position and role of Holy Spirit. This would enable them to guide those they inhabited into every manner of deviancy and destruction. But, how -- he no doubt wondered -- could he ever convince man to participate in this scheme? Pondering on this question, he recalled how easily Eve was deceived, giving in to the lust of the flesh. He no doubt recalled that *"When the woman saw that the Tree (of Knowledge*

of Good and Evil) was good for food, and pleasant to the eyes, something to be desired to make one wise, she took of the fruit thereof, and did eat" (Gen 3:6).

Based on woman's desire to care for her family, which separated from God, became her manifest weakness, perhaps her daughters could again be deceived -- duped into reaching for what was pleasant to the eye, that they were sure would make them wise. Perhaps, Satan must have thought, they could also be enticed by the beauty of the Watchers, if they were to reveal some of the mysteries of God, giving them knowledge in the use of charms, roots, herbs, plants, astrology and omens.

Demonic Possession Commences:
After enchanting them with this knowledge, the 'sons of God' (the Watchers) beguiled (seduced) the daughters of man and bare children by them (Gen 6:1-4). Having accomplished this, Satan's plan was fully implemented. Their offspring -- the Nephilim -- would have bodies of flesh, fashioned after their human mothers, but spirits originating from, and guided by, the fallen Watchers who gave their allegiance to him. **The demonic infestation and possession of mankind had commenced!**

With the interbreeding of species -- human and angelic -- The duality of authority emerged, represented by the two horns on the beast of Revelation 13:11 -- the beast that came up out of the earth. This duality of authority, according to God's Word, caused the woman to desire the man's role (the spirit male who impregnated her), and the man (the spirit) to exercise dominion, through power and control, over the woman. *"To the woman He said, "I will greatly increase your pains in childbearing; with pain you will give birth to children. And, your desire will be for your husband, and he will rule over you"* (Gen 3:16).

The word 'desire' used in this verse, when speaking of the woman, is a translation of the Hebrew word, *'teshuwquah'*, which means to stretch out after, or pursue, as in one participating in an athletic competition. Whereas the term, 'he shall rule over you,' in this text -- referring to the man -- is a translation of the Hebrew *w'huw yimshaal baak*, meaning, 'he will, by an oath, exercise dominion, or power, over, or against, you.'

In the Book of Enoch, the ancient patriarch describes acts of seduction that were engaged in by the women, in their competition with one another to attract the Watchers. Enoch also describes the oath that the Watchers made on Mount Hermon, to take dominion over mankind. This incident was so familiar to primeval and ancient mankind that the word 'hermon' became synonymous with taking an oath.

As the daughters of men satiated their lust through sexual encounters with the watchers; the watchers in turn carried out their oath to take dominion over man. What they could not do through influence, they accomplished through intercourse; their offspring bearing within them, their spirit of rebellion. Their descendants -- the Nephilim -- now began to emulate the likeness, or character, of the archetype of rebellion -- Satan. They worshiped him as their god, and began carrying out his scheme to destroy mankind. Satan's objectives in his scheme, are -- as described by Jesus -- to *"steal, kill and destroy"* (Jn 10:10). The Nephilim's supporting activity is described by Enoch, who wrote:

"And it came to pass when the children of men had multiplied that in those days were born unto them beautiful and comely daughters. And the angels, the children of the heaven, saw and lusted after them, and said to one another: 'Come, let us choose us wives from among the children of men and beget us children.' And Semjâzâ, who was their leader, said unto them: 'I fear ye will not indeed agree to do this deed, and I alone shall have to pay the penalty of a great sin.' And they all answered him and said: 'Let us all swear an oath, and all bind ourselves by mutual imprecations not to abandon this plan but to do this thing.'

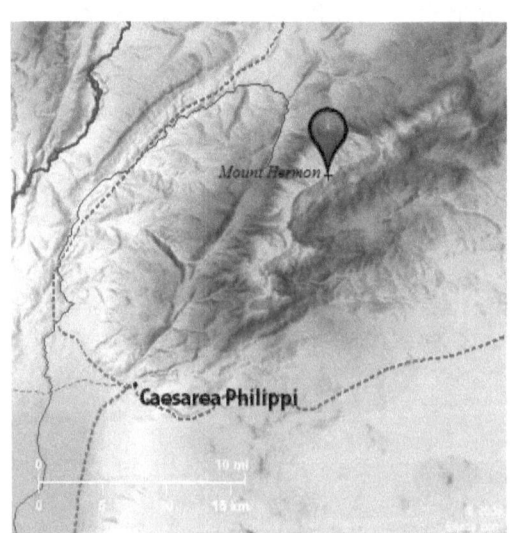

The Oath:
"Then sware they all together and bound themselves by mutual imprecations upon it. **And they were in all two hundred; who descended in the days of Jared on the summit of Mount Hermon** [located near Caesarea Philippi, as depicted in the adjacent map], and they called it Mount Hermon, because they had sworn and bound themselves by mutual imprecations upon it.

And these are the names of their leaders: Sêmîazâz, their leader, Arâkîba, Râmêêl, Kôkabîêl, Tâmîêl, Râmîêl, Dânêl, Êzêqêêl, Barâqîjâl, Asâêl, Armârôs, Batârêl, Anânêl, Zaqîêl, Samsâpêêl, Satarêl, Tûrêl, Jômjâêl, Sariêl. 8. These are their chiefs of tens" (En 6).

"And all the others together with them took unto themselves wives, and each chose for himself one, and they began to go in unto them and to defile themselves with them, *and they taught them charms and enchantments, and the cutting of roots, and made them acquainted with plants.* **And they became pregnant, and they bare great giants, whose height was three thousand ells**: *Who consumed all the acquisitions of men.*

And when men could no longer sustain them, the giants turned against them and devoured mankind. And they began to sin against birds, and beasts, and reptiles, and fish, and to devour one another's flesh, and drink the blood. *Then the earth laid accusation against the lawless ones"* (En 8).

These original Nephilim were destroyed in Noah's Flood. But, as we have seen, this was not the end of them. Moses' report of this primeval event acknowledged that this occurred both before, and after Noah's Flood, saying: *"The Nephilim were on the earth in those days --* **and also afterward** *-- when the sons of God [the Watchers] went into the daughters of men and had children by them"* (Gen 6:4).

Moses' report is consistent with the report of the twelve spies Moses commissioned to investigate the land of Canaan. They returned after spending forty days in the land of Canaan to report: *We saw the Nephilim there, the descendants of Anak. We looked like grasshoppers by comparison, and we looked that way to them too!"* (Nu 13:33). Verse 32 says, *"they will devour us."* The giants were, according to reputable historic accounts, cannibals!

Nimrod, the founding king of ancient Babylon, was a cannibal -- a giant tyrant who hunted men (Gen 10:8-10). So were the Babylonia kings that followed him. His followers, whom he encouraged to build cities blocking the highways into Canaan, thereby surrounding the promised land, were for the most part giants. They included kings, like Ishbi-benob, Goliath, Saph, Sippai and Og, the last of the Rephaites (a family of giants). It was the presence of these kings -- these giants -- and their declared intent to destroy the descendants of Shem -- the Israelites -- that motivated God to direct the Israelites to destroy them.

However, **while all of the giants within the promised land were destroyed, there is evidence that many that survived the fall of Babylon and migrated into other nations, and lived on for many decades.** [For additional information on these giants, see "Mysteries of the Bible: The Primeval Era", Potter, J.V., and P.M., Advocare Publishing, Redding, CA, 2009.] These surviving giants built cities fit only for giants, and perpetuated the beliefs and practices of the Mystery Religion established by Nimrod and his queen, Semiramis.

Thus was fulfilled the words recorded by John the Revelator: *"One of the seven angels who had the seven bowls came and said to me, "Come, I will show you the punishment of the great prostitute, who sits on many waters. With her the kings of the earth committed adultery and the inhabitants of the earth were intoxicated with the wine of her adulteries." Then the angel carried me away in the Spirit into a desert.*

There I saw a woman sitting on a scarlet beast that was covered with blasphemous names and had seven heads and ten horns. The woman was dressed in purple and scarlet, and was glittering with gold, precious stones and pearls. She held a golden cup in her hand, filled with abominable things and the filth of her adulteries.

This title was written on her forehead: **MYSTERY BABYLON THE GREAT THE MOTHER OF PROSTITUTES AND OF THE ABOMINATIONS OF THE EARTH"** (Rev 17:1-5).

Nations vs. Kingdoms:
The point we previously made concerning the distinction between a nation and a kingdom, is important to revisit here. That point is that nations have geographical boundaries while kingdoms do not. Ancient cities such as Babel and Nineveh had geographical boundaries; but the Kingdoms of Babylon, its successors, Babylonia and Assyria -- all of which supported the Mystery Religion of ancient Babylon -- had no boundaries. "The

inhabitants of the whole earth were intoxicated with the wine of her adulteries" (Rev 7:2).

Mystery Babylon "the beast which was, is now not, and yet is" (vs.. 8), is represented by the woman (the false mystery religion) riding the scarlet beast (Babylon, Babylonia and her successor, Assyria). The Assyrian people living today trace their origins to the population of the pre-Islamic Mesopotamia, the ancient Akkadian Empire -- an empire ruled by giants.

The Seventh Kingdom and its Ruler:
Concerning this seventh kingdom mentioned in Revelation 17, lets review what we know concerning its mark, or seal of authority.

1. The initial ruler's name was Nimrod. He appeared to be a man, but was in reality, a cross-species giant -- a descendant of the fallen watchers and mankind, one of the Nephilim -- who had a dual-nature: the flesh of a man and the spirit of a fallen angel.

2. His title: was King of Babylon while living, but upon his death, Queen Semiramis dubbed him Zoraster, the Sun God -- a name that has been translated into other languages as Baal, Bel, Baalim, Molech, The Great Life Giver, Eternal Father of Creation, etc. In short, Nimrod defied the God of Heaven, becoming, second only to Satan, as an archetype of the Lawless One.

3. His territory, identified by the names ascribed him, included the whole earth, indeed the cosmos! And those he claimed as his subjects -- as 'the great life-giver and eternal father of creation -- included every man, woman and child who has ever lived, who now lives, or shall in the future, live. What a succinct embodiment of one *"who was, is not now, and yet is; who shall ascend from the abyss and go to his destruction"* (Rev 17:8).

Listen to these words of John, as rendered in the Contemporary English Version: *"The beast you saw is one that used to be (exist) and no longer is (exists). It will return from the deep pit (abyss), but only to be destroyed. Everyone on earth, whose names are not written in the Book of Life before the time of creation will be amazed. They will see this beast that used to be, and no longer exists, but will be (exist) once more"* (Rev 17:8,9 CEV).

The Fatally Wounded Beast Returns:
It is this beast -- the Nephilim, or Giants, and the kingdom they ruled -- that received the fatal wound predicted to be healed: *"The beast which I saw was like unto a leopard, and his feet were as the feet of a bear, and his mouth as the mouth of a lion: and the dragon gave him his power, and his seat, and great authority.* **And I saw one of his heads as it were wounded to death; and his deadly wound was healed: and all the world wondered after the beast***"* (Rev 13:2,3).

In validation of our identification of this beast as the Kingdom of Assyria, consider the words of Nahum, the prophet: *"O king of Assyria, your shepherds slumber; your nobles lie down to rest. Your people are scattered on the mountains with no one to gather them.* ***Nothing can heal your wound; your injury is fatal.*** *Everyone who hears the news about you claps his hands at your fall, for who has not felt your endless cruelty?"* (Na 3:18-19).

The ancient civilization of Assyria was established by the Akkadians, also referred to as Anakims, descendants of Anak one of the families of giants (Num 13). It was centered on the Plain of Shinar, straddling the Tigris and Euphrates Rivers -- the area that encompasses the present-day nations of Iran and Iraq. Ancient Assyria encompassed the majority of Mesopotamia, controlling all of the Fertile Crescent, as well as Egypt, before succumbing to Babylon, that evolved into Neo-Babylonia, and still later, Persia.

Many think of Assyria and Babylon as separate and distinct cultures, but Babylon, the seat of Nimrod's kingdom, was the dominant city-state in ancient Mesopotamia. In fact, the name 'Babylon' is a Greek variant of an ancient Akkadian word, *'Babilu'*, meaning "Gateway of the gods." It was considered the "holy city" of Mesopotamia, the seat of the Babylonian Empire. Babylon, with its hanging gardens was considered one of the Seven Wonders of the Ancient World.

In precise fulfillment of biblical prophecy, the ancient kingdom of Assyria and Mystery Babylon -- the false religious system founded within its principle city-state -- and its rulers, giants all, received a fatal wound. The city-state of ancient Babylon was destroyed, the kingdom of Assyria, that eventually evolved into Persia, collapsed in 330 BC. Indeed, the Mystery Religion founded in ancient Babylon, seemed to have received a deadly wound as the Christian faith swept the world during the first through the fourth centuries, even becoming the official religion of the Roman Empire.

Based on the accuracy of these prophecies, is there any reason to doubt the future fulfillment of John's prophecy, that this deadly wound will be healed, and all the world will wonder after the beast? John, even provided a timetable of sorts for the fulfillment of this prophecy. Just prior to introducing the return of this beast, he says: *"He who has an ear, let him hear. ... This calls for patient endurance and faithfulness on the part of the saints"* (Rev 13:9,10). Or, as the Complete Jewish Bible has translated it: *"Those who have ears, let them hear! ... This is when God's people must persevere and trust!"*

In our next chapter, we will investigate more fully John's prophecy of the return of this beast who, the prophecy says, *"exercises all the authority of the first beast in its presence; and makes the earth and its inhabitants worship the first beast whose fatal wound had been healed"* (Rev 13:12).

Chapter Nineteen
The Image of the Beast

The Image:
Let's consider carefully each aspect of John's prophecy concerning this 'image to the beast':

1) *"Then I saw another beast, coming out of the earth.*
2) *He had two horns like a lamb, but he spoke like a dragon.*
3) *He exercised all the authority of the first beast on his behalf, and*
4) *made the earth and its inhabitants worship the first beast, whose fatal wound had been healed.*
5) *And he performed great and miraculous signs, even causing fire to come down from heaven to earth in full view of men.*

6) *Because of the signs he was given power to do on behalf of the first beast, he deceived the inhabitants of the earth.*

7) *He ordered them to set up an image in honor of the beast who was wounded by the sword and yet lived.*

8) *He was given power to give breath to the image of the first beast, so that it could speak and cause all who refused to worship the image to be killed.*

9) *He also forced everyone, small and great, rich and poor, free and slave, to receive a mark on his right hand or on his forehead, so that no one could buy or sell unless he had the mark, which is the name of the beast or the number of his name. This calls for wisdom. If anyone has insight, let him*

calculate the number of the beast, for it is man's number. His number is 666 [or 616]" (Rev 13:11-18).

The word, 'image' in verse 15, is a translation of the Greek word, *eiko'ni*, meaning a likeness, a representation, or resemblance of the original. Wikipedia defines an image as follows: *"An image (from Latin imago) is an artifact, for example a two-dimensional picture, that has a similar appearance to some subject — usually a physical object or a person."*

Healing the Fatal Wound:
To correctly identify the beast of Revelation 13:11, we must also identify the 'first beast' -- the one this beast sets up (or develops) an image of -- thereby giving life, or breath, to the first beast, which received a fatal wound, and yet lived. The beast of Rev 13:11 also enables the image of the first beast to speak and cause all who refuse to worship the image, to be killed. And, it is this same beast who forces everyone to receive the mark in order to carry our any commerce.

Comparing each of these factors to the beast of prophecy, who received the fatal wound, and yet lived, to rule another day, we must look for the following:

1. A kingdom that previously exercised control over mankind world wide, since *"he made the earth and its inhabitants worship the first beast, whose fatal wound had been healed"* (Rev 13:12).

2. This worldwide kingdom must have had, as its seat of power, a nation located within the boundaries of ancient Mesopotamia (vs.. 1-10).

3. This nation must have had a national religion -- a mystery religion -- which it is intent on imposing on all men, everywhere (vs. 13,14).

4. This nation must have a ruler (president or king) one in whom is vested a duality of authority, represented by the two horns (vs.. 11), who speaks (preaches or utters directions) like the dragon (Satan).

5. The ruler of this nation, while speaking like the dragon (Satan) must exhibit the characteristics of a lamb (man).

6. This ruler will exercise all the authority of the first beast -- on his behalf -- making the inhabitants of the earth worship the first beast (vs.. 12).

7. This ruler will *"perform miraculous signs, even causing fire to come down from heaven in full view of men"* (vs.. 13).

8. This ruler has the ability to force people to worship the image of the first beast (vs.. 15).

9. This ruler has the ability to force men to receive his 'mark' or seal of authority, in order to carry on any commerce.

10. The ruler of this nation, who commands a worldwide kingdom, and enforces the worship of Satan, is one of the Nephilim, like Nimrod, fulfilling Moses' prophetic word: *"The Nephilim were on the earth in those days — **and also afterward** — when the sons of God went to the daughters of men and had children by them"* (Ge 6:4). In Hebrew, this text reads: '**and again in like manner, hereafter, when more of the same breed of magistrates besieged against the daughters of the species mankind.**'

11. Finally, this ruler has a 'mark', or seal of authority, symbolized by the number 616 (alternatively 666).

Reflecting back on the nature of a ruler's seal of authority, it contains three essential components -- his name, his title and the territory he rules.

1. His name is **Man** [*"This calls for wisdom. If anyone has insight, let him calculate the number of **the beast**, for it **is man's number**"* (Rev 13:18)].

2. His title is **The Lawless One** [*"And then the lawless one will be revealed, whom the Lord Jesus will overthrow with the breath of his mouth and destroy by the splendor of his coming. The coming of the lawless one will be in accordance with the work of Satan displayed in all kinds of counterfeit miracles, signs and wonders"* (2 Th 2:8-9)].

3. His territory **The Earth** [*"All the world wondered after the beast. And they worshipped the dragon which gave power unto the beast"* (Rev 13:3-4)].

The Fatally Wounded Beast Lives Again!
Moses said: *"The Nephilim were on the earth in those days — **and also afterward** — when the sons of God went to the daughters of men and had children by them"* (Ge 6:4).

Jesus, apparently making reference to this ancient warning, told his disciples: *"And, **as it was in the days of Noah, so shall it be also in the days of the Son of man"*** (Lk 17:26). The Greek here is [Kai kathoo's ege'neto en tais heeme'rais Noo'e hou'toos e'stai kai' en tais heeme'rais tou Huiou' tou' Anthroo'pou], literally meaning: *"**Therefore, even as it came to pass during the time (years) of Noah, in like manner shall it be therefore during the time (years) of the son of certain man.**"*

Do these texts really suggest that the Nephilim will return once again -- before the end of time? To answer this, consider the rest of Luke's warning: *"**And, there shall be signs in the sun, and in the moon, and in the stars**; and **upon the earth distress of nations, with perplexity**; the sea and the waves roaring; **Men's hearts failing them for fear, and for looking after those things which are coming on the earth**: for the powers of heaven shall be shaken"* (Lk 21:25,26).

Compare the words of Christ, recorded here in Luke, with the words of the prophet, John:

- **Jesus** - *"As it was in the days of Noah, so shall it be also in the days of the Son of Man."*

- **John** - *"I saw another beast ... He had two horns ... He exercised all the authority of the first beast ... Whose fatal wound had been healed."*

- **Fact** - The Nephilim roamed the antediluvian world and were destroyed in Noah's Flood. They appeared once more after the flood and endeavored do destroy all the descendants of Shem (the Israelites).

- **Jesus** - *"And, there shall be signs in the sun, in the moon, and in the stars."*

- **John** - *"And he performed great and miraculous signs, even causing fire to come down from heaven in full view of men. Because of the signs he was given power to do ... He deceived the inhabitants of the earth."*

- **Fact** - Both the Book of Enoch, and the Book of Jubilees -- two ancient apocryphal writings -- describe how the Watchers came to earth in fiery chariots, deceiving the earth's inhabitants.

- **Jesus** - *"And upon the earth distress of nations, with perplexity ... Men's hearts failing them for fear, and for looking after those things which are coming on the earth."*

- Micah - The Old Testament prophet, Micah, also foretold of this time of great perplexity, and associated with the work of the Watchers: **"The day of the watchers has come**, *the day God visits you. Now is the time of their confusion*

- **John** - *"He caused all who refused to worship the image to be killed. He also forced everyone, small and great, rich and poor, free and slave, to receive a mark on his right hand, or in his forehead, so that no one could buy or sell unless he had the mark."*

- **Fact** - Here we have two distinguishing characteristics of this beast and the image he creates:

    1. He prohibits religious freedom, enforcing idolatry of the worst kind -- the worship of the dragon (Satan);

    2. He controls world commerce.

    3. He creates stark fear, or terror, in the hearts of men, causing them to focus on his lethal power and his probable future acts of terror.

Identifying the Terrorist(s):
The apostle, Paul, writing about these same events, said: *"Concerning the coming of our Lord Jesus Christ and our being gathered to him, we ask you, brothers, not to become easily unsettled or alarmed by some prophecy, report or letter supposed to have come from us, saying that the day of the Lord has already come. Don't let anyone deceive you in any way, for*

that day will not come until the rebellion occurs and the man of lawlessness is revealed, the man doomed to destruction. He will oppose and will exalt himself over everything that is called God or is worshiped, so that he sets himself up in God's temple, proclaiming himself to be God.

"Don't you remember that when I was with you I used to tell you these things? And now you know what is holding him back, so that he may be revealed at the proper time. **For the secret power of lawlessness is already at work;** but the one who now holds it back will continue to do so till he is taken out of the way. And **then the lawless one will be revealed**, whom the Lord Jesus will overthrow with the breath of his mouth and destroy by the splendor of his coming. **The coming of the lawless one will be in accordance with the work of Satan displayed in all kinds of counterfeit miracles, signs and wonders,** and in every sort of evil that deceives those who are perishing" (2 Th 2:1-10).

Jesus words in Luke 21:25,26: "*men's hearts failing them for fear'*, is explained in the following phrase: *"and for looking after those things which are coming on the earth"*, literally translated: "*therefore, in anticipation of he (that one, those) of the impending attack on the world."*

In another place, Jesus said: "*Think not that I am come to send peace on earth: I came not to send peace, but a sword. For I am come to set a man at variance against his father, and the daughter against her mother, and the daughter in law against her mother in law. And **a man's foes shall be they of his own household**" (Mt 10:34-36).

Jesus was on this occasion, apparently quoting from a prophetic warning given many years before by the prophet, Micah. This is the only other place this specific warning is mentioned in Scripture -- and it is associated with the Watchers. "***The day of the watchers has come***, the day God visits you. Now is the time of their confusion. Do not trust a neighbor; put no confidence in a friend. Even with her who lies in your embrace be careful of your words. For a son dishonors his father, a daughter rises up against her mother, a daughter-in-law against her mother-in-law — **a man's enemies are the members of his own household**" (Mic 7:4-6).

The Return of the Watchers:
In these Scriptures, **Moses, Luke, Micah, Jesus, the apostles, John and Paul,** all seem to be warning us that the

Watchers will return again and attack the earth in the last days, once more interbreeding with women. As a result of this, Micah warned, one may have an enemy of their soul (a Nephilim) in their own household. How could such a thing as this happen, since Scriptures, including the Book of Enoch, tell us that the fallen angels were cast into the abyss (bottomless pit)? Consider the following prophecy, recorded by John the Revelator:

"Then the fifth angel blew [his] trumpet, and I saw a star that had fallen from the sky to the earth; and to the angel was given the key of the shaft of the Abyss (the bottomless pit). He opened the long shaft of the Abyss (the bottomless pit), and smoke like the smoke of a huge furnace puffed out of the long shaft, so that the sun and the atmosphere were darkened by the smoke from the long shaft.

"Then out of the smoke locusts came forth on the earth, and such power was granted them as the power the earth's scorpions have. They were told not to injure the herbage of the earth nor any green thing nor any tree, but only [to attack] such human beings as do not have the seal (mark) of God on their foreheads. They were not permitted to kill them, but to torment (distress, vex) them for five months; and the pain caused them was like the torture of a scorpion when it stings a person. And in those days people will seek death and will not find it; and they will yearn to die, but death evades and flees from them"

"The locusts resembled horses equipped for battle. On their heads was something like golden crowns. Their faces resembled the faces of people. They had hair like the hair of women, and their teeth were like lions' teeth. Their breastplates (scales) resembled breastplates made of iron, and the [whirring] noise made by their wings was like the roar of a vast number of horse-drawn chariots going at full speed into battle. They have tails like scorpions, and they have stings, and in their tails lies their ability to hurt men for [the] five months.

Over them as king they have the angel of the Abyss (of the bottomless pit). In Hebrew his name is Abaddon [destruction], but in Greek he is called Apollyon [destroyer]" (Rev 9:1-12). In this prophecy, the angel of the fifth trumpet (a fallen angel) --

descends to earth with the key to the abyss, and opens this bottomless pit. **The words 'bottomless pit' in Greek is [fre'atos tees' abussou'] literally meaning: 'the abyss pit', referring to a cistern or well used as a prison.**

Remember, Satan and his fallen host were cast into the bottomless pit (the abyss). (Rev 20:3; En 6). **Once unlocked, smoke ascends out of the abyss, as from a furnace. The result is that the sun (light) is darkened (obscured), by reason of the smoke from the abyss.**

Remembering that this is prophetic, we need to examine the symbolism used. **Jesus is the light -- 'the light of the world'** (Jn 8:2). Prior to leaving this world, he commissioned his disciples to *"Go into all the world and preach the good news to all creation"* (Mk 16:15). **Satan's objective, as Paul declared, is to obscure Christ's message, blinding the minds of the lost.** He says: *"And even if our gospel is veiled, it is veiled to those who are perishing. The god of this age has blinded the minds of unbelievers, so that they cannot see the light of the gospel of the glory of Christ, who is the image of God"* (2 Cor 4:3-4).

John said: *"Out of the smoke locusts came forth on the earth, and such power was granted them as the power the earth's scorpions have."* Referring once again to the Greek, the word locust [akrides] means devourer. This is a clear description of Satan, of whom it is said: *"Your enemy the devil prowls around like a roaring lion looking for someone to devour"* (1 Peter 5:8). It may also be a reference to the return of the Nephilim, who hunted and devoured men.

The second phrase: *'and such power was granted them as the power the earth's scorpions have'*, is also significant. In the Greek, the term 'power was given unto them' is [edo'thee autais exousia] literally meaning: *'superhuman influence (power or right) was bestowed upon these.'* In the following phrase: *'as the power the earth's scorpions have'* the Greek is [hoos e'chousin hoi scorpions tee's gee's], meaning: *'in the manner that scorpions have mastery of the land'.*

Scorpions are opportunistic, predatory, nocturnal creatures, that hide from the light of the sun. There are more than 2,000 individual subspecies of scorpions, and their range (or kingdom) is essentially worldwide, South of 49 degrees latitude North (which basically follows the border between the US and Canada). They can survive both freezing temperatures and intense desert heat.

The species of scorpion most prevalent in the Middle East and North Africa -- therefore familiar to the prophet, John -- is named the 'deathstalker' (pictured left) due to its potent venom and the relatively high toll it takes in human life. The deathstalker scorpion from this region accounts for nearly seventy-five percent (75%) of all deaths attributed to scorpion stings.

The beings ascending from the abyss are commanded to hurt nothing, other than *"such human beings as do not have the seal (mark) of God on their foreheads. They were not permitted to kill them, but to torment (distress, vex) them for five months; and the pain caused them was like the torture of a scorpion when it stings a person."* The phrase 'the seal of God on their foreheads', is in Greek [tee'n sfragida tou' Theou' epi too'n metoo'poon], meaning: 'the stamp (or mark) of genuineness of Divinity within the forehead [mind] or upon their countenance'.

The beings that ascend from the abyss are not permitted to kill those without the seal of God, but, they are permitted (or directed) to vex, or torment them, for five months. In biblical prophecy, God uses one day to represent one literal year (Num 14:34; Eze 4:6). Based on this prophecy, the torment of the wicked, will after **'the return of the Nephilim' last 150 years!**

The torment of men, the text says, will compare to the torment of a scorpion when it strikes a man. In this phrase, the word 'torment' may also refer to the **'tormentor' (Satan).** The similarity between the work of these beings and that of a scorpion is seen in the Greek word translated 'it strikes' [paisee]. This word literally means 'to strike a single violent blow'. And, the Greek word translated 'man' (whom they strike) refers to mankind.

How could the tormentor, Satan, strike a single violent blow, sufficient in force that it will cause mankind to suffer for 150 years -- unless that 'blow' is in the form of an engrammatic' alteration (or mutation) of man's genetics? Whatever it is, this blow against humanity is such that those who are stricken will seek death. *"And in those days people will seek death and will not find it; and they will yearn to die, but death evades and flees from them"* (Rev 9:6).

Verse 7 is commonly translated to read: *"The locusts resembled horses equipped for battle. On their heads was something like golden crowns. Their faces resembled the faces of people"* [Joel 2:4]. *"They had hair like the hair of women, and their teeth were like lions' teeth."* The first sentence in Greek reads: [Kai ta' homoioo'mata too'n akri'doon ho'moia hippois heetoimasm'nois eis po'lemon]. Consider the following, more likely translation: *"And the resemblance [either in size or shape] of the devourers, (is) similar in appearance, or character, to horses made ready for the purpose of warfare."*

Horses or Large, Ferocious Beings?
Were what John saw in his vision really horses, or were they beings, the size and ferocity of horses armed for battle? The next two sentences appear to answer this. *"On their heads was something like golden crowns. Their faces resembled the faces of people."* Referring again to the Greek, the word 'crown' is [ste-fanoi] referring to a badge of honor that one wears conspicuously. The term 'like gold' may mean their badges of honor are made of gold, or something that looks like gold; or that these beings are adorned with golden ornaments. They also have faces resembling people. The Greek says *"their faces are as the faces of humans."* [And], *"They have hair like women, and their teeth are like the teeth of lions."*

Another clue to their identity is their intent to destroy mankind and the identity of their leader. *"Over them as king they have the angel of the Abyss (of the bottomless pit). In Hebrew his name is Abaddon [destruction], but in Greek he is called Apollyon [destroyer]"* (vs.. 11). Referring to the Greek, we read: *"They had over them a king [sovereign power], the angel [that messenger] of the bottomless pit [of the abyss], whose name in Hebrew, Abaddon [destroying angel], and in the Greek, hath name, Apollyon [destroyer]."*

Paul seems to be warning of these same beings in his letter to the Thessalonians: *"Concerning the coming of our Lord Jesus Christ and our being gathered to him, we ask you, brothers, not to become easily unsettled or alarmed by some prophecy, report or letter supposed to have come from us, saying that the day of the Lord has already come. Don't let anyone deceive you in any* *way, for that day will not come until the rebellion occurs and **the man of lawlessness** is revealed, **the man doomed to destruction**. He will oppose and will exalt himself over everything that is called God or is worshiped, so that he sets himself up in God's temple, proclaiming himself to be God"* (2 Th 2:1-4).

Identifying the Antichrist:
Many interpret Paul's comments concerning 'the lawless one' as a prophecy foretelling of a particular individual who will appear in the last days and set himself up as ruler over the world. However, a more careful examination of Paul's word, are inconsistent with such an interpretation. Paul says: *"Don't you remember that when I was with you I used to tell you these things? And now you know what is holding him back, so that he may be revealed at the proper time. For **the secret power of lawlessness is already at work**; but the one who holds it back will continue to do so till he is taken out of the way"* (2 Th 2:5-7).

The 'lawless one' is not Satan himself, for Paul tells us that the lawless one will work in concert with Satan (vs.. 9). Who then is the lawless one? What is holding back this one -- the one doomed to destruction? And, how long is he to be held back?

The Lawless Ones:
This 'man of lawlessness' appears to be one-in-the-same with the 'lawless ones' mentioned by Enoch: *"And all the others together with them (the Watchers) took unto themselves wives, and each chose for himself one, and they began to go in unto them and to defile themselves with them, and they taught them charms and enchantments, and the cutting of roots, and made them acquainted with plants. And they became pregnant, and they bare great giants, whose height was three thousand ells: Who consumed all the acquisitions of men. And when men could no longer sustain them, **the giants turned against them and devoured mankind**. And **they began to sin against birds, and beasts, and reptiles, and fish, and to devour one another's flesh, and drink the blood. Then the earth laid accusation against THE LAWLESS ONES**"* (En 7:1-6).

What, or whom, is holding the lawless ones back? John the Revelator seems to address this at the beginning of the prophecy we looked at concerning *"the star that had fallen from heaven to the earth ... (who) was given the key to the shaft of the abyss"* (Rev 9:1). He says: *"After this I saw four angels standing at the four corners of the earth, holding back the four winds of the* earth to prevent any wind from blowing on the land or on the sea or on any tree" (Rev 7:1).

John also answers our question pertaining to how long they will be held back, and when they will be released. **"They were told not to harm** the grass of the earth or any plant or tree, but **only those people who did not have the seal of God on their foreheads"** (Rev 9:4) ... "Then I saw another angel coming up from the east, having the seal of the living God. He called out in a loud voice to the four angels who had been given power to harm the land and the sea: **"Do not harm the land or the sea or the trees until we put a seal on the foreheads of the servants of our God"** (Rev 7:2-3).

When will this 'lawless one' commence his activity against mankind? Paul says: **"For the secret power of lawlessness is already at work**; but the one who now holds it back will continue to do so till he is taken out of the way. And **then the lawless one will be revealed**, whom the Lord Jesus will overthrow with the breath of his mouth and destroy by the splendor of his coming. The coming of **the lawless one will be in accordance with the work of Satan** displayed in all kinds of counterfeit miracles, signs and wonders, and in every sort of evil that deceives those who are perishing" (2 Th 2:7-10).

Comparing their characteristics and objectives, this 'lawless one' appears to be one-in-the-same with that entity described in Revelation 13:11-13: "Then I saw another beast, coming out of the earth. He had two horns like a lamb, but he spoke like a dragon. **He exercised all the authority of the first beast on his behalf, and made the earth and its inhabitants worship the first beast, whose fatal wound had been healed**. And **he performed great and miraculous signs, even causing fire to come down from heaven to earth in full view of men**.

"Because of the signs he was given power to do on behalf of the first beast, **he deceived the inhabitants of the earth**. He **ordered them to set up an image in honor of the beast who was wounded by the sword and yet lived**. He was given power to give breath to the image of the first beast, so that it could speak **and cause all who refused to worship the image to be killed"** (Rev 13:14-15).

John, after foretelling the history of nations, each represented by a beast, describes this beast, saying: "And the beast that was, and is not, even he is the eighth, and is of [literally 'out-of' or *proceeding from] the seven, and goeth into perdition"* [literally, *"endures for a while and then spiritually disappears forever"* (Rev 17:11). In other words, the power John is describing proceeds out of the seventh beast, which we have already established to be the ancient kingdom of Assyria, that evolved into Persia. Then, after enduring for a while, this beast disappears eternally.

Consider the Facts:

1. He is man
2. He proceeds out of Persia.
3. He has dual powers
4. He is the Lawless Ones - associated with the Watchers
5. His Kingdom or Domain is the earth
6. He received a fatal wound, but now appears -- healed
7. He accomplishes miraculous things
8. He orders mankind to worship the first beast
9. He threatens to kill all who refuse to worship the beast's image.
10. He controls the world commerce.
11. He employs terrorism.
12. He is associated with Babylon the Great, the Mother of Harlots -- the origin of the Mystery Religions

Paul said that the work of the lawless ones had already gone forth in the earth, and that when the lawless ones themselves come, they will work in concert with the dragon, Satan, performing great signs and wonders (2 Th 2). In our next chapter, we will identify this beast, his kingdom, the seat of his power, and the mystery religion he will impose upon all the inhabitants of the earth.

Chapter Twenty
The Beast, His Kingdom & His Religion

Picking our reading of Scripture up with the apostle, Paul's warning, we read: *"**For the secret power of lawlessness is already at work**; but the one who now holds it back will continue to do so till he is taken out of the way. And **then the lawless one will be revealed**, whom the Lord Jesus will overthrow with the breath of his mouth and destroy by the splendor of his coming. The coming of **the lawless one will be in accordance with the work of Satan** displayed in all kinds of counterfeit miracles, signs and wonders, and in every sort of evil that deceives those who are perishing"* (2 Th 2:7-10).

The original descendants of the Watchers and human women -- the Nephilim -- were destroyed during Noah's Flood. When the Nephilim died, their bodies -- like all flesh -- decomposed, but their spirits continued to live on. Being crossbreeds -- born of man and of angels -- the disembodied spirits of the deceased nephilim continue to carry out their lawless deeds within the spirit (unseen) realm -- as demons! Early Christian apologists understood this and taught that demons are the disembodied spirits of the giants, and the 'Seed of Satan'.

Of great importance in understanding demons is the fact that the bodies of the Nephilim are not to be resurrected: *"They are dead, they shall not live; they are deceased, they shall not rise: therefore hast thou visited and destroyed them, and made all their memory to perish"* (Is 26:14). Thus, Paul accurately stated that *"the secret power of lawlessness is already at work,"* even though the lawless ones themselves were not yet revealed. Their coming (or return) will be, as Paul indicated, *"in accordance with the work of Satan."* Only after he is given the key to the abyss and unlocks the bottomless pit, allowing the Watchers to once again attack mankind (interbreeding with women), will the Lawless Ones -- the Nephilim -- be loosed upon the earth.

[For more information on the origin, work and destiny of demons, see the book, "Mysteries of the Bible: The Primeval Era", Potter, J.V. and P.M., Advocare Publishing, Redding, California, 2009.]

The end-time relationship between men and demons is articulated by the prophet, John, who introduced the sixth angel. This angel declared: *"Release the four angels who are bound at the great River Euphrates,"* the four angels who had been kept ready for this very hour and day and month and year were released to kill a third of mankind. ... A third of mankind was killed by the three plagues of fire, smoke and sulphur"* Rev 9:14-18). This event is further detailed in Ezekiel 38 & 39, when the present-day counterparts of the ancient nations of Gog and Magog attack Israel. Following is a synopsis of this prophecy:

"I will send fire on Magog and on those who live in safety in the coastlands, and they will know that I am the Lord" (Eze 39:6). ... *"On that day I will give Gog a burial place in Israel, in the valley of those who travel east toward the Sea. It will block the way of travelers, because Gog and all his hordes will be buried there. So it will be called the Valley of Hamon Gog. For seven months the house of Israel will be burying them in order to cleanse the land"* (vs. 11-12). ...

"The Sovereign Lord says: Call out to every kind of bird and all the wild animals: 'Assemble and come together from all around to the sacrifice I am preparing for you, the great sacrifice on the mountains of Israel. There you will eat flesh and drink blood. You will eat the flesh of mighty men and drink the blood of the princes of the earth as if they were rams and lambs, goats and bulls — all of them fattened animals from Bashan" (vs. 17-18).

Then, John says, *"the rest of mankind that were not killed by these plagues still did not repent of the work of their hands, nor did they stop worshipping demons ... Nor did they repent of their murders, their magic arts, their sexual immorality or their thefts"* (vs. 20,21).

John essentially repeats this when describing the seven last plagues. After describing the first four plagues, he says: **"The** *fifth angel poured out his vial upon the seat of the beast; and his kingdom was full of darkness; and they gnawed their tongues for pain, and blasphemed the God of heaven because of their pains and their sores, and repented not of their deeds"* (Rev 16:10-11). The phrase, "and repented not of their deeds" suggests that God's mercy is still open were they to repent and turn to Him.

After describing the judgment that falls on the seat of the beast, John reveals where the seat of the beast is located. *"The sixth angel poured out his bowl on the great river Euphrates, and its water was dried up to prepare the way for the kings from the East"* (Rev 16:12).

To identify the seat of the beast and the origin of the Lawless Ones, a person need only a map of the Middle East and a bit of knowledge of the history of the nations that previously occupied that land, and those occupying it today. The following map clearly depicts the object nations described in this prophecy.

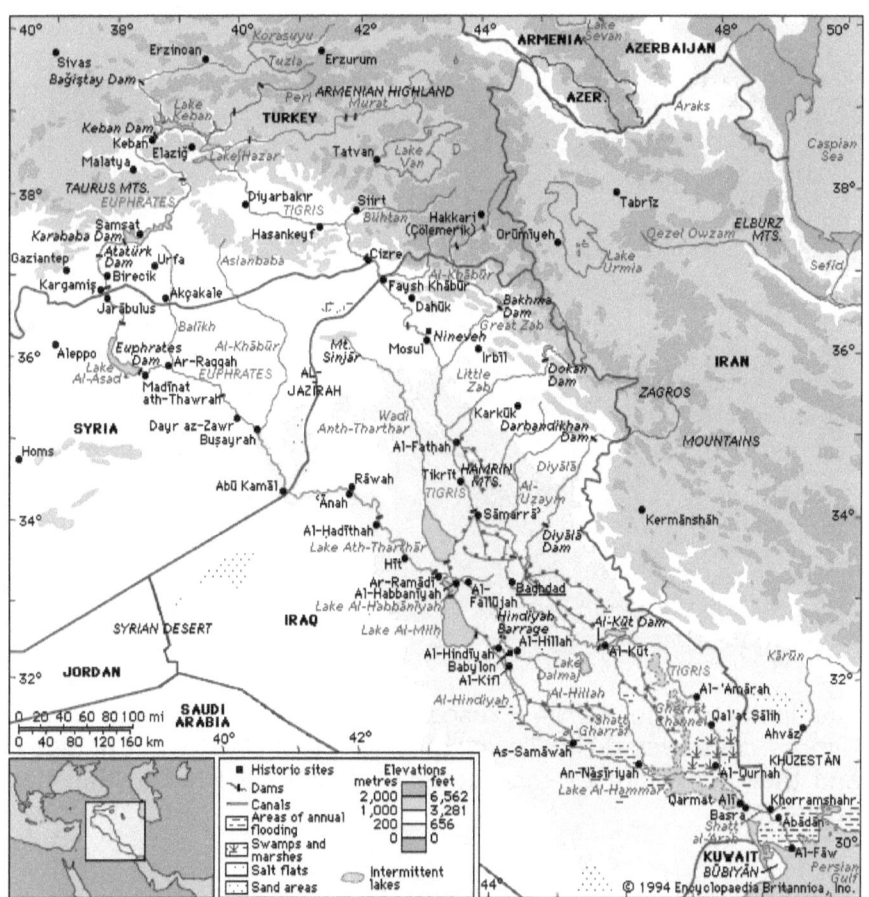

211

The seat of the ancient kingdom of Assyria, was the city of Babylon. The ancient city of Babylon was situate in the great Mesopotamia Fertile Crescent. Through this fertile valley flow the Tigris and Euphrates Rivers who have their headwaters in the Caucasus Mountains, and terminate in the Persian Gulf.

This area was the seat of the ancient kingdom of Assyria, the seat of ancient Babylon, the seat of the Old-Babylonians (the Akkadians and their descendants, the Semitic Amorites). It was the seat of the ancient Kingdom of Persia, before its collapse in 330 BC. This region was the home of Nimrod, Semiramis and many of the other Nephilim (giants).

This was the home of the ancient Mystery Religions that spread throughout Egypt, Asia Minor and the Middle East, as mankind began its migration after the fall of the Tower of Babel and the division of the earth in the days of Peleg (Gen 10:25). This was also the home of the patriarch, Job, the home of Terah, and the place where Abram began his migration into Canaan.

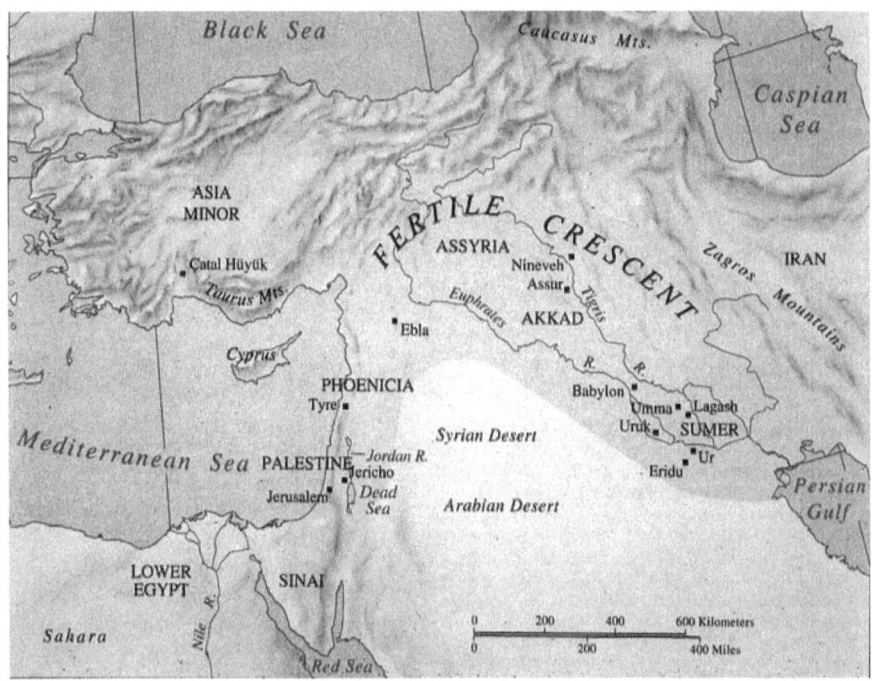

The limits of the Fertile Crescent, the City of Babylon, where Nimrod constructed the Tower of Babel, and Ur of the Chaldees; and their proximity to each other is clearly depicted in the map above.

John, the Revelator, states that this is the seat of the beast -- the seat of the kingdom that will be reestablished, representing an image, or likeness, of the nation that was before it. This area was the center of the second invasion of the Nephilim (giants), who entered history after the Watchers once again took wives of the daughters of men, and begat children. One of these children was Nimrod, a descendant of Ham, the youngest son of Noah.

It was the descendants of Ham, the Canaanites, of whom Noah declared, prophetically, that they would be cursed because of their moral and sexual deviancy. These were the descendants who founded the cities of Sodom and Gomorrah, who introduced sodomy and who were destroyed for their perversion, when God rained fire down on the Plain of Jordan, resulting in the Dead Sea -- the lowest elevation on planet earth.

Returning to John's prophecy concerning the identity of the beast, we read: *"The sixth angel poured out his bowl on the great river Euphrates, and its water was dried up to prepare the way for the kings from the East"* (Rev 16:12).

The 'drying up of the River Euphrates,' according to biblical symbolism already introduced, would suggest that the population base that once occupied this region, and the authority and power of the peoples of this region, would dry up, or materially diminish. History validates the fulfillment of this prophetic application. After the collapse of the Persian Empire, the region was subjugated, first to Greek and then to Rome. In the mid-sixth century, the ancient Persian Empire was divided into four quarters, one of which -- the most westerly -- was named Iraq. Thereafter, the region of Iraq, identified loosely as the 'island' -- that is, the land between the Tigris and Euphrates rivers -- was inhabited by Arabian tribesmen.

It was here, in the Great Fertile Crescent, that the Islam religion initially found a geographic foothold and flourished. Around 636, an Arab Muslim force under Sa`d ibn Abi-Waqqa-s defeated the main Persian army at the Battle of al-Qa-disiyyah and moved on to sack the capital of the Persian Empire, Ctesiphon. By the end of 638, the Muslims had conquered almost all of the Western Sassanid provinces (modern Iraq), and the last Sassanid Emperor, Yazdegerd III, fled to central and then on to northern Persia, where he was killed in 651.

This Islamic conquest was followed by a mass immigration of Arabs from eastern Arabia and Mazun (Oman) to Khvarva-ra-n. These new arrivals did not disperse and settle throughout the country; instead they established two new garrison cities, at al-Ku-fah, near ancient Babylon, and at Basrah in the south.

It was their intention that the Muslims should be a separate community of fighting men, their families living off of the taxes, or tribute, extracted -- by force if necessary -- from the local inhabitants. In the north part of northeastern Iraq, Mosul began to emerge as the most important city and the base of a Muslim governor and garrison. Apart from the Persian elite and the Zoroastrian priests, who never converted to Islam, thus losing their lives and property, most of the Mesopotamian peoples became Muslim and were allowed to keep their possessions.

Khvarva-ra-n, now became a province of the Muslim Caliphate, known as Iraq. The city of Baghdad was built during the 8th century and became the capital of the Abbasid Caliphate. During this period, Baghdad served as the intellectual center of the Muslim world for several centuries, enduring until the sack of Baghdad in 1258. Many famous Muslim scientists, philosophers, inventors, poets and writers were active in Iraq during the 8th to 13th centuries.

During the late 14th and early 15th centuries, the Black Sheep Turkmen ruled the area now known as Iraq. In 1466, the White Sheep Turkmen defeated the Black Sheep and took control of the region. In the 16th century, most of the territory of present-day Iraq came under the control of Ottoman Empire as the pashalik (territory) of Baghdad. Throughout most of the period of Ottoman rule (1533-1918) the territory of present-day Iraq was a battle zone between the rival regional empires and tribal alliances.

During the years 1747-1831 Iraq was ruled by the Mamluk officers of Georgian origin who succeeded in obtaining autonomy from the Sublime Porte. They suppressed tribal revolts, curbed the power of the Janissaries, restored social order and introduced a program of modernization of economy and military. In 1831, the Ottomans managed to overthrow the Mamluk regime and imposed their direct control over Iraq.

Ottoman rule over Iraq lasted until the World War I when the Ottomans sided with Germany and the Central Powers. In the Mesopotamian campaign against the Central Powers, the British forces invaded the country, suffering a major defeat at the hands of the Turkish army during the Siege of Kut (1915–16).

Britain imposed a Ha-shimite monarchy on Iraq and defined the territorial limits of Iraq without taking into account the politics of the different ethnic and religious groups in the country -- in particular those of the Kurds and the Assyrians in the north. During the British occupation, the Shi'ites and Kurds fought for independence. Although the monarch, Faisal I of Iraq was legitimized and proclaimed King by a plebiscite in 1921, nominal independence was not achieved until 1932, when the British Mandate officially ended.

In 1945, Iraq joined the United Nations and became a founding member of the Arab League. At the same time, the Kurdish leader Mustafa Barzani led a rebellion against the central government in Baghdad. After the failure of the uprising Barzani and his followers fled to the Soviet Union. In 1948, Iraq entered the 1948 Arab-Israeli War, fighting along side other members of the Arab League in order to defend Palestinian rights.

In February 1958, King Hussein of Jordan and `Abd al-Ila-h proposed a union of Ha-shimite monarchies to counter the recently formed Egyptian-Syrian union. The prime minister Nuri as-Said wanted Kuwait to be part of the proposed Arab-Ha-shimite Union. Shaykh `Abd-Alla-h as-Sali-m, ruler of Kuwait, was invited to Baghdad to discuss Kuwait's future. This policy brought the government of Iraq into direct conflict with Britain, which opposed granting independence to Kuwait. At that point, the monarchy found itself completely isolated. Nuri as-Said was able to contain the rising discontent only by resorting to ever greater political oppression.

Inspired by Nasser, officers of the Nineteenth Brigade, known as "Free Officers", with the leadership of Brigadier Abd al-Kari-m Qa-sim (aka. "az-Za`i-m", 'the leader') and Colonel Abdul Salam Arif, overthrew the Hashimite monarchy on July 14, 1958. The victor, and new government, proclaimed Iraq to be a republic and rejected the idea of a union with Jordan. Iraq's participation in the Baghdad Pact thus ceased.

Saddam Hussein Abd al-Majid al-Tikriri, known to the West simply as Saddam Hussein, played a key role in the 1968 coup that brought down the government, bringing the Ba'ath Party to power, which espoused a form of secular pan-Arabism and socialism. It was the key role Saddam played in this coup and other activities of the Ba'ath Party that eventually brought the party, and Saddam to power. Saddam Hussein served as President of Iraq from July, 1979 to his overthrow, during the US invasion, in April, 2003.

The Ba'ath Party's beliefs are a combination of Arab Socialism, Nationalism, and Pan-Arabism. The Party's vision, which Hussein shared, was to unite all Arab nations into a single, unified kingdom that could stand up to the Western powers. This vision, placed Iraq at odds with its neighboring countries, particularly Iran, who has always believed that they are the true remnant of the Persian Empire, and that the entirety of the Great Fertile Crescent, is rightfully theirs. It is this belief, and their ultimate plan to assert ownership over the region, that John apparently foresaw, when he penned the following:

"And the sixth angel poured out his vial upon the great river Euphrates; and the water thereof was dried up, that the way of the kings of the east might be prepared" (Rev 16:12).

The fifth of the seven last plagues is poured out on the 'seat of the beast' -- ancient Babylon -- which has politically, economically and socially 'dried up' or diminished in power. Now, with Iraq -- the present-day kingdom occupying the land of ancient Babylon -- weakened, the kings of the East, seize the opportunity and invade the region. Who are these 'Kings of the East'? One need only look at a map of the region to grasp the significance of this prophecy.

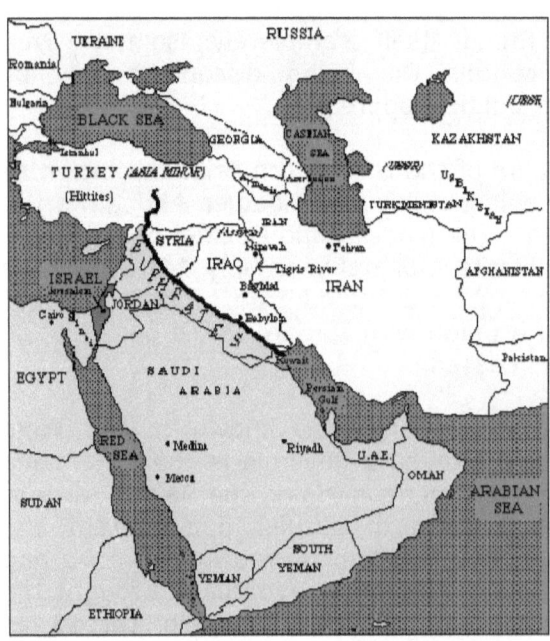

Immediately East of Iraq lies Iran, the seat of the remnant of the Persian empire, the stronghold of radical Islam, the sponsor of worldwide terrorism. A bit more easterly, and adjacent to Iran, lies Afghanistan, home of the Taliban; Kazakhstan, home of the Turkestan Liberation Organization, recognized as a terrorist organization, and the favored political ally of Russia and China; and Pakistan, homeland of the many radical Islam Madrassas. Collectively, Afghanistan, Kazakhstan and Pakistan, represent the seat of the Mujahideen and Al-Qaida, a multinational, stateless, fundamentalist movement.

Further East lie Russia and China, which Ezekiel, the Old Testament prophet, implicates as coconspirators with the afore mentioned group of nations, in the end-time battle of Gog and Magog against Israel.

This movement sponsors terror and calls for a global jihad to destroy every form of secular government and culture. Their avowed objective and purpose: to establish a one-world theocracy, based on radical Islam making Sharia law (Islamic religious law) the solitary, worldwide system. Sharia Law is the legal framework of Islam, which governs every public and private aspect of one's life. These Islamic principles of jurisprudence control virtually every aspect of day-to-day life, including politics, economics, banking, business, contracts, family relationships, sexuality, hygiene, and social issues.

To realize where we are on the universal clock, that is ticking away the seconds between time and eternity, consider these facts:

- The political and social structure that once governed Iraq and the Great Fertile Crescent has already died up, making way for the kings of the East.

- Capitalizing on this, Islamic Sharia Law has now become the most widely used religious law and one of the three most common legal systems in the world.

While this news may surprise and even alarm many, this is just the beginning. To fully comprehend where we are on this clock, consider what John foresaw, concerning the sixth of the seven last plagues. After mentioning that the River Euphrates dried up to make way for the kings of the East, John says:

"And I saw **three unclean spirits** like frogs come out of the mouth of **the dragon**, and out of the mouth of **the beast**, and out of the mouth of the **false prophet.** For they are the spirits of devils, working miracles, which go forth unto the kings of the earth and of the whole world, to gather them to the battle of that great day of God Almighty" (Rev 16:13,14).

Referring to the Greek, a transliteration of this would read: *"Then (or at this time), I beheld the weapon (by implication, words or language), proceeding from the dragon, and from the weapon (words or language) of the beast (monster), and from the weapon (words of language) of the religious impostor, three demonic (lewd and impure] spirits, with the speed of frogs, since they are spirits of devils (demons) bringing forth signs and wonders, who depart and proceed towards, overcoming the kings of entire earth, to convene together at the battle (war) that day (era), that great day (era) of God the Omnipotent One."*

This Scripture, presents an alliance, established between: **the dragon** (Satan), **the beast** [the political power that is an image, or resemblance, of Ancient Assyria], and **the false prophet** [the false religious system (Mystery, Babylon the Great, the Mother of Harlots,) (Rev 17:5).] Their weapons are in their mouths -- the weapon of words; and in the signs and wonders performed through demonic power.

 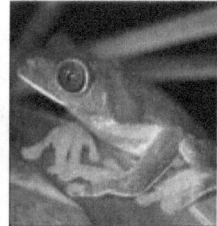 

They cover the earth like frogs, hopping rapidly from place to place, being unlimited geographically since they are evil spirits (or demons), rather than men. Going from place to place, they perform great signs and wonders, even making fire come down out of the heavens. **Their purpose, to overcome the kings of the whole earth,** in order to convene together a great army, sufficient -- in their minds -- to engage the Omnipotent One: God -- in a great cataclysmic battle, giving them control over the whole earth -- indeed, over the entire universe.

Preposterous? Overcoming the Omnipotent One is beyond their reach, but consider the intended outcome of their efforts. John, describing the vision given him, wrote: *"They (the nations of the earth) have only one purpose. So they give their power and authority to the beast. They will make war against the Lamb, but the Lamb will overcome them because he is Lord of Lords and King of Kings -- and with him will be his called, chosen, and faithful followers. ... For God has put it into their hearts to accomplish His purpose by agreeing to give the beast their power to rule, until God's words are fulfilled"* (Rev 17:13,14 & 17).

This demonic triad -- the dragon, the beast and the false prophet -- then *"gather the kings of the earth together, to that place that in the Hebrew tongue, is called Armageddon [the battle of Armageddon]"* (Rev 16:16).

**Har-Meggido - The Tel (Mound) of Megiddo
Israel, Megiddo, & The Valley of Jezreel**

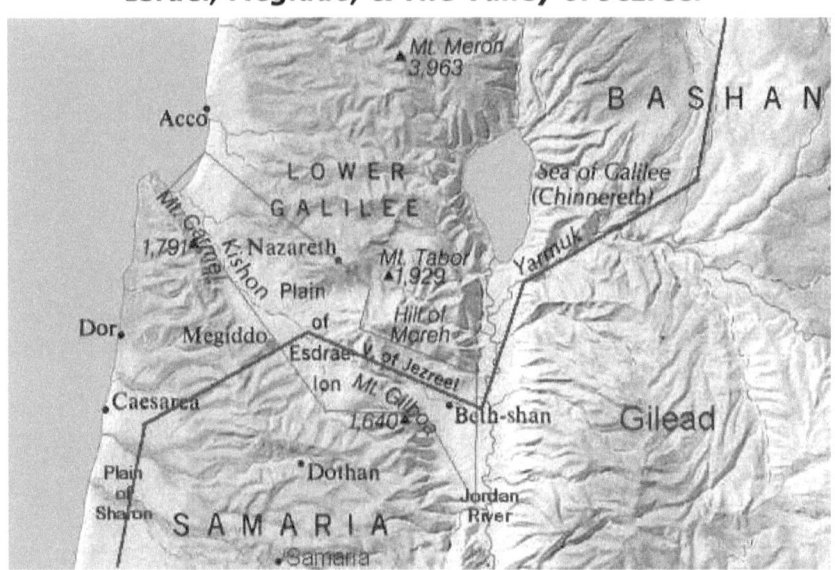

During this great cataclysmic battle -- the Battle of Armageddon -- the armies of the king of the earth assemble in the Valley of Jezreel, surrounding the mound, or tell of Megiddo (Har-Megiddo). The identity of the players in this worldwide conflagration, and the outcome of this battle of battles, are the subject of our next chapter.

Chapter Twenty-One
The Shadow of Armageddon
The Dragon, The Beast & The False Prophet

Megiddo is the jewel in the crown of biblical archaeology. Strategically perched above the most important land route of antiquity in the ancient Near East, the city dominated international travel and trade throughout ancient times. As civilizations rose and fell, sequential settlements on Har-Megiddo (the mountain, or tell of Megiddo) were built, each on the ruins of its predecessor. Over time, this created a multi-layered archaeological legacy abounding in unparalleled treasures, including monumental temples, lavish palaces, mighty fortifications, horse stables and remarkably-engineered water systems.

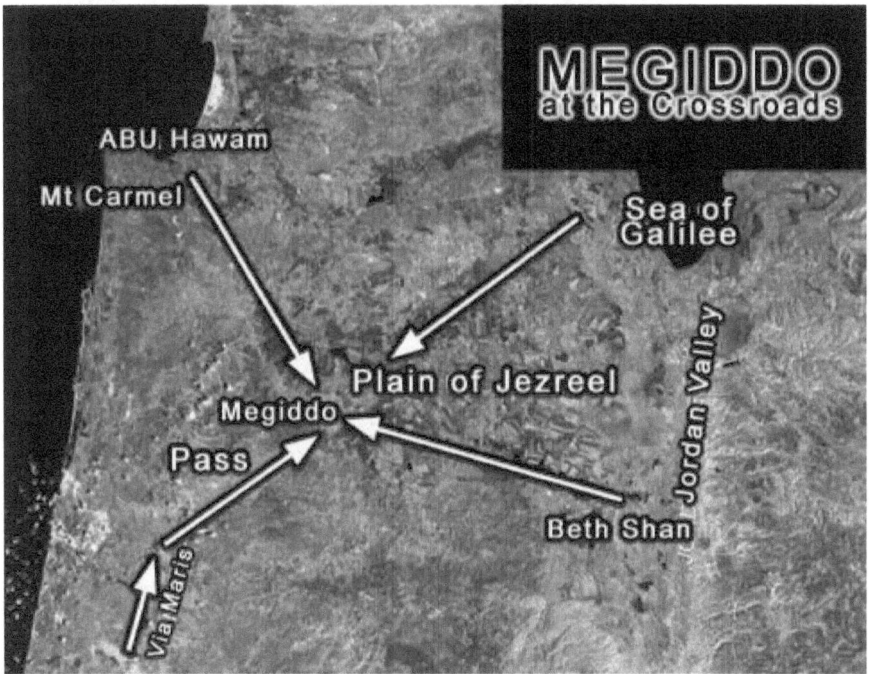

No Battle of Armageddon:
Nearly every one has heard talk of the Battle of Armageddon, referenced as being the final battle on earth, but this isn't exactly the case. The valley of Megiddo, now known as the valley of Jezreel, will according to Bible prophecy, serve as the gathering place; a place where the armies warring against Israel will assemble (Rev 16:16). The battle itself will actually take

place in Jerusalem and environs, and is called the "Battle of That Great Day of God Almighty" (Rev 16:14).

Megiddo has been a strong fortification dating back to ancient times. It is situated approximately 55 miles north of Jerusalem, a few miles south east of Haifa — a natural port and industrial center, that would provide ideal facilities for landing troops.

The ruins of Megiddo are located on a promontory overlooking the plain of Megiddo, an oval-shaped valley once called the Plain of Esdraelon, but now commonly referred to as the Valley of Jezreel. Megiddo provides a large flat area, ideal for assembling military equipment and personnel, while maintaining a watch on the surrounding countryside. The Valley of Jezreel is a flat land plane approximately 20 miles long by 14 miles wide, and is surrounded by mountains.

Har-Megiddo:

- The only site in Biblical lands with remains of 23 to 30 ancient cities, built one on top of each other.

- One of the most famous battlegrounds in the world. Historians believe that more battles have been fought at this site than anywhere else on earth: Assyrians, Canaanites, Egyptians, Greeks, Israelites, Persians, Philistines, and Romans have all fought to control Megiddo.

- Genghis Khan's army marched all the way here from Mongolia in an attempt to reach North Africa, and here they were defeated by the Mamelukes.

- It guards the most important highway of the ancient world, the Via-Maris that connected Egypt with Mesopotamia, controlling several vital land routes for travelers between Europe, Asia, and Africa.

- This site is linked to numerous great figures in world history, including: King Solomon, King Ahab, and King Josiah of late-monarchic Judah, Pharaohs Thutmose III, Shishak and Necho of Egypt and Kings Tiglath-pileser III and Esar haddon of Assyria, and the Antichrist.

- As recently as 1948, a battle occurred here -- the final defeat of the Arabs by the Jews -- indeed a fitting symbol for God's final war on his enemies.

- One of the most significant archaeological finds at Megiddo was the city's complex water system. It consists of a vertical shaft 120 feet deep connected by a tunnel 215 feet long to a spring located outside the city walls.

- One of Megiddo's claims to archeological importance is the fact that since 586 BC it has remained uninhabited, preserving the ruins of history, without newer settlements disturbing them.

Archaeologists excavating Megiddo have unearthed an incredible find of between twenty-three and thirty separate layers of settlements, built one, on top of another, that cover a period of thirty-five centuries. Settlement at Megiddo first emerged at least 5,000 years ago and continued to the Persian invasion of Palestine some 2,300 years ago. Today, however, nothing is left but the ruins of what once was the regional administrative and military center of Israel during the reign of King Solomon.

Megiddo is first mentioned in the Bible in Joshua 12:21. During Joshua's time, the city was inhabited by Canaanites but later came under the control of King Solomon. The Israelite connection to the city ended around 732 BC, when the Assyrians conquered Palestine. Although the city was destroyed and rebuilt several times after that, it gradually declined in significance. Most recently, Megiddo was the site where British General, Edmund Allenby, launched his attack against the Turks in 1917. It also served as a military base for Israeli Defense Forces during the 1948 war.

Armageddon -- An Anticipated Event:
The Battle of Armageddon, is a well known, long anticipated event among many cultures around the world. Conflicting cultures look forward to the battle, to resolve the issues between good and evil. It is, many believe, the site where the positive forces of the cosmos will engage in battle against the negative

forces; and in most legends surrounding this impending event, good will win out in the end.

Armageddon & Traditional Christianity:

In Evangelical and Fundamental Christian theology, the Armageddon encounter will take place between Christ and the Antichrist -- God and Satan. It will, Christians believe, finally clear the world of immorality once and for all. According to most traditional Christian interpretations, the Messiah, the "Lamb", will return to earth and defeat the Antichrist, the "Beast", during the battle of Armageddon. After that, Satan will be put into the bottomless pit or abyss for 1,000 years, known as the Millennial age. At the end of the millennial period, Satan is released from the abyss, and will gather Gog and Magog from the four corners of the earth, who will encamp surrounding the holy ones and the "beloved city".

After the powers of darkness surround the camp of the saints, intent on capturing it, fire will come down from God, out of heaven and devour Gog and Magog during this Battle of Armageddon. Then. the Devil who deceived them will be thrown into Gehenna (the lake of fire and brimstone) where the Beast and the false prophet have been since just before the 1,000 years.

Armageddon & Jehovah's Witnesses:

The Jehovah's Witnesses believe that Armageddon is a battle in which Satan unites the kings of the Earth against God's appointed King, Christ. Unlike other Christian groups, Witnesses teach that the Bible uses Megiddo as the "symbolic" place of gathering of all the kings of the Earth, where they will try to do battle against God and his forces. This action on the part of the kings of the Earth will be provoked, Witnesses believe, by expressions and signs inspired by demons. This they assert, will be followed by the establishment of God's kingdom on earth for a thousand years. The final judgment and purification of the Earth's sin occurs at the end of the Millennium, a prelude to Armageddon, and an attack on all religions, undertaken by the United Nations.

Armageddon & Seventh-day Adventists:

Seventh-day Adventists teach that the current religious movements taking place in the world are setting the stage for Armageddon. They are concerned by the growing unity between Spiritualism, American Protestantism and Roman Catholicism. A significant difference between Seventh-day Adventist and mainstream Protestant theology is their teaching that the events of Armageddon will leave the earth desolate for the duration of the millennium. They teach that the righteous will be taken to heaven at the beginning of the millennium, while the rest of humanity will be destroyed, leaving Satan with no one to tempt and effectively "bound" by circumstances. The final re-creation of a "new heaven and a new earth," will then follow the millennium.

Armageddon & Islam:
In Islamic theology, Armageddon is viewed as a spiritual battle or struggle in the present age between the forces of good, i.e. righteousness, purity and virtue (a world living under Sharia Law), and the forces of evil (the infidels -- all non-Muslims). The final struggle between the two camps comes about as satanic influence is let loose with the emergence of Gog and Magog. Satan gathers all his powers, and uses all his methods by which to mislead non-Muslim people, introducing an age where iniquity, promiscuity, atheism, and materialism abound. According to Islamic teachings, the present age has, as a result of its wickedness, been a witness to the wrath of God. Manifestations of His wrath include, they believe, the First and Second World Wars and the increasing frequency of natural disasters.

Muslims believe that God has appointed the coming Mahdi to be the promised Messiah, who will effect the spiritual reformation and moral redirection of mankind. They believe the moral teachings of Islam will eventually protect humanity from, and will overcome these evils, thereby establishing unity and sincere worship of God, ushering in an age of peace on earth. This age continues, they believe, for approximately one thousand years as per Judeo-Christian and Islamic prophecies of the Apocalypse. This era, they contend, will be characterized by the assembling of mankind under one faith (Islam, governed by Sharia Law).

Armageddon & Baha'i:
Baha'í literature provides three interpretations of the Battle of Armageddon, which they associate with events surrounding the World Wars. The first interpretation deals with a series of tablets written by Bahá'u'lláh, founder of the Baha'í Faith, to be sent to various kings and rulers. The second relates to events near the end of World War I involving General Allenby and the Battle of Megiddo (1918) during which World Powers are said to have drawn soldiers from many parts of the world to engage in battle with one another at Megiddo. The third interpretation reviews the overall progress of all World Wars, and the situation in the world before and thereafter.

The Military History of Armageddon:
You might be surprised to learn that other battles -- referred to as the battle of Armageddon -- have occurred here before, in fact, several times over the course of history. The term Armageddon is born of a location rather than an event -- a location that has seen its fair share of warfare and blood. During the past four thousand or so years, Meggido has seen more blood shed than any other place on earth.

As one secular writer stated: *"Whether or not the Battle of Armageddon, written about in the book of Revelation, is an actual event or symbolic, there is no denying that the battles at Har-Megiddo, that have already taken place, have spilled their share of blood, and have oft-times seen what people would consider a good faction battling against what people would consider an evil faction. If Armageddon is a prophecy of a real event, people who believe in it have reason to believe that Megiddo is where it will take place."*

Armageddon: A Fresh Look:
Setting aside these various interpretations for the moment, lets return to the words of John, the apocalyptic prophet, where we left off: *"They (the nations of the earth) have only one purpose. So they give their power and authority to the beast. They will make war against the Lamb, but the Lamb will overcome them because he is Lord of Lords and King of Kings -- and with him will be his called, chosen, and faithful followers. ... For God has put it into their hearts [the kings of the earth] to accomplish His purpose by agreeing to give the beast their power to rule, until God's words are fulfilled"* (Rev 17:13,14 & 17).

Reflecting on the last chapter, remember that the nation, represented by the beast referred to here, is a nation that lies East of the Great Fertile Crescent, through which the river Euphrates flows. This nation, according to John, will endeavor to resurrect the ancient Persian kingdom. Its objectives are expansive: it to dominate the entire earth. Its methodology is to employ a cataclysmic battle, and it will stop at nothing, including cooperation with the powers of darkness to accomplish its objective. Concerning this alliance, John said:

*"And I saw **three unclean spirits** like frogs come out of the mouth of **the dragon**, and out of the mouth of **the beast**, and out of the mouth of the **false prophet.** For they are the spirits of devils, working miracles, which go forth unto the kings of the earth and of the whole world, to gather them to the battle of that great day of God Almighty"* (Rev 16:13,14).

We have seen that these three entities will cover the earth like frogs, hopping rapidly from place to place. They are unlimited geographically because of their allegiance with evil spirits (or demons) who, traveling from place to place, perform great signs and wonders, even making fire come down out of the heavens. Their intent, to overcome the kings of the whole earth, which they accomplish when all nations of the earth surrender their power and authority. Then, as a worldwide kingdom, they will assemble a great military force, sufficient -- they believe -- to engage the Omnipotent One: God -- in a great cataclysmic battle, that will give them control over the whole earth.

A Nefarious Triune Kingdom:
To identify this nefarious kingdom, we need to connect the curious event of all the nations of the earth surrendering their power and authority of rule to the beast, with the next few words of John -- words that at first seem somewhat unrelated. *"The woman you saw is the great city that rules over the kings of the earth"* (Rev 17:18). Remember that the woman referenced here is identified a few verses earlier. John wrote:

"One of the seven angels ... said to me, "Come, I will show you the punishment of the great prostitute, who sits on many waters. With her the kings of the earth committed adultery and the inhabitants of the earth were intoxicated with the wine of her adulteries." Then the angel carried me away in the Spirit into a

desert. There I saw a woman ... This title was written on her forehead: **MYSTERY BABYLON THE GREAT THE MOTHER OF PROSTITUTES AND OF THE ABOMINATIONS OF THE EARTH"** (Rev 17:1-5).

The ruins of Babylon, pictured on the previous page, can be seen near present-day Al Hillah, in the Babil Province of Iraq, situated about 85 kilometers (55 mi.) south of Baghdad. All that remains today, of the once famed ancient city of Babylon, is a mound, or tell, of broken mud-brick buildings and debris scattered over the fertile Mesopotamian plain between the Tigris and Euphrates rivers.

Historical resources tell us that Babylon was initially a small town, that sprang up about the beginning of the third millennium BC (the dawn of the ancient dynasties). The town flourished, attaining prominence and political repute with the rise of the First Babylonian Dynasty. It was called the "holy city" -- the "gate of god" -- and one of the Seven Wonders of the Ancient World. Its demise, determined by God due to her heinous acts of idolatry and deviancy, was proclaimed through His prophet, Jeremiah.

Then, "The word the Lord spoke through Jeremiah the prophet concerning Babylon and the land of the Babylonians: "Announce and proclaim among the nations, lift up a banner and proclaim it; keep nothing back, but say, 'Babylon will be captured; Bel will be put to shame, Marduk filled with terror. Her images will be put to shame and her idols filled with terror.' A nation from the north will attack her and lay waste her land. No one will live in it; both men and animals will flee away" (Jer 50:1-3). ... *"Babylon will be a heap of ruins, a haunt of jackals, an object of horror and scorn, a place where no one lives"* (Jer 51:37).

Babylon, the seat of the ancient Assyrian Empire, fell into the hands of the Persians in 539 BC. After that, she slowly declined in magnificence and power until Alexander the Great endeavored to reestablish it as a center of learning and commerce. Following his untimely death in 323 BC, Alexander's kingdom was divided and most of the city's inhabitants were relocated to Seleucia.

This brought an end to the city as a center of influence, however, sacrifices were still carried out in its old sanctuary for nearly a century thereafter. By 141 BC, when the Parthians ruled the region, the ancient city of Babylon was in ruins and completely desolated. Pictured to the left, are the ruins of Babylon as of 1932; clearly a 'heap of ruins, a haunt of jackals, an object of horror and scorn, due to the horrendous things that had occurred there -- and a place where no one lives'.

However, despite its present condition, Persians, have long envisioned the resurrection of Babylon, and have fought many battles over the right to achieve this feat and restore her prominence and power. Saddam Hussein was the most recent individual to attempt this. In 1983, Saddam Hussein started rebuilding the city on top of the old ruins, investing in both restoration and new construction. He even inscribed his name on many of the bricks, thereby imitating Nebuchadnezzar. The inscription thereon reads: *"This was built by Saddam Hussein, son of Nebuchadnezzar, to glorify Iraq"*.

This is reminiscent of the ziggurat at Ur, where each individual brick was stamped with *"Ur-Nammu, king of Ur, who built the temple of Nanna"*. These bricks became sought after as collectors' items after the downfall of Saddam Hussein, since construction was stopped, the ruins no longer being restored to their original state. Saddam had also installed a huge portrait of himself with the ancient king, Nebuchadnezzar, at the entrance to the ruins, and had shored up Processional Way, a large boulevard of ancient stones, and had refurbished the Lion of Babylon, a black rock sculpture about 2,600 years old.

When the Gulf War ended in 1991, Saddam envisioned building a modern palace, over the ruins of ancient Babylon. It was designed in the pyramidal style of a Sumerian ziggurat and was to be named Saddam Hill. Construction commenced, and in 2003, with the palace nearly complete, Saddam was ready to begin construction on a cable tramway from modern Baghdad to ancient Babylon restored. But, the allied invasion halted the project.

History has witnessed the fulfillment of the prophecy of Jeremiah: *"Babylon will be captured; Bel will be put to shame, Marduk filled with terror. Her images will be put to shame and her idols filled with terror.' A nation from the north will attack her and lay waste her land. No one will live in it; both men and animals will flee away"* (Jer 50:2-3).

To Western powers, the removal of Saddam Hussein provided a doorway of opportunity -- i.e., the creation of a democracy in the middle East that might change the political landscape of the Moslem world. **For the Kings of the East, the allied invasion of Iraq, and the overthrow of Saddam Hussein, provided an all together different opportunity -- the realization of their dream to restore Babylon as the springboard to world domination.**

The Islamic Republic of Iran calculates that American and its allies have achieved what it could not -- the removal their most potent local enemy, Saddam Hussein -- making the recapturing of the seat of the ancient Persian and Assyrian Kingdom possible without a major battle. For now, Iran is content to take advantage of America and its allies dedication to stay in Iraq, allowing Iran to avoid losing face in the Moslem world, yet providing them the opportunity to indirectly inflict as much damage as possible on America and her allies, including their archenemy, Israel.

An article published in April 2006 states that the United Nations, working with Iraqi leaders, have plans for restoring ancient Babylon and converting it into a cultural center. But, there are others with different ideas.

Iran's Sinister Designs for Iraq:
Ayatollah Ruhollah Khomeini, in September 1981, said: *"War is a divine blessing, a gift bestowed upon us by Allah."*

In 1980, Iran's policy of spreading the "Revolution" to Iraq played a key role in the outbreak of the eight-year Iran-Iraq war. Iraq with its large population of Shiite Muslims, and their most sacred shrine, provided the ideal location to springboard the export of "Revolution" throughout the region. The porous 800-mile border between the nations, and the vast oil reserves of Iraq, made it a tempting target for the Iranian mullahs who sought to develop client Islamic Republics throughout the region. Official slogans abounded, such as "liberating Jerusalem through Karbala" reflected Iran's extraterritorial designs for Iraq.

The end of Iran-Iraq war in 1988, did not end the mullahs' dream of installing a fundamentalist regime in Iraq. When Iraq occupied Kuwait on August 2, 1990, Iran played both sides to advance its own goals. This war potentially offered Iran an opportunity to gain a foothold in the postwar Iraq. Although their attempts to install a Islamic regime in Iraq failed in 1991, Iran's leaders have not lost sight of their desire. Before the second Gulf war, with the prospect of a conflict looming, Iran's leaders decided to kill two birds with one stone: to collapse the Saddam Hussein' regime and establish an "Iraqi" government, over whom they could gain control.

Immediately after the fall of Saddam, Iran launched a multi-pronged campaign in Iraq. The infiltration of agents under the guise of local loyalists to Shi' (Shiite) religion, to consolidate their network. They accomplished this by providing direct and indirect support for foreign terrorists in Iraq, intending to make the postwar stabilization process so difficult for the United States and its allies, that they would abandon the Iraqi people.

In Iran's sinister strategy, when it comes to Iraq, they believe time is their ally and all they have to do is to be discreet, patient, keep their heads down, and, if necessary, even participate in the reconstruction efforts, while their secret agents carried out their subversive plans in Iraq.

The United States has cast a skeptical eye on Iran's plan to assist in the reconstruction of Iraq by flooding the country with hundreds of thousands of dinar-spending tourists and religious pilgrims. The Department of Defense says: *"There may be pilgrims who come for legitimate purposes but we've also raised concerned about (people coming) across for not-so legitimate purposes, either smuggling or people coming across to foment violence and to oppose the progress that's being made."*

A security officer in Kerbala said, *"(Iranian pilgrims) cross the border secretly and come in busloads The illegals are the source of all our problems. They are sent by the Iranian secret service to destabilize our country."*

Efforts to create a "second Iran" in Iraq
There are three grave Mideast dangers facing the United States and its allies. These risks include expanded terrorism, the new Iraq coming under the control of pro-Iranian Shiite extremists and an Iran already armed with ballistic missiles and intent on obtaining nuclear weapons. Iran is, in fact, already taking action to bring about a "second Iran" in Iraq in three distinct ways:

1. Iran is using Iraqi Shiite clerics, who agree that clergy should be the ruling power, to build a political power base through the mosques and their associated social services.

2. Iran has established "The Supreme Council for Islamic Revolution" in Iraq to build a political movement that could win elections or take power town by town with the help of covert Iranian funds and propaganda. This organization also has an Iranian-trained, armed paramilitary of about 30,000 and growing, which has been moving into Iraq.

3. Iran is working covertly with pro-Iranian, Iraqi extremist Muqtada al-Sadr, to use political and coercive means, including murder, to intimidate and take over the Shiite leadership in Iraq. The murders of several prominent Shiite clerical leaders who favored democracy and cooperation with the Coalition, replicated some of Iran's covert actions in post-Taliban Afghanistan, where a number of moderate Muslim clerics were killed.

   (Excerpts from an article by Constantine C. Menges, senior fellow with the Hudson Institute, formerly special assistant for national security affairs to the president.)

Iran's designs on Iraq go back a long, long way. In 1979, the year of the Iranian Revolution, Ayatollah Ruhollah Khomeini converted a very extreme version of Islam into state policy. Written into the Iranian constitution is the nation's obligation to *"constantly strive to bring about the political, economic, and cultural unity of the Islamic world."*

In real terms, this means exporting its extremist religio-political rule to the rest of the Middle East and the world. Neighboring Iraq — with its majority Shiite population and its 900-mile border with Iran — is a natural starting point for enforcing this extremist unity. Author and analyst Alireza Jafarzadeh compares Iraq's "geographic vulnerability" to Iran — which is quadruple its size with triple its population — to the situation between Lebanon and Syria, Lebanon being dominated by Syria for decades.

From the beginning, Khomeini saw Saddam Hussein as the number-one obstacle impeding the forward march of the Islamic revolution. He directly appealed to Iraqis to boot him out, calling him a "puppet of Satan." Saddam, feeling threatened, responded by invading Iran on Sept. 22, 1980. Khomeini viewed the resulting conflict as nothing less than a war over the future of his beloved religion. He is reported to have said: "*It is not a question of a fight between one government and another, it is a question of an invasion by an Iraqi non-Muslim Baathist against an Islamic country, and this is a rebellion of blasphemy against Islam.*"

The resulting war was brutal, devastating, and inconclusive, costing each side the lives of about a million people and about half a trillion dollars, without yielding either any appreciable gain. When a UN ceasefire brought an end to the conflict in 1988, Khomeini's military was sapped of strength and morale, and his country lay in economic ruin. Nevertheless, he and his regime never gave up its plans for Iraq. Iran simply began working out an alternative plan — a plan that involved what Jafarzadeh calls "a complex program of infiltration at every level."

Iran has poured vast resources into the region trying to destabilize Iraq from within by infiltrating it economically, politically, religiously and socially, as well as through propaganda, intelligence gathering and terrorism. Saddam single-handedly succeeded in turning Iraq into a blood enemy, and the Islamic Republic wanted nothing more than to see him gone.

The Iranian regime was inadvertently 'blessed' with an unwitting, unintended ally. When Saddam tried to replenish his depleted war chest by invading Kuwait, in 1991, a US led coalition punished him. Not only did the Gulf War diminish Saddam's resources, it also ruptured the secular Arab nationalist alliance movement Saddam symbolized. The resulting ideological vacuum left ample opportunity for Islamic extremism to flourish. Flourish it did. Iran moved to seize leadership of the burgeoning Arab movement by stepping up its support for terrorist groups throughout the region and the world.

This action caught the eye of Trumpet editor in chief, Gerald Flurry, who wrote: "*Much of the world is unaware of what a powerful and dangerous force the Islamic camp is becoming. Iran is a natural leader for many of them today. Iran also has a goal to lead this group.*"

Flurry's interest was triggered by his knowledge of the prophecy of Daniel 11:40 — an end-time prophecy — which Flurry believes represents the time we currently live in. This prophecy describes a geopolitical power, depicted as "the king of the South" (Dan 11), and as one of the kings of the East by the apocalyptic prophet, John (Rev 16). Based on their descriptions of critical sequence of end-time events, Mr. Flurry began to believe that Iran, leading the radical Islamist alliance, would fulfill that role. In the Trumpet a year later he wrote, *"I believe all indications point to radical Islam, headed by Iran as this king."* Flurry also suggested the possibility that Iran might attempt to take control over the oil of other Middle East oil producers (July 1993).

By 1994, Secretary of State Warren Christopher was calling Iran *"the world's most significant state sponsor of terrorism."* Its tendrils were extending deeper and deeper into the political hot spots in the region. In December of that year, Flurry wrote an article with this provocative headline: "Is Iraq About to Fall to Iran?" *"The most powerful [Muslim] country in the Middle East is Iran,"* he wrote. *"Can you imagine the power they would have if they gained control of Iraq, the second-largest oil-producing country in the world?"*

Flurry based his forecast on a prophecy imbedded in Psalm 83, which is explained in a booklet Flurry published, titled, "The King of the South," the first edition of which was printed about that time. As compelling an argument as this might be to some, considering how powerful as Iran was becoming, nothing boosted its bid for leadership within the region more than what commenced in 2003 -- the "war on terror" that emerged following the Sept. 11, 2001, attack on the World Towers in New York City, NY.

This event guided the White House to focus its attention more than ever on Iraq — and more specifically, on Saddam Hussein. Those planning the attack were optimistic about how the situation would play out if they simply eliminated Saddam. *"An explosion of joy will greet our soldiers,"* predicted Deputy Defense Secretary Paul Wolfowitz. *"There may be pockets of resistance, but very few Iraqis are going to fight to defend Saddam Hussein,"* he said. The Pentagon was easily convinced that the long-repressed Iraqi people would rise up against the Baathists and bring the war to an end "in weeks or even days." This idea incredibly underestimated two critical realities.

1. The importance of Saddam Hussein in holding together the patchwork of ethnic, national and religious groups that comprises Iraq. *"Iraq has never been a real country,"* wrote Yossef Bodansky. He believed that an assault on Iraq and the removal of Saddam Hussein and the Baath regime would discredit and effectively destroy the only mechanism holding mutually hostile entities together.

2. The second critical reality was the Iran factor. Donald Rumsfeld, US Secretary of Defense, in May of 2003 -- shortly after Saddam had been chased into his spider hole -- said: *"Iran should be on notice: Efforts to try to remake Iraq in Iran's image will be aggressively put down."*

As resolute as this sounded, Iran was already covertly invading Iraq, supporting more than 25,000 Iran-sponsored Shiite armed forces it had infiltrated into the country. One correspondent, Jafarzadeh, wrote, *"Immediately after the coalition invasion of March 2003, Iran's leaders exploited the situation and launched a no-holds-barred mission to control Iraq's elections, militias, and power structure at every level. The leaders in Tehran had been waiting for such an opportunity since the end of the Iran-Iraq War in the late 1980s, and the upheaval of Operation Iraqi Freedom was a gift beyond their wildest dreams. The door to Iraq flung open, they leapt at their chance to fulfill their long-held goal of installing an Islamic Republic in Iraq that mirrored their own."*

Iran's strategy was simply to underwrite enough terrorism — supporting terrorists from any group willing to cooperate — willing to destabilize Iraq and make it ungovernable. This would, they believed, convince the Americans to make an ignominious retreat, leaving behind a Saddam-free Iraq ripe for transformation into an Iranian protectorate. Their strategy has been an enormous success. The years since 2003 have seen a slow, bloody but inevitable march toward Iraq falling under Iran's influence.

Once Iran established that beachhead, it will proceed to export its revolution further afield. It is all happening exactly as the Bible said it would. Iran's march to establish additional, far-flung, beachheads, is well documented in our next chapter.

Chapter Twenty-two
The Armageddon Battle Plan

To comprehend Iran's battle plan against those they consider infidels, we need to reflect on several key Scriptures we have previously cited, concerning the worldwide conflagration that is commonly referred to as "The Battle of Armageddon.

Jesus said: *"**There will be signs in the sun, moon and stars**. On the earth, **nations will be in anguish and perplexity** at the roaring and tossing of the sea. **Men will faint from terror, apprehensive of what is coming on the world, for the heavenly bodies will be shaken**"* (Lk 21:25-26).

Paraphrasing the Greek text, we read: *"In the future, there will be **supernatural wonders on/in sun and moon and stars and upon the land/earth anxiety, anguish, distress of nations, together with a state of quandary (perplexity; confusion at sea and vibrations; [with] men's hearts failing because of exceeding fear (or terror) and apprehending after the impending attack of the earth**, because the powers of the kingdom of God (Christianity) shall be disturbed."*

The apostle, Paul, describing these same events, wrote: *"For the secret power of lawlessness is already at work; but the one who now holds it back will continue to do so till he is taken out of the way. And then the lawless one will be revealed, whom the Lord Jesus will overthrow with the breath of his mouth and destroy by* the splendor of his coming. **The coming of the lawless one will be in accordance with the work of Satan displayed in all kinds of counterfeit miracles, signs and wonders, and in every sort of evil that deceives those who are perishing"** (2 Th 2:7-10).

John, prophetically declared: *"Then I saw another beast, coming out of the earth. He had two horns like a lamb, but he spoke like a dragon. He exercised all the authority of the first beast on his behalf, and made the earth and its inhabitants worship the first beast, whose fatal wound had been healed. **And he performed great and miraculous signs, even causing fire to come down from heaven to earth in full view of men"*** (Rev 13:11-13).

Each of these Scriptures identifies supernatural events that produce anxiety, perplexity, confusion, fear and terror in mankind, deceiving the ungodly and causing disruption within the kingdom of God -- the church. In short, **they speak of an era of terrorism, just preceding the end of time.** It is a time during which the church, that previously held a place of honor worldwide, will be targeted as 'the enemy' by the sponsors of this terrorism. How could this happen, that the Church of Christ, that once enjoyed such broad acceptance, be thus denigrated -- its members sought out as enemies?

John seems to provide an answer to this question, writing: *"And I saw **three unclean spirits** like frogs come out of the mouth of **the dragon**, and out of the mouth of **the beast**, and out of the mouth of the **false prophet.** For they are the spirits of devils, working miracles, which go forth unto the kings of the earth and of the whole world, to gather them to the battle of that great day of God Almighty"* (Rev 16:13,14).

We mentioned earlier, the fact that these three unclean spirits are likened to frogs, symbolizes the rapid dispersion of the work of the dragon, the beast and the false prophet. As an unholy alliance, assisted by demons, they proceed to carry out worldwide, what the dragon (Satan) began, when he followed the church into the wilderness.

*"The beast was given a mouth to utter proud words and blasphemies and **to exercise his authority for forty-two months**. He opened his mouth to blaspheme God, and to slander his name and his dwelling place and those who live in heaven. **He was given power to make war against the saints and to conquer them. And he was given authority***

over every tribe, people, language and nation" (Rev 13:5-7).

We saw in a previous chapter, that this period of forty-two months represented the 1260 years of persecution the church endured following the collapse of the Roman Empire. We learned that the dragon (Satan) was the one who gave authority to the beast (this nation). In this Scripture, John notes that the beast the dragon now enables is given power to make war against the church worldwide -- over every tribe, people, language and nation.

As a result of the combined activity of the dragon (Satan) and the beast (the nation, who represents the healing of the deadly wound received by the Kingdom of Assyria), and the false prophet (the state religion of the nation or kingdom in question): *"All inhabitants of the earth will worship the beast — all whose names have not been written in the book of life belonging to the Lamb that was slain from the creation of the world"* (Rev 13:8). Now, having identified this demonic and treacherous triad, let's examine the astoundingly accurate fulfillment of these words that were received by John in vision, and recorded by him nearly two thousand years ago.

The History of Terrorism:

From the establishment of the ancient city-state of Babylon and the Assyrian kingdom to the present day, terrorism has played a role in the military warfare of various organizations, countries, and empires. From Nimrod and his Assyrian allies -- the giants -- to present-day Al Quida and its allied, the organized targeting of civilians has a long and bloody history. State endorsed terrorism has always been promoted by nations with religious based ideology, even in such horrific cases as Hitler and Stalin. Even the Aztecs terrorized their region of the world, in their quest for captives to sacrifice to their sun god, Quetzalcoatl.

Answering the call of clandestine political leaders, present-day Palestinian mothers send their children out with a suicide belts and the blessing of Allah, promising them 'a guaranteed passage into paradise' in return for mass killings. Irrespective of time, empire, or ideology, religion has served as the prime motivation for terrorism throughout history.

At first glance, the infamous Assyrians might appear to be an exception to religiously motivated terrorism. Why did they skin captives alive, entomb civilians into city walls, and impale captives on a spike through the anus into the bowels? Were the implementation of these excruciatingly slow deaths due merely to capricious sadistic urges, or were they religiously motivated? Shalmaneser I (1263 to 1234) bragged to have blinded 14,400 enemies in one eye. Assyrian wealth was envied and the Assyrians' cruelty feared as they deported captives to weaken possible rebellions. But, could there really have been a religious overtone to all this?

Inscriptions found among Assyrian ruins, and bas reliefs in the British museum depict the ruthless Assyrian king, Ashurbanipal, offering human sacrifices to his gods. Archeologists commonly find inscriptions depicting the Assyrian rulers praising their gods for the brutal conquests to which they have been divinely commissioned.

Their polytheism was inherited from the Babylonians, the Summerians and Akkadians before them. It enabled demonically motivated rulers to envision themselves as part of a capricious pantheon, and share in the pseudo-authority of the gods, which evolved to suit the political aims of the administration. Kings were believed to be the earthly embodiment of the god Ashur. It was from the midst of this early religious environment, that Abram answered the call of YAHWEH to separate himself and depart for the Promised Land.

Assyria rose to its golden age about the end of the sixth century BC, when Assyria's kings maintained a large, professionally trained, standing army. This arrangement gave Assyria remarkable military advantage over other countries. The Assyrians developed the world's first steel (Jer 15:12), the battering ram, chariots, and amassed a cavalry. Assyria's armies routinely terrorized towns throughout the neighboring lands, even defeating the Egyptians in 670 BC. The Kingdom of Assyria expanded over time, covering the entire Fertile Crescent, forcing tribute payment from Babylon, Israel, Egypt, and Phoenicia.

Aztec Terrorism:
Building upon the sacrificial rituals of other Meso-American tribes, the Aztecs are another "civilization" that was built on state terrorism. According to historian, Carroll Payne, the Aztecs were *"militant regimes that based their imperial power on the complete surrender of terrified subjects."* Their religion also *"exalted the act of volunteering as a human sacrifice."*

The Aztecs were feared because they were known to sacrifice thousands of victims each year in *"ritual religious ceremonies that often included cannibalism."* Their religion evolved to meet their political ends and religious ideology as their priests performed grotesque rituals as acts of service to their many gods: to appease their wrath, and for their empire to prosper. In the end, the Aztecs were conquered, their nation obliterated by Spanish explorer, Cortez.

Early Efforts to Recreate a Worldwide Kingdom:
Some of the most well-known terrorists of all time, include Mao Zedong, Adolf Hitler and Joseph Stalin, who were world renown for their cruelty and eccentric ideas. These rulers went about their task with religious fervency and ideology.

Mao Zedong
Mao Zedong came to power in China in 1949 and continued to rule until his death in 1976. During his reign of terror, Mao Zedong is credited with taking more than 30 million (30,000,000) lives. Historians of that era claim that many of his victims were subjected to having a red-hot gun-rod rammed into their anus. Others died from having their stomach cut open and their heart scooped out while still screaming in the pangs of death. A confidential report found that one quarter of the entire Red Army who served under Mao at the time, were later slaughtered, often after being tortured, to instill fear and absolute obedience among the others.

Hitler
Using the justification of social Darwinism, Hitler formed the Nazi party and with the help of the Roman Catholic church, gained by promising them he would make Catholicism the state religion, he won the 1933 election. Achieving a landslide victory, Germany gave him power to implement his religious ideas. By adding to Darwinism a grossly convoluted interpretation of Christian scriptures, Hitler considered the Jews to be an inferior race, and sought to completely exterminate them by horrific means.

In the end, Hitler's ideas, which were based primarily on Nationalist society ideals and objectives, cost the world nearly 60 million (60,000,000) lives. In the concentration death camps of the Holocaust, Hitler ordered such despicable experimentation and torture of humans, it would be inappropriate to even speak of them.

Stalin

Stalin also wanted to create a new society with a new human personality. His faith in the ideas of Marx and Darwin philosophy motivated him to reject his own religious upbringing and destroy the traditional religions of Russia. Stalin, directly or indirectly contributed to at least 30 million (30,000,000) deaths in the formation of his USSR. He reigned terrorism upon his own people as his KGB tortured political and religious dissidents. He sent millions to die in the icy work camps of the Gulag. Stalin's second wife was so horrified at the carnage her husband had caused, she took her own life in sorrow.

Saddam Hussein

Not far behind Mao, Hitler and Stalin is the more recent terrorist, who idolized these men. Saddam Hussein, in his glory days, relished the fact that he had invaded Kuwait, burned its oil fields in a dastardly act of eco-vandalism, killed some five thousand (5,000) of his own people with chemical weapons at Halabjah, and stuffed another four hundred thousand (400,000) or more of his constituents into mass graves. Saddam Hussein was all too familiar with terrorism.

In addition to terroristic acts individually directed by him, Saddam essentially owned and operated a full-service supermarket for global terrorists, complete with monetary exchange, cash contributions, diplomatic aid, safe havens, terror training, and even medical attention. Starting with money, Saddam Hussein's government supported terrorism by paying "bonuses" of up to $25,000 to the families of Palestinian homicide bombers.

Saddam Hussein's vice president, Taha Yassin Ramadan, is the man who Israeli intelligence found to be directly involved in funneling money from Baghdad to the hands of the families of the homicide bombers. Documents that the Israeli Defense Force captured in the Palestinian town of Ramallah indicate that Vice President Ramadan used the Arab Liberation Front, the Palestinian Liberation Front, and the Palestinian branch of the Iraqi Baathist party to deliver these funds into the hands of terrorists' families.

Three of these masters of terrorism -- Hitler, Stalin and Hussein -- shared a common ideology and objective: to breathe new life into the "Great Ottoman Empire."

The Ottoman Empire:
At the height of its power (16th to 17th century), the Ottoman Empire spanned three continents, controlling much of Southeastern Europe, Western Asia and North Africa. The Empire embodied 29 provinces and embraced numerous additional vassal states. Some of these states were later on, absorbed into the empire, while others gained autonomy over the course of centuries. The Ottoman empire temporarily even exercised authority over distant overseas lands through forced declarations of allegiance to the Ottoman Sultan and Caliph.

The empire was at the center of sociopolitical interactions between the Eastern and Western worlds for six centuries. With Constantinople (Istanbul) as its capital city, and its control of lands around the eastern Mediterranean, the Ottoman Empire was, in many respects, the initial Islamic successor to the Eastern Roman (Byzantine) Empire. The Ottoman Empire is to date, the longest lasting Muslim empire (1300 to 1922).

The efforts of present-day leaders to resurrect the authority and power of the Ottoman Empire made them the enemy of other Muslims -- principally the Iranians -- endeavoring to breathe new life into the ancient Assyrian/ Babylonian/Persian Kingdom. The plans for kingdom-building of Mao, Hitler, Stalin and Hussein have all exemplified the nefarious triad -- the dragon (Satan and his demons), the beast (a tyrannical political government) and the false prophet (a state sponsored religion: a state with a national religion, undergirded by satanic forces).

The Tool of Assassination:
The term 'assassin' comes originated with a Shiite Muslim sect, the Nizari Isma'ilis (also known as hashashins, or "hashish-eaters"), a secret order of assassins. This sect began fighting Sunni Muslims around 1090 to 1275 AD, then expanded their fight to include Christians during the Medieval Christendom Crusades era (1095 to 1291 AD).

The hashashins were known to spread terror by murdering innocent men, women and children. This Brotherhood of Assassins committed unthinkable terror, believing that they would, in exchange for their atrocities, gain paradise and seventy-two virgins if killed in battle; or should they survive the fight, receive unlimited hashish while on earth.

Present-day Efforts to Resurrect the Kingdom of Assyria:
State supported terrorism, with an overt religious foundation, has once again risen out of the Islamic based regions. From the seventh century, when Islamic terror swept out of Mecca, across Northern African and towards India, Muslims have continuously posed a world wide threat to peace and security. Millions were killed after Iran evoked Allah's blessing on their own youth who, believing the false promises of guaranteed passage to paradise, attacked Iraq. And, Saddam Hussien, who to the West put on a secular face, was intensely religious in his justification of genocide against the Kurds.

The Frog Begins to Hop:
Our key Scripture stated that John *"saw **three unclean spirits***

like frogs ... go out to the kings of the whole world" (Rev 16:13,14). Picking up on this phrase, lets examine the work of Iranian sponsored, or supported, Islamic extremism. Islamic terrorism is the common term for violence, rooted in Islamic fundamentalism, and aimed at defending, even promoting, Islamic culture, society, law and values in opposition to the political, allegedly imperialistic, and cultural influences of non-Muslims, the Western world in particular.

There are also political dimensions to the ideology, that point to the history of Western influence and control after the fall of the Ottoman Empire in 1918. The West's backing of Israel, and the growth of democracy, provided sufficient cause for those subscribing to Islamic ideology to justify and explain its use of violence as a resistive and retributive force against Western, non-Muslim imperialism and political influence.

Islamic terrorist acts have included airline hijacking, kidnapping, assassinations, suicide bombings, and mass murder. The most prominent act attributed to Islamic terrorism is the hijacking of commercial passenger airliners and their use in the destruction of the World Trade Center, in the US, on September 11, 2001, which claimed 2,998 lives. The United States and its allies responded by declaring a "war on terrorism," but the battle has been long and has not deterred the spread of Islamic ideology.

Organized Terrorism:
A list of international terrorist organizations developed by the US State Department, and considered to be active during the last five years, include the following:

Afghanistan: al Qaeda:
Established by Osama bin Laden in the late 1980's, al Qaeda's goals include the establishment a pan-Islamic Caliphate

throughout the world by working with other allied Islamic extremist groups to overthrow all regimes it deems "non-Islamic," and expelling Westerners and non-Muslims from Muslim countries.

Al Qaeda boasts several hundred thousand members and has a a worldwide reach through cells operating in a number of countries. It benefits from its ties to Sunni extremist networks. The founder, Osama Bin Laden, and his top associates, are believed to reside in Afghanistan and Pakistan. The group maintains terrorist training camps in both countries. Al Qaeda's worldwide network includes many Sunni Islamic extremist groups, such as the Egyptian Islamic Jihad, members of al-Gama'at al-Islamiyya, the Islamic Movement of Uzbekistan, and the Harakat ul-Mujahidin.

Al Qaeda is suspected to have been involved in the October 2000 bombing of the USS Cole in Aden, Yemen, the bombings in August 1998 of the U.S. embassies in Nairobi, Kenya, and Dar es Salaam, Tanzania, killing at least 301 persons and injuring more than 5,000 others, the U.S. helicopters that were shot down, killing U.S. servicemen, in Somalia in 1993, and three bombings that targeting U.S. troops in Aden, Yemen, in December 1992.

Algeria: Armed Islamic Group (GIA) & The Salafist Group for Call and Combat (GSPC)
Established in 1992, the GIA aim is to overthrow the secular Algerian regime and replace it with an Islamic state. Its strength is unknown, however, it has splinter groups abroad, many of whom reside in Western Europe, and provide financial and logistic support. The Algerian government has implicated Iran and Sudan as supporters of these Algerian extremists. The GSPC is known to have ties with both Iran and al Qaeda.

Cuba:
The Tri-Continental Conference hosted by Cuba in 1966, sponsored by the Soviet Union, saw the beginning of the internationalization of terrorism. Terrorist organizations, at that time dubbed "liberation groups" from Europe, Asia, Africa, the Middle East and Latin America began building alliances. Financial, political, operational and intelligence cooperation connected these terrorist groups across the world. International terrorism soon flourished. Europe suffered from a decade of terrorist activity as European and Middle Eastern terrorist groups worked together to bring attention to their Palestinian cause.

Egypt: Al-Jihad/Egyptian Islamic Jihad/Islamic Jihad

Established in the late 1970's this organization's stated goals are the overthrow of the Egyptian government to replace it with an Islamic state, from which they plan to attack the US, Israel and their interests in Egypt and abroad. The organization has close ties to al Queda and Iran.

Iraq: Abu Nidal organization (ANO) & the Palestine Liberation Front (PLF):
The ANO, a.k.a. Fatah Revolutionary Council, Arab Revolutionary Brigades, Black September, and Revolutionary Organization of Socialist Muslims all originated as splits off of the PLO in 1974. Their express goal, is to establish a Palestinian State. Their affiliations, from which they receive support, include the governments of Iran and Syria. The PLF, which began operations in the mid-1970's, has as its express goal, the creation of a Palestinian State and the overthrow of Israel.

Lebanon: Hezbollah, Hamas & Palestinian Islamic Jihad & The Palestinian Islamic Jihad:
Hezbollah - which in Arabic, means 'Party of God', is an Islamist Shiite militia based in Lebanon, and is a direct product of Iran. Formally established in 1982, following the Israeli invasion of Lebanon, Iran's aim was to uproot the PLO (Palestinian Liberation Organization) bases there. Iran sent Revolutionary Guard Corps members to assist in the war. A generation later, the relationship between Iran and Hezbollah is still not entirely transparent, but Hezbollah must be considered a full proxy for Iranian intentions, since Iran funds, arms and trains Hezbollah, through the IRGC.

Hezbollah had two goals when founded: 1) removing the Israeli presence in South Lebanon that remained following its 1982 invasion, and 2) establishing a Shi'a Islamic state in the image of the post-revolution Islamic state of Iran. Hezbollah later abandoned its goal of an Iranian-style Islamic state, and is now nationalistic and Islamic in its political orientation, although still supported by Iran and Syria.

Hamas - Iran's relationship with the Palestinian Islamist group Hamas has not been constant over time. It has waxed and waned according to common interests between Iran and Hamas at various times since the late 1980s. Hamas, the dominant political party in the Palestinian territories, has long depended on terrorist tactics, including suicide bombings, to register their protest against Israeli policies.

According to Cambridge University researchers, Iran's relationship with Hamas began in the 1990's when Iran's interest in exporting revolution coincided with Hamas' rejection of compromise with Israel. Iran has continually provided funding and training for Hamas since the 1990s. Iran also pledged to help fund the Hamas led Palestinian government after its parliamentary win in January 2006. Historically, Hamas has openly called for the destruction of the state of Israel, and refused to recognize it. Its manifesto contains strong, incendiary language, championing the requirement that Muslims wage jihad against all foreign usurpers of Muslim lands.

The Iranians and PIJ first established meaningful contact in the late 1980s in Lebanon. Subsequently, Islamic Revolutionary Guard Corps have trained PIJ members at Hezbollah camps in Lebanon and Iran has commenced funding the PIJ. The PIJ has been based in Damascus, Syria since 1989. The PIJ was originally based in Egypt, then later moved to the Gaza Strip. Following its exile from Gaza in the late 1980s, it moved to Lebanon, and later to Damascus. Its objective is to facilitate the establishment of a Palestinian Islamic state.

The PIJ's priority of putting the Palestinian cause before the Islamic cause, reflects a distinctive change from Islamist thought of the 1970s. At that time, most jihadist movements believed that a pan-Islamic revolution would have to precede uniting Palestine. PIJ reversed this thinking, focusing first on the Palestinian cause, believing it will serve as the catalyst for pan-Islamist revolution.

The Palestine Islamic Jihad (PIJ), organized in the 1970's, has as its primary goal the creation of an Islamic Palestinian state and the destruction of Israel through holy war. The organization receives financial assistance from Iran and limited logistic assistance from Syria.

Pakistan: Harakat ul-Mujahidin (HUM) & Jaish-e-Mohammed (JEM):
HUM was organized in the early 1990's. Its primary goal is to unite Kashmir with Pakistan, however, it operates an Afghanistan based terrorist training camp, and many of its members, trained in terrorism, have joined the Afghans, linking up with the Taliban and al Queda. The JEM, established in February, 2000 operates terrorist training camps in Peshawar. This organization also maintains close ties with the Taliban and al Queda.

Philippines: Abu Sayyaf Group (ASG):
ASG's primary goal is to promote the creation of an independent Islamic state in western Mindanao and the Sulu Archipelago. These areas in the southern Philippines are heavily populated by Muslims. The ASG officially started operations in 1991. The organization receives support from Islamic extremists in the Middle East and South Asia, and has ties to Mujahidin in Afghanistan.

South Africa: Qibla and People Against Gangsterism and Drugs (PAGAD):
Qibla began operations in the 1980s, and PAGAD in 1996. Their express goals are to establish an Islamic state in South Africa; PAGAD: Fight drug lords in Cape Town. Both organizations have ties to Islamic extremists in the Middle East. The two groups share an anti-Western stance and some of their members and leadership, promote a greater political voice for South African Muslims. PAGAD is suspected of conducting hundreds of bombings and other violent actions. Collectively, they have launched numerous anti-Western, anti-Christian and anti-Israel campaigns.

Sudan:
The state of the Sudan, located in Africa, became one of the first off-continent centers of Terrorism. Sudan is infamously known as an Islamic state which sponsors terrorism. Sudan "continues to be a used as a meeting place; a safe haven and training ground for international terrorists." The hostile state of the Sudan had long been suspecting of not only supporting various terrorists, but storing their destructive weapons, and providing a place to train for upcoming terrorism attempts. The government of Sudan allows Muslims to terrorize Christians despite the outcry from the international community.

Syria: Popular Front for Liberation of Palestine (PFLP) and The Popular Front for the Liberation of Palestine-General Command (PFLP-GC)
Started in 1967, the primary goal of these organizations is to inhibit negotiations with Israel and promote national unity. Both organizations receive safe haven, logistic and military support from Syria bolstered by financial support from Iran.

Turkey: Kurdistan Workers' Party (PKK):
Begun in 1974, the PKK's primary goal is the establishment of an independent Kurdish state in southeastern Turkey, where the population is predominantly Kurdish. Members of the group receive safe haven and financial aid from Syria, Iraq, and Iran.

Uzbekistan: Islamic Movement of Uzbekistan (IMU)
The organization's primary goal is to establish an Islamic state in Uzbekistan, however, they embrace terrorism as a 'tool of the trade' in accomplishing their objectives. Their members number in the tens of thousands and have frequently been found fighting along side other militants in Afghanistan and Tajikistan. Area of operation includes Uzbekistan, Tajikistan, Kyrgyzstan, and Afghanistan. They are affiliated with, and receive support from, other Islamic extremist groups in Central and South Asia.

Worldwide: Al Quida:

The Islamic organization called Al Quida founded and headed up by Osama bin Laden, is a radical group of suicidal terrorists, who had their beginnings under Saudi Arabian Whahabbism. They later found refuge under the former Taliban re of Afghanistan. They "perceive themselves making the ultimate sacrifice. In the end, they believe they will enjoy special rewards in the hereafter. Because of the architecture all human brains share, they have a sense of fulfillment for their peak experience -- created at death."

These terrorists, *"having a sense of being on a mission from God in dying, simply cannot imagine that they will not attain a peace which passes all understanding."* Having this religion based mindset, they destroyed the World Trade towers in New York, and partially damaged the Pentagon in Washington DC. With delusions that suicidal destruction will lead to happiness, the Taliban have created a very strong and dangerous society. Osama claims that millions of Muslims are trained and ready to volunteer for suicide missions, and that millions more Muslims will provide the essential financial backing.

Chapter Twenty-seven
The Intercontinental Leap

In 1995, after entering into an alliance of terrorism against the West, the Sunni and Shiite terrorists, through their new identity -- al Qaeda -- arrived in the Americas.

The Triangle of Terror: According to intelligence sources, **Osama bin Laden, the founder of al Qaeda, was the first member of his new terrorist organization to venture forth into the "New World."**

These sources learned that he spent several days in what has been named the "Triangle" (the tri-border area of Argentina, Brazil and Paraguay). There he visited mosques, met with leaders of local groups sympathetic to Hezbollah's cause, and attended meetings with the leaders of various international drug cartels.

The "Triangle" was first made known to most north Americans through the 1986 movie, "The Mission," that revealed the wonders of Iguacu Falls, a series of 273 cascades arranged in a horseshoe shape, that fall more than 350 feet. With the help of a native guide, one can still traverse the lush primordial rain forest suffused with giant trees and ferns, begonias and orchids, tropical lizards, capuchin monkeys, macaws, and parrots, and visit the falls.

Today, one must be very careful to stay on the jungle paths, not only to avoid hungry jaguars and wild dogs, but to avoid terrorists with semiautomatic machine guns strapped to their side.

Deep within the "Triangle," and only a few miles from Iguacu Falls, there are now, three large cities, whose primary residents are international terrorists. The principle city within the "Triangle" is Ciudad Del Este (City of the East), in Paraguay. It is renowned for its landing strips hidden below the canopy of the rain forest, and the region's cocaine that is transported to North America, via private planes using these landing strips. They provide a cash crop for area 'farmers' that is valued at more than twelve billion ($12,000,000,000) per year.

The stores and galleries in Ciudad Del Este, once filled with artifacts and native crafts to attract tourists, now display new wares: stolen goods of every imaginable sort, smuggled from the US, along with land mines, improvised explosive devices, antiaircraft guns, drugs and rare, endangered animals.

It is a thriving city of nearly a quarter million residents, served by fifty-five different banking organizations that help resident and tourist terrorists launder more than six billion ($6,000,000,000) in illegal funds, each year. But, should you decide to visit there as a Gringo Tourist, you need not worry too much; for it is far more likely that you will be killed by terrorists long before reaching the city center.

Radicalized Muslims began migrating to the "Triangle" in the mid- 1970's, and by 2005, their numbers had swelled to over sixty thousand (60,000). Hezbollah (the "Party of God") was the first Islamic terrorist organization to establish a base there, in 1983. Funded, trained and supported by the Iranian Revolutionary Guard, this group understood that the "Triangle" surrounded by almost impenetrable jungle, would serve as the ideal location to train new recruits and discreetly amass funds for their envisioned jihad against America and Israel.

Khalid Shaikh Mohammed, Bin Laden's Chief of Military Operations, came to the "Triangle" in March, 2003, to meet with Hezbollah leaders for the purpose of planning attacks against the US, Canada and Israel. Other al Qaeda 'luminaries' soon made their way to the "Triangle," including: Ramzi bin al-Shibh, one of the key planners of 9/11; Khalil bin Laden, Osama's younger brother; 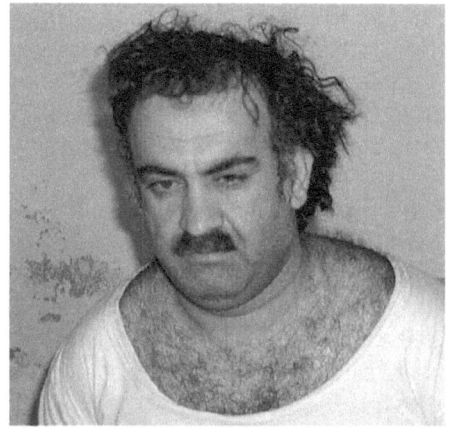 and al-Saiid Ali Hassan Mokhles, formerly an operator of terrorist training camps in Afghanistan; and many others.

Why has such a collection of terrorist luminaries assembled themselves in such a remote region? Bin Laden and his allies realize that this site, surrounded by almost impassible jungles, is far better suited for his operations than the mountainous terrain of Afghanistan or the remote desert of the Sudan. The "Triangle" offers unguarded borders, numerous waterways, innumerable jungle trails, and more than one hundred concealed airstrips. **The "Triangle," hidden in the Amazon Jungle, provides what Afghanistan could not:**

1. The world's fourth largest reserve of uranium,

2. A perfect place to establish laboratories for developing weapons of mass destruction,

3. The ideal location to serve as a launching pad for attacks against the US.

Proof of al Qaeda's and its allies' plans for 'crimes against humanity' came to light in August, 2004. Brazilian police seized a shipment of 1,320 pounds of uranium and thorium ore, bound for one of al Qaeda's allies, and coconspirator against the US and Israel. The shipment made its way to within seventy-five miles of Macapa, near the mouth of the Amazon River. One more day, and this radioactive material -- sufficient in mass to create a number of 'dirty bombs -- would have been on board a ship and well on its way to cause chaos and destruction.

A Marriage Made in Hell - Terrorists and Gangbangers:
Nearly everyone is aware that the numbers of gangs and gangbangers (members of gangs) in this country are on the rise, and that their acts are becoming increasingly more sinister and destructive. At the same time, relatively few are aware of the recent 'marriage made in hell' that took place between these gangbangers and radical Islamic terrorists.

Mara Salvatrucha, a.k.a. MS, MS-13, MS-18 & Mara:
Mara Salvatrucha, (MS-13 and MS-18), are similar, but competing criminal gangs. Both originated on the streets of Los Angeles. MS-13's origin dates back to the 1980's. **The word *mara* means gang in Caliche, and stems from the word, *marabunta*, the name of a species of large, fierce stinging wasps, indigenous only to South America.** "*Salvatrucha*" is a portmanteau of Salvadoran origin and trucha, is a Caliche term for being alert, used by the gangs to warn others to be prepared for carrying out a crime or to avoid capture by police.

MS-13:
The majority of MS-13 gang members are ethnically, Salvadorans, Hondurans, Guatemalans, and Nicaraguans. Initially localized, MS-13 quickly spread to Central America, when members were deported to their country of origin after being arrested. Returning to their native lands, these members recruited more members, many of whom made their way back into the US. This has led some contend that deportation policies have contributed to the increased size and influence of the gang both within the United States and Central America.

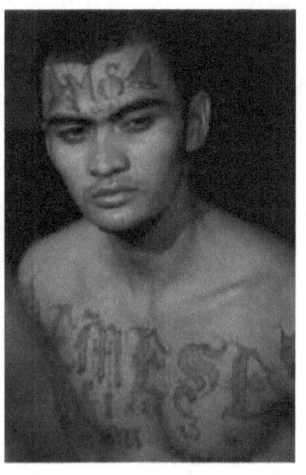

With little direction, and limited opportunities available to them locally, many Central American youth began admiring the returning MS-13 deportees, for their apparent power and expressed purpose, and commenced emulating their behavior. One deportee, interviewed after his re-arrest, reported that when he had been returned to his hometown, there were only he and two other MS-13 gang members in the area, but that the interest of local youth was so great, more than forty (40) local kids were 'jumped-in' (initiated into the gang) in a single day.

Even though getting 'jumped-in' consisted of getting severely beaten for thirteen (13) seconds, the gang quickly became the largest in El Salvador, rapidly spread to Honduras and Guatemala. **The gang's distinctive 'mark' of recognition is an 'MS' or 'MS-13' (6+1+6=13), proudly displayed in tattoos, most often on the forehead.** Similar tattoos may appear on biceps, chest, and hands, interspersed with tattoos of a skull and crossbones, 'devil horns,' or a devil head.

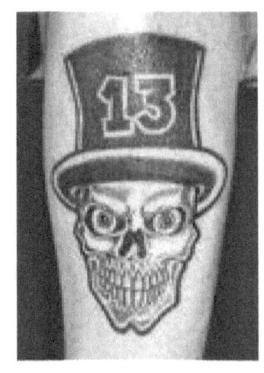

MS-13's original primary purpose was to protect Salvadoran and Honduran immigrants from other, better established gangs in the Los Angeles area, most of which were comprised predominantly of Mexicans, Hispanic-Americans and African-Americans. True to its objectives, the gang initially allowed only Salvadorans and Hondurans to join, but later began admitting other Central Americans as members.

As the gang has spread to other parts of the United States, and Canada, MS-13 has become one of the largest, most dangerous gangs in the North America. In 2005, MS-13 membership in the US alone, topped fifty thousand (50,000). Gang members became involved in a melange of criminal activities but specialize in illegal immigration documents, human smuggling, kidnappings, drug trafficking and gunrunning.

MS-18:
Back 'home' in Los Angeles, a number of MS-13's rival gangs, comprised primarily of Hispanic youth, coalesced to form the largest street gang in the city, boasting membership in excess of twenty thousand (20,000). In defiance of MS-13, the aggregated Los Angeles group adopted the name, MS-18. Through its Hispanic 'family' MS-18 quickly spread throughout Southern and Central California.

As MS-13 deportees and their recruits returned to Los Angeles and environs, MS-18, seeking to enlarge its numbers, became the first Hispanic gang to break the racial membership barrier. While membership was originally restricted to Mexican-Americans, its members today include Central Americans, African Americans, Middle Easterns, Asians, Caucasians, and Native Americans.

MS-18 is not the typical street gang of the 1960's to 1980's. It is a highly organized army of thugs. On the streets, they have their Lieutenants, who call the shots (also called Shotcallers), and the foot-soldiers who report to them, carrying out attacks against other gangs, and crimes against society. Members are required to abide by a strict set of rules. For example, while they may smuggle and traffic in drugs, members are forbidden to use crack cocaine and other hard drugs. Failure to obey a Shotcaller's directive, or failing to show a fellow gang member proper respect, results in disciplinary action, ranging from an eighteen (18) second beating up to execution, depending on the seriousness of the offense.

 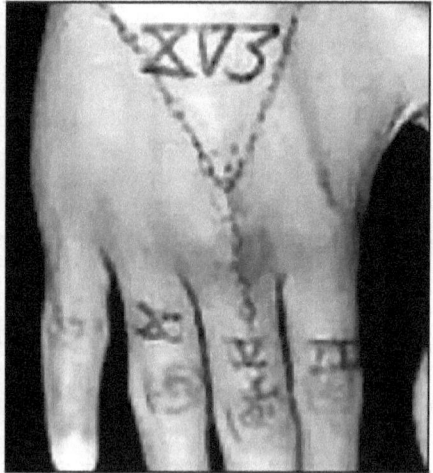

MS-18 has developed a higher level of sophistication and internal organization than any other gang. MS-18 is well networked, maintaining communication and liaison with its members throughout the US, Mexico and Central America. Its members have been linked to occurrences of murder, murder-for-hire, assaults, drug trafficking, extortion, vandalism, drug smuggling, prostitution, robbery, weapons trafficking, and a host of other crimes. Every gang has its identifying marks and MS-18 is no exception. **It's 'mark' which members wear proudly, are easily identified tattoos, the most common**

being the number 666 (6+6+6=18) tattooed on the back or fingers of the right hand.

Back in Salvador, MS-13 continues to grow and gain strength. Authorities there report that approximately 60% of prison inmates serving prison terms for gang-related crimes, either fled from prosecution in, or were deported from, the United States.

By 2005, MS-13 had expanded into Oregon, Texas, Nevada, Utah, Oklahoma, Illinois, Michigan, Maryland, Virginia, Florida, New York and Alaska. In recent years thousands of MS-13 gang members have moved into the Washington, DC area. The areas of Langley Park and Takoma Park near the Washington border have become centers of MS-13 gang activity.

The Criminal Courtship:
In 2005, Honduran Security Minister, Oscar Alvarez, and the President of El Salvador sounded an alarm, claiming that leaders of the Muslim terrorist organization, Al-Qaeda were meeting with leaders of MS-13 and other Central American gangs, and formulating plans to infiltrate the United States. FBI agents said that the U.S. intelligence community and governments of several Central American countries found no basis to suggest that MS-13 is connected to Al-Qaeda or other Islamic radicals. However, according to captured members of both al Qaeda and MS-13, there is little question that the next major terroristic attack against the US by al Qaeda, will have been made possible by the growing relationship between al Qaeda and this swelling horde of savage barbarians -- members of MS-13 and its rival, MS-18.

Migrant Mexican workers, seeking to cross the well-guarded 1,820 mile border between Mexico and the US, must first come to terms with the thousands of MS-13 and MS-18 gang members who watch over the area like a flock of vultures. Their reason for 'standing guard'?; to extract the 'safe passage fee' of five thousand dollars ($5,000.00), for each man, woman and child. Families without sufficient resources -- which represents the majority of those seeking passage -- are forced to surrender their every possession, including: watches, rings, family heirlooms, even their shoes, sombreros and coats, or serapes.

Those lacking adequate money and/or tangible goods are forced to engage in drug trafficking and prostitution. Those who resist payment in cash or in kind, are pushed off the fast moving trains transporting them to the border. If they fight back, they are commonly hacked into pieces, then thrown from the trains. **Salvadorian Consulate, Asdrubal Agulair Zepeda, recently reported that the area between the Guatemalan border and Tapachula, Mexico, is literally strewn with body parts of dead immigrants, too poor to pay the terrorists' protection fee.**

Controlling the border and extracting these fees is big, big business. Every day, there are 4,000 to 5,000 illegal immigrants seeking passage into the US -- enough to fill more than sixty jumbo jet passenger planes. By controlling the admission of immigrants into the New World, MS-13 has transmogrified into a multi-million dollar enterprise, and in so doing, it has developed into an international Mafia. After 9/11, and, as a result of their accumulating fortunes, MS-13 gained the attention of top al Qaeda leaders, who realized that the gang could -- for a price -- be relied on to smuggle sleeper agents, al Qaeda operatives, drugs, and weapons of mass destruction, across the border into the US.

A Marriage Made in Hell:
Thus, in 2002, the world's most notorious terrorist organization (al Qaeda), and the most violent criminal street gang in the Americas, entered into a marriage of convenience. Their **'prenuptial agreement'** was simple and straight forward. Al Qaeda, through its established cells in South America, agreed to

pay MS-13, $30,000 to $50,000 for each sleeper agent, that MS-13 equipped with acceptable *matricula consular*, and smuggle into the US. sneak

Matricula consular are official identification cards, issued by the Mexican government through its consular offices, to verify that the bearer is a Mexican citizen living outside of Mexico with government permission.

These consular identification cards can be used to obtain drivers' licenses, open bank accounts, board planes and trains, enter many security areas, and carry on virtually every form of commerce within the US. Counterfeit *matricula consular*s are astoundingly easy to come by, selling for as little as $100.00 to $150.00 on the streets in Los Angeles.

News of the marriage between al Qaeda and MS-13 prompted the Honduran government to adopt a zero-tolerance policy, making membership in the street gang illegal and, upon arrest and conviction, punishable by up to twelve years in prison. However, MS-13 was quick to fight back. They simply began beheading scores of political victims, leaving notes on their bodies which read, "Idiots, the end of the world is approaching." Naturally, this dimmed law enforcement agents' enthusiasm for enforcing their zero-tolerance policy.

Sleeper Agents:
Relying on this marriage of convenience, literally thousands of sleeper agents, referred to as "Special Interest Aliens (SIA's) have entered the US with the help of MS-13 and MS-18. These SIA's countries of origin are not in Central and South America, but from Saudi Arabia, Syria, Iran, Pakistan, Afghanistan, Egypt, Somalia, Yemen, Jordan, Lebanon and Iraq -- countries that pose major national security concerns to the US. Virtually overnight, the illegal immigrant passageway, once known as "Cocaine Alley," became littered with discarded Muslim prayer cloths, pages from the Qur'an, copies of Arabic newspapers, etc., prompting US border patrol agents to rename the passageway, "Terrorist Alley."

In 2003 alone, US Border Patrol agents apprehended 4,226 SIA's, and during the first nine months of 2004, they arrested 6,022, indicative of an alarming increase. But, since US prison space is at a premium, most were merely booked, given a hearing date, and released. Needless to say, more than ninety-five percent (95%) failed to appear for their scheduled hearing. When Border Parol agents and State law enforcement officers complained, they were admonished that their practice of rounding up these SIA's who appear to originate from the Middle East merely displays an attitude of cultural insensitivity and racial profiling. A recent report by the US Department of Homeland Security (DHS) reveals that forty-five thousand and eight (45,008) SIA's released between 2001 and 2005, have disappeared, melting into the general populace of the US.

The Mara Salvatrucha/al Qaeda Threat:
September 28, 2004, the Washington Times published an article claiming that a top al Qaeda lieutenant met with leaders of the violent Salvadoran criminal gang MS-13, with roots in Mexico and the United States -- including a stronghold in the Washington DC area, to seek their assistance in infiltrating the US - Mexico border.

Mara Salvatrucha members are not only actively involved in smuggling aliens, drugs and weapons, members in America also have been tied to numerous killings, robberies, burglaries, car-jackings, extortion, rapes and aggravated assaults -- including at least seven killings in Virginia, and a machete attack on a 16-year-old in Alexandria that severely mutilated his hands. The Salvadoran gang, MS-13, is thought to have established a major smuggling center in Matamoros, Mexico, just south of Brownsville, Texas, from where it arranges transportation into the United States for illegal aliens -- SIA's -- from countries other than Mexico.

Authorities say al Qaeda terrorists take advantage of the lack of detention space within the Department of Homeland Security that has forced immigration officials to release non-Mexican illegal aliens back into the United States. Adnan G. El Shukrijumah, a key al Qaeda cell leader for whom the U.S. government has offered a five million dollar ($5,000,000.) reward, was recently spotted in Honduras, meeting with leaders of El Salvador's notorious Mara Salvatrucha (MS-13) gang. Immigration officials claim this gang has smuggled thousands, if not tens of thousands, of Central and South Americans -- mostly gang members -- into the United States. U.S. authorities have also confirmed that al Qaeda operatives have been in Tegucigalpa planning attacks against British, Spanish and U.S. Embassies.

Known to carry passports from Saudi Arabia, Trinidad, Guyana and Canada, **El Shukrijumah** sought meetings with the Mara Salvatrucha gang leaders who control alien-smuggling routes through Mexico and on into the United States. El Shukrijumah, 29, who authorities said was in Canada last year looking for nuclear material for a so-called "dirty bomb" and El Shukrijumah, a former southern Florida resident and pilot, are thought to have helped plan the September 11 attacks, and were among seven suspected al Qaeda operatives identified by Attorney General John
Ashcroft as being involved in plans to strike new targets in the United States.

Mr. Ashcroft said at the time that El Shukrijumah posed "a clear and present danger to America." Robert Morales, a prosecutor for Guatemala, indicated to The Globe that some Central American gang members are seeking refugee status in Canada. Superintendent of the Canadian Royal Canadian Mounted Police, integrated gang task force, John Robin, stated in a recent interview:

"I think [gang members] have a feeling that police here won't treat them in the harsh manner they get down there (in the US)." Robin noted that Canadian authorities "want to avoid ending up like the U.S., which is dealing with the problem of Central American gangsters on a much bigger scale."

Connecting the Dots:
To connect the dots and correlate all of this to biblical end-time prophecies, consider the following facts:

- Scripture refers to the enemies of the church as the Lawless Ones, and state that while the Lawless One(s) themselves will not appear until the end-time, their work, supported by Satan, had, during the first century, already gone forth in the world (2 Th).

- For apparently very different reasons, Satan; Iran and its allies; al Qaeda and its radicalized Islamic allies; and the Mara Salvatrucha gangs, all advocate the overthrow of every present form of civil government.

- Contrary to the nations represented by beasts emerging from the sea, the beast John describes as ascending from the earth (Rev 13), is to be a kingdom without boundaries (covering the whole earth). Satan's kingdom of darkness, Iran's Islamic Kingdom under Sharia Law, and the al Qaeda/Mara Salvatrucha marriage, all envision worldwide domination.

- The demonic triad: the dragon, the beast and the false prophet, will be allies in the great battle against God (Rev 16). Satan comes as a thief to steal, kill and destroy (Jn 10:10). These are common goals of Satan, Iran and al Qaeda/Mara Salvatrucha.

- The demonic triad are depicted as spewing forth evil spirits which, like frogs, cover the whole earth (Rev 16:13,14). History bears out their united, demonic assault against every nation.

- They will make war against the church (Rev 16). Satan; Iran and her allies; and al Qaeda/Mara Salvatrucha are united in their quest to silence the Gospel of Christ and destroy the Christian church.

- **John says they are men who will be recognized by a 'mark' on their right hand or forehead** (Rev 13:16), and that the number of said mark is either 666 or 616.

  - ✓ **MS-18 members are recognized by tattoos on their right hand** that are either 6-6-6, or in Roman Numerals X-V-III, both equaling 18 and both fulfilling (Rev 13:18).

- ✓ **MS-13 members are recognized by tattoos on the forehead** depicting either MS, MS-13; or by the Roman Numerals X-!-!!, equaling 13.

John, the apocalyptic prophet, describing their demonic onslaught against the world, said: *"Out of the smoke [rising from the abyss] locusts came down upon the earth and were given power like that of scorpions of the earth. ... The locusts looked like horses prepared for battle ... and their faces resembled human faces. Their hair was like women's hair ... They had as king over them the angel of the Abyss, whose name in Hebrew is Abaddon, and in Greek, Apollyon"* (Rev 9:3-11).

Referring to the Greek, the phrase, *"Out of the smoke locusts came down upon the earth,"* the word translated *smoke*, is *kap-nos'* which refers to something that drifts in on the breeze, like smoke or an odor; and the word translated *locusts*, refers to a flying insect. These flying insects, John says, have a sting like a scorpion, the Greek word for scorpion (*skorpios*), meaning to pierce or sting.

The word *mara*, employed by the MS-13 and MS-18 gangs, means gang in Caliche, and stems from the word *marabunta*, the name of a species of large, fierce wasps, indigenous only to South America, and its sting can be fatal. Consider the parallel between this and the deathstalker scorpion, common to the region where John resided when he wrote the Revelation. Importantly, John does not identify the beings that come against the earth as scorpions. Rather, he states that they are given power like that of a scorpion, apparently employing the sting of a scorpion as a means for identifying the flying insect he saw, since the Salvatrucha is indigenous only to South America.

John says: *"The locusts looked like horses prepared for battle."* The Greek word for *looked like, (homoioma)*, refers to something that is abstractly similar, i.e., a vague resemblance, likeness or similitude. In other words, the being ascending (or drifting) from the abyss vaguely resembled a horse, or horseman, prepared for battle. Then, to make sure that his readers did not confuse these creatures with horses, John said: *"Their faces resembled human faces. Their hair was like women's hair."*

Members of the MS-13 and MS-18 gangs are commonly depicted with shaved heads, however, these pictures are generally of gang members who have had their heads shaved because they are incarcerated or on parole, and not permitted to exhibit gang appearances, wear gang related clothing, use gang gestures, etc. In sharp contrast, when in their home environment, these same gang members (other than those involved in the 'skinhead' movement) more often than not sport long, often unkempt, hair.

Bringing the prophecy given him to a conclusion, John says: *"They had as king over them the angel of the Abyss, whose name in Hebrew is Abaddon, and in Greek, Apollyon."* According to many published police reports, these gang members -- criminals involved with the drug trade -- are commonly engaged satanic worship, practice satanic abuse of their victims, offer sacrifices to Satan, even bringing children into the world for the express purpose of offering them as sacrifices to Satan.

Satanism Unmasked:

Satanism is really the exaltation of a person's own self. It's claiming one's self to be God, much like Lucifer did. It's example is depicted in several places in the Bible, the clearest example being in Isaiah 14.

The popular Satanist 'faith' was founded by Anton Szandor LaVey in 1966. He wrote the book, the "Satanic Bible" to outline the basic tenets of their beliefs. Basically, **they hold ego gratification to be paramount of all human activities.** They despise charity towards the weak and embrace the strong.

Satan worshippers are resolute in their determination to commit crimes against society and social order, which they despise. Teen Satan worshippers often arrange themselves in gangs they call "Covens", since it sounds more 'cool' than referring to themselves as 'gang' members. These 'covens' are usually led by smalltime criminals who operate them to meet young women, and to develop posses of other youth, who they commission to perform crimes for their benefit.

As these youth grow up, they will stop at nothing to demonstrate their individual power and supremacy. In a recent Russian police raid, they arrested eight members of a Satanic gang after they killed, roasted and ate, four other youths! The four teens that were killed were plied with alcohol before each was stabbed 666 times, then had their hearts, genitalia, breasts and limbs removed. The gang drank some of their blood, then roasted and ate some of the meat as part of a satanic ritual, after which they buried the remains under an inverted cross.

The prophet, John, says that the attack against mankind will ascend from the abyss, or bottomless pit (Rev 9:2), which in Greek is (*abussos - phrear*), literally referencing a bottomless cistern or well, used as a prison. He says that the fallen angel, whom he also refers to as a star fallen from heaven, is given a key, which he uses to open this prison, allowing flying creatures to ascend and strike man. This same terminology, we learned from the Book of Enoch, described the return of the Watchers -- the fallen angels who took human wives and had children by them: offspring who were the Nephilim -- the giants of old.

The apostle, Paul, warned of such things, saying: "***The secret power of lawlessness is already at work**; but the one who now holds it back will continue to do so till he is taken out of the way. And then the lawless one will be revealed, whom the Lord Jesus will overthrow with the breath of his mouth and destroy by the splendor of his coming.* **The coming of the lawless one**

will be in accordance with the work of Satan displayed in all kinds of counterfeit miracles, signs and wonders, and in every sort of evil that deceives those who are perishing" (2 Th 2:7-10).

To make certain that the church recognized the lawless ones, John wrote: *"This calls for wisdom. If anyone has insight, let him calculate the number of the beast, for it is man's number. His number is 666/616"* (Rev 13:18).

Since world domination is the goal, and the works of lawlessness (rebellion or terrorism) are the weapons of their warfare, is there any doubt that the alliance of Iran, the radicalized Islamic terrorists, and the members of MS-13, MS-18 and similar gangs, will welcome the coming lawless ones?" Being empowered by Satan, they will have supra-human strength and perform counterfeit signs and wonders. If they are willing to engage in human sacrifices, exterminate those they disagree with, and have children solely for human sacrifice, will they not welcome the return of the Watchers, who Micah identifies as the Lawless Ones?

Reflecting on this, we are reminded of an incident that demonstrates the accuracy of Paul's words. Two of our friends unwittingly became involved with 'the lawless ones' when the husband took his retirement fund and purchased an established wrecker service. After having invested their life savings in the business, they learned that it had been serving as a shield to cover up a drug-smuggling, drug-dealing, prostitution ring.

One of their most 'lucrative' business transaction involved trading drugs to prostitutes who then bore children for them to sell at auction! Even worse, the infants who because of disability or uncomliness failed to sell, were used for human sacrifice!

When this couple discovered the real nature of the business they had invested in, and tried to sell it, their 'employees' turned against them -- shooting their livestock, damaging their property and threatening their lives. In the end, their demonically motivated employees secured ownership of the business for less than ten cents on the dollar.

Our friends only recourse was to come out of retirement, go back to work, and turn over to law enforcement, a list they had compiled of nearly 100 lawless ones involved in the illegal trafficking.

Should there be any doubt in your mind that such things are happening, and are predicted to increase, it should be removed by the evidence we present in the next chapter.

CHAPTER TWENTY-FOUR
OUT OF THE ABYSS

"The fifth angel sounded his shofar; and I saw a star that had fallen out of heaven onto the earth, and he was given the key to the shaft leading down to the Abyss. He opened the shaft of the Abyss, and there went up smoke from the shaft like the smoke of a huge furnace; the sun was darkened, and the sky too, by the smoke from the shaft. Then out of the smoke onto the earth came locusts, and they were given power like the power scorpions have on earth" (Rev 9:1-3 CJB).

The Timing:
Within this Scripture are several keys for determining: **the timing of this event; the identity of the one who opens the abyss; the nature of the abyss, the events that occur when the abyss is unlocked; who or what ascends out of the abyss; and the physical location of the abyss.**

John begins the revelation of this particular event, writing: *"The fifth angel sounded his shofar ..."* This event occurs after the unnumbered multitude, who have washed their robes in the blood of Christ, are identified as those who have come out of the great persecution [tribulation] (Rev 7:9-14). Those coming out from (or having endured) the great persecution, appear -- from this Scripture -- to include all those who have washed their robes in the blood of Christ. The dialogue concerning these saints immediately follows the sealing of the 144,000, identified as being 12,000 from each of the twelve tribes of Israel.

To understand **the meaning of the 144,000**, we must consider the times and the culture referenced. To Old Testament Hebrews, the number 12 represented governmental and covenental completeness and perfection. The Hebrew economy and sociopolitical structure was not as complex as that of our day, so their need for large numerical values was not the same as it is today. The numerical value of 1,000, and multiples thereof, was the highest numerical value they employed. Thus, the 144,000 who were sealed symbolized the highest imaginable number from each of the twelve tribes, representing to the Hebrews, complete completeness, or perfect perfection.

The act of their being sealed is also very symbolic.
Ancient scrolls were sealed with wax that was embossed with the ring of the king or officer of the court, and was to be opened only by the party to whom it was addressed. Scrolls often had a number of seals, so that when one was opened, only that portion of the scroll was readable until the next seal was removed. Referring back to our Scriptural context, this event occurred after the sixth seal of (Rev 9:1-3) had been opened, but prior to the opening (or breaking) of the seventh seal. As we have previously noted, the number six (6) represents mankind -- particularly fallen man, whereas the number seven (7) represents divine perfection, spiritual completeness and restoration.

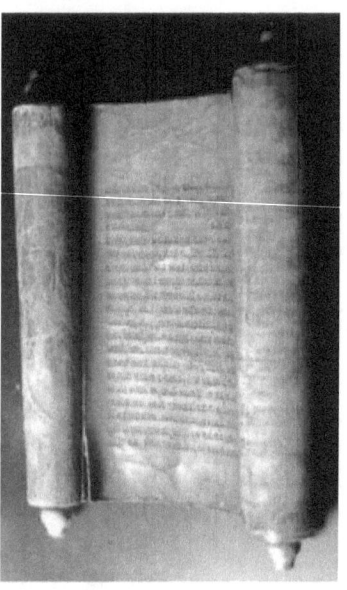

Events Marking the Opening of the 7th. Seal:
The era represented by the sixth seal, ended when the veil between the Holy and the Most Holy chambers, in Herod's Temple, was rent (torn) from the top to the bottom. This event occurred at Jesus' crucifixion when He declared from the cross, "It is finished." At that moment, the plan for the restoration of mankind, through the Hebrew nation and the Levitical Priesthood ended. At that same moment, the church age commenced with the Melchizedek Priesthood being restored to earth. Concerning this event, Christ's role in implementing the church and restoring the Melchizedek Priesthood, the author of the Book of Hebrews, wrote:

"If perfection could have been attained through the Levitical priesthood (for on the basis of it the law was given to the people), why was there still need for another priest to come — one in the order of Melchizedek, not in the order of Aaron? For when there is a change of the priesthood, there must also be a change of the law. He of whom these things are said belonged to a different tribe, and no one from that tribe has ever served at the altar. For it is clear that our Lord descended from Judah, and in regard to that tribe Moses said nothing about priests. And

what we have said is even more clear if another priest like Melchizedek appears, one who has become a priest not on the basis of a regulation as to his ancestry but on the basis of the power of an indestructible life. For it is declared: "You are a priest forever, in the order of Melchizedek." (Heb 7:11-17).

Only after this event could it be said that the saints had "washed their robes in the blood of Christ." Having birthed the church by restoring the Melchizedek Priesthood, Christ's work for the saints, is described in the final words of Revelation 7, just prior to the opening of the seventh seal. *"For the Lamb at the center of the throne will be their shepherd; he will lead them to springs of living water. And God will wipe away every tear from their eyes"* (Rev 7:17).

At this point in the events being revealed to John, the seventh seal is opened. The solemnity of this event was marked by a period of silence in heaven: *"When he opened the seventh seal, there was silence in heaven for about half an hour"* (Rev 8:1). When the seventh seal is opened, there are seven angels who appear, each having a trumpet.

After this, another angel appears, who has a golden censer filled with incense representing the prayers of the saints -- apparently referring to those innumerable saints who had washed their robes in the blood of Christ. This angel then fills the censer with fire and hurls it to the earth (Rev 8:5). This act is followed by peals of thunder, rumblings, flashes of lightning and a great earthquake.

The Great Tribulation:
This act appears to introduce the great tribulation period of the end times, since when each of the seven angels sounds his trumpet, great woes (tragedies, miseries, anguish) occur upon the earth. This fact is confirmed by the words of John, who, after describing the aftermath of the sounding of the fourth angel's trumpet, wrote: *"As I watched, I heard an eagle that was flying in midair call out in a loud voice: "Woe! Woe! Woe to the inhabitants of the earth, because of the trumpet blasts about to be sounded by the other three angels!"* (Rev 8:13). It is the first of these last three angels -- the fifth angel -- who introduces the event this chapter focuses on: the opening of the abyss.

We know that this is describing the end-time events, since when the sixth angel sounds his trumpet, the seven last plagues are poured out upon the earth, which is just prior to the second coming of our Lord and Savior, Jesus Christ -- Whose coming is announced by seventh angel blowing his trumpet. John confirms this, writing: *"But in the days when the seventh angel is about to sound his trumpet, the mystery of God will be accomplished, just as he announced to his servants the prophets"* (Rev 10:7). This mystery concerns Christ and His Body, the church (Eph 5:32), and is Christ in us, the hope of glory (Col 1:26,27).

The one with the key:
The key to the abyss is given to the star that had fallen from heaven. *"I saw a star that had fallen from the sky to the earth. The star was given the key to the shaft of the Abyss"* (Rev 9:1). This 'star' unquestionably represents Lucifer (now known as Satan), for Isaiah wrote: *"How you have fallen from heaven, O morning star, son of the dawn! You have been cast down to the earth, you who once laid low the nations! You said in your heart, "I will ascend to heaven; I will raise my throne above the stars of God; I will sit enthroned on the mount of assembly, on the utmost heights of the sacred mountain. I will ascend above the tops of the clouds; I will make myself like the Most High." But you are brought down to the grave, to the depths of the pit"* (Is 14:12-15).

The Abyss:

John says that Satan was given the key to the shaft of the abyss (Rev 9:1b). Referring to the Greek, Satan is given the key *(kleis)*, [literally the ability to unlock], the pit *(phrear)*, [literally a hole in the ground, i.e., a cistern, used as a prison], the one the one identified as the abyss *(abussos)*, [figuratively a fathomless deep, or bottomless inferno].

Several key facts are presented here:

- Satan is given the ability to unlock the abyss;
- The abyss is fathomless in its depth;
- The abyss is an inferno;
- The opening to the abyss is a shaft.

These keys to the precise identity of the abyss and its location, are discussed later in this chapter.

Events Occurring When the Abyss is Opened:
When the abyss is unlocked, smoke rises, as from a great furnace. It is important to understand that this is not actually speaking of smoke since the Greek word for 'as' is *(hos)*, meaning [in a manner similar to.] The Greek word translated "great furnace" is *(megalees kaminos)*, meaning [an exceedingly great, mighty or strong, furnace, or inferno.]

The King James Translation says "The sun and sky were darkened by the smoke from the abyss" (Rev 9:2). The Greek for this reads *(skotoo ho light)*, meaning [the light was obscured.] Remember, Jesus is the light of the world (Jn 8:12; 9:5) and it is Satan who opens the abyss, allowing something like smoke to obscure the sun and sky. This suggests that when Satan is allowed to unlock the abyss, letting what is trapped therein ascend, the Gospel of Jesus Christ will be obscured or veiled.

The apostle, Paul, comments on this very situation, saying: *"And even if our gospel is veiled, it is veiled to those who are perishing. The god of this age has blinded the minds of unbelievers, so that they cannot see the light of the gospel of the glory of Christ, who is the image of God"* (2 Co 4:3-4). Satan is clearly the 'god of this age' whom Paul identified as the one who crucified Christ:

"We do, however, speak a message of wisdom among the mature, but not the wisdom of this age or of the rulers of this age, who are coming to nothing. No, we speak of God's secret wisdom, a wisdom that has been hidden and that God destined for our glory before time began. None of the rulers of this age understood it, for if they had, they would not have crucified the Lord of glory" (1 Co 2:6-8).

Beings From the Abyss:
John said: *"Then out of the smoke onto the earth came locusts, and they were given power like the power scorpions have on earth"* (Rev 9:3). The beings that arise from the abyss are likened to locusts, the Greek word being *(akris)*, literally meaning, [to light on the top of vegetation]. These beings, according to the Greek, light (or appear) upon the whole earth *(eis ho gthay)*. Power was given them as scorpions have. The word 'power' is the Greek *(exousia)*, meaning [superhuman influence].

This power is similar to the power of *scorpions* a Greek word meaning [to pierce.] These beings are commanded to hurt nothing, nor to hurt any person, except those who are not sealed with the seal of God, which is identified as the indwelling Holy Spirit (Eph 4:30). These beings that rise from the abyss have a ruler -- the angel of the abyss, whose name in Hebrew is Abaddon (the destroying angel), and in Greek, Apollyon (the destroyer), a clear reference to Satan.

The apostle, Paul, also identifies those who this fallen angel (Satan) rules, saying: *"For our struggle is not against flesh and blood, but against the rulers, against the authorities, against the powers of this dark world and against the spiritual forces of evil in the heavenly realms"* (Eph 6:12). Referring to the Greek, it says: *"we wrestle against the chief among the powers (magistrates); against the ruler,"* [the Greek word used here for ruler is *(kosmokrator),* an epithet referring to Satan]. We struggle *"against the shady ones, against the (pneumatikos), supernatural spirits of wickedness of the heavens."* In other words, our struggle is against Satan, the chief, or ruler, of the supernatural spirits of wickedness of the heavens (the fallen angels).

When Satan is allowed to unlock the abyss, those under his rule, the fallen angels, will ascend to torment all who are not sealed by the seal of God -- the Holy Spirit. They ascend and strike the earth a single profound blow that will impact mankind for 150 years. This is the Watchers, the fallen angels who took wives of the children of men in the antediluvian world (Gen 6:1-4). According to the prophecy of Gen 6:4, they returned again after the flood.

Throughout the Old Testament, we read of giants, beginning with Nimrod, founder of ancient Babylon. David killed the last of the giants in the land of Canaan, however there are multiple biblical prophecies that indicate they will return again. Jesus himself, indicated that they will return in the last days, saying the latter times would be like the days of Noah. [For more information on this, see "Mysteries of the Bible: The Primeval Era", J.V. And P.M. Potter, Advocare Publishing, 2009.]

The Location of the Abyss:
John says this fallen angel (Satan) was given the key to the shaft of the abyss. If the abyss represents the fathomless, bottomless inferno, what might the shaft represent? Remember, the words in the original text referencing the 'bottomless pit' refers to a well, or cistern, used as a prison. In times of antiquity, it was a fairly common practice to use dry cisterns as prisons, the only access to the cistern being the well shaft descending from the surface. Prisoners were lowered down this shaft (well) into the cistern below. Then, when (and if) released, they were lifted back up through that same shaft.

The apocalyptic prophet, John, said: *"I saw three evil spirits that looked like frogs; they came out of the mouth of the dragon, out of the mouth of the beast and out of the mouth of the false prophet. They are spirits of demons performing miraculous signs, and they go out to the kings of the whole world, to gather them for the battle on the great day of God Almighty"* (Rev 16:13-14).

Drawing on the information presented in previous chapters, which identify: the beast as Iran, the false prophet as radicalized Islam, and the dragon as Satan -- who rules over the demons and fallen Watchers -- consider the following bit of history:

Islam & The Abyss:
The Islamic religion originated in the early seventh century AD, was founded by the false prophet, Muhammad, in the area known today as Saudi Arabia. Muhammad wrote the Islamic holy book, the Koran, which he claimed was revealed to him by the angel Gabriel. This new religion enjoyed rapid growth among the various nomadic tribes, unifying them and giving them an identity which endured until Muhammad's death.

Following Muhammad's death in 632 AD, Islam an theological split occurred, dividing Muslims into two main sects which remain to this day -- the Shiites and the Sunnis. The split between these groups focused on the issue of succession: i.e., who had the right to assume rule and interpret the Koran. Shiites maintained that only biological descendants of Muhammad can be infallible to rule and interpret scripture. In contrast to this, the Sunnis believe that any believer is qualified to rule, as long as there is general agreement among their religious scholars.

The formal split between these sects occurred on a battlefield near modern day Karbala, on October 10, 680. During this battle, the Shiite leader, Hussein -- a direct descendant of Muhammad -- was killed and decapitated. Following this event, there was a succession of Imams (leaders) all descendants of Ali and Fatima -- who were direct descendants of Muhammad. Each Imam interpreted the Koran somewhat different from his predecessor until the twelfth Imam, after which there was to be no further changes. This gave rise to what is known as the "Twelver Shiite Islam", which is considered the official religion of Iran.

This twelfth Imam's name was Abul Qasim Muhammad, also known as Muhammad al-Muntazar, meaning "Muhammad, the Awaited One", born in 868. When Abul Qasim Muhammad's father, Imam Hasan al-Askari, died, the religious scholars, unaware of the birth of his son, Abul Qasim Muhammad, approached the elder Imam's brother, Ja 'far, asking him to serve. But, as they were entering the house of the deceased, preparing to lead the funeral prayers, a young boy suddenly stepped forward and said: *"Uncle, stand back! For it is more fitting for me to lead the prayers for my father than for you."*

Following the funeral, people asked about the boy's identity but none seemed to know him. The boy was never seen again, and Shiite tradition maintains that from that moment on, he went into occultation, or hiding.

It is this doctrine of 'occultation' [a translation of the Persian word, *Ghayba*], that plays a central role in Shiite theology -- the belief in the coming Mahdi. According to their tradition, this boy -- the Mahdi -- went into hiding, thereby creating a dilemma for Imam succession. This was eventually resolved by adopting the doctrine of "The Hidden Imam." This doctrine teaches that this boy (the Twelfth Imam) never died, but went into hiding (disappearing in occultation) for an unspecified period of time.

The Shiite Twelvers believe that the hidden Imam, the Mahdi, went into hiding to protect his life from hostile enemies. They believe that he presently lives in a well -- a well that's located in a cave, in Samarra, Iraq. So strong is their belief, a Mosque was constructed over the cave, and the cave was partitioned off, guarded by a gate named the Gate of Occultation. Shiites regularly gather in the rooms of this cave to pray for the Mahdi's return. The time of his return, they believe, has been decreed by Allah, and they expect that when he returns, he will vindicate his faithful followers, leading them to victory in battle over all infidels, thereby ushering in a perfect Islamic society of justice and truth.

After the subsequent political partition of the region, and the creation of the Republic of Iraq, Iranian Shiites declared that the hidden imam was miraculously unocculted, or unhidden, for a brief moment, after which he took up residence in the Well of Request, in Jamkaran, Iran. Immediately, the Iranians began making preparation for his reappearance in Teran. Ahmadinejad, then the Mayor of Teran, donated $17 million, toward the construction of the Jamkaran Mosque, and authorized unlimited state expense to improve the designated route the Mahdi would take through the city.

According to Shiite tradition, if a faithful Muslim visits the mosque on forty Tuesdays in succession, without missing one, he will see the Mahdi. For believers, their devotion to the Mahdi is real. Tears stream down the cheeks of those waiting at the well for his reappearance, sometimes numbering more than 2,000, as their eyes stare upward, arms held wide open to receive Allah's promised salvation. Even President Ahmadinejad visits the site, and with the other devout Muslims, writes prayers and oaths on little slips of paper, then drops them down the well to be received -- and answered -- by the Mahdi.

Today, all sects of Islam believe in the Mahdi and look forward to his reappearance as their savior, who will appear at the end of days. His return, Muslems believe, will be preceded by cosmic chaos, including worldwide war and bloodshed. After a cataclysmic confrontation between Islam and the evil and darkness of infidels who reject Islamic Sharia Law, the Mahdi -- they believe -- will lead the world into an era of universal peace. Muslems believe that the Mahdi will be accompanied by Jesus Christ, who will be his lieutenant. Equally disturbing, is their belief that it is Muslims' divine assignment to provoke the cataclysmic chaos thus hastening the Mahdi's appearance, ushering in this 'utopian' age.

Ahmadinejad is a high ranking member of the clandestine, mystical Hojjatieh Society, a closed fraternity founded in 1953, by Sheikh Mahmoud Halabi, a radical cleric from the holy city of Mashhad, in northeastern Iran. The Hojjatieh Society is referred to locally as The Cult of the Mahdi. Its members believe they can encourage the Mahdi's appearance by stirring up chaos and conflict. This perilous precept is known as *taajil*, and the groups theology, when compared to the established Muslem faith, is comparable to the lunatic, end-time fringe group, the Branch Davidians, led by David Koresh, and mainline Christianity.

Shortly after his inauguration as president of Iran, in August, 2005, Ahmadinejad declared that the *real* ruler of Iran was the

Twelfth Imam, and that all government policies and decisions would be guided by the express objective to hasten his coming.
Ahmadinejad went on to say that he believes his role as president, *"demands contributing to the outbreak of chaos in the Middle East, sufficient in scope to usher in Armageddon and the Day of Judgment."*

Will Ahmadinejad be the one to lead Radical Islam to evoke a time of chaos and conflict sufficient to usher in Armageddon and the day of judgment, or are we to look for another? Before you answer this question, consider the evidence provided in the next chapter.

CHAPTER TWENTY-FIVE
THE GATHERING STORM

"Multitudes, multitudes in the valley of decision! For the day of the Lord is near in the valley of decision" (Joel 3:14).

The Old Testament Prophet, Joel, is a fairly obscure Hebrew, of whom little is known other than from a small book of prophecy, bearing his name. The Book of Joel, believed to have been composed sometime between the ninth and seventh centuries BC, contains two divisions: the first division provides a historical account of a plague of locusts and a drought that ravaged Judah. These events, according to Joel, were symbolic of God's final judgment.

The second division is a prophecy concerning God's final judgment of all the nations of the earth, which Joel said would be preceded by an outpouring of The Spirit of God. **"I will pour out my Spirit on all people.** *Your sons and daughters will prophesy, your old men will dream dreams, your young men will see visions. Even on my servants, both men and women, I will pour out my Spirit in those days. I will show wonders in the heavens and on the earth, blood and fire and billows of smoke. The sun will be turned to darkness and the moon to blood before* the coming of the great and dreadful day of the Lord. And everyone who calls on the name of the LORD will be saved" (Joel 2:28-32).

Joel's Prophecy and Pentecost:
Following his crucifixion and resurrection, Jesus "...*appeared to them [his disciples] over a period of forty days and spoke about the kingdom of God. On one occasion, while he was eating with them, he gave them this command: "Do not leave Jerusalem, but wait for the gift my Father promised, which you have heard me speak about. For John baptized with water, but in a few days you will be baptized with the Holy Spirit"* (Ac 1:3-5).

On this occasion, "*when they met together, they asked him, "Lord, are you at this time going to restore the kingdom to Israel?" He answered them: "It is not for you to know the times or dates the Father has set by his own authority. But you will receive power when the Holy Spirit comes on you; and you will be my witnesses in Jerusalem, and in all Judea and Samaria, and to the ends of the earth"* (Ac 1:7-8).

The apostles, together with more than one hundred other devoted disciples, trekked from the Mount of Olives -- the Mount of Christ's ascension -- back to Jerusalem, where they ensconsced themselves in the upper (or inner) room to fast, pray and wait. "*Then they returned to Jerusalem from the hill called the Mount of Olives, a Sabbath day's walk from the city. When they arrived, they went upstairs to the room where they were staying. Those present were Peter, John, James and Andrew; Philip and Thomas, Bartholomew and Matthew; James son of Alphaeus and Simon the Zealot, and Judas son of James. They all joined together constantly in prayer, along with the women and Mary the mother of Jesus, and with his brothers"* (Acts 1:12-14).

Then it happened! *"When the day of Pentecost came, they were all together in one place. Suddenly a sound like the blowing of a violent wind came from heaven and filled the whole house where they were sitting. They saw what seemed to be tongues of fire that separated and came to rest on each of them. All of them were filled with the Holy Spirit and began to speak in other tongues as the Spirit enabled them"* (Acts 2:1-4). On that day of Pentecost, after receiving the indwelling of Holy Spirit, the apostles left the upper room and went throughout Jerusalem, preaching to the crowds in "other tongues, as the Spirit enabled them" (Acts 2:4).

Some in the crowds listened, but others made fun of them and accused the apostles of being drunk. Peter responded to the crowds, saying: *"These men are not drunk, as you suppose. It's only nine in the morning! No,* **this is what was spoken by the prophet Joel:** *"'In the last days, God says, I will pour out my Spirit on all people.* *Your sons and daughters will prophesy, your young men will see visions, your old men will dream dreams"* (Ac 2:15-17).

The import of this event: its being the fulfillment of the second division of Joel's prophecy, and clarifying where mankind is on the clock of time, was immediately evident to Peter, who shared his revelation with Christ's other apostles and those who were accusing them of being drunk. Joel warned: *"Multitudes, multitudes in the valley of decision! For the day of the Lord is near in the valley of decision"* (Joel 3:14 KJV). This warning can be better understood by referring to the Hebrew text. Other versions have translated this more appropriately, to read: *"Huge numbers of soldiers are gathered in the valley where the Lord will hand down his sentence. The day of the Lord is near in that valley"* (NIrV).

This warning, sounded by Joel, is echoed in Zechariah's end-time prophecy (Zec 14:1-9), and John's apocalyptic prophecy (Rev 16). All seem to be warning of the same event -- the day of judgment and the battle of Armageddon. In our last chapter, we focused on the identity of the three evil spirits who conspire together to incite this great battle: The Dragon (Satan); the Beast (Iran and her allies), the false-prophet (radical Islamics), accompanied by the Lawless Ones [represented by Mara Salvatrucha (MS-13 and MS-18)].

In this chapter, we will endeavor to verify that Iran will be the prime-mover in this great conflagration, and go on to identify its allies. To accomplish this, we turn to another eschatological prophet -- Ezekiel.

Commencing in Eze 38:1, we read: *"The word of the Lord came to me saying, "Son of man, set your face toward Gog of the land of Magog, the prince of Rosh, Meshech, and Tubal, and prophesy against him, and say,' Thus says the Lord God, "Behold, I am against you, O Gog, prince of Rosh, Meshech, and Tubal. And I will turn you about, and put hooks into your jaws, and I will bring you out, and all your army, horses and horsemen, all of them splendidly attired, a great company with buckler and shield, all of them wielding swords; Persia, Ethiopia, and Put with them, all of them with shield and helmet; Gomer with all its troops; Beth-togarmah from the remote parts of the north with all its troops — many peoples with you. 'Get ready; be prepared, you and all the hordes gathered about you, and take command of them"* (Eze 38:1-7 NASB).

Nearly 2,600 years ago, the prophet, Ezekiel prophetically identified the member nations of a nefarious alliance that would, in the last-days, embark on a crusade that would make the holocaust pale in comparison -- the complete elimination of the Jewish race and her allies. These allied nations, we might refer to as God's "Ten Most Wanted" since Ezekiel highlights the fact that God has declared He is against them (38:3), and against their plan to obliterate the nation of Israel.

Chapters 38 & 39 of Ezekiel describe a future invasion of Israel by a vast coalition of nations -- nations that are her neighbors and surround it. Listening to current news, it's not too difficult imagine that this invasion prophesied over 2600 years ago, could be fulfilled in our lifetime. Prior to describing this great conflagration, Ezekiel made a prediction that seemed very unlikely -- the regathering of the Jews to the homeland of Israel (Chapters 36-37). Following Rome's invasion of Jerusalem in 70 AD, the Jewish people had no homeland, but were scattered throughout the world for 19 centuries.

Until May 14, 1948 there was no nation of Israel to invade. On that date, by proclamation of the United Nations (Resolution 181), the Nation of Israel was established -- And, on that same date, the Jewish people declared independence for Israel as a united, sovereign nation -- for the first time in 2,900 years! On that same day, the United States issued a statement recognizing Israel's sovereignty. Only hours beforehand, a United Nations mandate had expired, ending British control of the land. During the following 24-hour span of time, foreign control of the land of Israel formally ceased, Israel declared its independence, and its independence was acknowledged by other nations. Modern Israel was literally born in a single day, in precise fulfillment of the prophecy that God would roll back Israel's reproach and reestablish her in a single day (Is 66:7-8; Zec 3:9).

Isaiah's prophecy said the nation's rebirth would take place before there were labor pains. This is precisely what happened -- she was reborn just hours before the labor pains began. A movement called Zionism began in the 1800s, whose express purpose was to encourage Jews worldwide to move back to Israel, which at that time was called Palestine. Within hours after the declaration of independence in 1948, Israel was attacked by the surrounding countries of Egypt, Jordan, Syria, Lebanon, Iraq and Saudi Arabia.

With the nation of Israel now a reality, the labor pains had begun and the stage was set for the war that will usher in the tribulation and the rise of the Antichrist; a war that will end with the destruction of Israel's enemies by God Himself. With the rebirth of the nation of Israel, the surrounding nations aligned themselves within hours, to form a coalition against her. God had in ages past revealed this very thing, through His prophets. Now, the fulfillment of those prophecies seems more plausible than at any other time in history.

The first name on the register of "God's Ten Most Wanted List" is Gog. He is evidently a king over one or more of the nations mentioned, since the prophet, Amos, said: *"Thus the Lord showed me, and behold a swarm of locusts were coming, and, behold, one of the young devastating locusts was Gog, the king"* (Am 7:1). Comparing this with John's apocalyptic prophecy, which reads: *"And [the locusts] had a king over them, which is the angel of the bottomless pit, whose name in the Hebrew tongue is Abaddon, but in the Greek tongue hath his name Apollyon,"* it would appear that Amos and John are speaking of the same being -- **the demonic king, the prince of**

the powers of darkness -- **Satan.** Two other key players in this end-time prophecy are Rosh and Persia.

Persia as Iran:
As discussed in previous chapters, there is little doubt that the 'Persia' mentioned here is the ancient counterpart to modern day Iran. The first known civilization in Persia was that of the Elamites, who settled in the region sometime before 1200 BC Tribes of Medes and Persians wandered into this geographical region beginning about 900 BC. The Medes created the first state on the Persian plateau about 700 BC. The Median nation reached its zenith in the late 600's BC. The Persians gradually gained eminence over the Medes, and in 549 BC, Cyrus the Great, overthrew the Medes and developed a confederacy with the Persian people. It was this confederacy -- the Medes and Persians -- who conquered ancient Babylon in 539 BC.

The names Persia and Iran were used interchangeably to identify the Aryan empire until 1935, when the name was officially changed to Iran, a word meaning "Land of the Aryans." Modern Iran, as successor to Persia, is home to the oldest continuous civilization, and is the 18th largest country in the world.

The Land of Magog:
The kingdoms, or nations over which Gog (Satan) is to rule, are ten [God's Ten Most Wanted!] (Ez 38:1-7). The first nation mentioned, is the land of Magog. The more commonly accepted identity for Magog is in Central Asia. Jewish historian Josephus said, *"Magog founded the Magogians, called Scythians by the Greeks. The Scythians were a nomadic tribe who inhabited the ancient territory from Central Asia across the southern part of ancient Russia."* Today this area is inhabited by the former Soviet Republics of Kazakhstan, Kyrgyzstan, Uzbekistan, Turkmenistan, Tajikistan, and perhaps, the northern parts of Afghanistan.

All of these nations comprising the land of Magog have one thing in common - Islam. Militant Islam has been on the rise in these countries since the fall of the Soviet Union, when Islam no longer had to be practiced secretly. Radical Islamic groups such as the Islamic Renaissance Party, the Islamic Movement of Uzbekistan, and Hizb ut-Tahrir al-Islam, are working collectively to reunite central Asian nations and ultimately the entire Muslim world -- to breathe life into, or reestablish, the ancient Persian (Assyrian/Aryan) empire. It is out of this region of the world that a leader will arise, having as his express goal and objective, the reunification of the ancient Babylon (Assyrian/Aryan) empire and the destruction of Israel.

One more, very fascinating fact is that Gog and Magog are both mentioned in the Koran -- the Muslim holy book. The Koran refers to a battle called the War of Yajuj and Majuj; and these are specifically identified as Gog and Magog. According to Islamic doctrine, Gog and Magog were two tribes of Turks who spread corruption throughout the earth during Abram's time. Islamic mythology states, that to keep them in check, they were enclosed behind a great barrier, over which they have tried in vain to climb over, dig under, or break through, for centuries.

Islamics claim that they will remain their until Allah decrees their release. At Allah's decree, the barrier will collapse and Gog and Magog will pour forth in all directions, rushing into the land of Israel. Then, according to Islamic teaching, Jesus Christ (who returns as Mohammed's lieutenant), will pray against them and they will be smitten with a plague. If this sounds a bit familiar, it should be. Mohammed plagiarized that imagery from Ezekiel 38, making a few minor changes to fit his cosmology. Interestingly, these nations, which Muslims believe -- based on prophecies in the Koran -- will be destroyed, are all present-day Muslim nations.

Rosh as Russia:
Some versions of the Bible translate the Hebrew word 'Rosh' in verse 3 as a noun referring to a place in Russia. The least credible support for this view is that Rosh sounds like the modern-day name Russia and Meshech sounds like Moscow. In these versions, they treat Rosh as a proper name. The Greek translation translates Rosh as the proper name Ros. Because the ancient Sarmations were known as the Ras, Rashu, and Rus, and inhabited Rasapu which is now Southern Russia, many feel this verse points to Russia as the prince of Rosh. Additional support cited for this view is that verses 6 and 15 indicate that Israel's invasion will emanate out of the remote parts of the north. Russia is North, and quite remote by ancient standards, to the land of Israel.

According to Ezekiel's prophecy, Russia's allies in this invasion are ancient places that today are in Central Asia (Magog), Iran (Persia), Libya (Put), Turkey (Meshech, Tubal, Gomer, and Togarmah), and Sudan (Cush) — all being Islamic nations. A recent article sheds some fascinating new light on this subject. Mark Steyn at SteynOnline recently presented some alarming statistics concerning the rapidly changing demographics in

Russia. According to Steyn, there are ten million people in Moscow, twenty-five percent (25%) of them Muslim! The ethnic Russians are older; the Muslims are younger. The ethnic Russians are already in a net population decline; while the Muslim population has increased by 40% during the last 15 years alone. Seven out of ten Russian pregnancies among ethnic Russians are intentionally aborted; while in some Muslim communities, the fertility rate is ten children per woman.

Based on these trends, most political sociologists extrapolate that **by mid 21st century the population majority within the Russian Federation will be Muslim.** But one doesn't need to extrapolate. The Toronto Star (Canada's biggest-selling newspaper and impeccably liberal) recently noted that **by 2015 Muslims will make up the majority of Russia's army.** What will happen then in Russia? A remorseless evolution into a majority Muslim state? A Bosnian-style civil war? The secession of a dozen or so of Russia's 89 federal regions? A Muslim military coup? None of us knows for certain. However, we should know enough to know that we don't know, and be concerned. The Russia of 15 years ago is already ancient history.

By 2050, Russia will be, not only the principle Muslim nuclear power, it will be the first Muslim nation with a permanent seat on the United Nations Security Council. Assuming the accuracy of these facts, or anything even close, one can understand Russia's growing socioeconomic alliance with Iran and their future -- end-times -- participation in an Islamic invasion of Israel. Russia will be the ideal leader of this Islamic invading force, since Russia itself has the greatest military power and will be dominated by Muslims.

This is something that no one could have envisioned even a decade or two ago. Yet, it is happening right now, right before our very eyes. No one knows when the battle of Gog and Magog, mentioned in Ezekiel 38-39 will occur, but if several years in the future, this dramatic demographic shift in Russia could very well play a key role in setting the stage for this major end-time event.

Meshech and Tubal:
Meshech and Tubal (vs 2 and 6), were the names of the 5th and 6th sons of Japheth, the son of Noah (Genesis 10:2). Ezekiel 27:13 also identifies Meshech and Tubal as commerce trading partners with Tyre (Modern Lebanon). It's likely that Meshech and Tubal refer to the ancient Moshi/Mushki and Tubalu/Tibareni who dwelled in the area around the Black and Caspian Sea in

Ezekiel's day. Today these nations would include part of our modern country of Turkey, parts of Southern Russia and Northern Iran. All areas with a Muslim majority.

Gomer and Beth-Togarmah:
Verse 6 adds Gomer and Beth-Togarmah to the coalition. "Gomer" was the first son of Japheth. The Gomerites were the ancient Cimmerians. Expelled in 700 BC from the southern steppes of Russia, they settled in the area that is today called Turkey. "Togarmah" was the 3rd son of Gomer. Beth -- at the beginning of the name, Beth-Togarmah, is the Hebrew word for 'house' or 'place of'. In Ezekiel's time there was a city in Cappodocia (Modern Turkey) known as Tegarma, Tagarma, Til-garimmu, and Takarama.

The probability that four of the names mentioned in Ezekiel are now in Turkey makes a pretty strong argument for Turkey being a part of the horde that will invade Israel. Current circumstances in that country also lend credibility to this view. Since the breakup of the Soviet Union, Turkey has been making inroads into Central Asia (Magog). Turkey is also linked to Central Asia both ethnically and linguistically, and has a growing number of political parties that support opposition to Israel, establishment of a Turkish Islamic Republic, and the worldwide rule of Islam.

Persia, Cush and Put:
Verse 5 brings three more names into the mix. God tells us that "Persia, Cush and Put will be with them". Persia, as we have already noted, is pretty easily identified as modern day Iran. The ancient kingdom of Cush in Ezekiel's life time was the land just south of Egypt on the Nile River. Today this land is included within the nation of Sudan. Sudan is home to the National Islamic Front, and is ruled by an Islamic military dictatorship, a strong supporter of Iraq. Sudan was home to Osama bin Laden from 1991-1996, and has been the harborer of countless Islamic terrorist groups. Sudan easily fits into the coalition. It is already a close allies with Iran, trading military supplies for docking rights on the Red Sea shipping routes.

Ancient Put was the land just west of Egypt, the region known today as Libya. Libya has been another sponsor of terrorism -- a nation who openly refuses to recognize Israel's right to exist. When a military coalition against Israel is formed, Libya won't have to be asked twice to join.

Verse 6 adds *"and many people with you."* The nations listed specifically are all somewhat distant from Israel. By adding the phrase, "and many people with you", God may have been identifying those nations and peoples closer in proximity to Israel, who will join the Jihad. Some of these nations that might join the alliance are Iraq, Syria, Jordan, and Egypt. All of them are Islamic nations, all committed to the establishment of a worldwide Islamic kingdom, and all supportive of the destruction of Israel. No doubt all of these would join such a coalition, should such an opportunity present itself.

ANCIENT NAME	MODERN NATION	EXPLANATION
Rosh	Russia or Chief	Ancient Sarmatians known as Rashu, Rasapu, Ros, and Rus. OR Translated as the adjective Chief.
Magog	Central Asia and Russia	Ancient Scythians - Islamic southern republics of the former Soviet Union with a population of 60 million Muslims. This territory could include modern Afghanistan and Southern Russia North of the Black Sea.
Meshech	Turkey	Ancient Muschki and Musku in Cilicia and Cappadocia.
Tubal	Turkey (also southern Russia and Iran)	Ancient Tubalu in Cappadocia.
Persia	Iran	Name changed from Persia to Iran in 1935.
Ethiopia (Cush)	Sudan	Ancient Cush, south of Egypt.
Put	Libya	Ancient Put, west of Egypt.
Gomer	Turkey	Ancient Cimmerians - from the seventh century to first century BC in central/western Anatolia.
Beth-togarmah	Turkey	Til-garimmu - between ancient Carchemish and Haran (southern Turkey).
Many peoples with you	Other Islamic nations	Possibly Iraq, Syria, Jordan, and Egypt

The prophet, Joel, establishes some very important facts concerning this battle -- the time when Gog (Satan) and Magog (the end-times, Satanic kingdom, led by Iran and Radical Islam), together with the false prophet, march against Israel:

1. First, it is clear from the book of Joel, that these are end-time events, and that the 'end-times' commenced at the crucifixion of Christ and the birth of the church.

2. Second, salvation -- even to those aligned with the powers of darkness is still possible.

3. Third, There will be a tremendous outpouring of God's Spirit.

4. Fourth, the children of God will still be upon the earth when these events occur.

First ~ the timing ~ Joel says: *"Blow the trumpet in Zion; sound the alarm on my holy hill. Let all who live in the land tremble, for the day of the Lord is coming. It is close at hand — a day of darkness and gloom, a day of clouds and blackness. Like dawn spreading across the mountains a large and mighty army comes, such as never was of old nor ever will be in ages to come"* (Joel 2:1-2).

"Before them the earth shakes, the sky trembles, the sun and moon are darkened, and the stars no longer shine. The Lord thunders at the head of his army; his forces are beyond number, and mighty are those who obey his command. The day of the Lord is great; it is dreadful. Who can endure it?" (Joel 2:10-11).

Second ~ concerning salvation ~ of those in the enemy's camp: *"Even now,' declares the Lord, 'return to me with all your heart, with fasting and weeping and mourning.' Rend your heart and not your garments. Return to the Lord your God, for he is gracious and compassionate, slow to anger and abounding in love, and he relents from sending calamity"* (Joel 2:12-13).

Those warring against this demonic horde, apparently enjoy initial success, for God says: *"Blow the trumpet in Zion, declare a holy fast, call a sacred assembly. Gather the people, consecrate the assembly; bring together the elders, gather the children, those nursing at the breast. Let the bridegroom leave his room and the bride her chamber. Let the priests, who minister before the Lord, weep between the temple porch and the altar. Let them say, 'Spare your people, O Lord. Do not make your inheritance an object of scorn, a byword among the nations. Why should they say among the peoples, 'Where is their God?''* (Joel 2:15-17).

In response to their petitions, the Lord responds: *"I will drive the northern army far from you, pushing it into a parched and barren land, with its front columns going into the eastern sea and those in the rear into the western sea. And its stench will go up; its smell will rise"* (Joel 2:20).

Third ~ a spiritual revival ~ after this ceasefire there will be a great spiritual revival: *"And afterward, I will pour out my Spirit on all people. Your sons and daughters will prophesy, your old men will dream dreams, your young men will see visions. Even on my servants, both men and women, I will pour out my Spirit* *in those days. I will show wonders in the heavens and on the earth, blood and fire and billows of smoke. The sun will be turned to darkness and the moon to blood before the coming of the great and dreadful day of the Lord. And everyone who calls on the name of the Lord will be saved; for on Mount Zion and in Jerusalem there will be deliverance, as the Lord has said, among the survivors whom the Lord calls"* (Joel 2:28-32).

Fourth ~ God's People are still on the earth
At this same time, it appears that the nations under Gog, Magog and Persia (Iran), who have assembled their forces in the plane of Megiddo, initiate their assault against Jerusalem. The fact that God's people are still upon the earth at this time, and what happens next, is the subject of the following chapter.

Chapter Twenty-six
The Conspirators' Evil Scheme

Scripture warns us that: *"Satan will be released from his prison and will go out to deceive the nations in the four corners of the earth -- Gog and Magog -- to gather them for battle. In number they are like the sand on the seashore. They marched across the breadth of the earth and surrounded the camp of God's people, the city He loves"* (Rev 20:8-9).

Christians shouldn't be deceived monkeys.

God's people should not be among those who are deceived. However, **to avoid Satan's deception, we must: *"Study to show ourselves approved, workmen that need not be ashamed, rightly dividing the word of truth"*** (2 Ti 2:15). Or, as translated in the New International Readers Version, *"Do your best to please God. Be a worker who doesn't need to be ashamed. Teach the message of truth correctly."* This is our endeavor, as we present what is to many, a new slant on these age old prophecies.

In our last chapter, we identified Gog, demonic director of the nations in the of alliance with Magog: Rosh, the chief prince of Meschech and Tubal, and Persia (Iran) and its allies (Cush, Put, Gomer and Beth Togarmah). We learned of the underlying philosophy that will be employed in the development of this alliance -- the "Axis of Evil" if you please.

Assault on Israel:
As the nations assemble, God prophetically addresses them

through the prophet Ezekiel, saying: *"Get ready; be prepared, you and all the hordes gathered about you, and take command of them. After many days you will be called to arms. In future years you will invade a land that has recovered from war, whose people were gathered from many nations to the mountains of Israel, which had long been desolate. They had been brought out from the nations, and now all of them live in safety. You and all your troops and the many nations with you will go up, advancing like a storm; you will be like a cloud covering the land"* (Eze 38:7-9).

A Devious Imagination:
As these nations advance against Israel, confident in their success, this evil conspiracy expands its vision, goals and objectives. Prophetically disclosing this, God -- through Ezekiel -- said: *"On that day thoughts will come into your mind and you will devise an evil scheme. You will say, "I will invade a land of unwalled villages; I will attack a peaceful and unsuspecting people — all of them living without walls and without gates and bars. I will plunder and loot and turn my hand against the resettled ruins and the people gathered from the nations, rich in livestock and goods, living at the center of the land"* (Eze 38:10-12).

Referring to the Hebrew for clarity, we read: *['W haayaah bayowm hahuw' ya 'luw d baariym al l baabekka w chaashabtaa mach shebet raa aah]*, the literal translation being: **('it shall happen in that same era, exceedingly evil, cunning, or devious, imaginations will arise in your heart, and you will fabricate an evil thing')**; *['wchaashabtaa 'e'leh al 'erets p raazowt 'aabow' hashog tiym yosh beey laab etach, kulaam yoshbiym b 'eeyn chowmaah uwbriyach uwd laatayim 'eeyn laahem lishlol shaalaal w laaboz baz]*, literally meaning **('boastfully, you shall challenge, or charge, "come, let us rise up (or against the country of unwalled villages that dwell at rest (or in idleness) securely'); the whole [nation] dwelling without locked walls of protection, nor gates, to plunder, take spoil, and catch prey')**;

Continuing on, we read: *[l haashiyb yaad kaa al ch raabowt nowshaaqbot w 'el- 'am m' ucaap migowyim 'oseh miqneh w qinyaan yosh beey 'al- tabuwr haa 'aarets]*, the translation being **('then return to the starting point through the devastated places once inhabited towards the nation (or people) left behind; the Gentiles (or heathen) rich in substance and riches, that dwell above (or over) the summit in the middle land')**.

Unraveling the Divisive Scheme:
Taken together with the preceding verses, that describe the invasion of Israel, it would seem that the best translation of this section of Scripture might be: *"During the invasion of Israel, an exceeding evil, cunning, devious imagination will rise up in your heart, and you will devise an evil scheme. Boastfully, you will charge (your troops), saying: 'Come, let us advance against the nation of unwalled cities, that dwell in idleness and security -- that whole nation dwelling without walls of protection or locked gates; to plunder, spoil and take prisoners; then return through the devastated places once inhabited, towards the nation left behind, that dwell over the summit, in the middle land."*

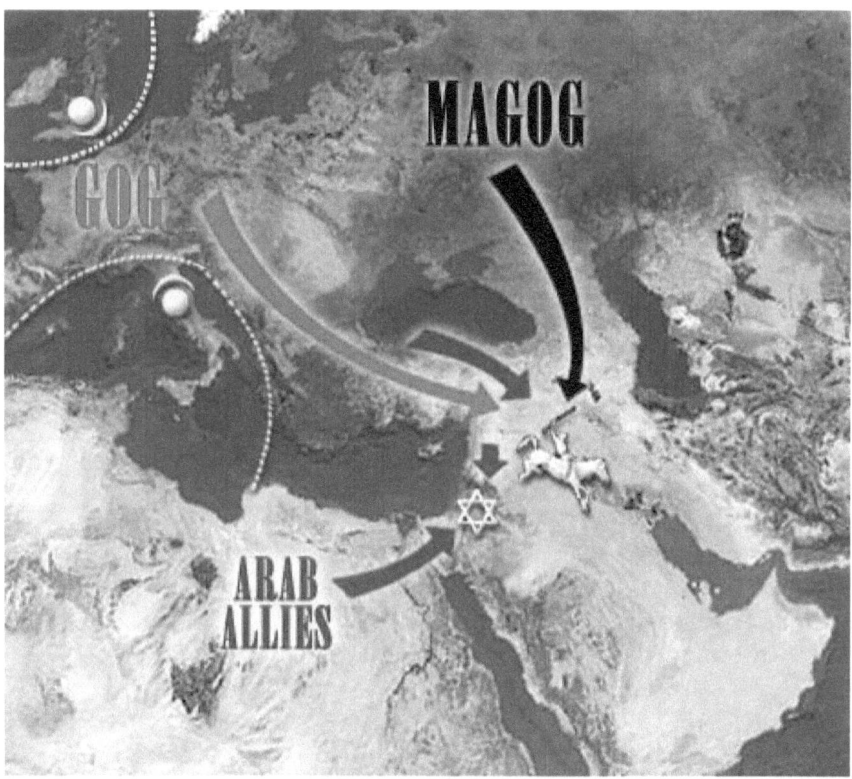

The first portion of this prophecy (Eze 38:1-9) should be crystal clear in light of our previous identification of the nations aligned against Israel, and current events. The battle-plan has already been drawn; only the timing of its implementation is uncertain. Iranian President, Mahmoud Ahmadinejad, a devout Shiite Muslim, and member of the clandestine, mystical Hojjatieh Society, that is referred to locally as The Cult of the Mahdi, declared after his inauguration in August, 2005, that the *real* ruler of Iran was the Twelfth Imam, and that all government policies and decisions would be guided by the express objective to hasten his return.

Ahmadinejad has stated publicly he believes his role as president, *"demands contributing to the outbreak of chaos in the Middle East, sufficient in scope to usher in Armageddon and the Day of Judgment."* He repeats in every public venue that will give him audience, that Israel has no right to exist, and should be wiped from the face of the earth. He has described Israel as a *"disgraceful blot"* that should be *"wiped off the face of the earth"*. Addressing a conference, titled "The World Without Zionism, he said: *"Anybody who recognizes Israel will burn in the fire of the Islamic nation's fury."*

This radical idea is not limited to Ahmadinejad. Over the last two decades, some Islamic nations, and international corporations, have begun removing Israel from their maps of the Middle East. The map of Palestine, distributed by the Palestinian Authority, depicts Jerusalem on its maps, however, the limits of the State of Israel have been omitted.

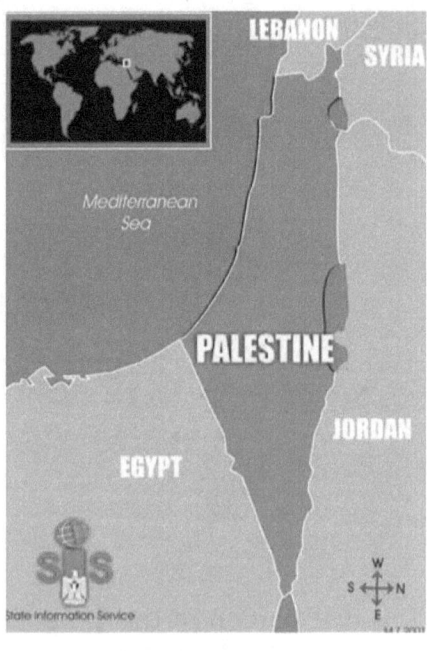

The Middle East map prominently displayed by the UN on November 29, 2005 at a public gathering at UN Headquarters, in the presence of all top three UN officials, the Secretary General, and the Presidents of the UN Security Council and the General Assembly, purported to be a "map of Palestine." Israel, a UN member state for 56 years, was not even on the map. Even the UN General Assembly partition lines, established on November 29, 1947 marking a Jewish and Arab state, which predate this 1948 map, do not appear.

Among major corporations, the British airline, BMI., has removed Israel from the electronic maps displayed to its passengers, claiming the reason being "to avoid offending Muslim passengers. However, these same maps depicted Mecca. The web sites of German auto-makers, BMW and Mercedez-Benz both display Middle East maps that leave the State of Israel unidentified.

"Palestinian Minister of Foreign Affairs Mahmoud al-Zahar, defends Iran's and Hamas' ultimate goal of destroying Israel and founding an Islamic state. In an address before the UN, he said: *"I dream of hanging a huge map of the world on the wall at my Gaza home which does not show Israel on it. I hope that our dream to have our independent state on all historic Palestine lands (including Israel) will become real one day. I'm certain of this because there is no place for the state of Israel on this land."*

Iranian and Israeli relations have materially deteriorated since the fall of the Pahlavi dynasty during the Islamic Revolution in 1979. Subsequent to the Islamic Revolution, led by Ayatollah Ruhollah Khomeini, Iran severed all diplomatic and commercial ties with Israel. Today, its government does not even recognize Israel as a country and refers to its government as the "Zionist regime". The lands delimited on most Middle East maps as Israel, are referred to by Iran, as "Occupied territories". The Iranian grand leader, Ayatollah Ruhollah Khomeini, has called Israel a *"cancerous tumor" that should be removed from the region."* He has emphasized that *"Palestine belongs to Palestinians, and the fate of Palestine should also be determined by the Palestinian people."*

Saber-rattling:

Since 1979, the conflict between Israel and Iran and its allies continues to intensify. During a military parade in Tehran, September 22, 2009, Iran's new 1,300 kilometer range Shihab-3 missiles bore the slogan **"Israel must be wiped off the map."** At an August, 2009 conference at Tehran University organized by the student committee for the Support for the Palestinian Intifada, a group headed by Hojatoleslam Ali Akbar Mohtashami-Pur, the final resolution called for *"annihilation of the Zionist regime."* During the August conference, speakers praised Palestinian suicide bombings in Israel, referring to them as "martyrdom operations."

"Israel is not standing idly by while Iran intensifies its threats. Israel is ready to bomb Iran's nuclear sites. The Israeli military has prepared itself to launch a massive aerial assault on Iran's nuclear facilities within days of being given the go-ahead by its government leaders. Israel wants the world to know that if its forces are given the green light, they can strike at Iran in a matter hours. They are presently making preparations at every level for this eventuality. Their message to Iran and to the world, is that their threat is not just empty words."

Iran is committed to continue its uranium concentration activities, leading to the development of weapons of mass destruction, to complement its growing arsenal of long-range missiles; making Iran a very real and present danger. Israel is equally determined to prevent Iran from developing nuclear weapons -- committed enough to take military action if necessary. In fact, according to Israeli governmental and military officials, military intervention is no longer a question of *'if necessary'*, but, *'when necessary'*.

No doubt the greatest deterrent against Israel taking action, that has served to maintain the current stalemate between Iran and Israel is a surprisingly little known fact beyond the Middle East. **Outside of Israel, the largest Jewish population concentration in the world is in Iran.** The size and influence of the Jewish population is so significant that the Iranian Jewish community is guaranteed one seat on the Majlis, Iran's consultative assembly. However, this fact does not insure a reciprocal deterrent.

According to Mohammed Ali Jafari, commander of the Army of the Islamic Revolution: *"If Israel military agresses against sovereignty and independence of the Islamic Republic of Iran, the country will use its right, established under international law which inevocably establishes the right to defend its sovereignty by all lawful means available to it. Moreover, if such aggression is penetrated, the United Nations will be obliged to repulse such an aggression towards its sovereign member".*

Israel, already a member of the nuclear nations, is believed to have an inventory of at least 200 nuclear warheads, and it is committed to prevent Iran from joining the international nuclear league. On September 17, 2009, Ze'ev Elkin, a member of the Israeli Knesset (Israel's legislative branch of government), said that the proposed delivery by Russia of S-300 missiles may prompt Israel to strike Iran. Should that happen, Russia will no doubt come to the aid of Iran -- one of its most important trade partners. The US will unquestionably respond, standing with Israel.

Gog and Magog vs. America:
Such an occurrence might well provide the impetus to redirect the military actions of Iran, Russia and their allies, as foretold by Ezekiel: *"During the invasion of Israel, an exceeding evil, cunning, devious imagination will rise up in your heart, and you will devise an evil scheme. Boastfully, you will charge (your troops), saying: 'Come, let us advance against the nation of unwalled cities, that dwell in idleness and security -- that whole nation dwelling without walls of protection or locked gates; to plunder, spoil and take prisoners."*

America in Prophecy:

Ezekiel's description of -- *'a nation of unwalled cities that dwell in idleness and security ... Without protective walls or locked gates'* -- fittingly describes the United States of America. Russia and Iran share a common interest in limiting the political influence of the United States in Central Asia. This common interest led the Shanghai Cooperation Organization -- an intergovernmental  mutual-security organization, founded in 2001 in Shanghai by the leaders of China, Kazakhstan, Kyrgyzstan, Russia, Tajikistan, and Uzbekistan -- to extend observer status to Iran in 2005, and full membership in 2006. Iran's relations with the organization, which is dominated by Russia and China, represents the most extensive international diplomatic ties that Iran has espoused since the 1979 revolution. Remarkably, the member nations of this organization include those very nations Ezekiel identifies (Eze 38:1-7).

Beyond this socioeconomic connection, there is an even more compelling reason for Iran, Russia and their allies to attack the US. All of the nations identified by Ezekiel are now, or soon will be, under Islamic rule. The Jewish people have once again been targeted for extinction -- this time by radical islamics. Iranian President Mahmoud Ahmadinejad, a rabid Holocaust denier, frequently calls for the annihilation of the State of Israel. During his recent speech before a United Nations meeting in September, 2009, Mahmoud Ahmadinejad denounced the Holocaust and Israel's "genocide, barbarism and racism" carried out under Germany's Hitler, calling it nothing but lies promulgated by Britain, the U.S., and others.

All the while, Ahmadinejad appears intent to replicate the tragedy he denies. Even his rhetoric mirrors that of Hitler before the Holocaust. Ahmadinejad is physically a small man, standing a diminutive five feet, four inches who smiles incessantly as he squintingly stares through his slit-like eyes. But, behind his inconsequential appearance, resides the heart of an international, genocidal terrorist. This bantam man of a man, Ahmadinejad, President of Iran, is probably the most dangerous man on earth.

Ahmadinejad has declared that: *"Islam is ready to rule the world. We must prepare ourselves to rule the world." ... " The wave of the Islamic Revolution will soon reach the entire world." ... "Israel is an illegitimate regime, there is no legal basis for its existence." ... "Anybody who recognizes Israel will burn in the fire of the Islamic nation's fury." ... "Israel must be wiped off the map" ... "The establishment of the Zionist regime was a move by the world oppressor against the Islamic world. The Islamic world will not let its historic enemy live in its heartland."*

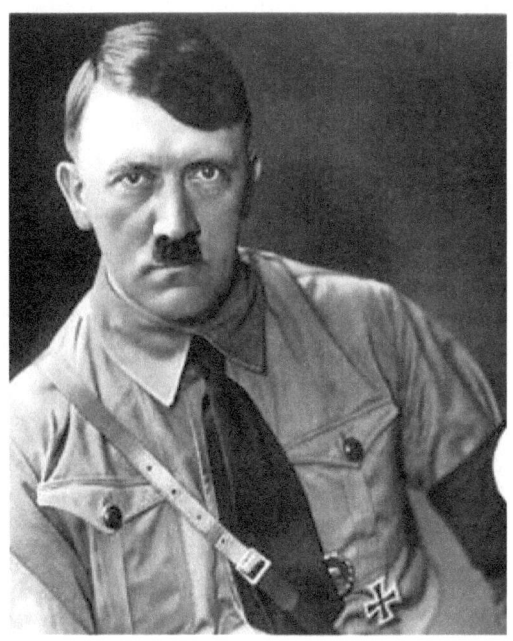

Keeping these comments in mind, listen to what Hitler said: *"I believe today that I am acting in the sense of the Almighty Creator. By warding off the Jews I am fighting for the Lord's work."* - Adolph Hitler, Reichstag speech in 1936. ... *"The personification of the devil as the symbol of all evil assumes the living shape of the Jew." ... "If only one country, for whatever reason, tolerates a Jewish family in it, that family will become the germ center for fresh sedition. ...*

"If one little Jewish boy survives without any Jewish education, with no synagogue and no Hebrew school, it [Judaism] is in his

soul. Even if there had never been a synagogue or a Jewish school or an Old Testament, the Jewish spirit would still exist and exert its influence. It has been there from the beginning and there is no Jew, not a single one, who does not personify it."

The Greatest Threat Since Hitler:
President Mahmoud Ahmadinejad's anti-Semitic and anti-Israel views place him and the Iranian regime among the foremost threats to Jews and the state of Israel since Hitler. His disregard for Israel is evident in the title he has given the nation, referring to Israel as the "little Satan"; while reserving the title, "the Great Satan", for the United States. To Ahmadinejad, Israel and the United States are the two principle roadblocks that must be obliterated to make way for the return of the Mahdi -- the Twelfth, Hidden Imam.

Hitler's and Ahmadinejad's radical anti-Semitism, their insatiable quest for power and world domination, and their deceiving diminutive stature, are not the only similarities between Ahmadinejad and Hitler. They share one other characteristic that reveal the depth of their sinister minds and malignant acts. Both **Hitler and Ahmadinejad, are themselves, of Jewish heritage.**

Hitler's Heritage:
Hitler's paternal grandfather was Jewish, a fact that was first disclosed in Paris, shortly before the Second World War. Hitler's cousin had tried to borrow money from him to finance his gambling habit and was rejected. In revenge, he broke the following story to the media.

- June, 1837: Alois (Adolf Hitler's father) was born, the illegitimate son of 42 year old Maria Schickelgruber, believed to have been impregnated by the 19 year old son of the prominent Frankenberger Jewish family of Graz, for whom Maria had been employed as a sewing-maid.

  Maria received financial support from the family up to Alois's birth, which, following Alois's birth was terminated with a substantial lump-sum payment.

  Alois' birth record in the parish baptismal register left the space for his father's name blank.

  Maria subsequently married a Johann Georg Hikler (Heider), who died before her son, Alois, began his career as an Austrian Customs Officer.

- 1868: Maria's son, Alois Hikler (Huetler/Heidler) had an illegitimate son.

- 1876: Alois' baptismal record at Dollersheim, Austria was amended by the parish priest, at the request of the seventy-seven (77) year old Nepomuk Hiedler, brother of the deceased J. G. Hikler (Hiedler), and attested to by two illiterate associates of dubious character, who testified that 'Alois' deceased foster-father, Johann Georg Hikler, had really been his biological father. [This was done to secure a career advantage for young Alois in the Austrian civil service.]

- 1880: Alois Hikler separated from his wife who was moneyed and fourteen (14) years his senior, and installed the barmaid of the Gasthaus, on the ground floor under his apartment, as his mistress.

- 1883: Alois' estranged wife died after which he married his mistress who, by this time, had already born him one child, and bears him one more before dying of tuberculosis two years later.

- 1885: Alois officially changed his surname to Hitler.

- C1886: Alois marries Klara Poizl, the seventh child of Nepomuk Hiedler's daughter Johanna, whose married name was Pölzl). She had worked for Alois as serving-maid before his separation from his first wife. He has six children by Klara (the first being born five months after their marriage, but only two survive their early years - Adolf and Paula).

- 1889: Saturday, April 20: In Brannau on the river Inn, Adolf is born, the fourth child of Klara.

- 1892: Alois, Adolf's father, is appointed to the Austrian Customs House in Passau, on the Bavarian side of the river Inn.

- 1900: Adolf, age eleven, graduates to the Realschule in Linz. He is forced to repeat his first year due to his low marks, his worst subjects being mathematics and German. He does a further year at the Realschule at Steyr near Linz. His teachers regard him as talented but lazy. The only class he places first in is Turnen (Physical Training).

- 1903: Alois dies of a stroke at Leonding near Linz, when Adolf is thirteen-years-old. His widow Klara, Adolf's mother, receives a generous pension and an educational allowance for her two children.

- 1909: Having by this time wasted his inheritances and educational allowance, Adolf takes up lodging in the Men's Home in the 20th Bezirk of Vienna, where he remains in seclusion, avoiding his Austrian military obligations, until 1913. During this time his anti-Semitism grows as he authors cheap anti-Semitic pamphlets and facilitates their general circulation.

- 1925: In Munich Germany, Adolf makes a final application to be deprived of his Austrian citizenship to avoid the possibility of deportation to Austria by the German police.

- 1946: October, in Nuremberg – while awaiting execution, Hans Frank [Hitler's attorney] confesses to a priest that after having been asked by Adolf Hitler to investigate his ancestry [after Hitler's nephew, William Patrick Hitler, had tried to blackmail him], he discovered Hitler's grandmother, Maria, had worked as a servant in Graz for a wealthy Jew named Leopold Frankenberger, who had a teenage son around 19 years old.

  According to Frank, the elder Frankenberger sent Maria regular child support payments until Alois was fourteen; the inference was that the payments were made because the younger Frankenberger had fathered Alois. Frank also claimed that there was a series of letters between Maria and the elder Frankenberger, which showed that the paternity of the younger Frankenberger was assumed by the correspondents. The letters were, understandably, never found.

- There is absolutely no indication that Alois' mother Maria even knew Hikler/Hiedler at the time of her son's conception; Quite the contrary. There is evidence that she lived in a different town (Graz) than Hikler/Heidler at the time of Alois' conception; and that; she received financial compensation for her pregnancy which, with its final settlement after the birth of Alois, was most certainly the price of her silence.

- This would make no sense at all, if it was a man whom she later married after the birth of Alois. But, it makes perfect sense if, in the strict social rules of that time, it was a person who would not -- or could not -- be named, such as the son and heir of her employer in Graz at the time of the boy's conception.

- Barring that cover-up then, the man history knows as Adolf Hitler might well have been known to us as Adolf Frankenberger, unless of course his name would have been too much an embarrassment to him and/or to his family.

The Image of the Beast: In mirror image fashion, Mahmoud Ahmadinejad is revealed to have Jewish past. According to a recent release in The Telegraph, Ahmadinejad's bitter hatred of Israel may stem from his desperately trying to hide his own Jewish past. The adjacent photograph of the Iranian president holding up his identity card during elections, March 2008, clearly shows that his family has Jewish roots. A close-up of the document reveals he was previously known as Sabourjian – a Jewish name meaning cloth weaver.

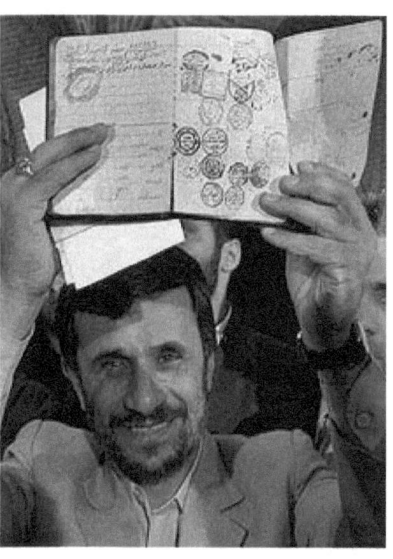

The short note scrawled on the card suggests his family changed its name to Ahmadinejad when they converted to Islam sometime after his birth. The Sabourjians traditionally hail from Aradan, Mr Ahmadinejad's birthplace, and their sir name derives from "weaver of the Sabour" -- the Sabour being the Persian name for the Jewish Tallit, or prayer shawl. His family name is included on the list of reserved names for Iranian Jews compiled by Iran's Ministry of the Interior.

Socio-cultural experts suggest that Mr Ahmadinejad's track record for hate-filled attacks against those of Jewish ethnicity stems from an overcompensation to hide his own past. Ali Nourizadeh, of the Centre for Arab and Iranian Studies, said:

"This aspect of Mr Ahmadinejad's background explains a lot about him. Every family that converts into a different religion takes a new identity by condemning their old faith. By making anti-Israeli statements he is trying to shed any suspicions about his Jewish connections. He feels vulnerable in a radical Shia society."

A London-based expert on Iranian Jewry said that the "jian" ending to the name, Sabourjians, clearly shows that the family had been religious-practicing Jews. *"He has changed his name for religious reasons, or at least his parents had,"* said an Iranian-born Jew living in London. *"Sabourjian is well known Jewish name in Iran."* A spokesman for the Israeli embassy in London said this information would not be drawn (recorded) on Mr Ahmadinejad's background. *"It's not something we'd talk about,"* said Ron Gidor, a spokesman.

The Iranian leader has not denied that his name was changed when his family moved to Tehran in the 1950's. However, he has never revealed what it was changed from, nor has he directly addressed the reason for their making the change. Relatives have previously indicated that a mixture of religious reasons and economic pressures forced his father Ahmad, a blacksmith, to change the family name, when Mr Ahmadinejad was aged four.

During his recent presidential debate, he was goaded while on television, to admit that his name had changed but he ignored the jibe. However after Mehdi Khazali, an internet blogger, called for a public investigation of Mr Ahmadinejad's ancestral roots, he was later arrested.

Unintentional Outcomes:
Hitler, driven by his boundless hatred toward his own kinsmen, actually played a key role in bringing to reality -- through unimaginable pain and suffering -- a homeland for the Jewish

nation. In an effort to assuage the horrors of the Holocaust and repatriate the Jewish people, the present Nation of Israel was born in a single day by proclamation of the United Nations, on May 14, 1948.

In remarkable imagery of the outcome Hitler's assault against the Jews, Iranian President, Mahmoud Ahmadinejad's obsession to facilitate the onset of Armageddon, is positioned to usher in the great and terrible day of the Lord (Joel 2:31), thereby making way for the Holy City, the home of the redeemed. There is another compelling reason why Iranian Present, Mahmoud Ahmadinejad is obsessed to destroy both Israel and the United States -- why he calls Israel, "Little Satan" and the United States, "The Great Satan." It is a reason that few, other than historians and practicing Jews, know much about. And, it is interwoven with Ahmadinejad's over-compensatory efforts to hide Jewish ethnicity.

The key to this Bible Mystery -- the United States' in biblical prophecy and end-time events -- is the focus of our next chapter.

Chapter Twenty-seven
The Diaspora

The Miracle of National Revival:
Much is said about the regathering of the Jewish people, and the restoration of their nation on their historic homeland -- the mountains of Israel. Indeed, the rebirth of Israel as a nation in a single day, was truly remarkable, clearly the handiwork of God. In contrast to this event, however, little has been written about or taught, concerning God's act of dispersing His chosen people throughout the nations, and His loving care and provision over them, during the nineteen centuries of their exile.

The ancient nation of Israel had more than sufficient warning that, unless she abandoned her idolatry and returned to God, her peoples would be scattered to the four winds. Speaking through his servant, Ezekiel, God had declared:

"Say to them, 'This is what the Sovereign LORD says: This oracle concerns the prince in Jerusalem and the whole house of Israel who are there.' Say to them, 'I am a sign to you.' "As I have done, so it will be done to them. They will go into exile as captives. ... I will scatter to the winds all those around him — his staff and all his troops — and I will pursue them with drawn sword. They will know that I am the Lord, when I disperse them among the nations and scatter them through the countries" (Eze 12:10, 14 & 15).

The prophet, Daniel, identified the reason for their disbursement, saying: *"Lord, you are righteous, but this day we are covered with shame — the men of Judah and people of Jerusalem and all Israel, both near and far, in all the countries where you have scattered us because of our unfaithfulness to you"* (Dan 9:7).

Although they were scattered, God continued to watch over them and care for them, as attested to by Ezekiel: *"Therefore say: 'This is what the Sovereign LORD says: Although I sent them far away among the nations and scattered them among the countries, yet for a little while I have been a sanctuary for them in the countries where they have gone"* (Eze 11:16-17).

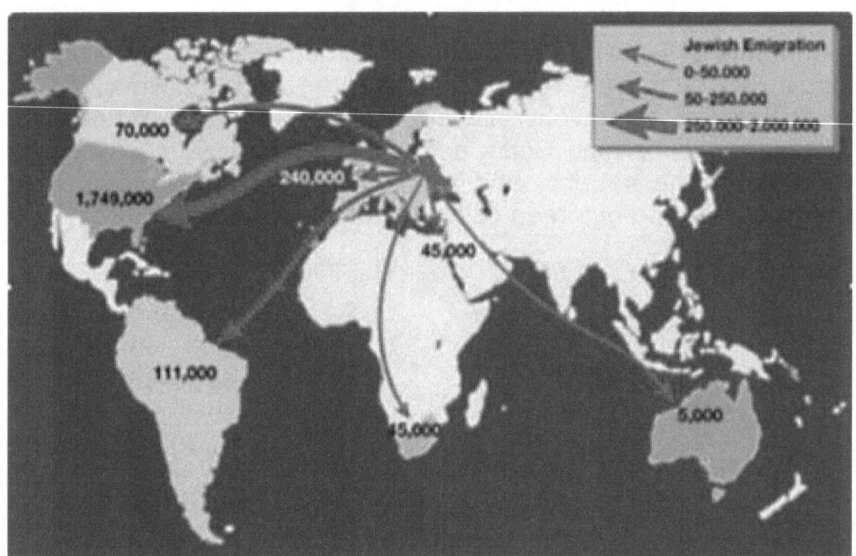

In God's omnipotence, He even used the Diaspora (Jewish dispersion) to spread the glad tidings of good news, to the Gentiles, wherever they went. *"James, a servant of God and of the Lord Jesus Christ, To the twelve tribes scattered among the nations: Greetings. Consider it pure joy, my brothers, whenever you face trials of many kinds"* (Jas 1:1,2); [and] *"Those who had been scattered preached the word wherever they went"* (Acts 8:4).

The Jewish presence outside of the Land of Israel is primarily the result of the expulsion of the Jewish people during the destruction of the First and Second Temple periods, and following the Bar Kokhba revolt. They later spread throughout the world by either migration or conversion. This migration, referred to as the Diaspora is commonly accepted to have begun with the 8th-6th century BC conquests of the ancient Jewish kingdoms, resulting in the expulsions of enslaved Jewish population.

A number of Middle Eastern Jewish communities were established then as a result of their host nations' tolerant policies and these remained notable centers of Torah life and Judaism for centuries to come. The defeat of the Great Jewish Revolt against Rome, in the year 70 AD and of Bar Kokhba's revolt in 135 AD against the Roman Empire notably contributed to the numbers and extent of the Diaspora.

Many Jews were merely scattered after losing their state, Judea, while others were sold into slavery throughout the empire. In 722 BC, the Assyrians under Shalmaneser V conquered the (Northern) Kingdom of Israel, resulting in many Israelites being deported to Khorasan. Since that time, well over 2,700 years ago, these 'Persian Jews' have lived in the territories of the modern day nation of Iran.

In 63 BC, Pompeii invaded Jerusalem, and Gabinius subjected the Jewish people to tribute. As early as the middle of the 2nd century BC, the Jewish author of the third book of the Oracula Sibyllina, addressing the "chosen people," wrote: *"Every land is full of thee and every sea."* The most diverse witnesses, such as Strabo, Philo, Seneca, Luke (the author of the Acts of the Apostles), Cicero, and Josephus, all mention that there were Jewish populations throughout the cities of the Mediterranean.

In 63 BC Palestine became subject to Rome. In that year the Roman general Pompeii marched on Jerusalem, and after a three month siege entered the city, went into the Temple, and even inspected the Holy of Holies — to the Jews, a terrible desecration of the Temple. He made Hyrcanus both high priest and local ruler, thus bringing the Hasmonean line to an end. During the next two troubled decades, Antipater emerged as the most powerful figure in Palestine, although he was never designated king.

Finally, in 40 BC, Herod, a son of Antipater, was named king of the Jews by Rome, although it was not until 37 BC that he entered Jerusalem and gained control of his kingdom. Herod was, politically speaking, the most competent Jewish king of this period, amply earning him the title, "Herod the Great," bestowed on him by historians. He was an able administrator, who loyally carried out the wishes of Rome. He kept the peace, reduced banditry in the land, and for his efforts was awarded additional territories to rule. His building endeavors were carried out on a lavish scale. Under his direction, massive public works projects were constructed, including: aqueducts citadels,, amphitheaters, the city of Caesarea, and most notably the new Temple in Jerusalem.

The temple, he restored to the grandeur of Solomon's time. Yet he never gained the approval of his Jewish subjects, who always regarded him as an alien. [After all he was an Idumean, or Edomite.] Herod dealt ruthlessly with real or suspected opponents, even having three of his own sons and his wife, Mariamne, murdered. The story of the massacre of the innocents (Matthew 2:16) is entirely characteristic of him. He died unmourned in 4 BC.

The New Testament dates the birth of Jesus from the reign of Herod (Mt 2:1); hence, the birth of Jesus must be dated in 4 BC or earlier. This chronological anomaly originated in the miscalculation of Herod's death by a fifth century Roman monk, Dionysius Exiguus, who was largely responsible for our present-day chronological system that dates events BC or AD (that is, before or after the birth of Jesus).

King Agrippa I (10 BC to 40 AD), in a letter to Caligula, enumerated that among the provinces of the Jewish Diaspora -- almost all the Hellenized and non-Hellenized countries of the Orient -- included Jewish settlements; and this enumeration was far from complete, since Italy and Cyrene were not included.

There is but scant information concerning the numerical significance of these diverse Jewish conglomerations. However, according to Josephus, outside of the Land of Israel and Babylonia, Syria had the densest Jewish population; particularly in Antioch, and in Damascus. It was in Damascus where, during the great insurrection, 10,000 Jews, (according to another version 18,000), were massacred. Philo gives the number of Jewish inhabitants in Egypt at that time as being 1,000,000; one-eighth of the nation's population. Alexandria was by far the most important Jewish community. Jews in Philo's time were inhabiting two of the five quarters (divisions) of the city.

To judge by the recorded accounts of wholesale massacres that occurred around 115 AD, the number of Jewish residents in Cyrenaica, at Cyprus, and in Mesopotamia were also very large. In Rome alone, at the commencement of the reign of Caesar Augustus, there had to be more than 7,000 Jews, since this is the number that escorted the envoys who came to demand the deposition of Archelaus. Finally, if the sums confiscated by the governor Lucius Valerius Flaccus in the year 62/61 BC represented the standard tax, a drachma per head for a single year, it would imply that the Jewish population of Asia Minor numbered 45,000 adult males, representing a total Jewish population of at least 180,000.

Roman orderly rule prevailed until the failed Jewish revolt of 66-70 AD, terminating in the capture of Jerusalem and the destruction of the Temple, the symbol of the national and religious life of Jews throughout the world. After this catastrophe, Judea formed a separate Roman province, governed by a legate, referred to at first as the "pro prætore," and later, "pro consule," who was also the commander of the army of occupation. The complete destruction of Jerusalem, and the settlement of several Grecian and Roman colonies in Judea, manifest the express intention of the Roman government to prevent the political regeneration of the Jewish nation.

Jewish revolt broke out in 66 AD and brought the Jews early hopes of success. However, it was put down by the overwhelming force of the Roman legions in 70 AD. At that time, Jerusalem was leveled and the Temple destroyed. Profound dislocations followed for the Jewish population, who were thenceforward obliged to function without the Temple and the associated religious ceremonies. Dislocations were also experienced by the Jewish Christians, for whom Jerusalem had been their center.

Years later, following a last desperate revolt by the Jews (132-135 AD), **a Roman colony was established on the ruins of Jerusalem, and a temple to Jupiter erected on the Temple Mount.** Jews were strictly forbidden to enter the city.

The sad separation between Jewish Christians and the Jewish synagogue, was finalized by the actions of Rome, who stipulated that Christians must renounce their belief in Jesus to remain in the city. [As is noted in the records of Jerusalem Conference (1) and Jerusalem Conference (2), the decision of Christ's apostles to approve a mission to the gentiles without the requirement of Torah observance, contributed to the ultimate separation between Christians and Jews.]

By 135 AD, the city of Jerusalem, now named "Ælia Capitolina," had become a Roman colony, a city that was markedly pagan boasting a temple to Jupiter, god of law and social order. Jews were even forbidden entrance to the city, under pain of death.

Long before these events occurred, God had declared, through His prophet, Isaiah, that when his chosen people were scattered, they would be called by a new name. *"The nations will see your righteousness, and all kings your glory;* ***you will be called by a new name that the mouth of the Lord will bestow"*** (Isa 62:2). ... *"The Sovereign Lord will put to death, those who forsake Him, but to **his servants he will give another [Hebrew 'acher, literally a strange] name**"* (Isa 65:15). In fulfillment of this prophecy, God's followers were given both a new secular and a new sacred name.

New Names:
As the fleeing Jews escaped up the face of Masada and over the Caucus Mountains, the Romans and their allies began referring to them as the Caucasians. A hundred or so years later, Christ's followers -- **"The disciples were first called Christians at Antioch" (Ac 11:26), and were no longer recognized as God's servants, but as His children**:

"How great is the love the Father has lavished on us, that we should be called children of God! And that is what we are! The reason the world does not know us is that it did not know him. Dear friends, now we are children of God, and what we will be has not yet been made known. But we know that when he appears, we shall be like him, for we shall see him as he is" (1Jn 3:1-2).

When the Roman army demolished Jerusalem, a great many Jews were killed; in addition, more than 90,000 were taken captive, including the famous historian Flavius Josephus who recorded the events of that era in his work, "Wars of The Jews". By 70 AD, According to him, Jerusalem and Judea were left desolate, most of its people either killed or taken into captivity -- unless they had earlier become refugees fleeing across the Caucus Mountains to remote lands. All who remained in Israel were ensconced in the defiant little garrison atop the mount at Masada, a fortress complex south of the Dead Sea, built by Herod the Great.

Thus, when the Temple was destroyed in AD 70 the period of the second exile began, referred to as the Diaspora. The Jewish people were soon scattered throughout the earth, and for the next 1900 years they had no right over, nor authority in, the land that God had given Abraham, Isaac, Jacob and their descendants.

During the Diaspora, the Jews outward migration accelerated. Meeting out the consequences for their rebellion, God declared that the garden spot of ancient Jerusalem, would become a wasteland -- a dry, parched land, barren of her peoples. *"I will strip her naked and make her as bare as on the day she was born; I will make her like a desert, turn her into a parched land, and slay her with thirst"* (Hos 2:3). The Jewish dispersion would be so complete, her peoples would forget their heritage as part of God's people, and take on a new name and new customs.

God declared further that: *"I will block her path with thorn bushes; I will wall her in so that she cannot find her way"* (Hos 2:6). Israel's inability to find her lovers and lose her way, God sovereignty used to redirect them to the lands He intended. Israel, now cut off from her sister nation, Judah, mingled with the peoples around her, so completely losing her way, she forgot both her heritage and customs.

However, God did not forsake them. He had promised, through His prophet, Ezekiel: *"But I will spare some, for some of you will escape the sword when you are scattered among the lands and nations. Then in the nations where they have been carried captive, those who escape will remember me — how I have been grieved by their adulterous hearts, which have turned away from me, and by their eyes, which have lusted after their idols. They will loathe themselves for the evil they have done and for all their detestable practices. And they will know that I am the Lord; I did not threaten in vain to bring this calamity on them"* (Eze 6:8-10).

Biblical historian, archaeologist, and educator, E. Raymond Capt has provided a very important archaeological link for the lost tribes of Israel, in his excellent work "Missing Links Discovered in Assyrian Tablets". In this work Capt has brought many fragments of information concerning the 'house of Israel' together. His work is based on the efforts of numerous researchers, historians, and archaeologists.

The conclusions Capt arrived at, based on his own and others' research, concerning the Behistun and Assyrian Tablet artifacts, is probably the single most important work concerning the identity of the 'Lost Tribes of Israel'. From a scientific point of view, he presents 'hard' evidence -- engraved in stone -- not just information from a biblical point of view. This scientific evidence is referred to as the "Jehu Stele" or "Black Obelisk". In 1846 AD, Sir Austin Henry Layard of England, found a stele in Kurkh on the Tigris river, that depicts Shalmaneser, king of Assyria, celebrating his triumph over Syria and portions of the Northern Kingdom of Israel (II Kings 17 & 18). It depicts among other things, one of Western Semitic dress bowing on all fours to Shalmaneser.

The text inscription above the scene states: *"The tribute of Jehu (Iaua) son of Khumri (Omri): I received from him silver, gold, a golden bowl, a golden vase with pointed bottom, golden tumblers, golden buckets, tin, a staff for a king, purukhti fruits."*

This 'Jehu' was the son of Jehoshaphat, one of the anointed kings over the 'house of Israel' (1 Kings 19:16). The word 'Khumri' in the "Jehu Stele" is the Assyria name for Omri. Thus, it is evident that the Assyrians called the kings of the 'house of Israel' at that time 'sons of Omri'. This 'Omri' was a captain of Northern Kingdom of Israel (the ten tribes) who the people appointed their king (1 Kings 16:16). Therefore, the word Khumri, which refers to Omri king of northern Israel, was the name used by Assyria for the ten tribes, or 'house of Israel'.

In 1847, English archaeologist Sir Austin Henry Layard discovered Sennacherib's palace, and the ancient capitol city of Nineveh, near Kiyunjik, as well as stores of clay tablets with

Assyrian cuneiform writing. An Assyrian translation of 1,471, discovered among the more than 23,000 clay tablets unearthed by Sir Austin Henry Layard, was published by R.F. Harper, and an English translation of the same, was made available in 1930, translated by Leroy Waterman, University of Michigan. These tablets cover that period of Assyrian history during the captivity of the 'house of Israel'.

The Assyrian name of Khumri for the **'sons of Omri'**, taken from the Jehu Stele mentioned above, was a pre-captivity name for the Israelites. These Assyrian Tablets further link the later Assyrian names for the 'house of Israel'. According to translations from these Assyrian Tablets, Khumri became changed to 'Gamir' and 'Gamera', during the house of Israel's captivity in Assyria. The Assyrian name "ga-me-ra-a-a" is translated to 'Cimmerian' by Prof. Leroy Waterman in Royal Correspondence of the Assyrian Empire, published by the University of Michigan in 1930. Thus, the word Cimmerian became one of the names that was used to identify the 'house of Israel'.

The Assyrian tablets provide proof for this Cimmerian marker in *"Letter 112 - Arad-Sin to the Overseer of the Palace"*, by connecting the Cimmerians with those of Gamir and Gamera. These Assyrian Tablets have provided a strong archaeological missing link to the tribes of Israel. Several ancient histories, such as those by Herodotus, Strabo, etc., mention the Cimmerians, yet their origins had previously been hard to determine without any archaeological foundation. The discovery of the Assyrian Tablets and their translation bridges the missing link.

Interestingly, the areas where Strabo said these Cimmerians migrated to, are all regions where Paul and the Apostles visited on their mission trips to preach The Gospel of Christ. Paul himself was from Tarsus, in Cilicia (Acts 9:11; 22:3). Christ told the Apostles in Matthew 10:5: *"...Go not into the way of the Gentiles, and into any city of Samaritans enter ye not: But go rather to the lost sheep of the house of Israel."*

Paul's commission, set forth in Acts 9:15 was to preach Christ to the Gentile, kings, and children of Israel. With Christ's command to go to the lost sheep, these nation and migration connections of the Cimmerians should become apparent. The seven Churches of Revelation were also located within the areas of Asia Minor where Strabo says the Cimmerians migrated to.

Another branch of the Israelites that can be traced to the Scythians are the 'Iskuza', also mentioned in the Assyrian Tablets. Since the term 'house of Isaac' is used to refer to the 'house of Israel' in Amos 7:16, this word 'Iskuza' was a natural Assyrian corruption of 'Isaac'. This label was further corrupted into the labels of 'Shuthae' by the Greeks and the word 'Sacae' by the Persians, both referring to the Scythians.

These two groups: the Cimmerians, which migrated first to Assyria, then west to Asia Minor and Western Europe; and the second group, the Scythians who migrated west later, taking over many of the Cimmerians' lands, represent the ancestry of the peoples of Europe and Asia Minor. These later divided themselves by family, becoming known later as: the Celts (Cimmerians), the Gauls, Normans, Norsk or Norse, Goths, and Germanic peoples.

The migration to ancient Britain by the Angles and Saxons (Isaac's sons), gave rise to several tribes, including: the Welsh, English, Scots, and Irish peoples. These various people groups, of seemingly different ancestry, have become interspersed to make up the ancestral nations of today's Europe. These people groups. who developed Europe all have one major trait in common. Though they have different names, and languages, they all make up the Caucasian race which settled in Europe, after having migrated from Assyria.

As one can determine from Britain's history, the various conquests of Britain by supposedly different nations of heritage, such as the Anglo-Saxons from Germany, the Danish and Norse, and then lastly the Normans of France, should -- it would seem -- have been made up of many different races. However, all the various people groups that invaded Britain were of one common ancestry, either descendants of the Cimmerians, or of the Scythians. They all have a common heritage -- part of the 'house of Israel'.

The name 'Caucasian' was itself derived from the people who first escaped Jerusalem and first held Masada and the routes through the Caucasus Mountains. Then, as Roman persecution intensified, Jews -- who by now were highly Christianized -- fled through the ancient aqueduct under the city, made their way up to Masada, and then migrated through the Caucasus Mountains, east of the Black Sea. It was their escape route, that earned them their "New Name" -- the "Caucasians".

These people -- the Caucasians -- subsequently migrated further west to the isles in Europe, and ultimately, into America. In II Esdras 13, in the Apocrypha, there appears to be another reference to this Passage in the Caucasus by the Cimmerians and Scythians.

Many of the Scythian migrants traveled further east, into the Orient. These 'Sok-wang', meaning 'Sakka princes', fled to a valley of the upper Indus, having Kashmir and Afghanistan as its borders. The historic migratory traces of the Sacae, the Scythians, and the Cimmerians, have been researched and documented by many historians, both ancient and modern. The evidence of their later migrations to Europe is plentiful. The only missing 'link' was that coupling them to those tribes of Israel, taken captive into Assyria, where their identity as Israelites was seemingly lost.

Israel had been warned by our Heavenly Father: *"I will punish her for the days she burned incense to the Baals; she decked herself with rings and jewelry, and went after her lovers, but me she forgot,"* declares the Lord. *"Therefore I am now going to allure her; I will lead her into the desert and speak tenderly to her. There I will give her back her vineyards, and will make the Valley of Achor a door of hope. There she will sing as in the days of her youth, as in the day she came up out of Egypt.*

"In that day," declares the Lord, *"you will call me 'my husband'; you will no longer call me 'my master.' I will remove the names of the Baals from her lips; no longer will their names be invoked.*

In that day I will make a covenant for them with the beasts of the field and the birds of the air and the creatures that move along the ground. Bow and sword and battle I will abolish from the land, so that all may lie down in safety.

Prophecy of Gentile Conversion:
"I will betroth you to me forever; I will betroth you in righteousness and justice, in love and compassion. I will betroth you in faithfulness, and you will acknowledge the Lord. "In that day I will respond," declares the Lord — "I will respond to the skies, and they will respond to the earth; and the earth will respond to the grain, the new wine and oil, and they will respond to Jezreel. I will plant her for myself in the land; **I will show my love to the one I called 'Not my loved one.'** *I will say to*

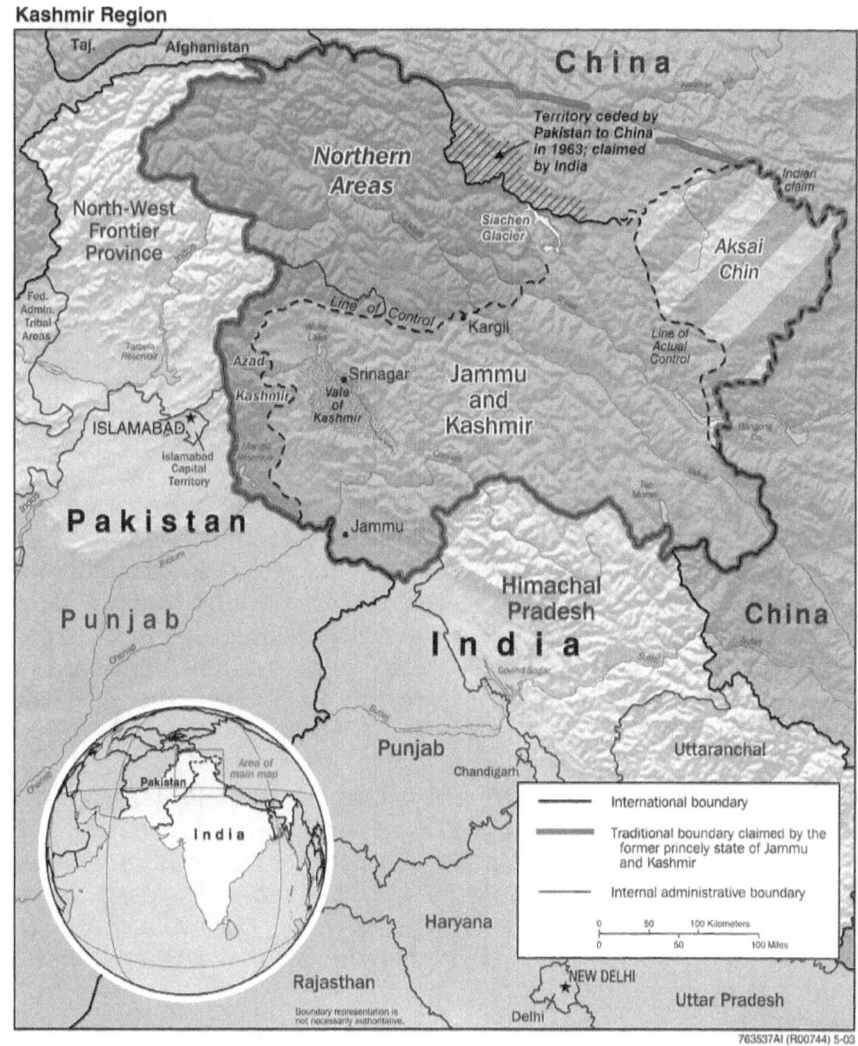

those called 'Not my people,' 'You are my people'; and they will say, 'You are my God.'" (Hos 2:13-23).

When the tribes of Israel finally migrated to their new lands, and the New Covenant was made available to them through Christ our Lord and Savior and his betrothed one -- the church, God took away the 'names of Baalim' out of their mouths which Assyria had given them. They became once again 'Ammi', God's People -- Christians (a contraction of two Greek words, meaning "children of the anointed one; or anointed children").

Unfortunately, paganism and the worship of false gods, which are not gods, is still prevalent among His People -- the church i.e., the 'house of Israel'. Once again God's People -- descendants of the 'house of Israel' -- are becoming lost, becoming once again identified as 'Lo-Ammi' (not My People). Another cycle of the same false religious, Babylon World Order, is now taking God's People into captivity. This time, however, that bondage is not geographical -- i.e., Babylon and Assyria -- this time the entrapment is that of our hearts and minds by the 'pleasures of sin', is luring us away from God and Christ, into spiritual captivity.

Only by yielding to this deception can one be taken into spiritual captivity in our day. Understanding The Mystery of God -- namely that **being adopted into the Family of God, through the incarnational life, death and resurrection to new life in Christ (Col 4:3), is the only way to prevent the slavery of deception entrapping so many today.**

Our founding fathers of the Western Christian Nations suffered religious captivity and battled for the freedoms that we have become so accustomed to. Let us not forget their struggles and slip again into bondage, for we are 'Ammi', His People, God's People. 'Ammi' includes all believers in Christ Jesus -- **God's people, who are known by a new name "Caucasian" (physical Israel) and "Christians" (representing spiritual Israel).**

It is this secret, This mystery of Christ -- Christ in us, and us in Him, the hope of glory (Col 1:27), the mystery of Christ and the church (Eph 5:32) that is *"the mystery that has been kept hidden for ages and generations, but is now disclosed to the saints. To them God has chosen to make known among the Gentiles the glorious riches of this mystery, which is Christ in you, the hope of glory"* (Col 1:26-27).

It is this mystery, hidden from God's people for ages, that is clearly understood by the powers of darkness. It is this mystery that the dragon, the beast and the false prophet (Rev 16:13,14) [Satan, Iran, Radical Islam & Mara Salvatrucha (the lawless ones)], are determined to keep hidden or annihilate. It is this mystery which Satan endeavors to keep us blinded to, so that we might not see the light of the gospel of the glory of Christ (2 Co 4:4) -- keeping us blinded to the light of the gospel while he entices us to partake of the wine of Mystery Babylon, the great harlot, mother of prostitutes (false religions), and of the abominations of the earth (Rev 14:8; 17:2 & 18:3).

Our goal is one with the goal expressed by the apostle, Paul: *"that you may be encouraged in heart and united in love, so that you may have the full riches of complete understanding, in order that you may know the mystery of God, namely, Christ, in whom are hidden all the treasures of wisdom and knowledge. I tell you this so that no one may deceive you by fine-sounding arguments"* (Col 2:2-4). *"Pray for us, too, that God may open a door for our message, so that we may proclaim the mystery of Christ, ... Pray that we may proclaim it clearly, as we should"* (Col 4:3-4). God's loving regathering of His people -- covered in the next chapter -- illuminates this mystery,

Chapter Twenty-eight
The Gathering

In our last chapter, we examined the cause and consequence of what has been called the Diaspora (the dispersion) of Israel into the nations of the whole earth. While, as a result of their rebellious spirit, God scattered his chosen people, the Israelites, He did not abandon them, Instead, He scattered them to discipline them (Jer 30:11), promising to gather them to Himself once again, when in distant lands, they remember Him (Zec 10:9, repent and return to Him. God promised not only to forgive their sins and heal their land (2 Ch 7:14); He promised to bring them back from their captivity (or exile), restore them to the land of their forefathers (Jer 30:3), and restore their fortunes (Jer 33:26).

To correctly understand the prophecies concerning the regathering of Israel, comprehend their import and apprehend their fulfillment, it is imperative to keep in mind that **from the creation of mankind, to his restoration into the family of God, the acts of God have been, and continue to be, multidimensional.** That is, there is always the archetype (the heavenly model or prototype); and the mirrored image manifestation: the type (the earthly image -- the replica of the archetype). Moreover, what happens concerning man in one dimension, occurs also in the other dimension (Mt 18:18).

For example, consider the instructions God gave Moses concerning the construction of the tabernacle. He told Moses to: *"Make this tabernacle and all its furnishings exactly like the pattern I will show you"* (Ex 25:9). ... *"Set up the tabernacle according to the plan shown you on the mountain"* (26:30). ... *"So, all the work on the tabernacle, the Tent of Meeting, was completed. The Israelites did everything just as the Lord commanded Moses"* (Ex 39:22).

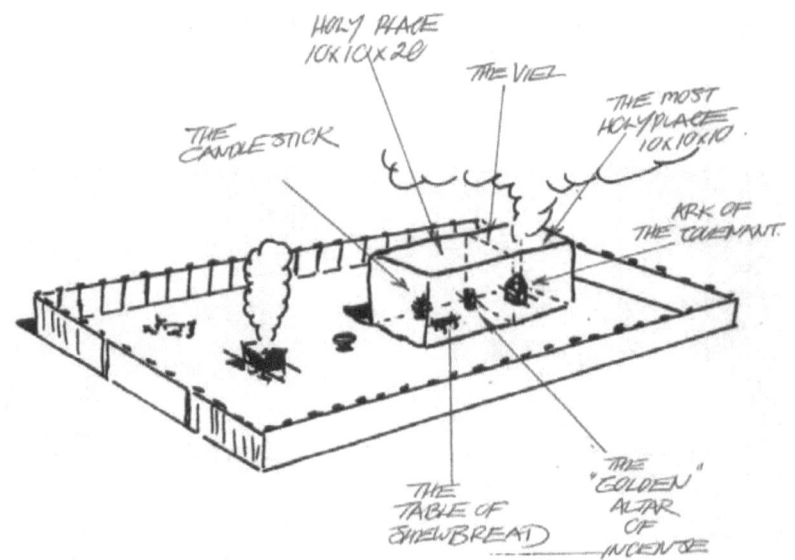

When the tabernacle components were complete, and the structure erected according to the pattern shown Moses, *"the cloud covered the Tent of Meeting, and the glory of the Lord filled the tabernacle"* (Ex 40:34). [And], *"the cloud of the Lord was over the tabernacle by day, and fire was in the cloud by night, in the sight of all the house of Israel during all their travels"* (Ex 40:38).

After the tabernacle was erected, and the glory of the Lord filled the tabernacle, the Levitical priesthood and sacrificial system were inaugurated -- all in accordance with the pattern first given to Abram and his descendants, then to Moses while on Mount Sinai. What was the pattern, or archetype of the tabernacle that Moses was directed to construct? The authors of the book of Hebrews and Revelation answer this question precisely. Concerning the sacrificial system, the author of Hebrews says:

"We do have such a high priest, who sat down at the right hand of the throne of the Majesty in heaven, and who serves in the sanctuary, the true tabernacle set up by the Lord, not by man. Every high priest is appointed to offer both gifts and sacrifices, and so it was necessary for this one also to have something to offer. If he were on earth, he would not be a priest, for there are already men who offer the gifts prescribed by the law. They serve at a sanctuary that is a copy and shadow of what is in heaven. This is why Moses was warned when he was about to build the tabernacle: "See to it that you make everything according to the pattern shown you on the mountain" (Heb 8:1-5).

Concerning the tabernacle itself, John wrote: "I saw in heaven another great and marvelous sign: seven angels with the seven last plagues — last, because with them God's wrath is completed. And I saw what looked like a sea of glass mixed with fire and, standing beside the sea, those who had been victorious over the beast and his image and over the number of his name. They held harps given them by God and sang the song of Moses the servant of God and the song of the Lamb: "Great and marvelous are your deeds, Lord God Almighty. Just and true are your ways, King of the ages. Who will not fear you, O Lord, and bring glory to your name? For you alone are holy. All nations will come and worship before you, for your righteous acts have been revealed."

"After this I looked and in heaven the temple, that is, the tabernacle of the Testimony, was opened. Out of the temple came the seven angels with the seven plagues. They were dressed in clean, shining linen and wore golden sashes around their chests. Then one of the four living creatures gave to the seven angels seven golden bowls filled with the wrath of God, who lives for ever and ever. And the temple was filled with smoke from the glory of God and from his power ..." (Rev 15).

Keeping in mind this two-dimensional reality (archetype and type; heaven and earth: spiritual and physical), consider the archetype of the rebellion and ultimate restoration of God's chosen ones -- his children -- mankind. The falling away of God's children began in the Garden of Eden, with the rebellion of Adam and Eve. Mankind's restoration will be completed at the last trumpet sound, when this perishable is clothed with the imperishable, and this mortal with immoralty: and death is swallowed up in victory (1 Cor 15:52-55). This falling away and the ultimate restoration of mankind to the Family of God, concerns the archetype or spiritual.

The physical type -- the mortal replica of the archetype of mankind's redemption and restoration -- began when God entered into covenant relationship with Abram, thereby selecting his descendants, the children of Israel, as His chosen people -- chosen, not because of their worthiness, but rather, chosen by God to demonstrate to worlds seen and unseen, His power of redemption. Israel was thus singled out by God, to model His plan of reconciliation and restoration to the universe. Through Israel, God's unfathomable love, His unconditional commitment to His children, would be made manifest to all -- both carnal beings (mortals) and spiritual beings (angels).

The children of Israel experienced something no other people had ever tasted since the Edenic rebellion. Through the covenant relationship between God and Abram, they were once more, children of God, rather than slaves of Satan (Ex 20:1,2; Dt 5:6). As His covenant children, they enjoyed the presence of God among them, guiding them, directing them in everything they undertook. However,

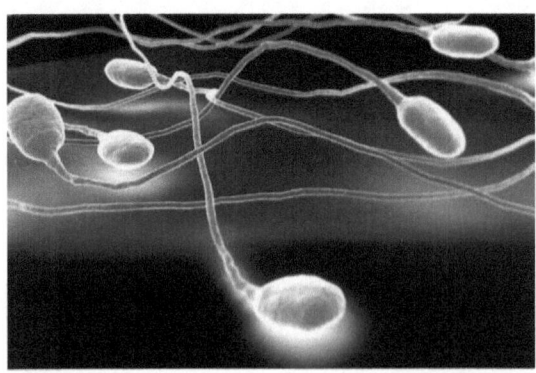

the spore of rebellion once sown into the family of man, remained, a seed so powerful, so deceptive, that regardless of God's great love and commitment, mankind again wandered astray. Worse yet, they seemed not to learn from their mistake.

Israel 'wandered away' from God over and over again. But, like a loving, unconditionally committed father, God pursued them, disciplined them, forgave them, and redirected them, again and again. However, after Israel time after time turned her back on God, became hardhearted and went lusting after her lovers (strange gods of idolatry), mocking God's messengers and scoffing at His prophets, it was necessary to resort to a more forceful intervention.

Thus, **"the wrath of the Lord was aroused against His people"** (2 Ch 36:16), until **the Lord rose up "to do His work, His strange work, and perform His task, His alien task"** (Is 28:21). After Israel had long turned her back on God, He turned His back on Israel, removing his protection of them as a nation, and of their homeland (the promised land), scattering them among the nations throughout the world (Lev 26:33; Neh 1:8).

God knew that the Children of Israel, after being scattered, forgetting their heritage and culture, and suffering persecution *"in the nations where they have been carried captive, those who escape will remember me — how I have been grieved by their adulterous hearts, which have turned away from me, and by their eyes, which have lusted after their idols. They will loathe themselves for the evil they have done and for all their detestable practices, and they will know that I am the Lord"* (Eze 6:9-10).

When this would occur, God promised: *"Then you will call upon me and come and pray to me, and I will listen to you. You will seek me and find me when you seek me with all your heart. I will be found by you,"* declares the Lord, *"and will bring you back from captivity. I will gather you from all the nations and places where I have banished you,"* declares the Lord, *"and will bring you back to the place from which I carried you into exile."* (Jer 29:12-14).

Signs and Wonders:
God promised that the regathering of Israel would be announced through wonders in heavens above and signs on the earth beneath (Acts 2:19. Christ, while on earth, warned his disciples that the Pharisees

and Sadducees (the religious leaders of his time) would likely miss the import of God's Signs of the Times, by looking only at the phenomenal (or natural) wonders in the heavens.

"The Pharisees and Sadducees came to Jesus and tested him by asking him to show them a sign from heaven. He replied, "When evening comes, you say, 'It will be fair weather, for the sky is red,' and in the morning, 'Today it will be stormy, for the sky is red and overcast.' You know how to interpret the appearance of the sky, but you cannot interpret the signs of the times" (Mt 16:1-3).

Heeding Christ's warning concerning the potential misinterpretation of signs, lets consider some of the prophecies pertaining to the regathering of Israel, beginning with the words of the prophet, Joel.

The Gathering Prophesied:
"Blow the trumpet in Zion; sound the alarm on my holy hill. Let all who live in the land tremble, for the day of the Lord is coming. It is close at hand — a day of darkness and gloom, a day of clouds and blackness. Like dawn spreading across the mountains a large and mighty army comes, such as never was of old nor ever will be in ages to come" (Joel 2:1-2). ...

"The Lord thunders at the head of his army; his forces are beyond number, and mighty are those who obey his command. The day of the Lord is great; it is dreadful. Who can endure it? 'Even now,' declares the Lord, 'return to me with all your heart, with fasting and weeping and mourning.' Rend your heart and not your garments. Return to the Lord your God, for he is gracious and compassionate, slow to anger and abounding in love, and he relents from sending calamity. Who knows? He may turn and have pity and leave behind a blessing — grain offerings and drink offerings for the Lord your God" (vs. 11-14).

Blow the trumpet in Zion, declare a holy fast, call a sacred assembly. Gather the people, consecrate the assembly; bring together the elders, gather the children, those nursing at the breast. Let the bridegroom leave his room and the bride her chamber. Let the priests, who minister before the Lord, weep between the temple porch and the altar. Let them say, 'Spare your people, O Lord. Do not make your inheritance an object of scorn, a byword among the nations. Why should they say among the peoples, 'Where is their God?" Then the Lord will be jealous for his land and take pity on his people. The Lord will reply to them: 'I am sending you grain, new wine and oil, enough to *satisfy you fully; never again will I make you an object of scorn to the nations"* (vs 15-19).

"Then you will know that I am in Israel, that I am the Lord your God, and that there is no other; never again will my people be shamed. **'And afterward, I will pour out my Spirit on all people. Your sons and daughters will prophesy, your old men will dream dreams, your young men will see visions. Even on my servants, both men and women, I will pour out my Spirit in those days.**

"I will show wonders in the heavens and on the earth, blood and fire and billows of smoke. The sun will be turned to darkness and the moon to blood before the coming of the great and dreadful day of the Lord. And everyone who calls on the name of the Lord will be saved; for on Mount Zion and in Jerusalem there will be deliverance, as the Lord has said, among the survivors whom the Lord calls" (vs. 27-32).

Joel's prophetic warning sets forth a number of important points:

1. The "Day of the Lord" is coming and is close at hand,
2. God's vast and mighty army comes to execute judgment,
3. God's people are exhorted to fast and pray,
4. God people are encouraged to repent and return to Him,
5. God offers blessings to all who respond to this call,

6. God's judgments can be forestalled by fasting and prayer,
7. God's people will be re-gathered to Him,
8. God's Spirit will be poured out in those days upon all flesh,
9. All who call upon God will be saved.

The Gathering Fulfilled:
This prophecy was fulfilled on Pentecost, when *"Peter stood up with the Eleven, raised his voice and addressed the crowd: "Fellow Jews and all of you who live in Jerusalem, let me explain this to you; listen carefully to what I say. These men are not drunk, as you suppose. It's only nine in the morning!* **No, this is what was spoken by the prophet Joel:**

"'In the last days, God says, I will pour out my Spirit on all people. Your sons and daughters will prophesy, your young men will see visions, your old men will dream dreams. Even on my servants, both men and women, I will pour out my Spirit in those days, and they will prophesy. I will show wonders in the heaven above and signs on the earth below, blood and fire and billows of smoke. The sun will be turned to darkness and the moon to blood before the coming of the great and glorious day of the Lord. And everyone who calls on the name of the Lord will be saved" (Ac 2:14-21).

Notice that **Peter says the prophecy of Joel was 'fulfilled' on the day of Pentecost.** He did not limit his comments to that portion of Joel's prophecy concerning the outpouring of God's Spirit on Pentecost. He included, by not delimiting the scope of his comment, that portion about there being wonders in the heaven and signs on the earth, thus declaring that these were also fulfilled. Today, we must be as careful as those in Jesus' day, to heed his warning -- to carefully interpret these wonders and signs from the perspective of their being signs of the times, rather than events in our phenomenal world.

Proper Prophetic Interpretation:
Many Bible prophecies are very familiar to us -- not so much because they are easily understood and their fulfillment readily recognized -- but simply because we've heard them repeated over and over again. Then, there are other prophecies -- prophecies that are vague -- not because they are difficult to understand -- but only in the sense that the infrequent mention

of them has obscured them in our minds. Traditions are prevalent within the church, and these traditions propose certain tenets, by stressing them over and over again while denying other teachings through neglect rather than rejection.

Jesus warned us of this, saying: *"In vain they worship me, teaching for doctrines the traditions of men"* (Mt 15:9; Mk 7:7). in another place, he said: *"They worship me in vain. Their teachings are but rules taught by men. They have let go the commands of God and are holding to the traditions of men"* (Mt 7:7-8). The apostle Paul also sounded a warning, writing: *"As I urged you when I went into Macedonia ... command certain men not to teach false doctrines any longer ..."* (1 Ti 1:3). ... *"If anyone teaches false doctrines and does not agree to the sound instruction of our Lord Jesus Christ and to godly teaching, he is conceited and understands nothing"* (1 Ti 6:3).

To avoid this tendency and insure proper interpretation of prophecy, we must search out all scripture on a given matter, to learn what Christ taught his Apostles and commissioned them -- as his initial ambassadors of truth -- to teach, when he said: *"go and make disciples of all nations, baptizing them in**a** the name of the Father and of the Son and of the Holy Spirit, and teaching them to obey everything I have commanded you. And surely I am with you always, to the very end of the age"* (Mt 28:19-20).

Some prophecies that deal with what many have interpreted to apply to the phenomenal, or physical, regathering of the nation of Israel to the middle eastern land of Palestine, were not interpreted as such by the apostles. They interpreted many of these prophecies to apply to the pneumenal, or spiritual regathering of God's people. If we consider ourselves to be Apostolic Christians -- basing our doctrines on the teachings of Christ and his Apostles -- then it is incumbent upon us to study the Apostles' interpretations of these prophecies and conform our theology to be consistent with their understanding.

Keys to Unlock God's Mysteries:
Several prophecies that have been touted to support a physical regathering of Israel to Palestine in our day and time, were not talking about that at all. Others have both a physical and spiritual application. Paul, and the author of Hebrews, quote several Old Testament prophecies concerning the regathering of Israel and applied them to their own apostolic experience of embracing the new birth and entering the kingdom of God -- in our day and time, as the church. These references and the apostolic interpretation thereof, have  become obscure in church traditions; something, we believe, that God would have us correct, to align our interpretation more closely to that which the Apostles taught.

Jeremiah's Prophecy of the Gathering:
The book of Hebrews is clearly speaking about the New Covenant, which the church presently represents and enjoys the benefits of. *"For if that first covenant had been faultless, then should no place have been sought for the second. For finding fault with them, he saith, Behold, the days come, saith the Lord, when I will make a new covenant with the house of Israel and with the house of Judah: Not according to the covenant that I made with their fathers in the day when I took them by the hand to lead them out of the land of Egypt; because they continued not in my covenant, and I regarded them not, saith the Lord.*

"For this is the covenant that I will make with the house of Israel after those days, saith the Lord; I will put my laws into their mind, and write them in their hearts: and I will be to them a God, and they shall be to me a people: And they shall not teach every man his neighbor, and every man his brother, saying, Know the Lord: for all shall know me, from the least to the greatest. For I will be merciful to their unrighteousness, and their sins and their iniquities will I remember no more. In that he

saith, A new covenant, he hath made the first old. Now that which decayeth and waxeth old is ready to vanish away" (Heb 8:7-13)

This citation is actually only part of a larger prophecy, found in Jeremiah, that deals with the regathering Israel after their being scattered. Exerts from Jeremiah's full prophecy follow:

"At the same time, saith the Lord, will I be the God of all the families of Israel, and they shall be my people. Thus saith the Lord, the people which were left of the sword found grace in the wilderness; even Israel, when I went to cause him to rest. The Lord hath appeared of old unto me, saying, Yea, I have loved thee with an everlasting love: therefore with loving kindness have I drawn thee. Again I will build thee, and thou shalt be built, O virgin of Israel: thou shalt again be adorned with thy tabrets, and shalt go forth in the dances of them that make merry.

"Thou shalt yet plant vines upon the mountains of Samaria: the planters shall plant, and shall eat them as common things. For there shall be a day, that the watchmen upon the mount Ephraim shall cry, Arise ye, and let us go up to Zion unto the Lord our God. For thus saith the Lord; Sing with gladness for Jacob, and shout among the chief of the nations: publish ye, praise ye, and say, O Lord, save thy people, the remnant of Israel. Behold, I will bring them from the north country, and gather them from the coasts of the earth, and with them the blind and the lame, the woman with child and her that travaileth with child together: a great company shall return thither" (Jer 31:1-8). ...

"Hear the word of the Lord, O ye nations, and declare it in the isles afar off, and say, He that scattered Israel will gather him, and keep him, as a shepherd doth his flock" (Jer 31:10). ...

"Is Ephraim my dear son? is he a pleasant child? for since I spoke against him, I do earnestly remember him still: therefore my bowels are troubled for him; I will surely have mercy upon him, saith the Lord. Set thee up way-marks, make thee high heaps: set thine heart toward the highway, even the way which thou wentest: turn again, O virgin of Israel, turn again to these thy cities" (Jer 31:20-21).

Continuing, here is the portion of the prophecy quoted in Hebrews: *"Behold, the days come, saith the Lord, that I will make a new covenant with the house of Israel, and with the* house of Judah: Not according to the covenant that I made with their fathers in the day that I took them by the hand to bring them out of the land of Egypt; which my covenant they broke, although I was a husband unto them, saith the Lord: But this shall be the covenant that I will make with the house of Israel; After those days, saith the Lord, I will put my law in their inward parts, and write it in their hearts; and will be their God, and they shall be my people. And they shall teach no more every man his neighbor, and every man his brother, saying, Know the Lord: for they shall all know me, from the least of them unto the greatest of them, saith the Lord: for I will forgive their iniquity, and I will remember their sin no more"* (Jer 31:31-34).

Beyond what the author of Hebrews quoted, Jeremiah continued, tells us that God will remember Israel forever: *"Thus saith the Lord, which giveth the sun for a light by day, and the ordinances of the moon and of the stars for a light by night, which divideth the sea when the waves thereof roar; The Lord of hosts is his name: If those ordinances depart from before me, saith the Lord, then the seed of Israel also shall cease from being a nation before me forever. Thus saith the Lord; If heaven above can be measured, and the foundations of the earth searched out beneath, I will also cast off all the seed of Israel for all that they have done, saith the Lord"* (Jer 31:35-37).

Grasping the full context of these scriptures, it is evident that many people, including a number of well meaning theologians, have erroneously interpreted these passages of Scripture, believing them to be speaking about the physical regathering of Israel to Palestine. However, correctly understood, it speaks of the regathering of God's people [His Children] through the cross of Jesus Christ.

These are the Scriptures, Christ's own Apostles interpreted as applying spiritually, to the New Covenant, and the day of the Lord (Jesus Christ).

Moses' Prophecy of the Gathering: Moses was warned by God that He would scatter Israel, but promised that He would return them under one condition. They must repent, humble themselves and obey the commandment of the Lord. *"And it shall come to pass, when all these things are come upon thee, the blessing and the curse, which I have set before thee, and thou shalt call them to mind among all the nations, whither the Lord thy God hath driven thee.*

"And shalt return unto the Lord thy God, and shalt obey his voice according to all that I command thee this day, thou and thy children, with all thine heart, and with all thy soul; that then the Lord thy God will turn thy captivity, and have compassion upon thee, and will return and gather thee from all the nations, whither the Lord thy God hath scattered thee. If any of thine be driven out unto the outermost parts of heaven, from thence will the Lord thy God gather thee, and from thence will he fetch thee: And the Lord thy God will bring thee into the land which thy fathers possessed, and thou shalt possess it; and he will do thee good, and multiply thee above thy fathers" (Dt 30:1-5).

The Key Condition:
God's promises are covenant promises in which each covenant party has responsibilities, or conditions, to meet. **One of the key conditions God gave for fulfilling His promise of the regathering of Israel, was that they must obey His voice.** Israel had in the past, strayed a number of times. And, only after they had suffered sufficiently to call on Him, repent of their wicked ways, humble themselves and enter into covenant obedience, did He gather them again to their homeland. A proper understanding of this prophecy must take into account the historic fact that **the people of Israel were never regathered by God, without first being in obedience to Him.** Applying this prophecy, we must understand that **He will not gather us -- His Children -- until we are walking in obedience: in a Father/child covenant relationship with Him.**

Continuing from where we left off in Deuteronomy note the words and terms cited by the Apostles in reference to our covenant and new birth experience. Moses said: *"And the Lord thy God will circumcise thine heart, and the heart of thy seed, to love the Lord thy God with all thine heart, and with all thy soul, that thou mayest live"* (Dt 30:6)

Paul in Romans quotes from Dt 30, when making reference to the Gospel: ***"For this commandment which I command thee this day, it is not hidden from thee, neither is it far off. It is not in heaven, that thou shouldest say, Who shall go up for us to heaven, and bring it unto us, that we may hear it,***

and do it? *Neither is it beyond the sea, that thou shouldest say, Who shall go over the sea for us, and bring it unto us, that we may hear it, and do it? But the word is very nigh unto thee, in thy mouth, and in thy heart, that thou mayest do it"* (Dt 30:11-14).

Reiterating what we said before: **Israel was never re-gathered while in disobedience.** God only regathered them during times of obedience. He waited again and again, until they returned to Him, before He would respond and guide them in any manner.

Challenging the 1948 Regathering:

Consider the following questions: In what manner did Israel repent, humble herself, confess her sins to the Lord, turn to Him and walk in obedience prior to 1948's alleged "gathering" of Israel to her homeland? In what ways have their sociopolitical decisions as a nation been orchestrated by God? None! Israel is still in disobedience. God never has, and never will, gather Israel while walking in disobedience. What is the commandment they must obey before God will re-gather them? Paul quotes Deuteronomy 30, to identify the commandment: **Israel must obey God before He will re-gather them as He promised.**

"But the righteousness which is of faith speaketh on this wise, Say not in thine heart, ***Who shall ascend into heaven? (that is, to bring Christ down from above:) Or, Who shall descend into the deep? (that is, to bring up Christ again from the dead.) But what saith it? The word is nigh thee, even in thy mouth, and in thy heart: that is, the word of faith, which we preach"*** (Rom 10:6-8). [Quoted from Deuteronomy 30.] In other words, Paul clearly identified the commandment that Israel must obey: the word of faith that Christ proclaimed and the Apostles preached!

Question for the 21st Century Church:

Has the church so long ago abandoned this Apostolic tenet that we, today are not even aware of it? By proposing that the commandment of God referenced in Deuteronomy is something other than what the Apostle Paul clearly interpreted it to be, is erroneous. Should the church today accept the interpretation of the Apostles, or rely on Baptist, Methodist or Plymouth Brethren dispensational traditions -- traditions that the Apostles never preached, traditions that have been around only about 200 years -- that predict some future gathering of Israel to Palestine, regardless of their disobedience?

Coming to Mt. Zion:
We have often heard it preached, that Israel coming to Mt. Zion with praise, and the nations coming to her, is a future event and that all Israel will gather back to the land of Palestine upon physical Mount Zion in the middle east after the church is removed from the earth. However, once again, the Apostles Epistles state in no uncertain terms, that we (the present-day church) are already at Mount Zion, and have been, since we have been born again and come into the New Covenant!

Isaiah's Prophecy of the Gathering:
"The word that Isaiah the son of Amoz saw concerning Judah and Jerusalem. And it shall come to pass in the last days, that the mountain of the Lord's house shall be established in the top of the mountains, and shall be exalted above the hills; and all nations shall flow unto it. And many people shall go and say, Come ye, and let us go up to the mountain of the Lord, to the house of the God of Jacob; and he will teach us of his ways, and we will walk in his paths: for out of Zion shall go forth the law, and the word of the Lord from Jerusalem" (Isa 2:1-3).

New Testament writers Clarify beyond a shadow of doubt that we do not have a covenant that was given from an earthly mountain that could not be physically touched -- an interpretation that makes no sense at all. We read of our New Covenant is as follows: *"But ye are come unto mount Zion, and unto the city of the living God, the heavenly Jerusalem, and to an innumerable company of angels, To the general assembly and church of the firstborn, which are written in heaven, and to God the Judge of all, and to the spirits of just men made perfect, And to Jesus the mediator of the new covenant, and to the blood of sprinkling, that speaketh better things than that of Abel"* (Heb 12:22-24).

God's children have -- according to the testimony of the apostles and the author of the book of Hebrews -- already come to Mount Zion! We have already come to the heavenly City, New Jerusalem, according to the messages preached by Christ's own Apostles. However, many in the church today have repeated words contrary to these Apostolic tenets -- words promulgated by various denominations, not by Christ nor by his apostles. We have carried these traditions -- these false doctrines, if you please -- far too long! It is high time for us to rid ourselves of these antichrist, anti-Apostolic interpretations.

The Righteous Judge:
Isaiah 11 speaks of Christ's coming as the Branch, the rod from the stem of Jesse. *"And shall make him of quick understanding*

in the fear of the Lord: and he shall not judge after the sight of his eyes, neither reprove after the hearing of his ears: **But with righteousness shall he judge** the poor, and reprove with equity for the meek of the earth: and he shall smite the earth with the rod of his mouth, and with the breath of his lips shall he slay the wicked" (Isa 11:3-4).

Jesus, Himself, repeated this righteousness judgment in (Jn 8:15-16), and told people to do likewise (Jn 7:24). *"Ye judge after the flesh (by human standards); I judge (pass judgment on) no man.* ***And yet if I judge, my judgment is true: for I am not alone, but I stand with the Father that sent me"*** (Jn 8:15-16). ... *"Judge not according to mere appearance, but make righteous judgments"* (Jn 7:24)

The Wolf and the Lamb:

We have often heard the passage, concerning the wolf laying with the lamb, interpreted physically, applying to a time when animals will be liberated from their carnivore instincts, that originated from when sin came into the world. However, this interpretation is inconsistent with the rest of the passage, that continues on into the 12th chapter, where we read:

"And in that day thou shalt say, O Lord, I will praise thee: though thou wast angry with me, thine anger is turned away, and thou comfortedst me. Behold, God is my salvation; I will trust, and not be afraid: for the Lord Jehovah is my strength and my song; he also is become my salvation. Therefore with joy shall ye draw water out of the wells of salvation" (Isa 12:1-3)

The Well of Living Water:
The literal transliteration of the Hebrew Name Yeshua -- translated Jesus -- is *'God is my Salvation.'* **The concept of our drawing waters from the well of salvation, refers to the New Testament covenant blessings of the Holy Spirit.** This interpretation was validated by Jesus' own words to the woman at the well.

"Jesus answered and said unto her, If thou knewest the gift of God, and who it is that saith to thee, Give me to drink; thou wouldest have asked of him, and he would have given thee living water. The woman saith unto him, Sir, thou hast nothing to draw with, and the well is deep: from whence then hast thou that living water? Art thou greater than our father Jacob, which gave us the well, and drank thereof himself, and his children, and his cattle? Jesus answered and said unto her, Whosoever drinketh of this water shall thirst again: But whosoever drinketh of the water that I shall give him shall never thirst; but the water that I shall give him shall be in him a well of water springing up into everlasting life" (Jn 4:10-14).

There is no question that this is speaking of Holy Spirit because, continuing on in John, we read: *"In the last day, that great day of the feast, Jesus stood and cried, saying, If any man thirst, let him come unto me, and drink. He that believeth on me, as the Scripture hath said, out of his belly shall flow rivers of living water. (But this spake he of the Spirit, which they that believe* on him should receive: for the Holy Ghost was not yet given; because that Jesus was not yet glorified.)" (Jn 7:37-39).

New Covenant Gathering:
Each of these prophecies speaks of a regathering of Israel. Each begins by speaking in New Covenant terminology. The church today -- 21st Century Christians -- need to recognize this and honor the Apostles' teaching. They referred to these terms as being New Covenant. The idea of the Virgin birth is readily known by all, because nearly every traditional denomination has proposed this concept. However, other concepts have been relegated into obscurity, so that most Christians are aware of only a part of the prophecies that concern the regathering of Israel.

Most Christians have failed to read, or are not familiar with, the entire cannon of Scripture, thus they fail to see that the terminology used in the Old Testament is explicitly cited by the Apostolic writers in the New testament as being indicative of our New Covenant relationship in Christ -- right here, right now -- not at some other time, some other place, some future physical gathering of Israel after the church is gone!

The Spiritual Gathering:
Gathering people to israel, God's servant, involves the gathering of people to the kingdom of God in and through Jesus, since **Jesus is actually called Israel, God's servant (Is 49).** *"Listen, O isles, unto me; and hearken, ye people, from far; The Lord hath called me from the womb; from the bowels of my mother hath he made mention of my name. And he hath made my mouth like a sharp sword; in the shadow of his hand hath he hid me, and made me a polished shaft; in his quiver hath he hid me; And said unto me, Thou art my servant, O Israel, in whom I will be glorified"* (Is 49:1-3)

Should there be any question concerning this, continue reading. Isaiah 49:6 is quoted in the New Testament as proof that this is indeed speaking of Jesus Christ. *"And he said, It is a light thing that thou shouldest be my servant to raise up the tribes of Jacob, and to restore the preserved of Israel:* **I will also give thee for a light to the Gentiles, that thou mayest be my salvation unto the end of the earth**" (Is 49:6)

The Apostles interpreted this very passage as being fulfilled when they, through the Spirit's direction that was given Paul and Barnabus, turned to the Gentiles to preach the Gospel: *"Then Paul and Barnabas waxed bold, and said, It was necessary that the word of God should first have been spoken to you: but seeing ye put it from you, and judge yourselves unworthy of everlasting life, lo, we turn to the Gentiles. For so hath the Lord commanded us, saying, I have set thee to be a light of the Gentiles, that thou shouldest be for salvation unto the ends of the earth"* (Acts 13:46-47)

Spiritual Israel:
This proves that Spiritual Israel is Jesus, and His Bride is the Church. In honoring Christ, we must accept the Apostles' interpretations of these verses, rather than endorse traditions of man derived from various denominational writings. Sadly, most have agreed with denominational theologians, that these things speak about some future gathering to the middle east, when the Apostles consistently applied the texts cited from these chapters to speak of their day, and of our day -- the Church Era!

Isaiah 49:6 spoke of restoring Israel. And the manner in which it would be done -- through the cross. Is 49:8 clarifies that this prophecy is speaking about the church-age. *"Thus saith the Lord, In an acceptable time have I heard thee, and in a day of salvation have I helped thee: and I will preserve thee, and give thee for a covenant of the people, to establish the earth, to cause to inherit the desolate heritage"* (Isa. 49:8)

Tradition has taught that these prophecies describe a future day, beyond our time. But the Apostles -- who learned their doctrines at the Master's knee, or by direct revelation -- taught differently! Listen to the words of Paul: *"We then, as workers together with him, beseech you also that ye receive not the grace of God in vain. (For he saith, I have heard thee in a time accepted, and in the day of salvation have I succored thee:* **behold, now is the accepted time; behold, now is the day of salvation.**)" (2 Cor. 6:1-2)

Paul, writing in his day, said the acceptable time and day that Isaiah spoke of was then a reality, indicating that it refers to the day of salvation, not some future regathering to a physical location! Righteousness and truth demand that we -- the church -- return to the teachings of the Apostles, who interpreted these things spiritually as applicable to the church, both in their day, and now.

To honor Christ then, we must conform our theology to theirs rather than 19th and 20th century theologians! Dare we disagree with the apostolic foundation upon which the church of Christ is built, in order to uphold some 'sacred-cow' theology

-- continuing to teach as doctrine man-made traditions that the apostles never taught, nor even spoke about?

Salvation Through Faith, Not Works:
Jesus Christ was given as the New Covenant to the people! His body and His blood themselves form the fabric of the New Covenant -- our covenant with God! We inherit God's promises to His children -- His heritage -- through faith in Christ in the New Covenant Church. All of the prophecies cited point to the cross and the church age, not to some post-church-rapture-age of Jewish salvation through works in the physical land in the east (Eph 2:9).

Jesus is the servant, Israel, (Acts 13:46-47). Thus the gathering of God's chosen people will be to Israel -- understood in the sense of Israel being Christ. *"Lift up thine eyes round about, and behold: all these gather themselves together, and come to thee. As I live, saith the Lord, thou shalt surely clothe thee with them all, as with an ornament, and bind them on thee, as a bride doeth"* (Is 49:18).

Little Children Who Make up the Kingdom:
Jesus said: *"Suffer the little children to come unto me and forbid them not, for of such is the kingdom of God"* (Mk 10:14). **God's people -- His chosen ones: are His Children -- who gather together in Jesus! Through the cross!** This is gathering of Spiritual Israel. The bride (the church, for the church is the bride), was birthed through the labor pains of Christ laying down his life for humanity: [the Archetype], even as Adam [the type] laid down his life and the woman -- his bride -- was taken from his side.

Reconciliation of Gentiles Prophesied:
This gathering of God's people raises a question, posed to teach us a lesson concerning when these prophecies were, or will be, fulfilled. *"The children which thou shalt have, after thou hast lost the other, shall say again in thine ears, The place is too strait for me: give place to me that I may dwell. Then shalt thou say in thine heart, Who hath begotten me these, seeing I have lost my children, and am desolate, a captive, and removing to and fro? and who hath brought up these? Behold, I was left alone; these, where had they been?"* (Isa 49:20-21)

He has children? But where did he get them? Others were lost in this gathering. But there are new children. Where did they come from? *"Thus saith the Lord God, Behold, I will lift up mine hand to the Gentiles, and set up my standard to the people: and they shall bring thy sons in their arms, and thy daughters shall be carried upon their shoulders"* (Isa 49:22)

This is the Church of Jesus Christ! Gentiles now enter the picture in this gathering of God's children to Israel -- Gentiles gathered to God's servant Israel -- declared to be Jesus himself (Acts 13).

As illustrated through the physical type -- the nation of Israel -- **Spiritual Israel [the church] will never be gathered by God while walking in disobedience.** God did not gather Spiritual Israel during the 1948 establishment of Israel as a nation. All of the Scriptures referencing the regathering of Israel begin by proclaiming New Testament covenant terms. This is clear, if one will just take time to read the entire prophecies. These are references the Apostles interpreted as indicative of the birth of the church age. Shall we believe and agree with the Apostles, or embrace and teach the traditions of men? Are we part of the Apostolic Church of Christ; or are we part of a man-breathed denomination?

Jesus called those in his day hypocrites, who taught for doctrines the commandments of men, and said, *"in vain do the worship me?"* (Mt 15:9; Mk 7:7). Would he not say the same about the church today, who being called by his name, teach for doctrines the commandments of men?

The Gathering and the Tabernacle of David:
"In that day will I raise up the tabernacle of David that is fallen, and close up the breaches thereof; and I will raise up his ruins, and I will build it as in the days of old" (Am 9:11).

The Council's Deliberations:
When the gentiles received the Holy Ghost, as Peter testified to before the council in Jerusalem, a scriptural basis was demanded to support of his claim, in order that the Apostles might know what to do about this unexpected situation, and know whether or not they were to require them to be circumcised according to the Old Testament law.

Peter's testimony before the counsel was outstandingly clear. In support of Peter, Paul witnessed to the council concerning God's work among uncircumcised gentiles. Still, it was not until James received a word from the Scriptures, that the council knew what to do. The Scripture highlighted by Holy Spirit to James, was Amos 9:11, which both he and the other apostles understood applied to the gentiles coming into the church in their day. James and the others in the council did not interpret it to refer to some future time when the Jews were restored to Palestine. Quite the contrary: he quoted that Scripture and explained that it referred to the then-present time of Gentiles coming into the church.

"And after they had held their peace, James answered, saying, Men and brethren, hearken unto me: Simeon hath declared how God at the first did visit the Gentiles, to take out of them a people for his name. And to this agree the words of the prophets; as it is written, After this I will return, and will build again the tabernacle of David, which is fallen down; and I will build again the ruins thereof, and I will set it Gentiles, upon whom my name is called, saith the Lord, who doeth all these things. Known unto God are all his works from the beginning of the world. Wherefore my sentence is, that we trouble not them, which from among the Gentiles are turned to God: But that we write unto them, that they abstain from pollutions of idols, and from fornication, and from things strangled, and from blood" (Act 15:13-20).

The context of this demands that we interpret Amos 9:11 as referring to that day long ago -- during the apostles lifetimes -- a time during which gentiles were first coming into the church. This is entirely the opposite of what much of our modern-day 'prophetic' teaching claims concerning the restoration of the Tabernacle of David. The restoration of the tabernacle, referred to by Amos, was applied explicitly by the apostles, to their own time -- and not some future age.

The Beginning of The Gathering:
It is not so much that the prophecies cited have been

spiritualized away. It is rather, that they have been obscured, becoming virtually unknown among us. **The regathering of Israel (God's children) actually began when God cut a covenant with Abram (Gen 15:8).** This was later confirmed through His prophetic words spoken to Abraham. *"I will bless those who bless you, and I will curse him who curses you; and in you all the families of the earth shall be blessed."* (Gen 12:3).

The words of this prophecy were expanded on through the Patriarchs, particularly through Jacob, in his farewell address to his sons. What did God say through Jacob (Israel) about the re-gathering of Israel? *"Concerning Judah, he says, The scepter shall not depart from Judah, nor a lawgiver from between his feet, until Shiloh comes; and to him shall be the obedience of the people"* (Gen. 49:10).

In other words, **the scepter of power (the kingdom) was to remain under the control of Judah until Christ returned to gather those people walking in obedience to himself.** These prophecies also foretold the division of the kingdom of David after the death of Solomon.

The 10 Northern tribes rebelled against God, committed idolatry and were carried off into Assyrian captivity in 721 BC, with only a small remnant remaining in Israel. Later in 586 BC, the Southern tribe of Judah, forsook God's Sabbaths and they too experienced seventy years of captivity and suffering in Babylon under Nebuchadnezzar. Later, by the decree of Cyrus in 536 BC, all who desired to do so were allowed to return to their land. But, this was not the 'last days regathering' spoken of by the prophets.

Ezekiel's Prophecy of the Gathering & the Holy Spirit:
Ezekiel, who prophesied shortly before they were carried off into Babylon, spoke about a regathering of Israel. It is this prophecy that much of the theological disagreement centers on. Many see Ezekiel's prophesy referencing either the return of the Jews from the Babylonian captivity, or a future return of Israel to modern day Palestine. Both of these views fail to correlate with the original prophecies (Gen 12:3, and 49:10), cited above.

These prophecies can only be brought into agreement when one realizes that Israel -- Spiritual Israel -- is re-gathered in fulfillment of the prophecy during the time of Christ. Ezekiel says God would take Israel from among the nations, and bring them into their own land (Eze 36:24-27). He said that at that time, God would sprinkle clean water on them, cleanse them from all their sins, put within them a new heart and put his Spirit within them. Spiritual Israel, therefore, could not be re-gathered at any time prior to, nor after, the age of the outpouring of the Holy Spirit. This again, pinpoints the time as the time of Shiloh, (Christ), for it is Jesus who pours out the Holy Spirit upon Israel in her last days of kingdom rule, (Joel 2:28-30, Acts 2:16-20).

Ezekiel 37, takes us even deeper into the era when the indwelling Holy Spirit would be a reality, (v. 14-28), clarifying this to be the time when Ephriam (the 10 Northern tribes) and Judah (the southern kingdom) will be joined together (re-gathered).

Ezekiel's Prophecy of the One King/One Shepherd:
"Surely I will take the children of Israel from among the nations, where they have gone, and will gather them from every side and bring them into their own land; and I will make of them one nation in the land, on the mountains of Israel; and one king shall be over them all; they shall no longer be two nations, nor shall they ever be divided into two kingdoms again" (Ez 37:21,22).

This prophecy once again focuses on the work of Shiloh, to whom the people would be gathered. Verse 24, speaks of "David," who would be the one king over them. "David" figuratively and prophetically refers to Christ. It would otherwise be a contradiction to say "one king shall be over them" and that they shall have one shepherd." Any other interpretation would suggest a co-regency between Christ and David, (son of Jesse and their former king), reigning together on God's throne. However, Christ made it clear, that David spoke, not of himself, but of the Lord. *"The Lord said to my Lord, sit at my right hand..."* (Psalms 110:1).

What Does God Say About the Re-gathering of Israel? *"At that time the sign of the Son of Man will appear in the sky, and all the nations of the earth will mourn. They will see the Son of Man coming on the clouds of the sky, with power and great glory. And he will send his angels with a loud trumpet call, and they will gather his elect from the four winds, from one end of the heavens to the other"* (Mt 24:30-31).

The Olivet Discourse:
In this Olivet discourse, Christ placed the regathering of Israel before that generation who was living while he was on earth all passed away. *"Now learn this lesson from the fig tree: As soon as its twigs get tender and its leaves come out, you know that summer is near. Even so, when you see all these things, you know that it is near, right at the door. I tell you the truth, this generation will certainly not pass away until all these things have happened"* (Mt 24:32-34).

Israel Regathered:
How can the gathering of Israel be going on today, or at some future date, when **according to Christ's own words, it was all fulfilled in the generation of his original Apostles?** This

means the regathering of Israel occurred within the first century AD. That was also the time of the initial ministry and indwelling of Holy Spirit. This interpretation accords perfectly with the teaching of Christ and his apostles, (Jn 10:16; 11:52; 2 Th 2:1; Heb 10:25). All of the acts mentioned occurred through the power of indwelling Holy Spirit.

Paul cites portions of Ezekiel 36 and 37, (2 Cor 6:1-2, 16-18), to explain that the church in his day fulfilled the prophecies of the new land and the new temple into which Israel was being re-gathered. Paul's conversion occurred about 36 AD -- after Christ's crucifixion, resurrection and ascension. Paul was, as a consequence for his stand for Christ, beheaded around 60 AD. He apparently never knew Christ personally, yet he makes it very clear that the regathering of Israel had already occurred. Moreover, his interpretation of these prophecies was never challenged by the other apostles.

Any attempt to align the Zionist movement, begun in the late 19th century, the nationalization of Israel and her return to Palestine in 1948, and/or the Zionist movement of today, that looks forward to the regathering of all Israeli descendants to the land of Palestine, with the regathering of Israel in the Bible is anachronistic. Such an alignment would constitute an error in time and be contrary to the Bible. Such teaching does not have Christ as it's center. It does not coincide with the apostles' teaching concerning the last days' outpouring of the Holy Spirit, occurring during their lifetimes, as recorded in Acts 2:16-20.

The Apostles clearly and explicitly referenced these prophecies as being fulfilled, the fulfillment commencing in their lifetimes and continuing throughout the church age. These references are those that many have mistakenly taken to reference the return to Palestine of a small number of Jews in 1948.

The gathering of Israel to Palestine in 1948, actually commencing before that time in steps and stages, has nothing to do with God's gathering of Spiritual Israel. The prophecies that speak of the regathering of Israel were all referenced by the Apostles as pertaining to the spiritual regathering of God's children, in and through Christ and His Bride: the church. As Christians, the Apostles' interpretations of Scripture are the ones the church should rely upon, and teach, rather than the traditions of men, espoused in books on prophecy and theological texts, the majority of which were written during the last 200 years.

There is no question that God worked in a miraculous way to bring a small number of Jewish people -- physical Israel -- back to her homeland. Certainly the birthing of the nation of Israel in a single day was a miracle. However, it is imperative that we understand that this miracle was limited to the physical [mortal] type of Israel -- not the [spiritual] archetype.

The prophecies of Israel being born in a single day (Is 66:7-8; Zec 3:9) are even more miraculous when applied to Spiritual Israel [The Archetype]. In a single day, at Pentecost -- more than 2,000 years ago -- when, as the apostles and others were assembled in an upper room, waiting and praying, as Christ had directed them, it happened -- Holy Spirit descended amidst them and indwelled them, and the church was born!

Comprehending the fact that a 'day' can also refer to an era -- or dimension of time and space -- it is scripturally correct to refer to our time as the Church Age, or Era. And, just as the New Testament Church Age on earth began in a single day, it will likewise culminate in a single day, at Christ's return. *"On that day his feet will stand on the Mount of Olives, east of Jerusalem, and the Mount of Olives will be split in two from east to west, forming a great valley, with half of the mountain moving north and half moving south. You will flee by my mountain valley, for it will extend to Azel. You will flee as you fled from the earthquake in the days of Uzziah king of Judah. Then the LORD my God will come, and all the holy ones with him.*

A Day Known Only to the Lord:
On that day there will be no light, no cold or frost. ***It will be a unique day, without daytime or nighttime — a day known to the Lord.*** *When evening comes, there will be light. On that day living water will flow out from Jerusalem, half to the eastern sea and half to the western sea, in summer and in winter. The Lord will be king over the whole earth. On that day there will be one Lord, and his name the only name"* (Zec 14:4-9).

This dramatic phenomenon is, of course, the long anticipated event -- the event that men of all ages have anticipated and looked forward to. However, while this day is the hope of glory for the redeemed, it is also the day most dreaded by Satan and those angels who rebelled with him, by the Watchers who abandoned their own home and took wives of the children of men (Jude 6), by the disembodied spirits of their offspring -- the demons, and by every man, woman and child who has failed to respond to Christ's invitation, *"Come, ye blessed of my Father, inherit the kingdom prepared for you from the foundation of the world"* (Mt 25:34).

This unique day -- when Jesus returns to earth -- to stand once again on the Mount of Olives, from which he ascended after making the ultimate sacrifice for mankind, is that day when the battle cry is heard around the world, and throughout the universe. It is Christ, issuing forth a proclamation of war for *The Battle of the Great Day of God Almighty* -- often referred to as The Battle of Armageddon. This battle is the focus of our next chapter.

Chapter Twenty-nine
Armageddon: the Battle of the Great Day of the Lord

Armageddon:
There has been a great deal of teaching in the church concerning "The Battle of Armageddon", most correlating it to the final conflict between Jesus Christ and the nations of the world. Armageddon, literally Har-Meggido, (Mount Megiddo), has seen more battles historically than any other place on earth. However, the final battle -- **the battle of Armageddon -- is merely a tradition of man, not a biblical truth.**

Examining Scripture carefully, one finds no reference to the Battle of Armageddon. Armageddon is identified as the gathering place for the nations' kings, in preparation for "the battle on the great day of God Almighty," not the location of the final battle. The following passage is the only biblical reference to Armageddon:

"The sixth angel poured out his bowl on the great river Euphrates, and its water was dried up to prepare the way for the kings from the East. Then I saw three evil spirits that looked like frogs; they came out of the mouth of the dragon, out of the mouth of the beast and out of the mouth of the false prophet. They are spirits of demons performing miraculous signs, and they go out to the kings of the whole world, to gather them for the battle on the great day of God Almighty. "Behold, I come like a thief! Blessed is he who stays awake and keeps his clothes with him, so that he may not go naked and be shamefully exposed." **Then they gathered the kings together to the place that in Hebrew is called Armageddon.** *The seventh*

angel poured out his bowl into the air, and out of the temple came a loud voice from the throne, saying, "It is done!" (Revelation 16:12-17)

Scripture states that Armageddon [Hebrew Har-Meggido] will be the gathering place for those nations that will participate in the battle prophesied to take place on "the great day of God Almighty." But, it is *not* the title of the battle.

John Sees Christ as the Coming Warrior & King

The Great Day of God Almighty:
The Great Day of God Almighty is the same as "The Day of the Lord." There are numerous Scriptures referring to that day, or era. Various Scriptures refer to "The Day of God", "The Day of the Lord", "The Day of the Lord Almighty", "The Great Day of the Lord", "The Day of Our Lord Jesus", "The Day of Christ Jesus", and "The Day of Christ".

This day is a day associated with both judgment and salvation: both destruction and deliverance. It is, according to the prophet, Zechariah, a unique day. He says: *"A day of the LORD is coming when your plunder will be divided among you. I will gather all the nations to Jerusalem to fight against it; the city will be captured, the houses ransacked, and the women raped. Half of the city will go into exile, but the rest of the people will not be taken from the city. Then the Lord will go out and fight against those nations, as he fights in the day of battle.*

"On that day his feet will stand on the Mount of Olives, east of Jerusalem, and the Mount of Olives will be split in two from east

to west, forming a great valley, with half of the mountain moving north and half moving south. You will flee by my mountain valley, for it will extend to Azel. You will flee as you fled from the earthquake in the days of Uzziah king of Judah. Then the Lord my God will come, and all the holy ones with him.

On that day there will be no light, no cold or frost. **It will be a unique day, without daytime or nighttime — a day known only to the Lord.** *When evening comes, there will be light. On that day living water will flow out from Jerusalem, half to the eastern sea and half to the western sea, in summer and in winter. The Lord will be king over the whole earth. On that day there will be one Lord, and his name the only name.* (Zec 14:1-9).

Judgment & Salvation:
On this day, God will fulfill His promises to destroy those nations that have attacked His chosen people (His Children); and on that same day, He will cleanse the House of David and the inhabitants of Jerusalem from their sin and impurity.

"On that day I will set out to destroy all the nations that attack Jerusalem. And I will pour out on the house of David and the inhabitants of Jerusalem a spirit of grace and supplication. They will look on me, the one they have pierced, and they will mourn for him as one mourns for an only child, and grieve bitterly for him as one grieves for a firstborn son. On that day the weeping in Jerusalem will be great, like the weeping of Hadad Rimmon in the plain of Megiddo" (Zec 12:9-11).

Clearly, **one can only grasp the significance of this Scripture, in the light of a two-dimensional reality.** Only then can one understand that this applies to Spiritual Israel -- not physical Israel. It should be clear, since the inhabitants of Jerusalem (New Jerusalem) will look on (behold) the presence of Christ, the One whom they pierced. This two-dimensional reality is further clarified by the phrase that *"on that day, the weeping in Jerusalem will be great, like the weeping of Hadad Rimmon in the Plain of Megiddo."*

While the spirit of grace and supplication is being poured out on the inhabitants of Spiritual Israel who are at this time in the New Jerusalem (in heaven) beholding Jesus, the One whom they pierced [the archetype]; back down on earth [the type] physical Israel and the kings of the earth, assembled on the plain of Jezreel, below the ancient city of Armageddon (Har Megiddo), will be weeping and/or gnashing their teeth (Mk 13:42).

"On that day a fountain will be opened to the house of David and the inhabitants of [New] Jerusalem, to cleanse them from sin and impurity" (Zec 13:1). On that same day, those of physical Israel, who did not accept Jesus as their Lord and Savior, will be thrown out where they will experience weeping and gnashing of teeth.

Jesus Clarified the Two Dimensional Reality:
Jesus clarified that Spiritual Israel and physical Israel are not one in the same. Jesus, in his response to the Roman Centurion who accepted him and sought him out to heal his servant, said: *"I tell you the truth, I have not found anyone in Israel with such great faith. I say to you that many will come from the east and the west, and will take their places at the feast with Abraham, Isaac and Jacob in the kingdom of heaven. But the subjects of the kingdom will be thrown outside, into the darkness, where there will be weeping and gnashing of teeth"* (Mt 8:10-12).

The book of Joel also speaks of this day -- the Day of the Lord -- and identifies the location of the final battle, describing it as taking place in the "Valley of Jehoshaphat." *"Blow the trumpet in Zion; sound the alarm on my holy hill. Let all who live in the land tremble, for the day of the Lord is coming. It is close at hand — a day of darkness and gloom, a day of clouds and blackness. Like dawn spreading across the mountains a large and mighty army comes, such as never was of old nor ever will be in ages to come"* (Joel 2:1-2).

Joel's prophecy addresses this two-dimensional reality, saying: *"I will show wonders in the heavens and on the earth, blood and fire and billows of smoke. The sun will be turned to darkness and the moon to blood before the coming of the great and dreadful day of the Lord. And everyone who calls on the name of the Lord will be saved; for on Mount Zion and in Jerusalem there will be deliverance, as the Lord has said, among the survivors whom the Lord calls.*

"In those days and at that time, when I restore the fortunes of Judah and Jerusalem, I will gather all nations and bring them down to the Valley of Jehoshaphat. There I will enter into judgment against them concerning my inheritance, my people Israel, for they scattered my people among the nations and divided up my land" (Joel 2:30-3:2).

Once again, Joel makes clear the fact that "The Day of the Lord" incorporates both the deliverance of God's chosen people -- *"everyone who calls on the name of the Lord"* -- on Mount Zion and the New Jerusalem; and the destruction of those who persecuted His people, scattering them among the nations. The nations to be judged will, according to Joel, be gathered together and then brought down to The "Valley of Jehoshaphat" for judgment.

We have seen, from the prophecy of John the Revelator, that **the nations will be gathered at a place called Armageddon [in Hebrew, Har-Megiddo],** a mound overlooking the Plain of Jezreel. Joel makes a point of the fact that Armageddon must be understood in the Hebrew tongue. **The Hebrew word Armageddon is actually comprised of three words [Armea, Gai and Dan]. Armea refers to a heap of sheaves; Gai refers to a valley; and Dan references judgment. Put together, these three root words mean, 'a heap of sheaves in a valley for judgment.'**

Joel 3:2 states that after the nations of the earth have been gathered at Armageddon (a heap of sheaves in a valley for judgment), they will be brought down to the Valley of Jehosaphat. In verse 3, Joel seemingly refers to a valley other than the Valley of Jezreel, when he says, **"Multitudes, multitudes in the valley of decision**, *for the day of the Lord is near in the valley of decision."* However, **the Hebrew word**

translated 'decision' is more accurately rendered 'concision' or 'threshing'.

Understanding this, a clear link can be established between this prophecy of Joel and that of John, who also mentions Armageddon: *"And he gathered them together into a place called in the Hebrew tongue, Armageddon"* (Rev 16:16).

Comparing these words of John to those of Joel, we read *"I will also gather all nations and will bring them down into the Valley of Jehosaphat"* (Joel 3:2) ... *"and let the heathen be wakened and come up to the Valley of Jehosaphat; for there I will sit to judge round about"* (vs. 12).

Illustrated below is Har-meggido [mistranslated as Armageddon] -- being the tel (mound) on which the ancient city of Meggido was built, overlooking the Valley of Jezreel, where the kings of the earth will assemble their armies in preparation of this battle. However, it is important to understand that this valley -- the Valley of Jezreel -- is not the same as the Valley of Jehosaphat.

Geographers tell us that there was never a physical location referred to as the Valley of Jehoshaphat. This seems at first glance to be an scriptural anomaly. However, on closer inspection, the reference to Jehosaphat appears to have an important association with Armageddon when one considers the connection between the references in Revelation and Joel.

Both refer to judgment and both to a battle of the Lord, unlike any battle ever before fought.

Searching the Scriptures for interpretative clues, we find that **Jehosaphat's name literally means "Yahweh will judge"** (2 Ch 20). In 2 Chronicles, it is recorded that Jehosophat witnessed a unique battle -- one that produced a decisive victory for God's people, yet required no human participation whatsoever.

As recorded by the chronicler (e.g., historian), enemy forces, led by Ammon, Moab and those from Mt. Seir assembled themselves in Engedi, to make war against Judah. The people of Judah were in great fear, and convened with Jehoshaphat, before the Temple in Jerusalem to pray, seeking Yahweh's help. They met together and invoked the prayer of Solomon, introduced at the time of the dedication of the Temple (1 Ki 8), when Jahaziel in "the spirit of Yahweh" revealed to them that *"the battle is not yours but God's"* (2 Ch 20:15). Jahaziel's name means *'he will be divided of el (i.e. God)'*.

On that occasion, Jahaziel, son of Zechariah, a Levite descendant of the sons of Asaph; and the people, were told to go out to the cliff of Ziz and once there to be *"still and see the salvation of Yahweh ... for Yahweh will be with you ... and Jehoshaphat bowed his head with his face to the ground: and all Judah and the inhabitants of Jerusalem fell down before Yahweh worshipping Yahweh"* (2 Ch 6:16-18).

The people fearfully trudged out to the wilderness of Tekoa, and climbed the cliff of Ziz, pictured. Having wearily climbed the hill where they could look down from the cliff, they were shocked to look down and see nothing but dead bodies in the valley below them! The assembled armies of Amon, Moab and Mt. Seir had -- by God's direction -- engaged in a fearsome battle among themselves. It is because of this historic battle, that we recall Jahaziel's name, which means: *"he will be divided of El."*

In the aftermath of this battle, during which Yahweh fought for the people, the children of Israel, together with Jehoshaphat, assembled themselves in the valley of 'Berachah' (a word meaning 'blessing'), where they "blessed Yahweh ... *"for Yahweh had made them to rejoice over their enemies"* (vs 20) This why that valley was subsequently called The Valley of Berachah, not The Valley of Jehoshaphat, for the victory was Yahweh's, not Jehoshaphat's.

The 'harvesting' of the multitudes in the valley of 'Decision' [concision or threshing] (Joel 3), and the Great Battle of The Day of the Lord, initiated by the kings of the earth assembled at Armageddon (Rev 16:16), have a close association, one that is worthwhile considering.

Referring back to previous chapters in this book, we provided evidence from (Eze 38), that the kings of the East (Iran and her allies), together with their armies, will invade the land of Israel (Eze 38:1-9). Then, after their armies cover the land like a cloud (vs 9), they will devise a plan to attack the land of unwalled cities (vs 10-13) -- a sentence which we believe applies to the United States of America, (referred to by Iran as the Great Satan). Then, while they are engaged in this battle, God will intervene!

"Thus says the Lord God, "Are you the one of whom I spoke in former days through My servants the prophets of Israel, who prophesied in those days for many years that I would bring you against them? "It will come about on that day, when Gog comes against the land of Israel," declares the Lord God, "that My fury will mount up in My anger. "In My zeal and in My blazing wrath I declare that on that day there will surely be a great earthquake in the land of Israel.

"The fish of the sea, the birds of the heavens, the beasts of the field, all the creeping things that creep on the earth, and all the men who are on the face of the earth will shake at My presence; the mountains also will be thrown down, the steep pathways will collapse and every wall will fall to the ground. "I will call for a sword against him on all My mountains," declares the Lord God.

"Every man's sword will be against his brother. With pestilence and with blood I will enter into judgment with him; and I will rain on him and on his troops, and on the many peoples who are with him, a torrential rain, with hailstones, fire and brimstone. "I will magnify Myself, sanctify Myself, and make Myself known in the sight of many nations; and they will know that I am the Lord" (Eze 38:17-23).

While this intervention of God appears to commence in the distant land (the United States), God declares that He will drive the invading armies back to the land of Israel, to carry out His prophesied judgment against them. *"Thus says the Lord God, "Behold, I am against you, O Gog, prince of Rosh, Meshech and Tubal; and I will turn you around, drive you on, take you up from the remotest parts of the north and bring you against the mountains of Israel"* (Eze 39:1-2).

The Battle of the Day of the Lord:
Once reassembled in the land of Palestine, God's great battle -- the day of judgment -- will commence: *"I will strike your bow from your left hand and dash down your arrows from your right hand. "You will fall on the mountains of Israel, you and all your troops and the peoples who are with you; I will give you as food to every kind of predatory bird and beast of the field. "You will fall on the open field; for it is I who have spoken," declares the Lord God.*

"And I will send fire upon Magog and those who inhabit the coastlands in safety; and they will know that I am the Lord. My holy name I will make known in the midst of My people Israel; and I will not let My holy name be profaned anymore. And the nations will know that I am the Lord , the Holy One in Israel. Behold, it is coming and it shall be done," declares the Lord God. "That is the day of which I have spoken" (Eze 39:3-8).

Bible students have often puzzled over the significance of the end-time prophesies in Isaiah. First, Isaiah prophesies about "that day" when the Lord will come down (from heaven) and battle supernaturally on Mount Zion in Jerusalem with "a sword, not of mortals."

*"This is what Yahweh says to me: "As a lion growls, a great lion over his prey-- and though a whole band of shepherds is called together against him, he is not frightened by their shouts or disturbed by their clamor-- so **Yahweh Almighty will come down to do battle on Mount Zion and on its heights**. Like birds hovering overhead, Yahweh Almighty will shield Jerusalem; he will shield it and deliver it, he will 'pass over' it and will rescue it." Return to him you have so greatly revolted against, O Israelites. For in that day every one of you will reject the idols of silver and gold your sinful hands have made. "Assyria will fall by a sword that is not of man; **a sword, not of mortals, will devour them.** They will flee before the sword and their young men will be put to forced labor. Their stronghold will fall because of terror; at sight of the battle standard their commanders will panic," declares Yahweh, whose fire is in Zion, whose furnace is in Jerusalem"* (Is 31:4-9).

In another place, Isaiah prophesied concerning the identity of the nations against whom God will enter into battle on that day, referring to them as the Edomites. *"Who is this coming from Edom, from Bozrah, with his garments stained crimson? Who is this, robed in splendor, striding forward in the greatness of his strength? "It is I, speaking in righteousness, mighty to save." Why are your garments red, like those of one treading the winepress? "I have trodden the winepress alone; from the nations no one was with me. I trampled them in my anger and trod them down in my wrath; their blood spattered my garments, and I stained all my clothing. For the day of vengeance was in my heart, and the year of my redemption has come"* (Is 63:1-4).

Edom is mentioned in Assyrian cuneiform inscriptions in the form "Udumi" or "Udumu"; three of its kings are known from the same source: K.aus-malaka at the time of Tiglath-pileser III (c. 745 BC), Malik-rammu at the time of Sennacherib (c. 705 BC), and K.aus-gabri at the time of Esarhaddon (c. 680 BC). According to the Egyptian inscriptions, the "Aduma" at times, extended their possessions to the borders of Egypt.

After the conquest of Judah by the Babylonians, the Edomites were allowed to settle in the region of Hebron. They prospered in this new country, that was called by the Greeks and Romans "Idumaea" or "Idumea", for more than four centuries, and were responsible for constructing the ancient city of Petra, carved from solid stone.

The historian, Strabo, writing around the time of Christ, stated that the Idumaeans, whom he identified as of Nabataean origin, constituted the majority of the population of Western Judea, where they commingled with the Judaeans and adopted their customs. Ethnically, they were descendants of Ishmael and Esau who had commingled, subsequently aligning themselves against Israel. They are the people who populate those nations described in Eze 38 & 39, from whence come the armies that will attack Israel and the United States.

The reference to these people in Isaiah 63, appears to suggest that when the Messiah returns to fight Yahweh's great battle against the nations, He approaches from the South, which may suggest a connection between Zechariah's vision and this vision, where Isaiah describes the Messiah coming from the South -- the area, where the most significant battle occurred during the reign of Jehoshaphat -- when God, had earlier intervened on behalf of His people.

Zechariah's mention of this great battle, details the destruction of the wicked and the salvation of the righteous. *"The burden of the word of the Lord for Israel, saith the Lord, which stretcheth forth the heavens, and layeth the foundation of the earth, and formeth the spirit of man within him. Behold, I will make Jerusalem a cup of trembling unto all the people round about, when they shall be in the siege both against Judah and against Jerusalem. And in that day will I make Jerusalem a burdensome stone for all people: all that burden themselves with it shall be cut in pieces, though all the people of the earth be gathered together against it.*

"In that day, saith the Lord, I will smite every horse with astonishment, and his rider with madness: and I will open mine eyes upon the house of Judah, and will smite every horse of the people with blindness. And the governors of Judah shall say in their heart, The inhabitants of Jerusalem shall be my strength in the Lord of hosts their God. In that day will I make the

governors of Judah like an hearth of fire among the wood, and like a torch of fire in a sheaf; and they shall devour all the people round about, on the right hand and on the left: and Jerusalem shall be inhabited again in her own place, even in Jerusalem.

"The Lord also shall save the tents of Judah first, that the glory of the house of David and the glory of the inhabitants of Jerusalem do not magnify themselves against Judah. In that day shall the Lord defend the inhabitants of Jerusalem; and he that is feeble among them at that day shall be as David; and the house of David shall be as God, as the angel of the Lord before them. And it shall come to pass in that day, that I will seek to destroy all the nations that come against Jerusalem.

"And I will pour upon the house of David, and upon the inhabitants of Jerusalem, the spirit of grace and of supplications: and they shall look upon me whom they have pierced, and they shall mourn for him, as one mourneth for his only son, and shall be in bitterness for him, as one that is in bitterness for his firstborn" (Zec 12:1-10). Zechariah tells us that "*Yahweh shall save the tents of Judah first.*" Jehoshaphat was king of Judah, and Judah was located in the southern part of Israel.

Compare the words of these prophecies uttered by Isaiah and Zechariah, with Ezekiel's description of this battle: "*Then those who live in the towns of Israel will go out and use the weapons for fuel and burn them up — the small and large shields, the bows and arrows, the war clubs and spears. For seven years they will use them for fuel. They will not need to gather wood from the fields or cut it from the forests, because they will use the weapons for fuel. And they will plunder those who plundered them and loot those who looted them, declares the Sovereign Lord.*

"*On that day I will give Gog a burial place in Israel, in the valley of those who travel east toward the Sea. It will block the way of travelers, because Gog and all his hordes will be buried there. So it will be called the Valley of Hamon Gog. For seven months the house of Israel will be burying them in order to cleanse the land. All the people of the land will bury them, and the day I am glorified will be a memorable day for them, declares the Sovereign Lord*" (Eze 39:9-13).

"*Son of man, this is what the Sovereign Lord says: 'Call out to every kind of bird and all the wild animals: Assemble and come together from all around to the sacrifice I am preparing for you,* the great sacrifice on the mountains of Israel. There you will eat flesh and drink blood. You will eat the flesh of mighty men and drink the blood of the princes of the earth as if they were rams and lambs, goats and bulls — all of them fattened animals from Bashan.

"At the sacrifice I am preparing for you, you will eat fat till you are glutted and drink blood till you are drunk. At my table you will eat your fill of horses and riders, mighty men and soldiers of every kind,' declares the Sovereign Lord. "I will display my glory among the nations, and all the nations will see the punishment I inflict and the hand I lay upon them. From that day forward the house of Israel will know that I am the Lord their God" (Eze 39:17-22).

The Old Testament prophets' descriptions of the Great Battle of the Day of the Lord, are all consistent with John's description in Revelation of the "Great and terrible Day of the Lord". "Then they gathered the kings together to the place that in Hebrew is called Armageddon. The seventh angel poured out his bowl into the air, and out of the temple came a loud voice from the throne, saying, "It is done!" Then there came flashes of lightning, rumblings, peals of thunder and a severe earthquake. No earthquake like it has ever occurred since man has been on earth, so tremendous was the quake. The great city split into three parts, and the cities of the nations collapsed. God remembered Babylon the Great and gave her the cup filled with the wine of the fury of his wrath. Every island fled away and the mountains could not be found. From the sky huge hailstones of about a hundred pounds each fell upon men. And they cursed God on account of the plague of hail, because the plague was so terrible" (Rev 16:16-21).

The Promised Restoration:
Following his description of the Great battle of the Day of the Lord, the prophet Ezekiel then focuses on the salvation of the righteous and their restoration to their promised land.

"Therefore this is what the Sovereign Lord says: I will now bring Jacob back from captivity and will have compassion on all the people of Israel, and I will be zealous for my holy name. They will forget their shame and all the unfaithfulness they showed toward me when they lived in safety in their land with no one to make them afraid. When I have brought them back from the nations and have gathered them from the countries of their enemies, I will show myself holy through them in the sight of many nations. Then they will know that I am the Lord their God, *for though I sent them into exile among the nations, I will gather them to their own land, not leaving any behind. I will no longer hide my face from them, for I will pour out my Spirit on the house of Israel, declares the Sovereign Lord"* (Eze 39:25-29).

Once again, the words of Ezekiel are consistent with the words of John in the Revelation. After describing the total destruction of spiritual Babylon [the alliance of the dragon (Satan), the beast (Iran and her allies), the false prophet (Radical Islam), together with the lawless ones (Mara Salvatrucha)], John describes Israel's restoration.

"Rejoice over her, O heaven! Rejoice, saints and apostles and prophets! God has judged her for the way she treated you.' Then a mighty angel picked up a boulder the size of a large millstone and threw it into the sea, and said: "With such violence the great city of Babylon will be thrown down, never to be found again. The music of harpists and musicians, flute players and trumpeters, will never be heard in you again. No workman of any trade will ever be found in you again. The sound of a millstone will never be heard in you again. The light of a lamp will never shine in you again. The voice of bridegroom and bride will never be heard in you again. Your merchants were the world's great men. By your magic spell all the nations were led astray. In her was found the blood of prophets and of the saints, and of all who have been killed on the earth."

"After this I heard what sounded like the roar of a great multitude in heaven shouting: "Hallelujah! Salvation and glory and power belong to our God, for true and just are his judgments. He has condemned the great prostitute who corrupted the earth by her adulteries. He has avenged on her the blood of his servants." And again they shouted: "Hallelujah! The smoke from her goes up for ever and ever" (Rev 18:20-19:3).

These prophecies all concern the destruction of spiritual Babylon (the ancient mystery religions) and the restoration of Spiritual Israel. The restoration spoken of is the restoration of God's People (His Children) into His heavenly kingdom, rather than the restoration of physical Israel to the Land of Palestine. This fact is made crystal clear in the words of John, which immediately follow.

"Then the twenty-four elders and the four living creatures fell down and worshiped God, who was seated on the throne. And they cried: "Amen, Hallelujah!" Then a voice came from the throne, saying: "Praise our God, all you his servants, you who

fear him, both small and great!" Then I heard what sounded like a great multitude, like the roar of rushing waters and like loud peals of thunder, shouting: "Hallelujah! For our Lord God Almighty reigns. Let us rejoice and be glad and give him glory! For the wedding of the Lamb has come, and his bride has made herself ready. Fine linen, bright and clean, was given her to wear." (Fine linen stands for the righteous acts of the saints.) Then the angel said to me, "Write: 'Blessed are those who are invited to the wedding supper of the Lamb!'" And he added, "These are the true words of God" (Rev 19:4-9).

The Physical Battle is Finished!
After the wedding of the Lamb (Christ) and his Bride (the Church) is consummated -- i.e., the church raptured and adorned with robes bright and clean (the saints' spiritual bodies of Shekinah Glory), they accompany Him on His final act against the enemies of God and His Children.

"I saw heaven standing open and there before me was a white horse, whose rider is called Faithful and True. With justice he judges and makes war. His eyes are like blazing fire, and on his head are many crowns. He has a name written on him that no one knows but he himself. He is dressed in a robe dipped in blood, and his name is the Word of God. The armies of heaven were following him, riding on white horses and dressed in fine linen, white and clean. "Out of his mouth comes a sharp sword with which to strike down the nations. "He will rule them with an iron scepter."

"He treads the winepress of the fury of the wrath of God Almighty. On his robe and on his thigh he has this name written: **KING OF KINGS AND LORD OF LORDS.**

"And I saw an angel standing in the sun, who cried in a loud voice to all the birds flying in midair, "Come, gather together for the great supper of God, so that you may eat the flesh of kings, generals, and mighty men, of horses and their riders, and the flesh of all people, free and slave, small and great." Then I saw the beast and the kings of the earth and their armies gathered together to make war against the rider on the horse and his army.

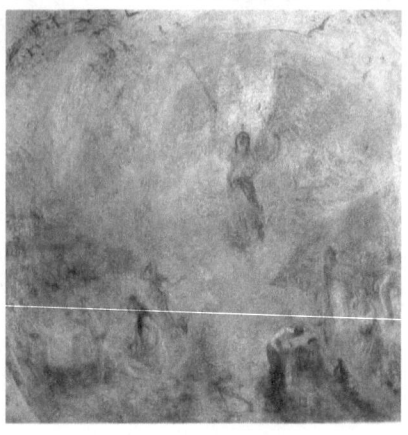

"But the beast was captured, and with him the false prophet who had performed the miraculous signs on his behalf. With these signs he had deluded those who had received the mark of the

beast and worshiped his image. The two of them [the beast (Iran and her allied nations) and the false prophet (radical Islam) -- which are inseparable] were thrown alive into the fiery lake of burning sulfur. The rest of them were killed with the sword that came out of the mouth of the rider on the horse, and all the birds gorged themselves on their flesh" (Rev 19:11-21).

In this prophecy, we see the end of the beast [the end-time political entities who have given their seat and authority to Satan (Rev 17:12-13)], however, the dragon -- (Satan), and his allied rebellious angels -- have yet to be dealt with. Satan had challenged God's authority and declared that he would establish his throne above God's (Is 14:12-15). Since this challenge was made in the heavenlies -- in the spirit realm -- it will be settled there, through divine Juris Prudence in the Court of Courts.

This necessitates the establishment of the Divine War Crimes Tribunal, and the related investigations in the Grandest, Grand Jury ever convened. This is the topic of our next chapter.

CHAPTER THIRTY
DIVINE 'WAR-CRIMES' TRIBUNAL

A tribunal is, in the general sense, any person, organization or institution given the authority to judge, adjudicate on, or determine claims or disputes — whether or not its title is referenced as a tribunal. For example, an advocate appearing before a court on which a single judge is sitting could describe that judge as 'their tribunal'. Many governmental courts titled 'tribunals' are described this way merely to emphasize the fact that they are not courts of normal jurisdiction.

Examples of this include: the International Criminal Tribunal for Rwanda. It was a body specially constituted under international law; In Great Britain, Employment Tribunals are bodies set up to hear specific employment disputes. Private judicial bodies are also often styled as 'tribunals'. The word 'tribunal' is not conclusive of a body's function. For example, in Great Britain, the Employment Appeal Tribunal is a superior court of record. The most recent trial demanding international attention and the convening of a tribunal, was the trial of Saddam Hussein, pictured above.

In this chapter, we will examine a tribunal of far greater interest to all, than that of Saddam Hussein's trial -- the Divine Tribunal, given universal authority to conduct an investigative judgment.

With the Battle of the Great Day of the Lord concluded; the righteous raptured into the heavens and the nations of the earth destroyed, it would seem that God's work on earth would be complete -- paradise lost restored. However, this is not the case. The perpetrators of the great spiritual conflict of the universe must still to be brought to judgment, and God, abiding by His profound justice, will give them their 'day in court', and include the perpetrators' victims in the court proceedings.

The apostle, Paul, tells us that all of creation eagerly awaits God's judgment of the wicked and the restoration of His children to their initial, glorious state. *"The creation waits in eager expectation for the sons of God to be revealed. For the creation was subjected to frustration, not by its own choice, but by the will of the one who subjected it, in hope that the creation itself will be liberated from its bondage to decay and brought into the glorious freedom of the children of God. We know that the whole creation has been groaning as in the pains of childbirth right up to the present time. Not only so, but we ourselves, who have the firstfruits of the Spirit, groan inwardly as we wait eagerly for our adoption as sons, the redemption of our bodies"* (Ro 8:19-23).

King David, long before, described creation's celebration when wickedness is destroyed and righteousness restored throughout the universe. *"Sing to the Lord, all the earth; proclaim his salvation day after day. Declare his glory among the nations, his marvelous deeds among all peoples. For great is the Lord and most worthy of praise; he is to be feared above all gods. For all the gods of the nations are idols, but the* L<small>ORD</small> *made the heavens.*

"Splendor and majesty are before him; strength and joy in his dwelling place. Ascribe to the Lord, O families of nations, ascribe to the Lord glory and strength, ascribe to the Lord the glory due his name. Bring an offering and come before him; worship the Lord in the splendor of his holiness. Tremble before him, all the earth! The world is firmly established; it cannot be moved.

"Let the heavens rejoice, let the earth be glad; let them say among the nations, "The Lord reigns!" Let the sea resound, and all that is in it; let the fields be jubilant, and everything in them! Then the trees of the forest will sing, they will sing for joy before the Lord, for he comes to judge the earth. Give thanks to the

Lord, for he is good; his love endures forever. Cry out, "Save us, O God our Savior; gather us and deliver us from the nations, that we may give thanks to your holy name, that we may glory in your praise" (1Ch 16:23-35).

Understanding what God's judgment of the world would usher in, David prayed: *"Rise up, O God, judge the earth, for all the nations are your inheritance"* (Ps 82:8); *"Rise up, O Judge of the earth; pay back to the proud what they deserve"* (Ps 94:2). To the righteous, David counseled: *"Let them sing before the Lord, for he comes to judge the earth. He will judge the world in righteousness and the peoples with equity"* (Ps 98:9).

Isaiah, prophesied concerning this same tribunal, saying: *"The Lord takes his place in court; he rises to judge the people. The Lord enters into judgment against the elders and leaders of his people: "It is you who have ruined my vineyard; the plunder from the poor is in your houses. What do you mean by crushing my people and grinding the faces of the poor?" declares the Lord, the Lord Almighty"* (Is 3:13-15).

Identifying Christ's role in this tribunal, Isaiah wrote: *"A shoot will come up from the stump of Jesse; from his roots a Branch will bear fruit. The Spirit of the Lord will rest on him — the Spirit of wisdom and of understanding, the Spirit of counsel and of power, the Spirit of knowledge and of the fear of the Lord — and he will delight in the fear of the Lord. He will not judge by what he sees with his eyes, or decide by what he hears with his ears; but with righteousness he will judge the needy, with justice he will give decisions for the poor of the earth. He will strike the earth with the rod of his mouth; with the breath of his lips he will slay the wicked. Righteousness will be his belt and faithfulness the sash around his waist"* (Is 11:1-5).

Paul, testifying before the Council in Thessalonica warned his listeners of this coming judgment, and Christ's role: *"For he has set a day when he will judge the world with justice by the man he has appointed. He has given proof of this to all men by raising him from the dead"* (Ac 17:31).

The Type (Mortal) and the Archetype (Spiritual) Tribunals: As previously indicated, God has given us -- his children -- on earth, a type of the archetype in the heavenly. He gave us the sanctuary, or tabernacle, representing both the heavenly temple and the human soul (the temple of God). He gave us the sacrificial system, given to serve as "a shadow of things to come, whose reality is in Christ." This was given to help us understand

God's redemptive work for mankind, including Christ's incarnation in human flesh, his sacrifice on the cross. He gave the righteous, the indwelling of Holy Spirit, which is but a token, or down payment of all that God has in store for us in heaven! (2 Co 5:5).

These earthly types were all descriptive of the archetype (spiritual) -- patterns of heavenly things.

He gave us Solomon's temple, built by Solomon, only after his father, David, had conquered the last of the giants and seized control of the ancient city of Salem. Salem, once the seat of Melchizedek's kingdom, had been taken over by the Amorites. But about 1000 BC, David subdued the Amorites, preempted their dominion, and renamed the city 'New Salem' (Jerusalem). Jerusalem and Solomon's Temple then served as the earthly type -- a physical model -- of the heavenly (spiritual) archetype: 'New Jerusalem' [New-new-Salem], the seat of the temple of God almighty.

In similar fashion, after Solomon had completed the Temple, God directed him to construct The King's Palace, that was connected to The Throne Hall, and the Hall of Justice; and a separate Queen's Palace, for his bride: the daughter of Pharaoh -- all being earthly types of the heavenly archetypes.

"He built the Palace of the Forest of Lebanon a hundred cubits long, fifty wide and thirty high, with four rows of cedar columns supporting trimmed cedar beams. It was roofed with cedar above the beams that rested on the columns — forty-five beams, fifteen to a row. Its windows were placed high in sets of three, facing each other. All the doorways had rectangular frames; they were in the front part in sets of three, facing each other. He made a colonnade fifty cubits long and thirty wide. In front of it was a portico, and in front of that were pillars and an overhanging roof.

"He built the throne hall, the Hall of Justice, where he was to judge, and he covered it with cedar from floor to ceiling. And the palace in which he was to live, set farther back, was similar in design. Solomon also made a palace like this hall for Pharaoh's daughter, whom he had married" (1Ki 7:2-8).

In the archetype (spiritual) setting, the redeemed serve God day and night in His temple. Of these, one of the elders, explained to John, that *"These in white robes ... are they who have come out of the great tribulation; they have washed their robes and made them white in the blood of the Lamb. Therefore, "they are before the throne of God and serve him day and night in his temple; and he who sits on the throne will spread his tent over them. Never again will they hunger; never again will they thirst. The sun will not beat upon them, nor any scorching heat. For the Lamb at the center of the throne will be their shepherd; he will lead them to springs of living water. And God will wipe away every tear from their eyes"* (Rev 7:14-17).

Judging Spiritual Perpetrators (Fallen Angels):
The apostle and prophet, John -- author of the Revelation -- describes this investigative judgment: this 'war-crimes tribunal' as follows: *"And I saw an angel coming down out of heaven, having the key to the Abyss and holding in his hand a great chain. He seized the dragon, that ancient serpent, who is the devil, or Satan, and bound him for a thousand years. He threw*

him into the Abyss, and locked and sealed it over him, to keep him from deceiving the nations anymore until the thousand years were ended. After that, he must be set free for a short time.

"I saw thrones on which were seated those who had been given authority to judge. And I saw the souls of those who had been beheaded because of their testimony for Jesus and because of the word of God. They had not worshiped the beast or his image and had not received his mark on their foreheads or their hands. They came to life and reigned with Christ a thousand years.

"(The rest of the dead did not come to life until the thousand years were ended.) This is the first resurrection. Blessed and holy are those who have part in the first resurrection. The second death has no power over them, but they will be priests of God and of Christ and will reign with him for a thousand years." ... "Then I saw a great white throne and him who was seated on it. Earth and sky fled from his presence, and there was no place for them.

"And I saw the dead, great and small, standing before the throne, and books were opened. Another book was opened, which is the book of life. The dead were judged according to what they had done as recorded in the books. The sea gave up the dead that were in it, and death and Hades gave up the dead that were in them, and each person was judged according to what he had done" (Rev 20:1-6 & 11-13).

The Lord is Just:
The Psalmist refers to this divine tribunal, saying: **"The Lord is known by his justice; the wicked are ensnared by the work of their hands.** The wicked return to the grave, all the nations that forget God. But the needy will not always be forgotten, nor the hope of the afflicted ever perish. Arise, O Lord, let not man triumph; let the nations be judged in your presence. Strike them with terror, O Lord; let the nations know they are but men" (Ps 9:16-19).

The apostle, Paul, discussing the appropriate protocol for Christians to resolve conflicts between themselves, made reference to this end-time divine war-crimes tribunal: *"If any of you has a dispute with another, dare he take it before the ungodly for judgment instead of before the saints?* **Do you not know that the saints will judge the world? And if you are to judge the world, are you not competent to judge trivial cases? Do you not know that we will judge angels? How much more the things of this life!**" (1Co 6:1-3).

Why does God grant men a role in judging angels? Because angels were created to serve as *"ministering spirits, sent forth to minister (or care for) them who shall be heirs of salvation (God's children: mankind)"* (Heb 1:14). Matthew, discussing the elect, referring especially to the newly baptized elect, whom he refers to as *"one of these little ones"* (i.e., a small innocent child not yet baptized), says that *"in heaven their angels see the face of My Father who is in heaven"* (Mt 18:10). This implies that one of the tasks of angels is to look after each person who has responded to God's call, has responded and been baptized, as well as little spiritual children (those young in the Lord). These Scriptures are incidentally, among those that support the concept of each person having a guardian angel.

Angels - Mortal or Immortal?
Some have contended that angels are immortal -- not able to die. This seems to be mere conjecture since there is no Scripture that states such. The angel's body at the present time is made up of light -- an antimatter, or spiritual substance (Lk 24:4). They were created beings and have been given the ability to choose -- to obey, or defy -- the Law of God and His voiced commands.

In his vision, Ezekiel (28:11) presents an interesting discussion that initially seems to refer to the King of Tyrus (Tyre). But, the end of verse 12 clarifies the context, making it plain he is speaking of the leader of the fallen angels, Satan (the Devil). He is compared to the King of Tyrus (Tyre), walking in the midst of the stones of fire at the throne of God on his holy mountain (Mount Zion in New Jerusalem). Ezekiel continues to explain that Satan's heart was lifted up with pride over his beauty and position, resulting in him defiling God's sanctuary 'by the multitude of his iniquities'.

Everlastingly Burned ~ Not Burned Everlastingly:
Note that in Eze 28:18, God says he will make Satan ashes. This sounds like angelic beings can be destroyed, even though they are made of Spirit (antimatter). With God all things are possible (Mt 19:26, Mk 10:27; 14:36).

Ezekiel (18:20) tells us the soul that sins shall die (or cease to exist, according to the meaning of the Hebrew word *'muwth'*. The word, soul, often translated as referring to the life-force (i.e., man's intellect, emotions, beliefs, etc.), suggests it may refer to angelic beings and humans alike. Only God can prevent humans from being resurrected into a new body containing that life-force; and only God can remove this life-force from angels.

Jude 6 states that fallen angels are kept in everlasting chains, in utter darkness, unto (until) the judgment of the great day. Jude does not indicate their ultimate disposition, and we can find no scriptural support for the concept that they will be kept alive, in torment or torture forever and ever.

We are told in Scripture that one very highly favored angel called Heylel, holding the rank of cherub, -- or, as his name is more correctly translated -- Lucifer [(Is 14), [The story of Hylel being an alternate account of this same being], chose to sin and disobey the Law of God. He apparently convinced one-third of all the angelic beings to do the same (Rev 12:4), resulting in their being cast out of heaven, and thrust into [not onto] the earth (Eze 28:17). They have, therefore, been incarcerated, confined in the abyss, or bottomless pit, until such time that the Father permits their release to complete His plan according to His will. (Jude 6)

When the elected (redeemed) saints have been transfigured, restored to their spiritual bodies at the first resurrection, they will, according to Paul, ascend to heaven to participate in the investigative judgment (1 Co 6:1-4). And, if saints are capable of judging angels, Paul contends. they should be able to tell whether or not anyone is obeying or defying the Law and Will of God while still in the flesh (as physical beings).

Angels Long to Know:
Angels, enjoy God's presence. They know a great deal, but they do not know all there is to know. **Angels look forward to the day when the elected saints (the redeemed) will be able teach them the deep things of God.** 1 Peter 1:12 tells us that they want to understand these things but **they do not even understand why they are doing what they are doing!** *"It was revealed to them that they were not serving themselves but you, when they spoke of the things that have now been told you by those who have preached the gospel to you by the Holy Spirit sent from heaven."*

Angels were not, according to the author of Hebrews, promised to rule the world, nor to become Sons and Daughters of God. *"For if the message spoken by angels was binding, and every violation and disobedience received its just punishment, how shall we escape if we ignore such a great salvation? This salvation, which was first announced by the Lord, was confirmed to us by those who heard him. God also testified to it by signs, wonders and various miracles, and gifts of the Holy Spirit distributed according to his will.*

"It is not to angels that he has subjected the world to come, about which we are speaking. But there is a place where someone has testified: "What is man that you are mindful of him, the son of man that you care for him? You made him a little lower than divine beings; you crowned him with glory and honor and put everything under his feet." *In putting everything under him, God left nothing that is not subject to him. Yet at present we do not see everything subject to him.*

"But we see Jesus, who was made a little lower than the angels, now crowned with glory and honor because he suffered death, so that by the grace of God he might taste death for everyone. In bringing many sons to glory, it was fitting that God, for whom and through whom everything exists, should make the author of their salvation perfect through suffering. Both the one who makes men holy and those who are made holy are of the same family. So Jesus is not ashamed to call them brothers.

"He says, "I will declare your name to my brothers; in the presence of the congregation I will sing your praises." And again, "I will put my trust in him." And again he says, "Here am I, and the children God has given me." Since the children have flesh and blood, he too shared in their humanity so that by his death he might destroy him who holds the power of death — that is, the devil — and free those who all their lives were held in slavery by their fear of death"

*"***For surely it is not angels he helps, but Abraham's descendants***. For this reason he had to be made like his brothers in every way, in order that he might become a merciful and faithful high priest in service to God, and that he might make atonement for the sins of the people. Because he himself suffered when he was tempted, he is able to help those who are being tempted"* (Heb 2:2-18).

The Divine Tribunal's Purpose:
"God did not spare the angels when they sinned, but sent them to hell, putting them into gloomy confinement, to be held for judgment" (2 Pet 2:4). When God cast these angels (the allies of Satan) out of heaven (the spiritual realm), and thrust them into the earth (the physical realm), He placed restrictions on their powers, limiting them to "their proper domain" or "first estate," that is, within the earth. There, they await their judgment for their rebellion.

The word translated 'Hell' in 2 Peter 2:4 is *'tartaroo'*, referring to a place of restraint for the wicked. Though Satan himself may have appeared before God's throne in heaven, it was at God's summons. Satan, the fallen angels, and the demons who he directs [the offspring of the Fallen Watchers and daughters of men (Gen 6:1-4)], can do only what God permits, according to His sovereign purpose and plan. (Job 1:6-12; 2:1-7).

There will come a day that even the angelic world will be judged to see whether they have obeyed, or defied the Will and Laws of God. **Why do angels need to be judged?** Because at least one third of them have sinned and deserve death. **Who will do this judging?** Those who have entered into the Kingdom of God as spirit-born children of God. As the prior victims of the fallen angels, the redeemed have the unique ability to sit in seats of judgment in this Divine War-crimes Tribunal. **Where will this judgment take place?** In the judgment hall of God's Temple, in the heavens.

When will this take place? In the end-times, after Christ has returned to rapture (remove) His church, and judge the wicked, resulting in their self-imposed deaths as they cry for the rocks and mountains to fall on them (Rev 6:16). **How long will this tribunal last?** At Christ's second coming, the redeemed who are dead come to life (Rev 20:4), and those who are still alive, *"shall be caught up together with them in the clouds, to meet the Lord in the air"* (1 Th 4:17). Collectively they will conduct this investigative judgment for 1,000 years (Rev 20:4) -- often referred to as the Millennium.

What function will the redeemed have in this tribunal? Under the guidance and authority of Jesus Christ, the resurrected, redeemed, saints will help to judge the world. Just as we are being judged now, we will, throughout the Millennium, judge those who have tormented us. We will, during this era, also judge the angels who rebelled against God under Lucifer (I Co 6:3; II Pet 2:4; Jude 6; Is 14:12-15).

The Investigative Judgment:
This investigative judgment might well be called 'The Great Grand Jury', for compared to our earthly judicial system, this investigative judgment is equivalent to our Grand Jury, when convened. Grand Juries have supreme authority within their judicial jurisdiction. In this case, the redeemed, under the guidance of Jesus Christ, who suffered, leaving us an example (1 Pe 2:21), will have authority over the universe.

Grasping this concept -- that the redeemed will investigate the conduct of the angels -- one can better understand Peter's admonition, when he wrote: *"Humble yourselves, therefore, under God's mighty hand, that he may lift you up in due time. Cast all your anxiety on him because he cares for you. Be self-controlled and alert. Your enemy the devil prowls around like a roaring lion looking for someone to devour. Resist him, standing firm in the faith, because you know that your brothers throughout the world are undergoing the same kind of sufferings. And the God of all grace, who called you to his eternal glory in Christ, after you have suffered a little while, will himself restore you and make you strong, firm and steadfast. To him be the power for ever and ever. Amen"* (1 Pe 5:6-11).

This Divine 'War-Crimes Tribunal' is this investigative judgment; the Grand Jury of the cosmos. The final, executory judgment -- the subject of our next chapter -- belongs to the Lord.

CHAPTER THIRTY-ONE
HELL FIRE AND BRIMSTONE

The Millennium:
In our last chapter, we pictured the return of our Lord -- commonly referred to as 'The Second Coming'. At that moment, those who died in the Lord will be resurrected and ascend, to be joined in the clouds by the righteous who are still alive on the earth at that time. Together, they will be raptured into the heavens. At this same time, or immediately preceding this, Satan (the Devil) is bound, with a great chain and cast into the abyss which is sealed over him, to prevent him from deceiving the nations of the earth, until the thousand years are finished (Rev 20:1-3).

The Millennial Activities of the Redeemed:
In the last chapter, we saw the Divine War-Crimes Tribunal convened, and the redeemed seated on this tribunal, charged with the investigative judgment of those rebellious, lost mortals, and the fallen angels. We also learned that this judicial responsibility will be the principal occupation of the redeemed for a thousand years -- often referred to as the Millennium. **Heaven, however, is not the final home of the redeemed.**

Moreover, there are still the wicked dead and the fallen angels back on earth to deal with.

During the Millennium, things on earth are seemingly at a standstill. Satan and his host of fallen angels are confined to the abyss. Satan: formerly known as Lucifer. the standard-bearer of the holy colors and leader of the heavenly worship, now awaits his final destiny. In addition to being cast into the abyss (elsewhere in Scripture defined as the world in chaos), Satan is bound with a great chain. That chain, is apparently of a spiritual, and circumstantial nature: the wicked are all dead, so there is no one to deceive, and the righteous -- both those who had been resurrected and those still living when Christ returns -- have been raptured, leaving Satan no one to tempt or torment.

The Millennial Activities of the Fallen Angels:
Satan has a thousand years to look upon the destruction he has caused, a millennium to reflect on all he has lost and the certain destruction that awaits him, and a painfully long time to listen to and answer the mournful complaints of the host of angels who joined him in his rebellion, only to see his boastful claims dashed, and their prideful ambitions, dashed. The prophet, Isaiah, describes this era as follows:

"The grave below is all astir to meet you at your coming; it rouses the spirits of the departed to greet you — all those who were leaders in the world; it makes them rise from their thrones — all those who were kings over the nations. They will all respond, they will say to you, "You also have become weak, as we are; you have become like us." All your pomp has been brought down to the grave, along with the noise of your harps; maggots are spread out beneath you and worms cover you.

"How you have fallen from heaven, O morning star, son of the dawn! You have been cast down to the earth, you who once laid low the nations! You said in your heart, "I will ascend to heaven; I will raise my throne above the stars of God; I will sit enthroned on the mount of assembly, on the utmost heights of the sacred mountain. I will ascend above the tops of the clouds; I will make *myself like the Most High." But you are brought down to the grave, to the depths of the pit.*

"Those who see you stare at you, they ponder your fate: "Is this the man who shook the earth and made kingdoms tremble, the man who made the world a desert, who overthrew its cities and would not let his captives go home?" All the kings of the nations lie in state, each in his own tomb. But you are cast out of your tomb like a rejected branch; you are covered with the slain, with those pierced by the sword, those who descend to the stones of the pit. Like a corpse trampled underfoot, you will not join them in burial, for you have destroyed your land and killed your people. The offspring of the wicked will never be mentioned again" (Is 14:9-20).

Reinforcing this vision, Isaiah later declared God's warning and promise concerning these last-day events, saying: *"Go, my people, enter your rooms (or, enter your inner-room) and shut the doors behind you; hide yourselves for a little while until his wrath has passed by. See, the Lord is coming out of his dwelling to punish the people of the earth for their sins. The earth will disclose the blood shed upon her; she will conceal her slain no longer. In that day, the Lord will punish with his sword, his fierce, great and powerful sword, Leviathan the gliding serpent, Leviathan the coiling serpent; he will slay the monster of the sea"* (Is 26:20-27:1).

The 'inner-room' Isaiah references in this Scripture, where God's people are to hide until His wrath has passed by, seemingly refers to their own inner-beings -- their spirits. In other words, the righteous will have reached that point where they have submitted their bodies a living sacrifice to God (Rom 12:1), freeing themselves, through the power of the indwelling Holy Spirit, from the desires of the flesh (Eph 2).

Spirit Demons Punished:
The three entities Isaiah mentions, whom God will punish in that day are: [the gliding serpent, the coiling serpent, and the monster of the sea]. These correlate with those three entities mentioned by John, in Revelation: *"Then I saw three evil spirits that looked like frogs; they came out of the mouth of the dragon, out of the mouth of the beast and out of the mouth of the false prophet. They are spirits of demons performing miraculous signs, and they go out to the kings of the whole world, to gather them for the battle on the great day of God Almighty"* (Rev 16: 13-14).

In Hebrew, the words translated 'gliding serpent', are *[haqaashaah liwyaataan]*, more correctly translated 'the obstinate, stiff-necked, stubborn serpent' -- clearly speaking of the dragon, or Satan. The term 'coiling serpent', stems from the Hebrew *[w.hack-zaaqaah w-al baariach naachaash]*, that is more properly translated, 'the violent and crooked hissing one', correlative with the false prophet in Revelation. And the term translated 'monster of the sea', stems from the Hebrew *[liv-yaw-thawn naachaash]*, is more properly translated, 'the hissing monster of the sea'. which correlates with the beast of (Rev 16), referring to the evil 'hissing' kingdom of Persia, that will be made up of many peoples [represented by the waters, or sea, since waters prophetically symbolize nations and peoples -- multitudes of many tongues] (Rev 17:15).

Christ will slay the monster of the sea [the wicked people of the nations of the earth (Is 27:1)] at his second coming. However, the complete annihilation of the gliding serpent, the dragon (or Satan) and the coiling serpent, the false-prophet (the mystery religions of Babylon the Great) which are undergirded by Satan, will not take place until after the Millennium.

Isaiah said: *"In that day the Lord will thresh [harvest] from the flowing Euphrates to the Wadi of Egypt, and you, O Israelites, will be gathered up one by one. And in that day a great trumpet will sound. Those who were perishing in Assyria and those who were exiled in Egypt will come and worship the Lord on the holy mountain in Jerusalem"* (Is 27:12-13). At his second coming, Christ will thresh the nations, as testified to by the prophecies of Joel and Revelation, previously cited. At that time, He will also rapture his church.

The Israelites who are being gathered up one by one (vs 12), have in entering the kingdom of God and of His son, Christ, come to worship the Lord on the Holy Mountain, since -- as His Word states, the church is His kingdom, that holy mountain. Thus, this prophecy of Isaiah correlates with Christ's prophecy of them entering his kingdom one by one, recorded by both Matthew and Luke:

"But as the days of Noah were, so shall also the coming of the Son of man be. For as in the days that were before the flood they were eating and drinking, marrying and giving in marriage, until the day that Noah entered into the ark, and knew not until the flood came, and took them all away. So shall also the coming of the Son of man be. At that time, there shall two be in the field; the one shall be taken, and the other left. Two women shall

be grinding at the mill; the one shall be taken, and the other left"* (Mt 24:37-41; Lk 17:34-36).

Post-millennial Activities:
Returning to John's revelatory vision, where we left off, we read: **"The rest of the dead did not come to life until the thousand years were ended.** *This is the first resurrection. Blessed and holy are those who have part in the first resurrection. The second death has no power over them, but they will be priests of God and of Christ and will reign with him for a thousand years"* (Rev 20:6).

John states that the nations of the earth who, in the end-times, attack God's people, will -- along with the devil and the false prophet -- be thrown into the lake of burning sulfur.

"When the thousand years are over, Satan will be released from his prison and will go out to deceive the nations in the four corners of the earth — Gog and Magog — to gather them for battle. In number they are like the sand on the seashore. They marched across the breadth of the earth and surrounded the camp of God's people, the city he loves. But fire came down from heaven and devoured them. *And the devil, who deceived them, was thrown into the lake of burning sulfur, where the beast and the false prophet had been thrown. They will be tormented day and night for ever and ever"* (Rev 20:5-8).

The last verse, which has been translated in the King James Version, *"They will be tormented day and night for ever and ever"* is very enlightening, when one carefully reviews the Greek text. The Greek says *[kai basanistheesontai heemeras kai nuktos eis tous aioonas toon aioonoon]*. A transliteration of this would read: *"Then vexing torment dawn and night (midnight) continually for the perpetuity -- that perpetuity."* One translation renders this Scripture: 'they will be forever tormented through the ages of ages' (AMP). Another renders it, They will all suffer eternally.

In an effort to resolve this, consider the following Scriptures:

- **"The Lord rained down burning sulfur on Sodom and Gomorrah** — *from the Lord out of the heavens"* (Gen 19:24).

- *"It was the same in the days of Lot. People were eating and drinking, buying and selling, planting and building.*

But the day Lot left Sodom, **fire and sulfur rained down from heaven and destroyed them all**" (Lk 17:28-29).

- "**He condemned the cities of Sodom and Gomorrah by burning them to ashes, and made them an example of what is going to happen to the ungodly**" (2 Pe 2:6).

- "Sodom and Gomorrah and the surrounding towns gave themselves up to sexual immorality and perversion. **They serve as an example of those who suffer the punishment of eternal fire**" (Jude 7).

When God rained down burning sulfur on the ancient cities of Sodom and Gomorrah, they were not merely burned, they were burned up -- not only reduced to ashes, but totally destroyed. The Dead Sea, also called the Salt Sea -- the site of ancient Sodom and Gomorrah -- is now the lowest elevation on earth: 1385 feet below mean sea level.

Sodom and Gomorrah have been given us as an example of what will happen to the ungodly -- an example of eternal fire. Beyond the shadow of a doubt, Sodom and Gomorrah are not still burning: they are covered by approximately 900 feet of water! Based on this Scriptural evidence, it is apparent that the 'eternal hell fire' mentioned in Revelation 20, must be understood as a fire that consumes everything for eternity [once and for all], rather than as a fire that burns eternally.

Who Suffers the Second Death in Hell Fire?
Jesus made it clear that Hell Fire -- which he referred to as **'the eternal fire' was prepared for the devil and his angels** (Mt 25:41). He also made it crystal-clear that only those humans who choose to join them by living their lives in rebellion to God -- defying His authority and refusing his proffered salvation (redemption and restoration to His family), will share in this eternal fire.

"Then he will say to those on his left, 'Depart from me, you who are cursed, into the eternal fire prepared for the devil and his angels" (Mt 25:41).

Ezekiel, speaking prophetically of the ultimate destruction of Satan, wrote: *"Your heart became proud on account of your beauty, and you corrupted your wisdom because of your splendor. So I threw you to the earth; I made a spectacle of you before kings. By your many sins and dishonest trade you have desecrated your sanctuaries. So **I made a fire come out from you, and it consumed you, and I reduced you to ashes** on the ground in the sight of all who were watching. All the nations who knew you are appalled at you; you have come to a horrible end and will be no more"* (Eze 28:17-19).

The prophet, Malachi, declared that the wicked people -- every evildoer -- will burn like stubble when God destroys the earth with fire. *"**Surely the day is coming; it will burn like a furnace**. All **the arrogant and every evildoer will be stubble**, and that day that is coming will set them on fire," says the Lord Almighty. "Not a root or a branch will be left to them. But for you who revere my name, the sun of righteousness will rise with healing in its wings. And you will go out and leap like calves released from the stall. **Then you will trample down the wicked; they will be ashes under the soles of your feet on the day when I do these things**," says the Lord Almighty"* (Mal 4:1-3).

The Timing:
Malachi's description of the end-time events is consistent with the prophecies of both Ezekiel and John. Ezekiel wrote: *"Son of man, prophesy against Gog and say: 'This is what the Sovereign Lord says: **I am against you, O Gog, chief prince of Meshech and Tubal. I will turn you around and drag you along. I will bring you from the far north and send you against the mountains of Israel.** Then I will strike your bow from your left hand and make your arrows drop from your right*

hand. On the mountains of Israel you will fall, you and all your troops and the nations with you.

"I will give you as food to all kinds of carrion birds and to the wild animals. You will fall in the open field, for I have spoken, declares the Sovereign Lord. **I will send fire on Magog and on those who live in safety in the coastlands, and they will know that I am the Lord.** I will make known my holy name among my people Israel. I will no longer let my holy name be profaned, and the nations will know that I the Lord am the Holy One in Israel. It is coming! It will surely take place, declares the Sovereign Lord. This is the day I have spoken of" (Eze 39:1-8).
...

"Son of man, this is what the Sovereign Lord says: Call out to every kind of bird and all the wild animals: 'Assemble and come together from all around to the sacrifice I am preparing for you, the great sacrifice on the mountains of Israel. There you will eat flesh and drink blood. You will eat the flesh of mighty men and drink the blood of the princes of the earth as if they were rams and lambs, goats and bulls — all of them fattened animals from Bashan. At the sacrifice I am preparing for you, you will eat fat till you are glutted and drink blood till you are drunk. At my table you will eat your fill of horses and riders, mighty men and soldiers of every kind,' declares the Sovereign Lord. I will display my glory among the nations, and all the nations will see the punishment I inflict and the hand I lay upon them" (Eze 39:17-21).

The Lake of Fire"
Referring once again to John's revelatory prophecy, we read: "I saw the beast and the kings of the earth and their armies gathered together to make war against the rider on the horse and his army. But **the beast was captured, and with him the false prophet who had performed the miraculous signs on his behalf. With these signs he had deluded those who had received the mark of the beast and worshiped his image. The two of them were thrown alive into the fiery lake of burning sulfur"** (Rev 19:19-20).

"When the thousand years are over, Satan will be released from his prison and will go out to deceive the nations in the four corners of the earth — Gog and Magog — to gather them for battle. In number they are like the sand on the seashore. They marched across the breadth of the earth and surrounded the camp of God's people, the city he loves.

But fire came down from heaven and devoured them. And the devil, who deceived them, was thrown into the lake of burning sulfur, where the beast and the false prophet had been thrown. They will be tormented day and night for ever and ever.

The Sentencing Judgment:
Following the investigative judgment, conducted by Christ and the redeemed in the Divine War-Crimes Tribunal during the Millennium, it is time for the sentencing of the lost. This is a function reserved unto God Almighty. *"There is,"* as testified by Christ's brother, James, *"only one Lawgiver and Judge, the one who is able to save and destroy"* (Jas 4:12). After all the testimony has been presented during the Millennial Tribunal,

"The Lord will rise up as he did at Mount Perazim, **He will rouse himself as in the Valley of Gibeon — to do his work, his strange work, and perform his task, his alien task"** (Isa 28:21).

Imagine yourself in the heavenly judgment hall, with the Divine Judge -- Almighty God -- presiding. The task He is about to undertake is alien to His loving nature -- a task the prophet, Isaiah, refers to it as God's strange work: His alien task. All of heaven has awaited this moment: the restoration of God's family.

Before the judgment seat of God Almighty, stands His First Begotten Son -- our Elder Brother, Jesus Christ. **He stands before His Father in the heavenly tribunal to testify on our behalf -- as the advocate of the redeemed.** It was, after all, for these -- the saints: you and I -- that he died. John, the apocalyptic prophet, describes this galvanizing episode as follows:

"I looked and there before me was a great multitude that no one could count, from every nation, tribe, people and language, standing before the throne and in front of the Lamb. They were wearing white robes and were holding palm branches in their hands. And they cried out in a loud voice: "Salvation belongs to our God, who sits on the throne, and to the Lamb." All the angels were standing around the throne and around the elders and the four living creatures. They fell down on their faces before the throne and worshiped God, saying: "Amen! Praise and glory and wisdom and thanks and honor and power and strength be to our God for ever and ever. Amen!"

"Then one of the elders asked me, "These in white robes — who are they, and where did they come from?" I answered, "Sir, you know." And he said, "These are they who have come out of the great tribulation; they have washed their robes and made them white in the blood of the Lamb. Therefore, "they are before the throne of God and serve him day and night in his temple; and he who sits on the throne will spread his tent over them. Never again will they hunger; never again will they thirst. The sun will not beat upon them, nor any scorching heat. For the Lamb at the center of the throne will be their shepherd; he will lead them to springs of living water. And God will wipe away every tear from their eyes." (Rev 7:9-17).

"Then I saw a great white throne and him who was seated on it. Earth and sky fled from his presence, and there was no place for them. And I saw the dead, great and small, standing before the throne, and books were opened. Another book was opened, which is the book of life. The dead were judged according to what they had done as recorded in the books. The sea gave up the dead that were in it, and death and Hades gave up the dead that were in them, and each person was judged according to what he had done" (Rev 20:3-6).

Concerning the redeemed, whom the oppressor (Satan) has held captive, refusing to let them go, it was prophesied: *"Let the wicked forsake his way and the evil man his thoughts. Let him turn to the Lord, for he will have mercy on him, and to our God, for he will freely pardon"* (Isa 55:7). Now fulfilled, it is proclaimed: *"Their Redeemer is strong; the Lord of hosts is His name. He will surely and thoroughly plead their case and defend* their cause, that He may give rest to the earth, and unrest to the inhabitants of Babylon" (Jer 50:34).

The Executory Judgment:
Common to most Hebrew and Greek Scriptures, the end result, or outcome, is expressed first, followed by the process through which it takes place. According to this custom, John looking at the final result, says: **"Then death and Hades were thrown into the lake of fire. The lake of fire is the second death. If anyone's name was not found written in the book of life, he was thrown into the lake of fire"** (Rev 20:7-15).

The events leading up to this climactic moment, are themselves profound. The nations of the earth, who first attacked the nation of Israel, then turned their demonic fervor against the United States and her allies, have been led back to Israel, back to the Land of Palestine. As indicated by both Ezekiel and John, the battle has been fearsome, the outcome almost unbelievable. Ezekiel and John both indicate that the Lord will intervene at this moment, on behalf of His chosen ones. But only the prophet, Zechariah, describes the incredulous results of this aftermath.

"In the whole land," declares the Lord, "two-thirds will be struck down and perish; yet one-third will be left in it. This third I will bring into the fire; I will refine them like silver and test them like gold. They will call on my name and I will answer them; I will say, 'They are my people,' and they will say, 'The Lord is our God" (Zec 13:8-9).

"Then the Lord will go out and fight against those nations, as he fights in the day of battle. On that day his feet will stand on the Mount of Olives, east of Jerusalem, and the Mount of Olives will be split in two from east to west, forming a great valley, with half of the mountain moving north and half moving south. You will flee by my mountain valley, for it will extend to Azel. You will flee as you fled from the earthquake in the days of Uzziah king of Judah. Then the Lord my God will come, and all the holy ones with him. On that day there will be no light, no cold or frost. It will be a unique day, without daytime or nighttime — a day known to the Lord. When evening comes, there will be light" (Zec 14:3-7).

Satan's Last Challenge:
As Christ descends with ten thousand times ten thousand, and thousands upon thousands of angels, together with the million of

saints, now redeemed and restored to the Family of God, other events are occurring upon the earth.

"When the thousand years are over, Satan will be released from his prison and will go out to deceive the nations in the four corners of the earth — Gog and Magog — to gather them for battle. In number they are like the sand on the seashore. They marched across the breadth of the earth and surrounded the camp of God's people, the city he loves" (Rev 20:7-9).

At that point in this universal drama of the ages, that prophecy Solomon in Ecclesiastes, is fulfilled: *"For God will bring every deed into judgment, including every hidden thing, whether it is good or evil"* (Ecc 12:14). The apostle, Paul, seems to be making reference to this when he wrote: *"For no one can lay any foundation other than the one already laid, which is Jesus Christ. If any man builds on this foundation using gold, silver, costly stones, wood, hay or straw, **his work will be shown for what it is, because the Day will bring it to light. It will be revealed with fire, and the fire will test the quality of each man's work**"* (1Co 3:11-13).

As Satan, his host of fallen angels, the kings of the earth, the false prophet, and all those who have defied the will and law of

God, surround the camp of the saints, planning to besiege it, they will have their every deed -- whether good or evil -- displayed before the universe.

God's Sentence Pronounced:

The shock is too much for them. In an instant, *"every hand will go limp, every knee become as weak as water"* (Eze 7:17). *"Every knee will bow ... Every tongue confess to God"* (Rom 14:11; Php 2:10). Then Jesus Christ -- King of Kings and Lord of Lords -- will address them, declaring: ***"It is done.*** *I am the Alpha and the Omega, the Beginning and the End. To him who is thirsty I will give to drink without cost from the spring of the water of life. He who overcomes will inherit all this, and I will be his God and he will be my son.*

"But the cowardly, the unbelieving, the vile, the murderers, the sexually immoral, those who practice magic arts, the idolaters and all liars — their place will be in the fiery lake of burning sulfur. This is the second death" (Rev 21:6-8).

This event was prophesied long ago by Zephaniah: *"The great day of the Lord is near — near and coming quickly. Listen! The cry on the day of the Lord will be bitter, the shouting of the warrior there. That day will be a day of wrath, a day of distress and anguish, a day of trouble and ruin, a day of darkness and gloom, a day of clouds and blackness, a day of trumpet and battle cry against the fortified cities and against the corner towers. I will bring distress on the people and they will walk like blind men, because they have sinned against the Lord. Their blood will be poured out like dust and their entrails like filth. Neither their silver nor their gold will be able to save them on the day of the Lord's wrath.* **In the fire of his jealousy the whole world will be consumed, for he will make a sudden end of all who live in the earth"** (Zep 1:14-18).

Hell Fire -- Sulfur and Brimstone:
The scope of this fire has been illustrated for us -- God having provided us an example of eternal fire in the destruction of ancient Sodom and Gomorrah. Referring to this example, the apostle, Peter, declared:

"But the day of the Lord will come as a thief in the night; in the which **the heavens shall pass away with a great noise, and the elements shall melt with fervent heat, the earth also and the works that are therein shall be burned up***. Seeing then that all these things shall be dissolved, what manner of persons ought ye to be in all holy conversation and godliness, Looking for and hasting unto the coming of the day of God, wherein* **the heavens being on fire shall be dissolved, and the elements shall melt with fervent heat?***"* (2 Pe 3:10-12).

Notice, Peter says even the elements -- the building blocks of our solar system -- will melt, as well as all the works therein. They will be dissolved, passing away with a great noise! This is amazing when one considers that planet earth was made to last. It is, according to astronomers and astrophysicists, a 4,550,000,000 (four and a half million) year-old, 5,973,600,000,000,000,000,000 (that is 5.974 Sextillion) ton ball of iron and stone. It has taken more devastating asteroid hits in its lifetime than you've had hot dinners, and lo, it still orbits our sun, merrily undisturbed.

Destructive Possibilities:
What might be sufficient to cause the sky to be rolled up like a scroll (Is 34:4; Rev 6:14), and the very elements of the earth melt? Considering the possibilities of science, there are a number ways the earth might be destroyed.

1. **The Black Hole --**
   When stars grow old, they are drawn toward one of the massive black holes in the universe, which suck the star in and consume it. If one could create a black hole, one could then simply place the black hole on the surface of the Earth and wait. Black holes are of such high density that they

pass through ordinary matter like a stone through the air.

The black hole would plummet through our planet, eating its way to the center of the Earth, then all the way through, coming out on the other side. Then, it would oscillate back and forth -- over and over -- like a matter-absorbing pendulum. Eventually it would come to rest at the core, having absorbed enough matter to slow it down. At this point, one would merely need to wait, while their black hole sits and consumes the remaining matter until the whole Earth is gone.

One problem, black holes are not eternal, they evaporate over time, due to Hawking radiation. Thus, since the destruction of the earth and everything thereon is prophesied to be eternal, the black hole concept cannot be applied.

2. **A Solar Flare** -- Scripture says that the earth will melt with fervent heat; so it seems reasonable to consider just how much heat this would require, and how one might achieve this. If the earth were composed entirely of iron and stone, the problem might not be too great, since the boiling point of iron is only 5,182 degrees Fahrenheit.

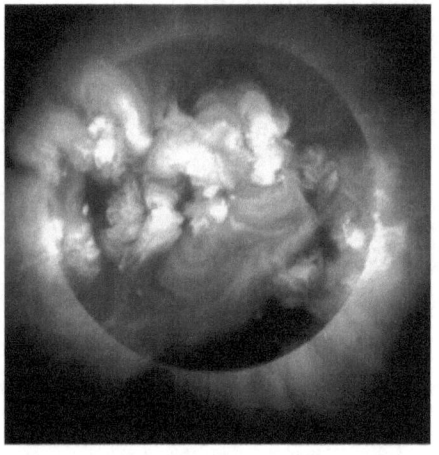

However, iron would be the least of our problems since the boiling point of tungsten and rhenium two of the heavy metals -- is over 10,000 degrees F. To reach this temperature one would need a state of the art solar furnace that was roughly two trillion (2,000,000,000,000) square kilometers -- hardly a feasible idea.

Moreover, there is another problem. Were one able to accomplish this feat, the earth would not really be destroyed, but merely converted to an intensely hot gigantic gaseous cloud -- which, if allowed to cool, could again form a planet.

3. **Super Spin --**
4. Another idea would be to somehow increase the rotational pattern of the earth to the point the gravitational pull is overcome and it literally flies apart. This would require affixing massive rockets at the earth's equator, all facing in the same direction, with sufficient thrust to  increase the earth's rotation from once in twenty-four hours to once each eighty-four minutes, or faster.

Obviously, there is no known rocket, or combination of rockets, that would produce sufficient thrust to accomplish this. But were it possible to produce such rockets, thereby increasing the rotation of the earth to the requisite speed, it would merely break apart into fine particles -- not disappear as prophesied.

5. **A Massive Explosion --** Another scheme might be to blow the earth up, with some supra-powerful explosive. However, this scheme has similar inherent problems. Blowing the earth into smithereens would still leave behind a massive number of minute particles -- unless, of course, one could use antimatter.

6. **Antimatter Attack --** Antimatter, the most explosive substance known to man, has been manufactured in small quantities using a large particle accelerator. But, one large enough for this job would

take a preposterous amount of time to produce. If one could develop the appropriate equipment, it would then be necessary to manufacture an earth-sized mass of antimatter and then somehow "flip" it through a fourth spatial dimension.

Antimatter is also the most costly substance in existence, with an estimated cost of about $25 billion per gram for positron produced antimatter, and about $62.5 trillion per gram for anti-hydrogen produced antimatter. This is because production is extremely difficult -- only a few antiprotons are produced in reactions conducted in particle accelerators. According to scientific experts, it cost several hundred million Swiss Francs to produce about 1 billionth of a gram (the amount used so far for all scientific particle/antiparticle collisions).

Assuming, however, one generated a sufficient amount of antimatter -- estimated to take at least 1,246,400,000,000 (1.25 Trillion) tons, the next, rather significant problem would be to launch it en-masse towards Planet Earth. Could this obstacle be overcome, the resulting release of energy upon collision [obeying Einstein's famous mass-energy equation, $E=mc^2$] would be equivalent to the amount of antimatter our own Sun produces in about 89 million (89,000,000) years.

Earth's Final resting place:

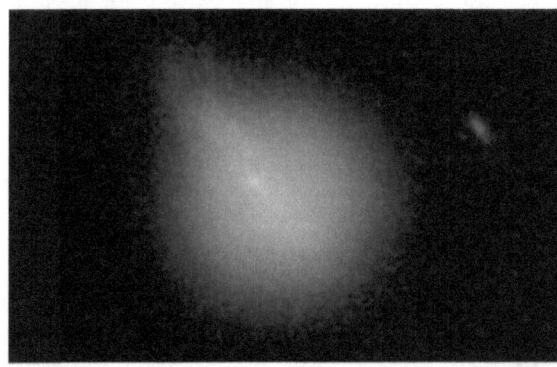

When matter and antimatter collide, they completely annihilate each other, leaving nothing but pure energy. In other words, could this scheme be carried out, all that would remain of planet Earth would be a single, scintillating flash of light, that would expand across the universe forever. This method is unquestionably the most permanent, and most nearly achieves the prophesied result since, the very matter (the elements which make up the Earth) would cease to exist, making it impossible to ever reassemble planet Earth again.

Such a collision would in fact, produce the effects mentioned in Scripture:

1) The sky would appear to be rolled up like a scroll (Is 34:4; Rev 6:14),

2) There would be a deafening noise (2 Pe 3:10), that would dwarf the sound produced when an airplane or rocket breaks the sound barrier.

3) The heat generated would be more than sufficient to melt the elements of the earth.

4) It would produce "a unique day, without daytime or nighttime -- a day known only to the Lord (Zec 14:7).

5) The only remaining trace of the event would be the light produced at impact, that would expand across the universe forever.

6) And time shall be no more! *"And he swore by him that liveth for ever and ever, who created heaven, and the things which are therein; and the earth, and the things which are in it; and the sea, and the things which are therein: That time shall be no longer"* (Rev 10:6 D-R)

The one complicating factor is this -- the antimatter required to produce this effect, would also cease to exist in that same, ever expanding, flash of light. However, this may not be a problem, since, before there was light, there was God. It was God who said, *"Light Be"* (Gen 1:2). The light produced, when God said, *"Light be: and Light was"* (ibid), was -- according to the translation of the Hebrew word *'owr'* -- the photon (the basic unit of the universe, which can be manifest as both matter and antimatter.

At the moment of creation, the entire Godhead (Father, Son and Holy Spirit) were present, and so it will be on that unique day, when the sky is rolled up like a scroll, the elements of the earth melt with fervent heat, and only light remains.

So it will be on this last day of planet earth: *"there came flashes of lightning, rumblings, peals of thunder and a severe earthquake. No earthquake like it has ever occurred since man has been on earth, so tremendous was the quake. The great city [the massively large residence (the earth)] split into three parts, and the cities of the nations collapsed. ... Every island fled away and the mountains could not be found"* (Rev 16:18-20).

The redeemed have been restored to God's Family; those who defied God's will and law have been destroyed, along with the fallen angels and demons; and the earth has disappeared. This event is the end -- yet, earth's end is also the genesis of a new beginning -- a new beginning described in our next and final chapter.

Chapter Thirty-two
New Beginnings

The Final Word for Scoffers:
The Great day of the Lord has come. For generations, mankind feared that day, but in the earth's later years, mankind had begun to scoff, saying: *"Where is the promise of his coming?"* They had, as Christ's apostle, Peter, noted, began using the reasoning that *"since the fathers [of Israel] fell asleep, all things continue as they were [indeed], from the beginning of the creation"* (2 Pe 3:4). Peter accused the masses of being willingly ignorant of the destiny of planet earth, reminding them of those who lost their lives during the great flood in Noah's days (vs. 5-6). Still, only a few responded.

Concerning those scoffing, Peter had warned those nay-sayers, saying: *"The Lord is not slack concerning his promise, as some men count slackness; but is long-suffering to us-ward, not willing that any should perish, but that all should come to repentance. But the day of the Lord will come as a thief in the night; in the which the heavens shall pass away with a great noise, and the elements shall melt with fervent heat, the earth also and the works that are therein shall be burned up"* (2 Pe 3:9-10).

Many heard the warnings of Peter, the other apostles and their disciples, who became known as Christians, but few took their warnings to heart. They even scoffed the more when Peter and the others declared: *"Nevertheless we, according to his promise, look for new heavens and a new earth, wherein dwelleth righteousness"* (2 Pe 3:13).

Then, *"as a thief in the night,"* it happened! The heavens passed away with a great noise, and the elements [both of heaven and earth] melted with fervent heat ... being dissolved (2 Pe 3:10-12). The words of Jesus Christ now came into remembrance among the redeemed and the angelic host: *"Heaven and earth will pass away, but my words will never pass away. "No one knows about that day or hour, not even the angels in heaven, nor the Son, but only the Father"* (Mt 24:35-36).

The apostle, John, and the redeemed -- those who thankfully had listened to him and others seeking to warn them -- recalled John's words: *"The world and its desires pass away, but the man who does the will of God lives forever. Dear children, this is the last hour; and as you have heard ... the antichrist is coming, even now many antichrists have come. This is how we know it is the last hour"* (1 Jn 2:17-18). Sadly, of all those who heard the warnings, so few had listened.

Cosmic Residue:
Now, there was nothing left but cosmic residue -- nothing but stunning silence and a shimmering light that radiated across the cosmos. In this silence, the redeemed, the holy angels and the twenty-four elders recalled the words of Isaiah -- the prophet of ancient times -- who, proclaimed the word of the Lord, saying:

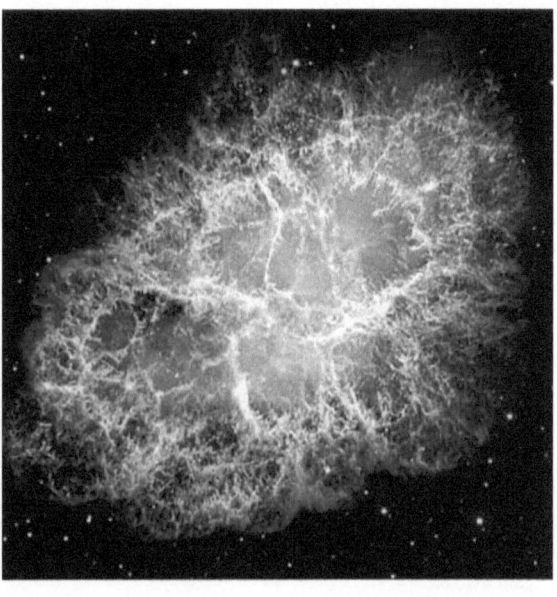

"Behold, I will create new heavens and a new earth. The former things will not be remembered, nor will they come to mind. But be glad and rejoice forever in what I will create, for I will create Jerusalem to be a delight and its people a joy. I will rejoice over Jerusalem and take delight in my people; the sound of weeping and of crying will be heard in it no more. Never again will there be in it an infant who lives but a few days, or an old man who does not live out his years. ...

"They will build houses and dwell in them; they will plant vineyards and eat their fruit. No longer will they build houses and others live in them, or plant and others eat. For as the days of a tree, so will be the days of my people; my chosen ones will long enjoy the works of their hands. They will not toil in vain or bear children doomed to misfortune; for they will be a people blessed by the Lord, they and their descendants with them. Before they call I will answer; while they are still speaking I will hear. The wolf and the lamb will feed together, and the lion will eat straw like the ox, but dust will be the serpent's food. They will neither harm nor destroy on all my holy mountain," says the Lord" (Is 65:17).

Now, the redeemed, the angels and the elders took heed as God broke the silence, once more calling things into existence. It was happening -- just like Christ's apostle, John, had envisioned and declared long ago!

"*Then I saw a new heaven and a new earth, for the first heaven and the first earth had passed away, and there was no longer any sea*" (Rev 21:1). Out of nowhere, appeared pristine celestial bodies, as the apostle, Peter had long ago declared: "*it was by God's Word alone, that long ago there were created heavens, and land arose out of water and existed between the waters*" (2 Pe 3:5).

One of these newly created celestial orbs somewhat resembled planet Earth, before it had vaporized. It was a sparkling blue planet, partially veiled by light clouds drifting through the atmosphere surrounding it, through which one could -- from time to time -- catch brief glimpses of inviting, verdant green land, interspersed with beautiful hills, mountains, lakes and rivers.

Noticeably, there was no seas. Suddenly, all understood the words recorded by John long ago: "*He that sat upon the throne said, 'Behold, I make all things new*" (Rev 21:5) and *there were no more seas*" (Rev 21:1).. As they descended from the heavens above; as the light pierced the veil created by the luminescent clouds, the redeemed behold beautiful, pristine mountains, rivers and valleys, where neither man nor angel has yet set fool upon. Truly, everything has been created anew, according to, and by, the Word of God Almighty.

Then, precisely as John had prophesied more than three thousand years before, another miracle occurred. "*I saw the Holy City,*" John said, "*the new Jerusalem, coming down out of heaven from God, prepared as a bride beautifully dressed for her husband*" (Rev 21:2). ... "*And there came up to me one of the seven angels which previously held the seven vials full of the seven last plagues, and talked with me, saying, Come hither, I will show thee the bride, the Lamb's wife*" (vs. 9).

"And he carried me away in the spirit to a great and high mountain, and showed me that great city, the holy Jerusalem, descending out of heaven from God; Having the glory of God: and her light was like unto a stone most precious, even like a jasper stone, clear as crystal" (Rev 21:10-11).

"And [the city] had a wall great and high, there were twelve gates, and posted at the gates twelve glorious angels, and the gates had names written above each, which are the names of the twelve tribes of the children of Israel. On the east are three gates; on the north three gates; on the south three gates; and on the west three gates" (Rev 21:12-13).

"And the angel speaking with me had a gold measuring-rod with which to measure the city, its gates and its wall. The city is laid out in a square, its length equal to its width. With his rod he measured the city at 12,000 Stadia -- the length, width and height the same. He also measured its wall, which was 144 cubits thick, according to man's, which the angel was using" (Rev 21:15-17).

The original units of measurement were clearly derived from the human body - the finger, hand, arm, span, foot, and pace. Since these measures differ somewhat between individuals, they must be reduced to a certain definite standard for general use. The Israelite system that evolved used divisions of [the finger breadth (Hebrew: Etzba; plural etzba'ot), the palm (Hebrew:

Tefah/Tefach; plural Tefahim/Tefachim), the span (Hebrew: Zeret), the ell (Hebrew: Amah, plural Amot), the mile (Hebrew: Mil; plural milin), and parasang (Hebrew: Parasa). The latter two being loan words from Latin and Persian. The Israelite measurements were interrelated as follows:

- 4 finger breadths (Etzba) = 1 palm (Tefah)
- 3 palms (Tefah) = 1 span (Zeret)
- 2 spans (Zeret) = 1 ell (Amah)
- 2000 ells (Amah) = 1 mil (Mil)
- 4 mils (Mil) = 1 parasang (Parasa)

The biblical ell is closely related to the cubit. However, two different cubit measurements are given in the Bible. Ezekiel's measurements imply that the ell was equal to 1 cubit plus 1 palm (Tefah), while elsewhere in the Bible, the ell was equated with 1 cubit exactly. Ezekiel's ell, by which he gave measurements of the Jerusalem Temple, was thus one sixth larger than the standard ell, an explanation of this seemingly suggested in the Book of Chronicles; the Chronicler writes that Solomon's Temple was built according to cubits following the first measure, suggesting that over the course of time the original ell was supplanted by a smaller one.

The cubit is the first recorded unit of length and was one of many different standards of measurement used through history. It was originally based on the measurement of one's forearm length. There is an Egyptian hieroglyph for the unit showing that it was eventually standardized. This unit of measurement was employed throughout Antiquity, during the Middle-Ages, and right up to Early Modern Times, especially for measuring cords and textiles, timbers, stone and volumes of grain.

The earliest attested standard measure is from Egypt and was called the royal cubit (mahe). It was 523 to 525 mm (20.6 to 20.64 inches) in length, and was subdivided into 7 palms of 4 digits, giving a 28-part measure in total. Secure evidence for this unit is preserved through architectural ruins, dating back at least to the construction of the Step Pyramid of Djoser, around 2,700 BC.

To this somewhat simple system of measurements, the Talmud adds a few more: namely the double palm (Hebrew: hasit), the pace (Hebrew: pesiah), the chord (Hebrew: hebel), the stadium (Hebrew: ris), the day's journey (Hebrew: derekh yom), and an unknown quantity named the garmida (Hebrew:). The stadium (plural stadia) appears to have been adopted from Persia, while the double palm seems to have been derived from the Greek dichas. The relationship between four of these additional units and the earlier system is as follows:

- 1 double palm (hasit) = 2 palms (tefah)
- 1 pace (pesiah) = 1 ell (amah)
- 1 stadium (ris) = 1600 palms (2/15 mile) (tefah)
- 1 day's journey (derekh yom) = 10 parasangs (parasa)

Measuring The New Jerusalem:
Based on this information, one can interpret with fair accuracy, that the measurements of the New Jerusalem will be as follows:

- The thickness of the wall - 144 cubits x 20.6 inches = 247 feet.

- The width, depth and height of the city wall - 12,000 stadia = 12000 x 2/15 = 1,600 miles.
- The land area (on the ground floor) 1600 x 1600 = 2,560,000 square miles @ 640 acres per square mile = (2,560,000 x 640) = 1,638,400,00 acres (one billion, six hundred thirty-sight million, four hundred thousand, acres)!

Based on the present United States census, there is an average of fifteen (15) residences per acre, with an average of 3.8 persons per residence. Thus, calculated on only the ground floor of the New Jerusalem, the capacity of the New Jerusalem would be: (1,638,400,000 x 15) 3.8 = 93,388,800,000 persons (ninety-three billion, three hundred eighty-eight million, eight hundred thousand redeemed saints)!

The map above, centered on present-day Jerusalem in Israel, depicts the approximate land coverage of the New Jerusalem, if it were situated at that location. The concept that some hold -- of the New Jerusalem descending from Heaven and lighting on the mountains of physical Israel -- is easily refuted by actual physical evidence. When it comes to the New Jerusalem, our idea of a city, is -- like our understanding of God -- far, far too small.

To try and envision a city of these dimensions, imagine traveling from Los Angeles, California to Kansas City, Kansas, which is 1,618 miles by road. Now, keep in mind that this would be but one side of the city, the width of which would be equidistant, as would its height into the skies. Try to imagine what a city -- what anything for that matter -- would look like, projecting 1,600 miles into space! The orbit of the International Space Station is only 216 miles above earth. Thus, the top of the wall of New Jerusalem will be 7.5 times higher than the space station's orbit.

Once you have begun to catch a vision of the size of the Holy City -- New Jerusalem -- consider its construction. "*And the wall of the city had twelve foundations, and on the foundations was written the names of the twelve apostles of the Lamb. ... The building of the city wall was of jasper: and the city was pure gold, like unto clear glass. And the foundations of the wall of the city were garnished with all manner of precious stones. The first foundation was jasper; the second, sapphire; the third, a chalcedony; the fourth, an emerald; The fifth, sardonyx; the sixth, sardius; the seventh, chrysolite; the eighth, beryl; the ninth, a topaz; the tenth, a chrysoprasus; the eleventh, a jacinth; the twelfth, an amethyst*" (& 17-21).

"*And the twelve gates were twelve pearls; every several gate was of one solid pearl: and the street of the city was pure gold, as it were transparent glass*" (Rev 21:12-14 & 17-21). Gold, refined to .9999 is beautiful, but imagine if it were transparent!

"*And I saw no temple therein: for the Lord God Almighty and the Lamb are the temple of it. And the city had no need of the sun, neither of the moon, to shine in it: for the glory of God did lighten it, and the Lamb is the light thereof*" (Rev 21:22-23). ...

"*And the nations of them which are saved shall walk in the light of it: and the kings of the earth do bring their glory and honor into it. And the gates of it shall not be shut at all by day: for there shall be no night there. And they shall bring the glory and honor of the nations into it. And there shall in no wise enter into it any thing that defileth, neither whatsoever worketh* abomination, or maketh a lie: but only they who are written in the Lamb's book of life" (Rev 21:22-27).

"And he showed me a pure river of water of life, clear as crystal, proceeding out of the throne of God and of the Lamb. In the midst of the street of it, and on either side of the river, was there the tree of life, which bare twelve manner of fruits, and yielded her fruit every month: and the leaves of the tree were for the healing of the nations" (Rev 22:1-2). ... "And there shall be no night there; and they need no candle, neither light of the sun; for the Lord God giveth them light: and they shall reign for ever and ever" (Rev 22:5).

Even the nature of the wild beasts is changed, being restored to their original; nature before the fall. "The wolf and the lamb will feed together, and the lion will eat straw like the ox, but dust will be the serpent's food" (Is 65:25).

"And I heard a loud voice from the throne saying, "Now the dwelling of God is with men, and he will live with them. They will be his people, and God himself will be with them and be their God. He will wipe every tear from their eyes. There will be no more death or mourning or crying or pain, for the old order of things has passed away." He who was seated on the throne said, "I am making everything new!"

Then he said ... "It is done. I am the Alpha and the Omega, the Beginning and the End. To him who is thirsty I will give to drink without cost from the spring of the water of life. He who [has] overcome will inherit all this, and I will be his God and he will be my son" (Rev 21:1-7)

"Behold, I am coming soon! My reward is with me, and I will give to everyone according to what he has done. I am the Alpha and the Omega, the First and the Last, the Beginning and the End. "Blessed are those who wash their robes, that they may have the right to the tree of life and may go through the gates into the city" (Rev 22:12-14).

"The Spirit and the bride say, Come. And let him that heareth say, Come. And let him that is athirst come. And whosoever will, let him take the water of life freely" (Rev 22:17). ... *"He which testifieth these things saith, Surely I come quickly. Amen. Even so, come, Lord Jesus. The grace of our Lord Jesus Christ be with you all. Amen"* (Rev 22:20-21).

Additional Titles Available

Soul Car & Psychospiritual Counseling: An Introduction to Pastoral Care, *by James V. Potter, Ph.D.* This volume provides an introduction to Pastoral Care through Pastoral Counseling. It examines the histories and differences between Biblical and psychological soul care, reviews a number of well known integrative therapies, and provides a unique integrative approach incorporating sound psychotherapeutic techniques within a Biblical Counseling framework. Scriptural support is provided for the techniques thus incorporated. Soul Care is an excellent guide for churches and individuals desiring to provide effective Christian Counseling.

Mastery Over Anger, *by James V. Potter, Ph.D.* Here is a Biblically based manual to help those struggling with anger problems gain the skills to effectively control their anger and use it appropriately. It teaches the student to resolve problems rather than create them, and demonstrates how to heal, rather than hurt the ones they love. In eight information-packed lessons, the author provides keys to stop angry outbursts, to get below anger into the underlying emotions, to examine the injustices that gave rise to such emotions, and how to release the emotions and resolve old injustices. The volume closes with a comparison of ineffective "dirty-fighting" techniques and a proven Ten Step approach to effective conflict resolution. This volume can be used as a course text, a facilitator guide in the therapy setting, or for self-help.

Assertiveness, Individuation & Autonomy, *by James V. Potter, Ph.D.*, is an excellent, faith-based, assertiveness training manual. Have you ever said yes to someone's request when you really didn't want to? Do you feel like other's owe you certain help, favors, love, etc., or that you owe these to others? Do you ever feel like your partner, or another, is trying to control you? Do you feel trapped, possessed and dominated? Do you ever feel like your being treated like a piece of property in your relationships, rather than a unique child of God? Do you ever tell a "white lie" or just not answer to avoid conflicts? If you answered yes to any of these questions, you definitely need this nine lesson book. Applying the principles taught therein will change your life. God desires a relationship *with* us, not ownership *of* us. And, our relationship with God should serve as the model for all our relationships. Suitable for a course text, as a facilitator guide in therapy, or for self-help.

Conquering Codependency, *by James V. Potter, Ph.D.*, is an excellent faith-based guide for breaking free from codependency. Do you sometimes feel like "you're walking on egg shells" around those you love, in order to avoid arguments? Do your partner's emotions (i.e., anger, sadness, depression, etc.), often affect your own emotional state? Do you sometimes have trouble knowing where your boundaries end and another person's begin? Are there areas of your life where you lack healthy personal boundaries, or you have such rigid boundaries in some areas that you easily offend others? Do you need help understanding and developing healthy personal boundaries and limits? Do you tend to focus on other people's negative characteristics rather than their positive characteristics? And, do you have trouble surrendering your life to God? If so, this volume is for you. Suitable for a course text, as a facilitator guide in therapy, and for self-help.

Jekyll & Hyde: Arrested Development: Breaking Bondages, Restoring Wholeness, *by James V. Potter, Ph.D.*, provides an excellent introduction into the problem of arrested development and an understanding of the associated personality disorders. If you have ever been accused of having a Dr. Jekyll/ Mr. Hyde personality, or live with someone who does, this volume is for you. This title examines process of personality development, through a life-span analysis, demonstrating how one's personality can become bent, predisposing that person to various personality disorders and an inability to develop healthy bonding.

It reveals the underlying cause of most dysfunctions -- the loss of love -- and the resulting manifestations of rejection and rebellion that give rise to addictions, compulsions and other life-controlling problems. This volume also lays the groundwork for answering some of life's most important questions, such as: Who am I? What is the meaning of my life experience? What is my purpose? Where am I going? And, How do I get there? It closes with a powerful exercise that, when practiced, can help break any compulsivity or addiction. Suitable as a course text and a therapeutic guide for therapists, counselors and facilitators.

Healing Inner-Child Wounds: Breaking Life-Commandments, *by James V. Potter, Ph.D.*, is a faith-based introduction of inner-healing. This volume commences earlier than most books on the subject, embarking on the subject where one should -- in the womb -- at the beginning of human development. Each chapter begins with a reexamination of one of a specific stage in life's developmental, then examines the developmental tasks of that stage, factors that can sabotage developmental progress, and aberrant adult behavior that often results from failure to successfully traverse this path.

Each chapter closes with age-appropriate exercises and meditations that help bring closure to that stage of life and facilitate movement toward maturity. Topics include: overcoming rejection and abandonment issues, developing trust, hope, love and faith, defusing obstinate-defiant thoughts and behavior, giving up magical thinking and restoring creativity and, developing self-awareness and competence. Suitable as a course text and for self-help. Ideal for use by therapists, counselors and facilitators in inner- child workshops.

Toxic Shame and the Journey Out, *by James V. Potter, Ph.D.,* is a faith-based guide designed to aid one in discerning the differences between guilt, false guilt, healthy shame and toxic shame. This volume employs the powerful twelve step approach to break one of life's most controlling, most destructive problems -- toxic shame. Below every addiction, compulsivity and/or other life-controlling problems, including codependency, lies toxic shame. Shame, unlike guilt, is not about what I have done, but rather, about who I am. Shamed to the very core, we develop a negative self-image and a corresponding poor self-worth. Then, because each of us needs affirmation and approval -- if only from ourselves -- we act-out our negative self-concept, thereby exacerbating our shame. Toxic Shame and the Journey Out, provides a gentle, faith-based approach to recovery. Suitable as a course text, as a therapeutic guide for therapists, counselors and facilitators, and as a self-help guide.

Growing Beyond Our Genetics: Adolescence & Beyond, *by James V. Potter, Ph.D.,* offers a much needed guide for understanding adolescent dysfunction and for facilitating re-parenting. Adolescence is a troubling, mystifying period of development commencing around thirteen and continuing until one reaches about twenty-six. It is a season of life during which we leave childhood and journey toward maturity, a time during which we acquire many life-management skills: some positive and some rather dysfunctional. It is a stretch during which we may experience positive parental guidance or profound abuse, either of which will impact every significant relationship we may develop, as well as our own self-acceptance and parenting skills.

Have you ever wondered about the effect of your genetics on your personhood -- your aptitudes, attitudes, characteristics, and behavior? This volume examines the life-span development tasks and pitfalls of adolescence; the effect of genetics vs. environment; the development and healing of Misogynists (men who hate and fear women), Misandrists (women who hate and fear men), Misogmists (persons who hate and fear marriage). Moving on from this beginning, we scrutinize the impact of our family lineage on the development of misbeliefs, life-commandments and disorders, employing a Family Time Line and Family Genogram to illustrate the impact of genetics. The volume closes with a study on the "new birth" which literally means to be **re-gened**, and demonstrates through Biblical and scientific reference the enormity of change possible if we just believe. Suitable as a course text, as a therapeutic guide for therapists, counselors and facilitators, and for self-help.

Bonding vs. Bondage: Keys to Marriage Intimacy & Oneness, *by James V. Potter, Ph.D.,* offers one of the most successful affair-prevention strategies known. The selection of a life-partner is the greatest decision that any of us ever makes. This decision is of such magnitude that it affects not only the remainder of one's own life, but that of generations yet to come. Unfortunately, it is -- more often than not -- made on the basis of emotional arousal, with little or no consideration for posterity, and in the absence of any specific training.

It is little wonder that more than fifty percent (50%) of all marriages in America end in divorce. Nor, is it surprising that children from divorced families are far more inclined to develop addictions, have more emotional problems, experience a higher school dropout rate, and are more at-risk to spend a part of their adult life in jail, prison or a mental health facility. What is surprising to many, is the fact that the single greatest contributing factor in familial dysfunction is a lack of bonding between married partners, and between parents and their children.

The lack of bonding inevitably results in one or both spouses, and one or more of the children, feeling trapped -- as though they are in bondage: a prison that they can escape only by leaving their family. This text provides an understanding of the tools and techniques needed to break free from this bondage and develop the deep bonding that will insure marital intimacy and oneness. Suitable for a course text, as a therapeutic guide by therapists, counselors and facilitators, as a guide for school counselors, and as a self-help guide.

Counseling Addicts & Offenders: A Guide to Criminal Justice Counseling, *by James V. Potter, Ph.D.,* is designed specifically to help addiction, criminal justice counselors and others working with alcoholics, addicts, and criminal justice offenders, effect meaningful and lasting change in this change-resistant population. Anyone who has spent any time in this field of counseling has seen many more clients experience relapse after relapse than those who achieve full recovery. Addiction and Criminal Justice Counselors are all too familiar with the judicial system's merry-go-round of arrest, conviction, incarceration, release, arrest, conviction, etc., etc. Why, understanding this system and knowing the outcome do addicts and offenders keep on doing the same old things?

Many counselors, pastors, chaplains, spouses and friends, trying to help these individuals have found this experience so discouraging that they have given up on the addict or offender. Others, who have excelled in other areas of ministry and counseling have even questioned their own ability as a counselor or facilitator after working with this population. While it is true that a counselor must frequently reassess his or her therapeutic skills, it is also true that the population addiction and criminal justice counselors have chosen to serve, can be more taxing, more demanding, and more resistive to change than almost any other group.

In this volume, you will see why this population is so resistive to change. You will learn just how differently they process information; distinctly different from other people. Their intellectual and affective thought processes are different, their foundational beliefs and value systems are different, and alas, their goals, objectives, purposes and motivations are different.

Attempting to correct addicts' and offenders' problematic behaviors through behavior-modification therapy is much like trying to cover up a skin cancer with a band-aid. Endeavoring to come along side an addict or offender and effect change through affirmation and exhortation is seen by them as a manifestation of weakness and a sure sign that the person can be easily manipulated.

In this volume, you will learn to understand the mental processes of addicts and offenders, learn how to "hook" those game-players who just want to satisfy the courts, discover new therapeutic techniques that have proven to be successful with this population, learn how to select the most appropriate treatment setting, treatment team, therapeutic approach and treatment interventions to increase the probability got change, and insure its durability over time.

Spiritual growth is a major focus within this course, and the curriculum draws upon information from other Psychospiritual development programs such as: Victor Frankl's *"Logotherapy"*, Solomon's *"Spirituotherapy"*, Bruce Thompson's *"The Divine Plumbline"*, John and Paula Sandford's *"Transformation of the Inner Man"* and *"Healing the Wounded Spirit"*, The Children of Alcoholics Foundation program *"Discovering Normal"*, and John Bradshaw on *"Homecoming"*.

This volume is suitable as a course text, as a therapeutic guide for therapists, counselors and facilitators, a guide for judiciary, probation and parole personnel. It is also an excellent guide for clergy, family members and friends of addicts and criminal justice offenders, improving their understanding and guiding them in their interactions to insure that they are helpers and not enablers.

Substances of Abuse, *by James V. Potter, Ph.D.,* is one of the volumes in the "Living Sober: Living Free" series. The "Living Sober: Living Free" series provides a Psychoeducational educational substance abuse and addiction prevention and treatment program -- a program based on an integrative approach -- integrating sound psychological principles and biblical truths. The series is designed for students participating in licensing or certification programs; those seeking college or continuing education credits; substance abuse counselors; school counselors; recovery program personnel, nurses, and others seeking information on substance abuse prevention and treatment.

People abuse substances such as drugs, alcohol, and tobacco for varied and complicated reasons, but it is clear that our society pays a significant cost for this abuse. The toll for substance abuse can be seen daily in our hospitals and emergency rooms, through the direct damage to abusers' health, and its link to physical trauma. Jails and prisons daily record the connection between crime and alcohol and drug dependence and abuse.

Volumes in this series include:
- Substance Abuse & Addiction: A Biblical Perspective
- Addiction: Demonic, Deviance, or Disease? (Models of Addiction)

- Substances of Abuse
- Addictive Activities & Compulsivities
- Substance Abuse Legislation, Regulation & Judicial Sanction
- Counseling Addicts & Offenders: A Guide to Criminal Justice Counseling
- Mastery Over Anger (Addiction & Domestic Violence)
- Assertiveness, Individuation & Autonomy
- Conquering Codependency
- Toxic Shame & The Journey Out (A 12-Step Journey)
- Bonding by Design (Reconciling & Restoring Couples)
- Socioeconomic Reentry & Relapse Prevention

About The Authors

Dr. James V. Potter and Paula M. Potter, MA, are Christian authors, counselors, educators and ordained ministers. Dr. And Paula Potter are semi-retired. They serve as adjunct faculty members with Vision International University, intercessory prayer leaders and teachers in their local church. They make their home in Northern California.

Dr. and Mrs. Potter have previously served with the Family Ministries School, University of the Nations, Youth With A Mission (YWAM) in Hawaii; as Associate Pastors with The New Covenant Churches and the Gospel of Salvation Ministries, in Hawaii. They founded and operated Hawaii Family Care Centers, a network of community-based Christian Counseling Centers in Hawaii, Agape Family Services, Alliance Recovery Services, Advocare Family Skills Institute, and Advocare Publishing Company, in California.

In addition to being pastors and educators, Dr., and Paula Potter are both Certified Christian Marriage and Family Therapists, Certified Clinical Pastoral Counselors, Certified Addictions Prevention and Rehabilitation Specialists, and Certified Domestic Violence Specialists. They are also certified Prepare/Enrich counselors and trainers.

Dr. Potter was the recipient of the prestigious Fellow Award by the American College of Forensic Counselors, and is a Diplomate of the National Board of Certified Christian Therapists and the American Association of Christian Therapists. Dr. Potter is listed in Who's Who in America, Who's Who in Religion, Who's Who in Education, Who's Who in the World. The International Biographical Centre and Men of Achievement.

Dr. James Potter, and Paula, Potter can be reached at:
Jubilee Enterprises
PO Box 994114
Redding, California 96099
www.jubileeenterprises.com

www.ingramcontent.com/pod-product-compliance
Lightning Source LLC
Chambersburg PA
CBHW030132170426
43199CB00008B/45